AUTHENTIC FAKES

David Chidester · AUTHENTIC FAKES

Religion and American Popular Culture

University of California Press

Berkeley Los Angeles London

University of California Press
Berkeley and Los Angeles, California

University of California Press, Ltd.
London, England

©2005 by the Regents of the University of California

Library of Congress Cataloging-in-Publication Data

Chidester, David.
    Authentic fakes : religion and American popular
culture / David Chidester.
        p.   cm.
    Includes bibliographic references and index.
    ISBN 978-0-520-24280-7 (pbk. : alk. paper)
    1. Popular culture—Religious aspects.   2. Popular
culture—United States.   3. Impostors and imposture.
I. Title.
BL65.C8C455   2005
201'.7'0973—dc22   2004008504

Manufactured in the United States of America
13   12   11   10   09   08   07   06
10   9   8   7   6   5   4   3   2

CONTENTS

PREFACE

American popular culture produces fakes, not only things that are made up and invented, but also people who are frauds and charlatans. Often, these fakes are religious fakes, because they involve artificial or fraudulent religious claims about transcendence, the sacred, or ultimate human concerns. In this book, I argue that despite their fraudulence, these religious fakes still do authentic religious work in and through the play of American popular culture. As a matter of urgency, in order to recover the religious, creative, and imaginative capacity of America, we need to understand and appreciate the religious work and religious play of "authentic fakes" in American popular culture.

This book explores religious dimensions and dynamics of popular culture. What is religion? There is no single, substantial definition. On the one hand, academics in the study of religion have defined their key term in many ways, some of which we will consider. We will test these academic definitions of religion against the evidence of popular culture to see how that culture might count as religion. On the other hand, in popular, ordinary language usage of the term, people have defined religion in many ways, which we will also consider. We will test popular usage of the term *religion* in American popular culture to see the different meanings that people give to the term.

Although we will consider all these possibilities, I do have a working definition of religion: *Religion* is a generic term for "ways of being a human person in a human place." I define religion as discourses and practices that negotiate what it is to be a human person both in relation to the superhuman and in relation to whatever might be treated as subhuman. Since being a person also requires being in a place, religion entails discourses and practices for creating sacred space, as a zone of inclusion but also as a boundary for excluding others. Accordingly, religion, in my definition, is the activity of being human in relation to superhuman transcendence and sacred inclusion, which inevitably involves dehumanization and exclusion. Religion, therefore, contains an inherent ambiguity. Although I have no intention of moralizing, religion does raise the moral problem of doing harm. As a humanizing, inclusive activity, religion protects people from harm. As a force of dehumanization and exclusion, religion does harm. Moralizing, while it might do no harm, also does no one any good, so I will not moralize. Instead, I will use the term *religion* as a point of entry into the meaning, power, and values at work in the production and consumption of authentic fakes in American popular culture.

This book is all about fakes. It deals with fakes from start to finish. I consider cultural activities that are not formally or legally recognized as religious institutions but nevertheless look like religion. For example, participants in popular culture have described the sport of baseball, the consumer product of Coca-Cola, and the musical genre of rock 'n' roll as if they were religions (chapter 2). Certain things that are plastic and fluid in their transformations have been described by enthusiasts as if they were religions, such as Tupperware and the Human Genome Project (chapter 3). None of these things are religions, of course. Except: people say they are; they fit "classic" academic definitions; and they do authentic religious work by negotiating what it means to be a human person in relation to transcendence, the sacred, or ultimate human concerns. As a kind of religious activity in American popular culture, these are all authentic fakes, doing real religious work in forging a community, focusing desire, and facilitating exchange in ways that look just like religion.

If we want to get real, touching, not seeing, is believing, but American popular culture has drawn upon the sense of touch in political rhetoric, firewalking, alien abductions, faith healing, and other forms of religion under pressure (chapter 4). Ultimately, the religious and political rhetoric of America calls upon the supreme visceral commitment, sacrificing one's life, as the ultimate test of authenticity, as illustrated by a "fake" religious leader, Jim Jones, and a simulated or media-generated political leader, Ronald Reagan, who revitalized an ideology of redemptive sacrifice for America (chapter 5). In the end, the really real in America, money, hard cold cash, the bedrock of values, is also an arena of trickery, fraud, and deception, even when money speaks the language of religion, "In God We Trust" (chapter 6). Again, as a kind of religious activity in American popular culture, these discourses and practices of life, death, and ultimate values are all authentic fakes, simultaneously simulations and the real thing.

Going global, we see that American popular culture, with its authentic fakery, is not confined to the territorial boundaries of the United States. Acting like missionary religions, Coca-Cola raises problems of intercultural translation, McDonald's raises problems of intercultural rationalization, and Disney raises problems of intercultural imagination, all of which are doing a kind of globalizing religious work in the world (chapter 7). This global exchange, however, goes both ways, since Africans—from the American movement in central and southern Africa of the 1920s to the criminal gang known as the Americans in Cape Town of the 1990s—have claimed to know the real meaning of America (chapters 6 and 8). In the midst of these transatlantic exchanges, where the authenticity of religious, cultural, and social practices is at stake, we find a genuine fake, the Zulu shaman Credo Mutwa, described in his own country as a "fake, fraud, and a charlatan" but celebrated in the United States as an authentic spiritual leader who is doing real, authentic religious work, like Coca-Cola, McDonald's, and Disney, by enabling people to reimagine what it is to be a human person in a rapidly globalizing human place (chapter 9).

As the most blatant, shameless illustrations of religious fakery, the virtual religions on the Internet have to be considered; these invented, transparently fake religions include such remarkable organizations as the Discordians, the Church of the SubGenius, the Wauists, the Church of the Covert Cosmos, the Church of Elvis, the Church of the Almighty Dollar, and over 150 others (chapter 10). Here are fake religions, as I will argue, doing real, authentic religious work in cyberspace by negotiating what it means to be a human person in a human place.

In conclusion, a review of what can be learned from considering authentic fakes in American culture—popular culture, consumer culture, political culture, and global culture—highlights how authentic fakes can generate power and creativity in American religion.

Raising the question of authenticity, this book shows that the term *religion* puts that question at stake in its most urgent formulation: What is it to be a human being? Some commentators have decried the inauthenticity of popular culture; others have celebrated its authenticity; and some have tried to finesse the question, such as cultural analyst Lawrence Grossberg, in an ironic mode, by referring to its "authentic inauthenticity." I will address the question of authenticity as the central problem of religion in American popular culture.

Although I live outside the United States, I have a deep attachment to America, not only because I was born there, but also because I have family, friends, colleagues, and collaborators living there. On a recent visit, one of my colleagues, who is also a collaborator, phoned me at 7 A.M. and woke me up, saying: "Man, you've got to check this out. Turn on channel 18. They've got an infomercial selling something called Super Blue Stuff." So, in a very blurry condition, I tuned into the television program advertising this product, which, according to the testimonials of many satisfied, even ecstatic, customers, was able to relieve otherwise unrelievable pain. Following all the personal testimonials about the life-transforming power of Super Blue Stuff, a brief disclaimer came up on the screen, which read, to the best of my recollection, something like: "Super Blue Stuff should not be used for the treatment, alleviation, or cure of any medical condition." In other words, if I understood the point of this disclaimer, truth in advertising required the makers of the product to admit that Super Blue Stuff did absolutely nothing. Nevertheless, while I was still trying to assimilate this admission that the product was useless, the inventor of Super Blue Stuff suddenly appeared on the screen, smiling, to declare, "It's a miracle!"

As seen on TV, this miracle of Super Blue Stuff, I could not help thinking, resonates with many other miracles of the United States of America, with all of the Super Red, White, and Blue Stuff that has made America such a mystery in the world. Like this healing product that doesn't work but is still a miracle, America is a mystery. By exploring American popular culture, in its mystery and mystification, in its media and miracles, I hope to outline a popular history of the American present, informed by a sense of the past, which is poised on the edge of a future, full of fear and terror, perhaps, but also pregnant with the possibility of new kinds of authenticity.

I can acknowledge here only a few of my debts incurred in the process of making this book. With friends in America, I have been able to test out quite a lot of the material in this book at festive academic occasions across the length and breadth of the United States. Over the past few years, I have spoken about popular culture; baseball, Coca-Cola, and rock 'n' roll; the sense of touch; blood and money; globalization; neoshamanism; Internet religions; and other things in this book at academic gatherings and invited lectures in Philadelphia, Boston, Princeton, Syracuse, Poughkeepsie, Richmond, Nashville, Gainesville, and Santa Barbara. All right, I admit that I stuck pretty much to the East for these events, but only because it is closer to Cape Town. I also tested some of this material in Cape Town, South

Africa; Toronto, Canada; Tsukuba, Japan; Hamburg and Hannover, Germany; and Stirling, Scotland.

I conducted my most intensive testing, however, at the annual meeting of the Farmington Institute—University of Maine, Farmington—where Professor Jennifer Reid has mobilized (and organized) a congenial group of colleagues and students for in-depth and sustained consultations on religion, materiality, and modernity. I thank Jennifer Reid and her family for providing this home for the study of religion.

In the process of making this book, I have been helped by the research assistance of Thomas Alberts, a collaborator in the study of religious authenticity, and other colleagues in the Institute for Comparative Religion in Southern Africa. I have benefited from critical and constructive readings by Edward T. Linenthal, Bruce Forbes, and anonymous reviewers. At the University of California Press, my editor, Reed Malcolm, has been an extraordinary colleague, a friend, and a collaborator in the work of authenticity. I have drawn inspiration from his ongoing commitment to infusing authenticity not only into books but also into his role as Paul McCartney in his Beatles tribute band. Fake? No, not at all. Entirely authentic. I also thank my wife, Careen, and the Board of Directors, as always.

So, we have a book. It was written under the working title *Holy Shit*, but obviously the book would never have been published under such a title by a reputable academic press. It would never have been able to go out into the world and do whatever good work it might do. I thank everyone at the University of California Press, in every capacity, for letting this book out into the world.

Although I have reworked and revised everything for this book, I have incorporated material from some of my discussions of religion and American popular culture that have appeared elsewhere. I thank other presses for giving permission to use material they have already let out into the world:

By permission of Lexington Books, I have used material from "Crosscultural Religious Business: Cocacolonization, McDonaldization, Disneyization, Tupperization, and Other Local Dilemmas of Global Signification," in Jennifer I. M. Reid, ed., *Religion and Global Culture: New Terrain in the Study of Religion and the Work of Charles H. Long* (Lexington, MA: Lexington Press, 2003), 145–66.

By permission of Taylor & Francis, I have used material from "Haptics of the Heart: The Sense of Touch in American Religion and Culture," *Culture and Religion* 1 (2000): 61–84, www.tandf.co.uk/journals/titles/01438301.html.

By permission of Oxford University Press, I have used material from "The Church of Baseball, the Fetish of Coca-Cola, and the Potlatch of Rock 'n' Roll:

Theoretical Models for the Study of Religion in American Popular Culture," *Journal of the American Academy of Religion* 64 (1996): 743–65.

By permission of Indiana University Press, I have used material from "'A Big Wind Blew Up during the Night': America as Sacred Space in South Africa," in David Chidester and Edward T. Linenthal, eds., *American Sacred Space* (Bloomington: Indiana University Press, 1995), 262–312.

And by permission of University of California Press, which has graciously granted permission to itself in this instance, I have used material from "Saving the Children by Killing Them: Redemptive Sacrifice in the Ideologies of Jim Jones and Ronald Reagan," *Religion and American Culture: A Journal of Interpretation* 1 (1991): 177–201, ©1997 by The Center for the Study of Religion and American Culture.

Although this is my first book with the University of California Press, I feel as if I am coming home. As a graduate student, I was trained and taught to think at the University of California, Santa Barbara. Every day I am aware of my enduring connection to the people of that place.

Many years ago in conversations, an editor for the University of California Press and I planned a book about values in American society that are not solely or accurately determined by the market. People value their lives, their families, their integrity, and their authenticity in ways that could never be determined by the pricing mechanisms of the capitalist market. For that book, we came up with a great title, *Not For Sale*. But that was the end of the project. Not a bad title, you might think, because our authenticity, as human beings, is certainly not for sale. But imagine a book, in a bookstore, sitting on the shelf or displayed in the window, advertising itself as "not for sale." No one would buy it. Who would buy a book that is not for sale?

Many years later, appearing under a different title, this book does pretty much what we wanted to do. This book is about values. Real values. We trust that you, the reader, will see all of the religious fakery in this volume as an occasion for thinking about authenticity.

Introduction

The Web site Adherents.com, which compiles statistics on the membership of religious groups, includes entries for the religions of television, sports, Disney, McDonald's, Coca-Cola, and Elvis worship. What is going on? They cannot possibly be serious.

Religion is serious. According to the great psychologist of religion William James, religion "signifies always a *serious* state of mind."[1] Popular culture, by contrast, is not serious. Or is it? In this book, I posit that it certainly is. Through the idea of religion, I will engage the compelling political, social, and economic realities of America, at home and abroad, as expressed in American popular culture.

Situated between the state and the market, between political power and economic exchange, religion is an arena of human activity marked by the concerns of the transcendent, the sacred, the ultimate—concerns that enable people to experiment with what it means to be human. Religious ways of being human engage the transcendent—that which rises above and beyond the ordinary. They engage the sacred—that which is set apart from the ordinary. And they engage the ultimate—that which defines the final, unavoidable limit of all our ordinary concerns.

Popular culture, for its part, encompasses the ordinary—the pleasures of our lives, which we may even take for granted, such as the creative and performing arts, sports, and leisure activities. If we want to think about the relationship between religion and popular culture, we have to ask: How does the serious work of religion, which engages the transcendent, the sacred, and the ultimate meaning of human life in the face of death, relate to the comparatively frivolous play of popular culture?

From the most intimate embodiment of personal subjectivity to the most public institutions of social collectivity, what I call religion is at work and at play. It is at work in the disciplines of the body, the regulation of one's conduct, and the legitimization of political, social, or economic power. It is at play in the creative improvisations, innovations, transformations, and transgressions of all that serious religious work. Of course, sometimes work can seem like play, so this initial opposition between religious work and religious play will blur.

In this book, I dwell in detail on the ways in which religion animates popular culture. Thus I concentrate less on how specific religious groups deal with popular culture than on how popular culture works in characteristically religious ways. Without denying the importance of organized religions or their relations with popular culture, I want to highlight the ways in which the production, circulation, and consumption of popular culture can operate like religion.

COMMUNITIES, OBJECTS, AND EXCHANGES

What difference does it make to call any cultural activity "religion"? As we will see, *religion* can be a useful term for understanding the ways in which transcendence, the sacred, and the ultimate are inevitably drawn into doing some very important things that happen in and through popular culture: forming a human community, focusing human desire, and entering into human relations of exchange.

Social cohesion, in forming a sense of community, is reinforced by religious resources. Rising above the everyday course of life, traces of transcendence seem necessary for instilling a sense of continuity with the past. Set apart from the ordinary world, traces of the sacred seem necessary for establishing a sense of uniformity in the present. In the play of popular culture, religious techniques for creating sacred time and sacred space have generated a sense of community within a diverse array of cultural enterprises, such as the church of baseball, the pilgrimage to Graceland, the devotion to Star Trek, and the proliferation of invented religions on the Internet. Originating in the United States, these sacred communities often assume a global significance, as witnessed by the frequent claims that something in American popular culture has established a new "mecca." According to its Web site, the Baseball Hall of Fame and Museum in Cooperstown, New York, is the "Mecca of baseball." The Coca-Cola Company's museum in Atlanta has been described as the "Mecca of Coca-Cola." Various claimants, including the cities of Memphis, New York, Los Angeles, and Cleveland, home of the Rock 'n' Roll Hall of Fame, have vied for recognition as the "Mecca of Rock 'n' Roll." Examples of the "meccanization" of American popular culture abound. All suggest that popular culture adopts religious resources not only for forming a sense of community but also for expanding that sense of community like a transnational, missionizing religion.

In a globalizing world, human identity and community, as celebrated in American popular culture, have been focused on material objects, the powerful commodities of a market economy. Directing attention toward the consumer product as the ultimate object of human desire is an important part of the religious work of American popular culture. Invested with transcendent power and sacred significance, the consumer product has emerged as the modern fetish, the object of religious desire in a capitalist economy. The fetish of Coca-Cola, for example, has been placed within arm's reach of desire all over the world, registering as an animated object of global religious attention. American popular culture has brought many inanimate objects to life, not only as commodities, but also as religious relics, icons, and even deities. In the global expansion of Disney and McDonald's, as cultural analyst Andrew Ross has observed, "the Mouse and the Golden Arches are almost as ubiquitous on the earth's crust as the Christian cross or the Muslim crescent."[2] On the Internet, "virtual" religions have deified any number of consumer products—we find the Church of the Twinkie, the Church of Volkswagenism, and the First Church of the Fisher-Price Record Player, for example. With regard to American popular culture, Karl Marx's "fetishism of commodities" seems to be a redundant phrase. The commodity is the fetish.

Although the notion of the fetish calls attention to an important religious activity—the formation and focusing of human desire—the term itself has a problematic pedigree. Long before the word *fetish* was applied to a consumer product such as Coke, European explorers, traders, and merchants in West Africa used it to denigrate African religions for their lack of any "authenticity" that might provide a stable system of values. In the work of W. E. B. Du Bois, the great African American sociologist, political activist, and, as I hope to show, historian of religions, the fetish posed a crucial problem for understanding the role of religion in American culture. Initially, Du Bois tried to rehabilitate African fetishism from its European denigration, but eventually he realized that the very notion of fetishism was a European invention. Accusing Africans of worshiping objects, Europeans masked the actual workings of slavery, which turned living human beings into objects, into commodities, for the transatlantic slave trade.

Like Du Bois, other theorists of modernity, following the lead of Karl Marx or Sigmund Freud, have turned the critique of African fetishism back on the West and its obsessions with material objects. While tracking such Western obsessions, however, we must avoid the denigrating, prejudicial dismissal of the religious interest in objects as fetishism. Lively objects, as focal points of desire, can create meaningful religious worlds.

In the life of material objects, human beings must participate by engaging in rituals of exchange, which bear traces of religious practices and performances. This suggests another important religious aspect of American popular culture. When compared with the buying, selling, and speculating done in the productive economy, the economic exchanges in religious rituals seem nonproductive.

To adopt a phrase coined by the unconventional sociologist Georges Bataille, popular culture celebrates ritualized *expenditure* in nonproductive economic activity. Not for profit, as Bataille argued, expenditure is economic activity in which the loss must be as great as possible in order to certify a claim on ultimate meaning. Ritual expenditure occurs in a gift, a display, or a performance of wealth. But expenditure also takes place in the waste, the destruction, or the irrecoverable loss of valued objects, including the highly valued "object" of human life. In many contexts, such as the performance of rock 'n' roll or the mystery of the global economy, we will see ritual expenditure, in Bataille's sense, operating within religion and American popular culture.

Money, of course, makes the world go around. But money is not what it used to be. Although economics textbooks still define it rather austerely as a medium of exchange, a unit of accounting, and a store of value, money has taken on a life—and religious proportions—of its own. As a system of symbols, money might be regarded as a religion, even as the "religion of the market"; it also has inspired a range of religious initiatives in American popular culture. For example, economic exchange has been transformed into the gospel of prosperity by religio-economic corporations such as Amway; the gospel of money by television ministries, which appeal to their viewers for funding, promising miraculous financial returns to the donors; and even the religious devotion to money in the online Church of the Profit$, which claims to be the only honest, authentic religion in America because it openly admits that it is only in it for the money.

Raising the stakes in these religio-economic exchanges, money and blood have become interchangeable within the calculations of the state and the market in American life and culture. Like money, human blood, in the symbolic economy of culture, is exchanged as a payment (colonizers shed it to authorize their claims on

America), as a waste (we squander it in wars), or as a debt that can never be paid (we owe a sacrificial debt to our country whose ultimate payment would require our own life). Clearly, after the devastation of September 11, 2001, this sacred economy of blood and money was revitalized in the United States, but it has had a long, sustained life in American history, one with a deep religious undercurrent.

These, then, are three reasons for investigating religion in American popular culture: religious activity is at work in forming community, focusing desire, and facilitating exchange.

RELIGION AND POPULAR CULTURE IN EMBODIED, NATIONAL, AND GLOBAL SPHERES

By exploring case studies in some depth and detail, I hope to present more than a survey. Perhaps the cases I consider will seem arbitrary. Still, the locations of these case studies are important, because I want to focus attention on religion and American popular culture as embodied, as national, and as global. These three spheres overlap in producing religious significance for America.

As a religion of the body, the religion of American popular culture involves the most basic, visceral engagements with the world. Sex, drugs, and the pulsating rhythms of rock 'n' roll embrace the body in an immediacy, an intensity, although the mind and soul might subsequently follow. Mediated through the senses, especially through the physical sense of touch, the embodied character of religion in American popular culture appears in the binding, burning, moving, and handling of religious meaning and power, but it also registers as religion under pressure, as a pervasive sense of anxiety, distraction, and stress in a world that seems to be spinning out of control.

Although I take the human body as the basic ground of religion, it also is important to recognize that much of the creativity of popular culture involves changing or leaving the body. Many ways of modifying the body—piercing and tattooing, plastic surgery and liposuction, cross-dressing and transsexual surgery—have increasingly become part of the American way of life. At the same time, Americans have sought to leave their bodies, flying out of this ordinary world into cyberspace, or virtual reality, unencumbered by the physical pull of planetary gravity or the physical weight of human embodiment. In these efforts, echoes of shamanism, the archaic "techniques of ecstasy," reverberate.

In religious trance, divine possession, or sacred ecstasy, the shaman can leave the body. I discuss shamans such as the African shaman Credo Mutwa, the American shaman Jim Perkins, and the divinely inspired electric shaman of rock 'n' roll, Jim Morrison. I also consider the possibility that the most important shaman in American popular culture, with his roots in ancient traditions of Siberian shamanism, might actually turn out to be not Jim Morrison but Santa Claus. In any event, this substratum of shamanic religion in American popular culture evokes a transcendence of space, place, and embodiment that has had a powerful appeal. Focusing on the body, therefore, calls for attention to the plastic, shape-shifting, and ecstatic attempts to transcend the body in American popular culture.

Within the United States, popular culture might be generalized as a kind of public religion. In the 1960s, sociologist Robert Bellah argued that the United States was animated by a collective, public, or civil religion, an understanding of the nation's historical destiny in the light of transcendence, which served as a religious warrant for American nationalism. Although civil religion, as Bellah defined it, still operates in America, these national religious impulses have thoroughly diffused through popular culture. As a result, Americans assimilate their civil religion less through the constitutional arms of the U.S. government—the executive, legislative, or judicial branches—than through the productions of film, television, radio, and other media of popular culture.

Nevertheless, as Bellah proposed, the presidents of the United States have played a central role in the formation of an American civil, public, or popular religion. Endowed with transcendent, sacred, and perhaps even ultimate power, American presidents have assumed authoritative roles not only in the public sphere but also in popular culture. In the chapters of this book, their exhortations have punctuated my explorations in American popular culture. With a definite historical interest, I have tried to situate cultural creativity within the horizon of political necessity evoked by presidents of the United States.

Starting with President Ronald Reagan, who revitalized the American ideology of redemptive sacrifice, American presidents have operated in a potent symbolic economy of blood and money that is mediated through the popular cultural outlets of film, television, and radio. As an actor, Reagan was already adept at the studied simulations required for such media transmissions and cultural transactions in America. His successors, however, forced to simulate his simulations, have only further entrenched the U.S. presidency in the media of popular culture. As a result, whether they have liked it or not, all subsequent presidents of the United States have had to operate in Ronald Reagan's world. Despite never having been movie stars, all subsequent presidents have been required to act as authentic, true-to-life replicas of American presidents on film.

In this book, I discuss U.S. presidents who have invoked civil religion, perhaps, but have also tried to establish the political horizon, the terms and limits, that might contain the proliferation of religious meanings in American popular culture. They have failed. Although Ronald Reagan revitalized a sacrificial ideology for America, celebrating the sacrifice of human lives for the social collectivity, his initiative was shadowed by Jim Jones, who led his following into mass death for the sake of a community.

Described by foreign journalists as the most powerful man in the world, President George Bush, who during his administration declared the dawn of the New World Order, became the primary suspect of conspiracy theorists during the 1990s. He was believed not only to be participating in a global conspiracy to rule the world but also to be performing human sacrifices and drinking human blood as a shape-shifting reptile, the offspring of reptilian extraterrestrials.

President Bill Clinton, who was included in this global conspiracy, tried to reinvigorate American popular culture by invoking the New Covenant for America, entering into a new transatlantic partnership with Africa, and announcing the opening of a new scientific frontier with the completion of the Human Genome Project, which he touted as holding enormous religious significance because it enables humans to learn God's language of creation.

Finally, President George W. Bush has also drawn the attention of conspiracy theorists, from his initiation into the Skull and Bones Society to his subsequent global agenda for U.S. military, economic, and cultural power in a war against terrorism.

Although the discussion of these U.S. presidents does not unfold in chronological order, their appearance in this book has a kind of coherence, because each represents the central religious commitment to redemptive sacrifice that animates American nationalism.

As an imaginative, imaginary realm, American popular culture is preoccupied with death, dying, and the dead, especially with heroic, redemptive sacrifice, which is a recurring motif of popular films, television, and other media. Clearly, death pervades American popular culture; from blockbuster entertainment to the nightly news, the body count is high. As a "cult of death," American popular culture, like American religious nationalism, seeks redemption in sacrificial death, so a consideration of death must be part of our exploration of religion and American popular culture.

All over the world, American popular culture has been disseminated and diffused into a vast array of local settings. Globalization, which is more than just a transnational mode of economic production, also expands the scope of the production and consumption of cultural forms. Clearly, America stands at the center and extends to the periphery of this globalizing network. Although critics of globalization decry the Americanization of global culture, pointing to the homogenizing effects of the Cocacolonization, McDonaldization, or Disneyization of the world, which seem inevitably to lead to the destruction of local legacies of human diversity, people all over the world seem to like it. From the perspective of consumers, who often find creative ways to localize American popular culture, its productions are not necessarily perceived as alien. Yet, even if the globalizing extensions of American popular culture are often experienced as "glocal"—both global and local—this process of cultural expansion has nevertheless reinforced certain economic, social, and political relations that entrench American power. Touching briefly on several foreign locations of American popular culture, including Russia, India, and Argentina, I focus more directly on developments in Japan and South Africa.

In the science of intercultural business communication, especially as it was designed to assist Americans in conducting global business, Japan emerged as a typical "type B" culture, according to a manual on intercultural negotiation, the opposite of the "type A" culture of America. Operating like transnational religions, Coca-Cola, McDonald's, and Disney have entered the Japanese markets on a mission to make conversions. However, despite the cultural imperialism of these quasi-religious missions, Japanese cultural entrepreneurs, as well as consumers, have found ways to convert these enterprises to suit their own interests.

The idea that the Japanese have converted these businesses instead of being converted by them recalls the argument advanced by W. E. B. Du Bois: that Africans, especially those enslaved in America, did not convert to Christianity but converted Christianity to the basic themes, rhythms, and interests of African religion. Important features of American popular culture, especially pop music, can be traced back to Africa. However, the transatlantic cultural exchanges in both religion and popular culture have been ongoing in relations between America and Africa.

I discuss several specific and crucial transatlantic exchanges between the United States and South Africa, for instance, America's popular interest in a South African political leader, Nelson Mandela, who was enthusiastically received on his visit to the States during 1990 as if he were a religious figure of mythic proportions, variously proclaimed as an African messiah, Moses, a pope, or a hero-of-a-thousand-faces. In counterpoint to Nelson Mandela, I also consider a South African religious leader, the Zulu shaman Credo Mutwa, who has gained a following in the United States among enthusiasts of New Age spirituality, representing the indigenous authenticity of African religion. According to one of his American supporters, Mutwa's religious vision supplemented Mandela's political leadership, "filling out and complementing Mandela's political journey with Mutwa's mythology."[3] At the very least, this interest in Mandela and Mutwa suggests the vitality of ongoing exchanges between America and Africa in the field of religion and popular culture.

In South Africa, powerful cultural images of America have assumed religious proportions. Nelson Mandela warned on several occasions during the 1950s that American imperialism was most dangerous because it came to Africa "elaborately disguised" not only as diplomacy and foreign aid but also as religion and popular culture.[4] However, visions of America have promised redemption as well. The American movement, with its expectation that the arrival of Americans would bring about a liberating apocalypse, emerged during the 1920s and 1930s as a popular African religious movement focusing on America as the hope of salvation. A different social movement, the criminal gang known as the Americans, which has been interpreted locally as if it were a religion, has located the meaning and power of America within the impoverished townships of Cape Town, South Africa. Coming to prominence in the 1990s, the Americans gang has advanced an alternative reading of the meaning and power of America as the sacred truth of blood and money in a globalizing world. In reviewing these transatlantic exchanges, I join the American movement and the Americans gang in South Africa in asking, "Where is America?"

Throughout this book, I confront the problem of authenticity. Although the productions of popular culture might in many ways look, sound, smell, taste, and feel like religion, there is a distinct possibility that they are not actually religious. Baseball is not a religion; Coca-Cola is not a religion; and rock 'n' roll is not a religion. But then all kinds of religious activity have been denied the status of religion, including indigenous religions labeled as superstition and alternative religious movements labeled as cults. What counts as religion, therefore, is the focus of the problem of authenticity in religion and American popular culture. Making the problem worse, some religious activity appears transparently fake, including the proliferation of invented religions on the Internet, but even fake religions can be doing a kind of symbolic, cultural, and religious work that is real.

At work and at play, human authenticity is at stake in American religion and popular culture. Religion is the real thing, but, as we already know from the world of advertising, Coca-Cola is also the real thing. Baseball and rock 'n' roll, McDonald's and Disney, Tupperware and Nike, along with all the other permutations of the popular, have artificially produced a real world. Religion, mediated through popular culture as ordinary leisure and entertainment but also as human possibility and experimentation, has appeared in the traces of transcendence, the sacred, and the ultimate in these cultural formations.

On August 25, 1998, at 7:20 P.M., an electronically triggered pipe bomb ripped through the American restaurant Planet Hollywood in the popular Waterfront shopping mall of Cape Town, South Africa, killing two people and seriously injuring twenty-six. Through the medium of talk radio, responsibility for the bombing was initially claimed that night by a self-professed member of the group Muslims against Global Oppression (MAGO) as an act of retaliation—fighting "fire with fire," he said—against the United States for its missile attacks the previous week on alleged terrorist installations in Afghanistan and Sudan. Although the leadership of MAGO subsequently disowned responsibility for the bombing, media speculation continued to focus on the possible motives for local Muslim retaliation against the United States.

During the second half of the 1990s in South Africa, several militant Muslim organizations emerged—MAGO, Muslims against Illegitimate Leaders (MAIL), and People against Gangsterism and Drugs (PAGAD)—that generally perceived the United States as a worldwide religious problem. As an icon of the American entertainment industry and, by extension, of the United States, Planet Hollywood seemed a fitting symbolic target. Earlier that year in the streets outside Parliament, in protest of President Bill Clinton's visit to South Africa, MAGO had staged a peaceful demonstration that featured the ceremonial burning of American flags. Burning the American flag, blowing up Planet Hollywood—these acts seemed to be part of a consistent pattern of religiously motivated opposition to the United States.

Like many people, I suppose I developed a heightened sensibility for danger in the wake of the bombing, even when I was not wondering whether I myself constituted a suitable American target. Sometime after the bombing, when I was walking through the Waterfront mall, I was startled by a rolling, thundering noise, like the sound of roaring waters. "Oh no, another bomb," I thought. "We're all going to die." Seconds later, however, as a swirling, screaming mass of humanity swept by me, I realized that it was not a bomb after all but only the American entertainer Michael Jackson, surrounded by an entourage of about twenty-five uniformed sailors from the South African Navy and chased by excited fans.

A regular visitor to South Africa, Michael Jackson had just been a special guest at Nelson Mandela's eightieth birthday celebration on July 18, 1998. The previous year he had toured the country, performing sold-out concerts, with proceeds going to his Heal the World Foundation. In every city he played during that tour, a huge inflatable statue was set up, reminding South Africans that Jackson is bigger than life. The frenzy I witnessed showed that the charismatic superstar certainly had an enthusiastic following in Cape Town. Despite widespread opposition to U.S. global politics, people of the city could still be devoted to this idol of American popular culture.

Jackson's artistry has drawn on the resources of religious symbols, myths, and rituals. According to cultural analyst Michael Eric Dyson, Jackson's performances are a "festive choreography of religious reality" that "communicates powerful religious truths and moral themes." In songs such as "We Are the World" (1985), "Heal the World" (1991), and "The Lost Children" (2001), Jackson's music has held out a mythic promise of redemption from human suffering. In the drama of his concerts, as Dyson notes, Jackson has turned the stage into a "world-extending sanctuary" in which audiences can ritually participate in this drama of redemption.[1] Devotion to Jackson, despite allegations of child abuse, suggests that many fans have a faith in the superstar that borders on religious faith.

In this chapter, I take Planet Hollywood and Michael Jackson as only points of departure for exploring our basic terms—*religion, the popular,* and *popular culture.* Charting a preliminary map, I set out different ways for understanding religion, for analyzing the popular, and for locating popular culture between the coercion of the state and the demands of the market. I touch on some of the key religious themes, from the religion of the body to the religious significance of globalization, which will be developed in greater detail in subsequent chapters. Everything will depend, of course, on what we mean by *religion.*

RELIGION

Religion is a difficult term to define, because everyone already "knows" what it means. What passes for common knowledge about religion tends to be organized according to binary oppositions: people know their own religion (as opposed to other religions), true religion (as opposed to false religion), or real religion (as opposed to fake religion). In exploring religion and American popular culture, we need to develop a more complex sense of what we mean by the term *religion*. Without belaboring the issue of definition, we are confronted with the ambiguity of a word that can be used in a conventional sense as a generic term for distinct religious traditions, communities, institutions, or movements, or in an analytical sense as a generic term for any kind of activity engaged with the transcendent, the sacred, or the ultimate concerns of human life. Both of these senses are important for exploring religion and popular culture. The first focuses our attention on specific religious groups in relation to popular culture; the second directs our attention to potent religious symbols, myths, and rituals that might animate cultural formations.

Fitting the conventional sense of the term, the Muslim organizations in Cape Town, as voluntary religious associations, form part of the rich, complex fabric of Islam in South Africa. Like any religion, Islam embraces a diversity of political positions—progressive, reactionary, and everything in between—in relation to the local social environment. In a globalizing world, it also reflects political positions that its adherents adopt in relation to the pervasive presence and power of the United States. Mobilizing in the mosques, some Muslim organizations have taken their religious interests to the streets in opposition to U.S. foreign policy. One of these organizations allegedly bombed Planet Hollywood, a symbol not only of American popular culture but also of a kind of global religion that has generated powerful symbols, myths, and rituals that seem to operate throughout the world like a religious mission. The franchise of Planet Hollywood, which has been described in tourist literature as "the Mecca of movie memorabilia," has restaurants in London and Paris, Jakarta and Tokyo, Dubai and Riyadh, Acapulco and Cancun, and, until 1998, in Cape Town, South Africa, occupying all the major zones of the clashing civilizations identified by political scientist Samuel Huntington as the fractures of conflict in a globalizing world. The bombing in Cape Town appeared to be another violent clash between Muslims and the West, or at least between Muslims and the West that could be imagined as centered in America, a religiously motivated attack on American sacred symbols.[2]

In the aftermath, however, Muslim leaders in Cape Town denounced the bombing. On behalf of the Muslim Judicial Council, Sheikh Achmed Seddik, while acknowledging that Muslims in Cape Town held "heavy anti-American sentiments," strongly condemned the bombing as terrorism. Likewise, a spokesman for Muslims against Global Oppression distanced his organization from the bombing, saying, "This is an act of terror."[3] Although the event was presented in the local and global media as an anti-American act, these Muslim leaders in Cape Town insisted that such an act of terror should also be understood as an anti-Muslim act, since terrorism is inconsistent with the basic religious values of Islam. Nevertheless, while the crime remained unsolved in South Africa, the U.S. State Department placed Muslims against Global Oppression on its list of terrorist organizations.

Back in the United States, meanwhile, religious controversy was generated by the representation of Muslims in Hollywood films. Anticipating the opening of *The Siege* (1998), which depicts a Muslim terrorist group planning bombings in New York, American Muslim groups protested the negative stereotypes about Islam, Muslims, and Arabs that are consistently perpetuated by Hollywood. A prominent Arab American, the disk jockey Casey Kasem, who for decades kept America tuned in to the latest hits in popular music on his radio show *American Top 40*, condemned Hollywood's tradition of vilifying Muslims. A film like *The Siege*, Kasem argued, "will leave the audience with the idea that Arabs and Muslims are terrorists and the enemies of the United States."[4]

Coincidentally, *The Siege* stars Bruce Willis, one of the owners of Planet Hollywood. In a thoughtful essay entitled "Bruce Willis versus Bin Laden," published in the Cairo weekly *Al-Ahram* in November 1998, Tarek Atia argued as a Muslim against the extremes represented by both men. In a world saturated by global media, he wrote, "Bruce Willis and Bin Laden have come, more than any other two people alive, to represent the extremes of human existence, pitted against each other. They are, in many ways, the most accessible archetypes of religious and secular extremism." Rejecting both of these extremes, Atia situated his struggle as an effort to lead a moral, spiritual life that is defined by neither fundamentalism nor secularism.[5]

According to Atia, Hollywood is not religiously neutral in this struggle. On the one hand, he argued, specific religious interests, including anti-Muslim interests, are being advanced by the "Jews who invented and remain in charge of Hollywood." Featuring in many conspiracy theories about the secret rulers of the world, Jewish control of Hollywood seems, at first glance, confirmed by history, since four out of five heads of the major film studios founded in the 1920s were from Jewish backgrounds. However, they tended to identify themselves less with Judaism than with Christianity and American nationalism. Louis B. Mayer, head of MGM, changed his birthday to the Fourth of July and attended a Catholic church that was also attended by Harry Cohn, head of Columbia Pictures. Asked to donate money to a Jewish relief fund, Cohn reportedly exclaimed: "Relief for the Jews? How about relief from the Jews? All the trouble in this world has been caused by Jews and Irishmen."[6] Although they exerted a powerful influence on the imagery of religion, race, and America, these Hollywood moguls were not advancing Jewish interests.

On the other hand, Atia maintained, secularist extremism, as embodied in an action hero such as Bruce Willis, can be regarded as a kind of secular religion promoted by Hollywood. Although he identified Willis as an archetype of secularism, Atia recalled sufficient evidence from Willis's popular films to suggest that the actor plays a quasi-religious role in American popular culture as the country's "savior" from criminals, gangsters, terrorists, and even asteroids. In *The Siege,* he seems to be saving America from Muslims.

Although entertainment is certainly an industry, it has produced superstars such as Bruce Willis and Michael Jackson, who display transcendent or sacred qualities in American popular culture. Following the sociologist Max Weber's definition of charisma, we might recognize these superstars as embodying that "certain quality of an individual personality by virtue of which he is set apart from ordinary men and treated as endowed with supernatural, superhuman and at least specifically exceptional powers and qualities."[7] Although we might want to draw other conclusions about them, we can at least recognize traces of religion—superhuman transcendence, the sacred as set apart from the ordinary—that seem to cling to the charismatic superstars of American popular culture.

In Michael Jackson's case, such traces of religion seem to be consciously mobilized, not only in maintaining his aura of mystery, but also in advancing promises of redemption. Saving the children, healing the world—these are redemptive promises that elevated Jackson to at least quasi-religious status in American popular culture. Still, we need to ask: Does it make sense to call any of this religion? Most important, does it make any difference to call any of this religion?

RELIGIOUS WORK

How does religion work? Classic definitions of religion have focused on its importance as a way of thinking, as a way of feeling, and as a way of being human in relation to other human beings in a community. As a way of thinking, according to E. B. Tylor's minimal definition, religion depends upon "belief in supernatural beings." More recently, Melford Spiro qualified this definition by stipulating that religion involves "culturally patterned interaction with culturally postulated superhuman beings." By this account, religion deals with the supernatural, which by definition cannot be confirmed or disconfirmed by ordinary sensory perception or scientific experimentation. According to this classic definition, religion works to identify certain persons as supernatural, superhuman, or at least as greater in power than ordinary humans. By this account, religion generates beliefs and practices for engaging transcendence.[8]

As a way of feeling, religion cultivates a range of intense emotions, from holy fear to sacred intimacy, which have also received attention in its classic definitions. Following Friedrich Schleiermacher's contention that religion is not a way of thinking but a way of feeling, specifically a feeling of absolute dependence upon a Supreme Being, F. Max Müller, the putative founder of the study of religion, defined it as an essentially emotional, even romantic "faculty of apprehending the Infinite." Similarly, focusing on personal feeling, Rudolf Otto defined religion as a feeling of holy awe, combining avoidance and attraction, before a mystery; William James defined religion as a personal response, in solitude, to whatever might be regarded as divine; and Paul Tillich defined it as a person's "ultimate concern" in the face of death.[9]

As a way of being in society, religion is more than merely a matter of personal thoughts and feelings. Religion involves beliefs and practices, but always in the context of social relations. In fact, as Émile Durkheim argued, religion might very well be central to the formation of society. Accordingly, Durkheim defined religion as beliefs and practices in relation to the sacred, with the "sacred" defined simply as that which is set apart from the ordinary, but in such a way that it serves to unify people who adhere to those beliefs and practices into a single moral community. Religious thinking and feeling, action and experience, in Durkheim's formulation, realize their function in the construction of any human society around the sacred.[10]

Social cohesion, according to Durkheim, depends on shared beliefs, practices, experiences, and interactions that can usefully be defined as religious. Generally, most scholars of religion have followed Durkheim in seeing religion as multidimensional, as a complex system of mythic and doctrinal belief, of ritual and ethical action, of personal and social experience.[11] Religion has been defined by Clifford Geertz as a "symbolic system" that generates powerful moods and motivations and clothes those dispositions in an aura of factuality so that they seem uniquely real in forming personal subjectivity and social solidarity.[12]

All of these classic definitions of religion percolate through this book. In part, I want to test them against the evidence of the beliefs and practices, the personal experiences and social interchanges that are actually going on in popular culture. In other words, I want to see if these "classic" definitions of religion actually matter.

At the same time, the meaning of the term *religion* is determined by usage. As the great linguist Émile Benveniste taught us, religion has been used as a highly charged marker of difference, defined precisely by its opposition to "superstition." Whatever the word might have meant in ancient Greco-Roman discourse, the term *religio* was consistently used to refer to an authentic human activity in opposition to *superstitio,* an inauthentic, alien, or even less than fully human activity that was allegedly based on ignorance, fear, or fraud.[13]

In the past I have focused on this oppositional character of the term *religion* in the cult controversies of modern America and the denial of indigenous religions of Africa under colonial conditions. I have tried to show how the term raises the stakes of human recognition, since it is inevitably used as a crucial marker in struggles over human recognition and denial. In the cult controversies, a religious movement such as the Peoples Temple of Jim Jones was denied the status of religion by being stigmatized as a cult. In European explorations of Africa, indigenous religious life was denied the status of religion by being denigrated as superstition.[14] As a marker of difference, in these cases *religion* was used as an instrument of denial.

Here I am interested not in the denial of religion but in the performative extensions of the term to the production, consumption, and artifacts of popular culture. In an essay I wrote in the mid-1990s on the church of baseball, the fetish of Coca-Cola, and the potlatch of rock 'n' roll, which I have integrated into this book, I was willing to consider these activities as religious, not because I said they were, but because participants, real people, characterized their own involvement in these enterprises as religious. Baseball players, Coca-Cola executives, and rock 'n' rollers testified that what they were doing was a kind of religion.[15] In counterpoint to the classic definitions of religion, I am interested in how the term has actually been used by people to make sense out of their lives. What did they mean when they used the term *religion* to describe their attachment to a sport, a consumer product, or an entertainment industry?

Designating popular culture as religion does not always mean accepting its religious legitimacy. Conventional religious institutions, especially conservative coalitions, have sometimes identified a competing cultural formation as religion to raise the stakes in the cultural contest. In recent years, conservative Christian groups have argued that humanism, secularism, and the scientific theory of evolution should all count as religions and therefore should be excluded from public schools. If the Christian religion cannot be established in public institutions, they have argued, then these other "religions" should also be removed in accordance with the First Amendment prohibition of any government-established religion.

Even Walt Disney productions have been subjected to such a strategic definition of religion. On June 18, 1997, the Southern Baptist Convention passed a resolution to boycott the Walt Disney Company. Arguing that the company had abandoned "its previous philosophy of producing enriching family entertainment," the convention accused Disney of promoting "immoral ideologies such as homosexuality, infidelity, and adultery." In launching a crusade against Disney, the Southern Baptist Convention argued that Disney was not merely a cultural force working against conservative Christian beliefs, values, and sexual ethics; it was also actually promoting an alternative religion, an earth-based, pagan, and pantheistic religiosity as celebrated in animated features such as *The Lion King* and *Pocahontas,* which represented a religious threat to Christianity. The Southern Baptist Convention boycotted Disney, not only because it presented a secular alternative to religion, but also because the corporation was allegedly advancing a religion of its own, in competition with Christianity.[16]

As this religious crusade against Disney suggests, popular culture can appear from different perspectives as religion. As I maneuver between classic academic definitions and actual popular uses of the term *religion,* I must admit that I do have a working definition of my own. In my view, something is doing religious work if it is engaged in negotiating what it is to be human. Classification, orientation, and negotiation—these are the processes that I look for when I study religion and religions: the processes of classifying persons into superhuman, human, and subhuman; the processes of orienting persons in time and space; and the contested negotiations over the ownership of those classifications and orientations.

In the world of Walt Disney, these patterns and processes of religious work are certainly evident. Although Disney's animated films evoke supernatural persons, such as fairies and genies, ancestral spirits and celestial kings, their religious work concentrates on playing with conventional distinctions among humans, animals, and machines. Religious classifications of persons put these distinctions at stake: What is it to be a human being, not only in relation to superhuman powers, but also in relation to beings classified as less than human? Consistently, Disney engages in a kind of religious work by trying to clarify these classifications.

At the same time, religious orientations in time and space serve to situate persons in place. In films, television, theme parks, and consumer products, the Walt

Disney Company has advanced a temporal orientation based on a poignant nostalgia for a bygone era and an unbounded optimism in scientific progress. Anchoring this temporal orientation, Disney theme parks have provided multiple sacred sites for ritual pilgrimage to the heart of a symbolic, cultural, and arguably religious sense of orientation in the world.

Classification and orientation, person and place, are inevitably negotiated in religion and popular culture. By negotiation, I refer to the relational, situational, and contested character of the production of religious meaning and power in popular culture. Negotiating the sacred does not occur in a vacuum. These struggles over the production, significance, and ownership of sacred symbols take place within a political economy of the sacred.

By using the phrase "political economy of the sacred," I want to focus attention on the ways in which the sacred is produced, circulated, engaged, and consumed in popular culture. Not merely a given, the sacred is produced through the religious labor of interpretation and ritualization. As I explore the political economy of the sacred, I want to highlight three things: First, I want to focus on the means, modes, and forces involved in the production of sacred values through religious labor. By definition, the sacred might be "set apart," but it is set apart, as Karen Fields has observed, "by doing."[17] In the political economy of the sacred, this sacred doing, or doing of the sacred, is not merely religious practice, symbolic performance, or social drama. It is a kind of religious work.

Second, I want to focus on the transformations of scarcity into surplus, the processes by which scarce resources, including symbolic capital, are transformed through religious work into sacred surpluses, especially the surplus of meaning generated through the religious work of interpretation.

Third, I want to focus on the struggles over legitimate ownership of sacred symbols, symbols made meaningful through the ongoing work of interpretation but also made powerful through appropriation, through the inevitably contested claims that are made on their ownership.

So this is what I mean by the "political economy of the sacred"—the terrain and resources, the strategies and tactics, in and through which the sacred is negotiated.[18]

THE POPULAR

According to a quantitative definition, popular culture is popular because it is mass produced, widely distributed, and regularly consumed by a large number of people.[19] Demographically, the popular might be simply understood as a measure of popularity. A cultural form is popular, in this sense, because many people like it. Implicit in this quantitative definition of the popular is a distinction between "high" culture, maintained by a numerically small social elite, and "low" culture, supported by the majority of people in a society. As a result, the popular, whether in popular culture or popular religion, has tended to be located among the laity rather than the clergy and among rural folk rather than city dwellers or among urban lower classes rather than urban elites.[20] In cultural studies, however, the popular has come to refer to a much more complex range of social positions within the production and consumption of culture.

The mass *production* of popular culture calls attention to what critical theorist Theodor Adorno called the "culture industry," the machinery of mass cultural production in a capitalist economy. Instead of assuming that popular culture is mass-produced because many people like it, Adorno argued that people like it because they basically have no choice. Effectively, the culture industry beats them into submission. Readily available and immediately accessible, mass-produced popular culture emerges as the only option within capitalist relations of production. As cultural production becomes an industry, artwork is transformed into a commodity that is created and exchanged for profit. In the process, the distinction between high culture and popular culture dissolves, since both "bear the stigmata of capitalism."[21]

The culture industry produces two basic effects in popular culture: uniformity and utility. Rather than meeting the diversity of popular desires for leisure or entertainment, the culture industry creates a new uniformity of desire. "Culture now impresses the same stamp on everything," Adorno and his colleague Max Horkheimer complained. "Films, radio and magazines make up a system which is uniform as a whole and in every part." Within the capitalist system of cultural production, leisure is integrated into the cycle of productive labor. Leisure, entertainment, and amusement are extensions of work, employments of "free" time that are organized by the same principle of utility that governs the capitalist system of production. As an integral part of the capitalist economy, the culture industry provides popular cultural diversions that the masses seek "as an escape from the mechanized work process, and to recruit strength in order to be able to cope with it again." In this production-oriented model, therefore, popular culture serves the interests of capital—profitability, uniformity, and utility—by entangling people in a culture industry in which a character such as "Donald Duck in the cartoons . . . gets his beating so that the viewers can get used to the same treatment."[22]

The popular reception, or *consumption,* of cultural forms, styles, and content calls attention to the many different ways people actually find to make mass-produced culture their own. Following the critical theorist Walter Benjamin, many cultural analysts argue that the reception of popular culture involves not passive submission but creative activity. Although recognizing the capitalist control of mass-produced culture, Benjamin nevertheless found that people develop new perceptual and interpretive capacities that enable them to transform private hopes and fears into "figures of the collective dream such as the globe-orbiting Mickey Mouse."[23]

Where Adorno insisted that the productions of the culture industry are oppressive, Benjamin looked for the therapeutic effects, such as the healing potential of collective laughter and even the redemptive possibilities in the reception of popular culture. In the case of Mickey Mouse, for example, Benjamin suggested that audiences are able to think through basic cultural categories—machines, animals, and humans—by participating in a popular form of entertainment that scrambles them. As Benjamin observed, Mickey Mouse cartoons are "full of miracles that not only surpass those of technology but make fun of them." Against the laws of nature and technology, these "miracles" of transformation—changing shape, defying gravity—occur spontaneously "from the body of Mickey Mouse, his partisans and pursuers." For an audience "grown tired of the endless complications of the everyday," Benjamin concluded, these miracles promise a kind of "redemption" in an extraordinary world.[24]

Without necessarily subscribing to the proposition of a therapeutic capacity or a redemptive potential of popular culture, cultural analysts adopting the reception-oriented model have concentrated on the creative activity of interpretation as itself a means of cultural production that takes place in the process of cultural consumption. As people actively decode cultural content through interpretation, they also participate in rituals of consumption, rituals of exchange, ownership, and care, through which the arts and artifacts of popular culture are personalized.[25]

In between cultural production and consumption, the space of popular culture is a contested terrain in which people occupy vastly different and often multiple subject positions grounded in race, ethnicity, social class, occupation, region, gender, sexual orientation, and so on. As the cultural theorist Stuart Hall has established, popular culture is a site of struggle in which various alternative cultural projects contend with the hegemony of the dominant culture. Subcultures develop oppositional positions, perhaps even methods of "cultural resistance," thereby creating alternative cultural formations, which social elites work to appropriate and assimilate into the larger society. Not a stable system of production and consumption, popular culture is a battlefield of contending strategies, tactics, and maneuvers in struggles over the legitimate ownership of highly charged cultural symbols of meaning and power.[26]

BETWEEN STATE AND MARKET

For the most part, recent research on religion and popular culture has focused on leisure pursuits. Analysts examining film, television, music, sports, and recreation for traces of religion have discovered religious symbols, myths, and rituals operating in all of these forms of popular culture. They have found myths of apocalypse in the movies of Stanley Kubrick and myths of a promised land in the music of Bruce Springsteen; rituals of confession in the courtroom television show of Judge Judy and rituals of pilgrimage at the theme parks of Walt Disney; powerful religious symbols of communal solidarity in the mainstream sports of baseball and football as well as in countercultural events such as the annual Burning Man celebration in the Nevada desert, a festival dedicated to the "creative power of ritual" in forming a temporary sacred community. All of these readings have helped us to see how religion is at play in American popular culture.

Participation in popular culture, as in a religious community, can be located between the power of the state and the demands of the market. From the perspective of the consumer, enjoying popular culture is different from paying taxes or working for wages. Beyond any rationale of the state or necessity of the market, popular culture appears to belong to a realm of desire, the space of leisure, enjoyment, and fun. All of this cultural play, however, is directly related to the serious work of the state and the market. In practice, the three spheres of state, market, and popular culture blur into each other. Paying attention to religion, I argue, helps in understanding the mixing and merging of political, economic, and cultural interests in American popular culture.

As Max Weber proposed, the state, by definition, is the organized exercise of violence over a territory. The state is a concentration of force asserting a privileged monopoly on the exercise of "legitimate" violence, whether overt or subtly coercive, through its military, legislative, policing, and tax-collecting institutions within the geography of a particular social space. But the legitimacy of the violence exercised by any state cannot simply be assumed. Inevitably, legitimacy is underwritten by a civil religion, a political religion, or a religious nationalism that confers a transcendent, sacred, or ultimate aura of necessity upon the state's exercise of violence. In these terms, any state, including a superstate such as the United

States, draws upon religious symbols, myths, and rituals in support of its ultimate claims on the exclusive exercise of violence over a territory.[27]

Also according to the insights of Weber, the capitalist market has not been merely an economic arena of competition in which individuals seek to maximize profits and minimize losses. In the history of the emergence of capitalism, religious interests were also at stake. If a capitalist economy was going to develop in the Christian West, the sin of usury had to be transformed into the virtue of capital investment. Without rehearsing the whole history of this religious transformation, we can still recognize that the emergence of capitalism as an economic order required certain religious dispositions of self-discipline (in productive labor) and self-denial (in postponing enjoyment of the fruits of labor by investing any accumulated resources in capital markets). By positioning the religious dynamics of American popular culture between the inherent violence of the state and the insistent demands of the market, we can track both the play of meaning and the work of power within the same political economy of the sacred.

Exploring religion and American popular culture can be fun. We enjoy watching baseball, drinking Coca-Cola, and listening to rock 'n' roll. For real excitement, we participate in firewalking rituals, go on guided tourist pilgrimages in Japan, Russia, and Africa, and are abducted by aliens from outer space. In the new frontiers of science, technology, and communication at the beginning of the twenty-first century, we are amazed at the instruction manual that God used to create the world, as mapped and sequenced by the Human Genome Project, and we are delighted by our apparently unlimited capacity to create new religions in cyberspace—the Discordians and the Church of the SubGenius, the Church of Elvis and the Church of the Almighty Dollar, the Church of the Bunny and the Church of Virus, not to mention the Kick-Ass Post-Apocalyptic Doomsday Cult of Love.

Seriously, however, the religious dynamics of American popular culture are not all fun and games. At stake in all this play is a profound question: How does personal subjectivity intersect with a social collectivity? In other words, how are we supposed to be human beings in relation to other human beings? How do our lives, but also our deaths, make sense?

REDEMPTIVE SACRIFICE

Religion, I argue, provides media for bridging the personal and the social, for connecting individual subjects with larger social collectives, such as clans, communities, and nations. Religious symbols, myths, and rituals are resources for merging the first person singular into a first person plural, for transforming any particular "I" into a collective "Us."

In the history of religions, the most ancient and widely distributed religious ritual is sacrifice—the consecration, offering, display, and consumption of a sacrificial victim. However, sacrifice is also a modern ritual. As the philosopher Slavoj Žižek has recently argued, sacrifice is the essence of a Christian legacy worthy of preserving in the modern West. As the highest expression of Christian love, or *agape*, sacrifice is the destruction of a loved object, according to Žižek. Under normal conditions, the ritual of sacrifice offers that loved object to God. In situations of violent conflict, however, sacrifice occurs for a different reason: now the loved object is sacrificed to avoid capture by an enemy.

According to Žižek, under such conditions, destroying the beloved object might be regarded as redemptive for two reasons. First, the loved one who is sacrificed might be saved from a fate worse than death. In this regard, a sacrificial death can be better than an unacceptable life. Second, the sacrificer, in killing the loved object, gives up his stake in the world that tied him to the social order. By sacrificing what is most precious, the sacrificer "changes the co-ordinates of the situation in which [he] finds himself; by cutting himself loose from the precious object through whose possession the enemy kept him in check, the subject gains the space of free action."[28]

This horrible calculation of killing and being killed, underwritten by a religious promise of redemptive sacrifice, moves through the political, economic, and cultural spheres of America. This same calculation of redemptive sacrifice occurs not only in the Christian nationalism of a U.S. president such as Ronald Reagan but also in the countercultural, communist strategies of Jim Jones, who led his community into a mass suicide in the interest of keeping their perceived U.S. enemy in check and gaining a free space for a fully human identity. Strikingly, ritualized sacrifice has registered as a recurring theme in the formation of states, markets, and popular culture.

In the late nineteenth century, in the midst of European nation building, Ernest Renan asked, "What is a nation?" A nation, he suggested, is formed out of a spiritual quality, a spirit, a soul, a collective soul, which is continuous with the past and uniform in the present. Continuity and uniformity, as Renan recognized, might be established on the tenuous basis of national ignorance, prejudice, and xenophobia, thereby defining a nation as a group of people who misunderstand their own history and hate their neighbors. Regardless of that, sacrifice, according to Renan, is the essential unifying feature of a nation. Whatever people might understand (or misunderstand) about their past or think about their neighbors, they have participated in a shared, collective national identity by virtue of sacrifice. According to Renan, a nation is "a large-scale solidarity, constituted by the feeling of the sacrifices that one has made in the past and of those one is prepared to make in the future."[29] Past, present, and future, in this view, become a national collectivity— continuous with the past, uniform in the present, open to the future—only because individuals are prepared to perform sacrifices before the altar of the nation.

Critics of the capitalist market economy have emphasized the sacrificial nature of its economic activity: the sacrifice of any immediate gratification of personal desires for self-discipline in productive labor and for self-denial in the deferment of present rewards in the hope of future profits. Many critics of capitalism—Karl Marx and Georges Bataille, Jim Jones and David Icke—for all their differences, agree that the basic, underlying function of the capitalist economy is to sacrifice human beings and suck their blood for financial gain. This interchange between blood and money is a recurring theme in controversies over the meaning of capitalism.

As a ritual, sacrifice attends to the body; it involves setting apart the physical body of a victim, consecrating it, killing it, and consuming it. The human body, therefore, is important in explorations of religion and popular culture that also bring in the state, the market, and the ideology of redemptive sacrifice. Other accounts of religion and American popular culture have paid attention to the senses of seeing and hearing, especially as they are employed in the audiovisual media of film, television, and even the Internet. Embodied human beings, however, have the capacity for engaging a richer sensory field than merely sight and sound. We are enveloped in a sensory world that is intimately tactile, drawing on the sense of touch as a register of contact and caress, binding and heat, motion and manipulation, tangibly involving our personal subjectivity within a larger world of contact. Accordingly, the sensory dynamics of tactility, the intimacy of human contacts, caresses, and shocks, require examination within the scope of religion and American popular culture.

RELIGION OF THE BODY

Although the human body might be vulnerable to being sacrificed in the interests of the state or the market, it can also be enjoyed as a personal domain of sensory, intimate, and desirable experiences. As material site, malleable substance, and shifting field of relations, the body is situated at the center of the production and consumption of religion and popular culture. As William R. LaFleur has observed, the body "has become a critical term for religious studies whereas 'mysticism,' for instance, has largely dropped out."[30] Displacing earlier concerns with religious beliefs and doctrines, with inner experience and spirituality, this interest in the body signals a new engagement with materiality—perhaps a new materialism— in the study of religion and popular culture.

Certainly, the body provides sensory media—seeing, hearing, tasting, smelling, and touching—that make both religion and popular culture possible. Nothing enters the human mind, culture, or religion, as the ancient Greek philosopher Aristotle insisted, unless it first passes through the embodied senses.

Although Aristotle regarded the sense of touch as the lowest human sense, as the most material, animal, and servile, tactility provides an excellent avenue into the embodied sensibility of popular culture. Basically, popular culture is regarded as good if it feels good, if it provides pleasurable sensations along the tactile register of the body. Tactility involves three things: the feelings of the flesh, the movements of the body, and the handling of objects by the body, especially the hands, in any sensory, perceptual, cultural, or religious environment. If we want to understand religion and popular culture, we need to pay close attention to these tactile engagements with the binding, burning, moving, and handling of the world that are simultaneously human, cultural, and religious.

The human body is a sensory field, sensing what is present and also what is absent. Introducing a series of essays, *About Religion,* theologian Mark C. Taylor observes—poetically, enigmatically—that religion is "about a certain about" that inevitably eludes our conceptual grasp. According to Taylor, it is "impossible to grasp what religion is about—unless, perhaps, what we grasp is the impossibility of grasping." Neither quite there nor exactly not there, religion is "always slipping away."[31] However, even this slippage that signals the impossibility of touching, holding, or conceptually grasping religion forces us back to the body, to its sensory media and metaphors and the kinds of knowledge that can be gained only by the body. Given the centrality of the body in human life, we might ask: What do the hands know about grasping that scholars of religion and culture do not know? This book examines the sense of touch as an avenue for entering the embodied, visceral, and material field of religion and popular culture.

Out of the sensory, sensual resources of the body, desire emerges as a driving force in religion and popular culture. Desire, it must be noted, is an essentially religious problem. Every religion has its own logic of desire. In the Christian universe outlined by Dante in his *Divine Comedy,* desire is a force that has to be directed away from the world and toward God. In the Buddhist universe outlined in the Bardo Thödol, the Tibetan Book of the Dead, desire is a force that has to be eliminated, thereby extinguishing all personal attachments to the world in order to enter the spiritual liberation known as Nirvana. As these brief allusions to Christian and Buddhist logics of desire can only suggest, religious traditions have wrestled with desire as the fundamental human dilemma.[32]

However, human desire also poses a problem in the popular culture of mass media, entertainment, and advertising. Modern American advertising, which has been characterized as "Adcult USA," conveniently solves that problem by creating an imaginary world in which people get what they want because they want what they get, that is, by persuading people to desire all kinds of things they do not actually need.

As the body is sensory, so is it gendered. Males, females, and other gendered possibilities are drawn into popular culture as consumers but also as subjects of representation. Women, characteristically, have been subjects of representation in advertising, cast as objects of desire but not always as personal subjects possessing an agency of their own.

Sexuality as well is at play in popular culture, but it is also at stake in the formation of states and markets. The public affairs of state are inevitably entangled in the most intimate affairs of gender and sexuality. Religious fundamentalists, shoring up boundaries they perceive to be threatened, inevitably focus on sex. But they also focus on money, trying to limit the promiscuous flows of capital across national boundaries. Sex and money, as highly charged symbolic forms, drawing upon embodied human desires, coalesce in contemporary struggles over the meaning, power, and control of the modern state in a globalizing world.[33]

AMERICA IN A GLOBALIZING WORLD

Recently, scholars have argued that the terms *religion* and *religions* are so damaged by their colonial, imperial, and globalizing legacy that they should be abandoned in cultural analysis.[34] At the same time, other scholars have employed conventional sociological models of religion and religions in the context of globalization.[35]

Neither of these approaches is satisfactory. In the first instance, we require rigorous conceptual terms for analyzing authoritative discourses and practices that transact with the transcendent, the sacred, or the ultimate in all areas of human life. For better or worse, the terms *religion* and *religions* can be useful in highlighting these meaningful and powerful human formations.

However, conventional models of religion fail to account for the dynamic transformations of religious resources and strategies in the making, unmaking, and remaking of religious worlds. By isolating religion as a separate, distinct, and differentiated social institution, conventional models cannot effectively track its dispersions and diffusions throughout the complex field of globalizing social, political, economic, and cultural relations.

To illustrate this problem, we can refer to the simple distinction that Peter Berger, director of the Institute for the Study of Economic Culture at Boston University, made among four processes of cultural globalization—the economic integration of Davos culture, the human-rights initiatives of faculty club culture, the Americanization of global popular culture, and the worldwide expansion of evangelical Protestantism.[36] The last cultural process explicitly registers as religion, suggesting for Berger the salience of an ongoing relation between a certain kind of religious orientation and economic development, a globalizing of the Protestant ethic and the spirit of capitalism in which "Max Weber is alive and well and living in Guatemala." However, all four of these global cultural processes bear strong traces of religious patterns and processes.[37]

The globalizing economy has been portrayed as the "religion of the market," driven by a "theology of the market," in the service of "'the market' as the modern god," and, in South African president Thabo Mbeki's observation, as "a supernatural phenomenon to whose dictates everything human must bow in a spirit of powerlessness." In the same vein, multinational corporations have been analyzed as missionizing religions, with globalization invoked as a mythic charter for opening up new markets all over the world. In a recent discussion of religious missions in Africa, analysts of Christian proselytization observed that "the Coca-Cola executive, committed to a profit margin for Atlanta, is no less a missionary than the American Baptist who teaches science in a high school in Nigeria."[38]

Transnational social movements for human rights have been analyzed as inevitably entangled with religion, whether human rights discourse is regarded as irreducibly religious, in conflict with religious loyalties, or in productive counterpoint to religious commitments. In drafting the Universal Declaration of Human Rights in 1948, delegates debated the role of religion. One delegate advocated reference to God in the preamble, arguing that nonbelievers could simply ignore that section, but most agreed that no part of the text should be ignored by anyone, arguing against such reference. Accordingly, this foundational document of the human rights movement is not religious, although it might still be regarded as bearing traces of religion, even operating as a "secular religion," in its appeal to transcendent norms and values, its assumptions about the sacred, inviolable character of every human being, and its status as the ultimate standard of personal rights and collective responsibility in the world.[39]

Likewise, globalizing popular culture, especially in its Americanizing expansion, has been analyzed as both displacement and reconfiguration of religious impulses. Popular culture has a lot to do with how Americans in the United States think about America, but it has also been dispersed and diffused throughout the world to make America a template for imagining human possibility in ways that bear traces of religion.[40]

Clearly, we need new intellectual resources for dealing with this complex, shifting terrain for the analysis of religion and religions in a globalizing world. Because the notion of "religion" can be stretched so far as to lose any analytical usefulness, especially if we think we can use it to refer to anything and everything, our understanding of religion requires critical and creative reworking in response to new challenges posed by globalization.

All over the world, people have sought to mold American popular culture to serve their own religious interests. In this process, local cultural formations are also molded in American style, but not necessarily in ways that are controlled by corporate headquarters in the United States. Within the United States, new forces and discourses beyond any centralized control have shaped cultural formations on frontiers, in the borderlands, and through processes of creolization; at the same time, much of what is regarded as distinctively "American" culture can be traced in origin to Africa, Asia, Europe, or elsewhere.[41]

In all of these cultural exchanges, the term *religion* identifies a layer, dimension, strand, or thread of culture that bestows a certain degree of urgency upon questions of human identity. In the constellation of discourses and forces shaping America at the beginning of the twenty-first century, popular culture operates at the intersection of new technologies of cultural production, new modes of cultural consumption, and new strategies for imagining human possibility. These new elements have made a dramatic difference in the ways that popular cultural formations overlap with religion, not only in the United States, but also in the world. At the center and the periphery of these formations, the United States—as Planet Hollywood, as Planet America—has assumed a popular cultural presence of religious proportions. In the chapters that follow, I explore the multiple meanings of *religion* in American popular culture.

CHAPTER TWO · Popular Religion

Whether defined as a specialized social institution dealing in the supernatural or as a symbolic system revolving around the sacred, religion represents resources and strategies for being human. The conventional view of religion defines it as a separate, distinct type of social institution that maintains traditional beliefs and practices in a community. According to this definition, three basic relationships have been established between religion and popular culture: religion appears in popular culture; popular culture is integrated into religion; and religion is sometimes in conflict with the production and consumption of popular culture.

First, we frequently encounter representations of religion in the productions of popular culture. During the twentieth century, the explosion of electronic media expanded the scope of religious representations through radio, film, television, and the Internet. On December 24, 1906, the first wireless radio broadcast in the United States consisted of a religious program of devotional music and Bible reading.[1] Although electronic media have certainly been exploited by religious groups for their own interests, the culture industry has also been actively involved in representing religious themes.

In American popular culture, the secular and commercial productions of Hollywood films have played a powerful role in shaping public perceptions of religion. Some representations of religion can be explicit. For instance, popular films depict recognizable religious characters—priests and nuns, evangelists and rabbis, gurus and lamas—in developing their narratives, which can be drawn from the story lines of religious traditions, especially from the Bible. Often other representations of religion in film are implicit. According to many cultural analysts, basic religious motifs of sin, sacrifice, and redemption, for example, can structure the plots of ostensibly secular films.[2]

Second, we observe the integration of popular culture into the practices of conventional religions. Successful religious groups generally adopt the material culture, the visual media, the musical styles, and other features of popular culture.[3] In American culture, the prominence of religious broadcasting on television has demonstrated the success of Christian evangelicals in appropriating an advanced communication technology in the service of the "great mandate" to preach their gospel to all nations. More recently, religious groups have established their presence on the Internet, exploring the potential of cyberspace for religious mobilization.

Drawn into the service of transmitting religion, the media of popular culture present both new possibilities and new limits for the practice of religion. In the entire range of electronic media, the transmission of religion is exclusively visual and auditory, developing new forms of visual piety and new styles of preaching, praying, and singing. But electronic media religion is devoid of all the smells, tastes, and physical contacts that feature in conventional religious ritual and religious life.

While converting popular culture to religious purposes, religious groups are also converted by the pervasive culture of consumerism in American society. As a prominent if not defining feature of American popular culture, consumerism has resulted in "selling God," transforming religious holy days into "consumer rites," and even fostering "religio-economic corporations," such as Amway, Herbalife, and Mary Kay Cosmetics, which merge business, family, and a Christian gospel of prosperity into a "charismatic capitalism."[4]

Third, we often find tensions between religious groups and the productions of popular culture. Frequently, conservative Christians complain about the moral relativism and spiritual corruption of American popular culture in general. With particular intensity, they single out rock, rap, and other forms of popular recorded music as being dangerously immoral, antisocial, and antireligious. Religious campaigns to censor, label, or otherwise influence popular music are periodically waged by conservative Christian activists and organizations. Going beyond the music and lyrics, these critics attack the imagery, values, and lifestyles associated with these popular art forms.

In this cultural conflict over popular music, evangelical Christians have created a successful commercial industry in Christian rock music—or contemporary

Christian music—which is unified less by musical style, rhythm, or performance than by the explicitly religious content of the lyrics. Conflict between a particular religious grouping and the productions of popular culture, therefore, can result in the emergence of alternative cultural movements, which can even establish a place within the culture industry.[5]

As conventional religious groups interact with popular culture in these ways—through representation in its media, adoption of its techniques, and rejection of its productions—the dividing line between religion and popular culture blurs. While popular media are telling religious stories and religious groups are appropriating popular media, culture wars engage intense religious interest. The very term *religion* becomes part of the contested terrain of popular culture. As suggested by the Southern Baptist Convention's crusade against the Walt Disney Company in accusing it of advancing an alternative pagan religion, participants in cultural struggles can engage in popular culture from different perspectives as if it were religion. Along similar lines, religious critics occasionally attack rock music for promoting the alternative religions of Satanism or pantheism. In these exchanges, it is hard to tell where religion leaves off and popular culture begins. Participants in popular culture often report that religious interests are at stake. Does it make sense to say that popular culture can operate as religion?

POPULAR CULTURE AS RELIGION

In considering popular culture as religion, everything depends, of course, on what we mean by religion. The academic study of religion draws on an intellectual legacy of competing definitions. Recall that E. B. Tylor, the founder of the anthropology of religion, defined religion as beliefs and practices relating to the supernatural, while Émile Durkheim, the founder of the sociology of religion, defined religion as beliefs and practices relating to a sacred focus that unifies people as a community.[6] For our purposes, these academic definitions share an interest in setting religion apart from everyday or mundane aspects of human life. Religion is cast as superhuman and sacred, as transcendent and ultimate, as highly charged and extraordinary. Looking at popular culture, however, we find ordinary cultural production and consumption. How could such ordinary activity be regarded as extraordinary?

In fact, the testimony of a number of participants in popular culture includes claims about its religious character. Reflecting on baseball after a lifetime of devotion to the sport, Buck O'Neil asserted, "It is a religion." On behalf of the Coca-

Cola Company, advertising director Delony Sledge declared, "Our work is a religion rather than a business." Responding to the extraordinary popularity of the Beatles, John Lennon observed that popular music seemed to be replacing Christianity in the field of religion because the Beatles were "more popular than Jesus." Perhaps many participants in the popular culture of rock 'n' roll would subscribe to rock critic Dan Graham's statement of faith, "Rock My Religion."[7] Still, the problem remains: What do we mean by religion? Although all of these participants in popular culture use the term *religion,* they use it in different ways. We need to understand these different constructions of religion in popular culture.

Baseball is a religion because it defines a community of allegiance, the "church of baseball." In both the past and the present, this sport has operated like a religious tradition in preserving the symbols, myths, and rituals of a sacred collectivity. Certainly, other sports provide a similar basis for sacred allegiance. As one wrestling journalist observed, a television exposé of the alleged fakery in the World Wrestling Federation (WWF) was contemptible because it tried to reveal "the 'secrets' of our sacred 'sport.'" While this journalist qualified the term *sport* with quotation marks, he did not similarly qualify the term *sacred.* Although staged, contrived, and faked as if it were a sport, WWF wrestling may still be regarded as sacred because it enacts a popular American contest of good against evil. As ritual rather than sport, WWF wrestling can be regarded as religion because it reinforces a certain kind of sacred solidarity in American popular culture.[8]

Like sports fans, the fans of Hollywood films, television shows, and popular music can participate in similar kinds of sacred solidarity, especially when that community of allegiance is focused on the extraordinary personality of a celebrity. Elvis Presley, of course, has emerged as the preeminent superhuman person in American popular culture, celebrated as an extraordinary being throughout the country, from the official sanctuary of Graceland to the unofficial Web site of the First Presleyterian Church of Elvis the Divine. Devotees collect, arrange, and display Elvis memorabilia, participate in the annual rituals of Elvis week, and go on pilgrimage to the shrine at Graceland, finding in the King not only a religious focus of attention but also a focus for mobilizing an ongoing community of sacred allegiance.[9] Similarly, fans of the *Star Trek* television series and movies have created a community of sacred solidarity that has assumed the proportions of a popular religion, with its own myths and rituals, its special language, and regular pilgrimages.[10] It is the sacred solidarity evoked in all these cases that renders the term *religion* appropriate.

Coca-Cola is a religion because it involves a sacred object, an object of global religious attention. In addition, as a consumer product that no one needs but everyone desires, Coke is an icon of the American way of life, a way of life that is celebrated at the pilgrimage site of the World of Coca-Cola in Atlanta, Georgia, but has also been diffused throughout the world. Coke is a sacred object at the center of a cultural religion that is both American and global, within arm's reach of desire all over the world, according to former company president Roberto Goizueta. In its materiality, the religion of Coca-Cola recalls the importance of icons, relics, and other sacred objects in the history of religions.

Certainly, American popular culture enjoys a rich diversity of sacred icons, such as Disney's mouse, the McDonald's arches, Nike's swoosh, and Barbie, "the image, the ideal." As many cultural analysts have observed, these icons have been established by an advertising industry that has functioned like a religion, a religious enterprise that one critic has called Adcult USA. The sacred materiality of these icons, however, reminds us of the importance of material culture in religion. In the production and consumption of popular culture, even ordinary objects can be transformed into icons, extraordinary magnets of meaning with a religious cast. In conjunction with these objects of popular culture, the term *religion* seems appropriate because it signals a certain quality of attention, desire, and even reverence for sacred materiality.[11]

Rock 'n' roll is a religion because it enacts an intense, ritualized performance—the "collective effervescence," as Durkheim put it—which is generated by the interaction between ritual specialists and congregants or, in this case, between artists and audiences. Recent research on religious ritual has focused on the dynamics of performance. From this perspective, ritual is sacred drama. In performance, ritual is also an interactive exchange, a dynamic process of giving and receiving. According to rock critic Dave Marsh, rock 'n' roll is religious because it involves precisely such a sacred ritual of exchange, a ritual of giving and receiving, exemplified by the break in the archetypal rock song "Louie, Louie," when the singer screeches, "Let's give it to 'em, right now!"[12] This giving is a pure gift, transcending the prevailing American value system that is based on maximizing profits and minimizing losses within an overarching system of capitalist market relations. American popular culture valorizes gift giving—at birthdays, weddings, and other ritual occasions—in ways that the market cannot valuate. In such rituals of giving and receiving, where value in the exchange is not determined solely by the market, popular culture preserves important aspects of traditional religious life. For these ritualized occasions of gift giving, the term *religion* seems appropriate in describing performances, practices, or events of sacred exchange.

To explore in more detail these claims that a competitive sport, a consumer product, and a type of musical entertainment might be regarded as religions, let us return to the testimonies of participants. "What has a lifetime of baseball taught you?" Buck O'Neil is asked in an interview for Ken Burns's television series on the history of the American national pastime. O'Neil, the great first baseman of the Kansas City Monarchs in the 1930s, served baseball for over six decades as player, coach, manager, and scout. "It is a religion," he responds. "For me," he adds. "You understand?"

Not exactly, of course, because we have no idea what O'Neil means by the term *religion*. As Ken Burns would have it, baseball is a religion because it operates in American culture like a church, "the church of baseball." Is that how we should understand religion in American popular culture, as an organized human activity that functions like the more familiar religious institution of the Christian church?

To complicate the matter, consider this: A religion is not a specific institution; rather, a religion is "a system of symbols." So says anthropologist Clifford Geertz; so also says author Mark Pendergrast in his account of a new religion that was founded in America but eventually achieved truly global scope, the religion of Coca-Cola. In his popular history *For God, Country, and Coca-Cola*, Pendergrast concludes that the fizzy, caramel-colored sugar water stands as a "sacred symbol" that induces "worshipful" moods that animate an "all-inclusive world view espousing perennial values such as love, peace, and universal brotherhood."[13] According to this reading, religion is about sacred symbols and systems of sacred symbols that endow the world with meaning and value. As Pendergrast argues, Coca-Cola—the sacred name, the sacred formula, the sacred image, the sacred object—has been the fetish at the center of a popular American system of religious symbolism.

But we can complicate things even further by revisiting the line that singer Joe Ely screams before the instrumental break in the Kingsmen's 1963 rock classic, "Louie, Louie." In the midst of the clashing, crashing cacophony, with lyrics that are mostly unintelligible at any speed, we are struck by the strained screech of Ely's exhortation, "Let's give it to 'em, right now!" What kind of "gift" is this?

In his book-length history of the song, which explores "the secret" of "Louie, Louie," rock critic Dave Marsh proposes that one useful model for understanding this kind of gift giving appears in the ritualized display, presentation, and destruction of property associated with the potlatch, performed by indigenous American societies in the Pacific Northwest. This analogy with a Native American ritual, Marsh argues, can illuminate what he calls the "socioreligious" character of

"Louie, Louie" in American culture. In this sense, however, religion is not an institution; it is not a system of symbols; it is the gift.

Church, fetish, potlatch—these three terms represent different models for representing religion. By examining the recent usage of these terms in popular accounts of baseball, Coca-Cola, and rock 'n' roll, I will explore some of the consequences of using these models to locate religion in American popular culture. As we will see in greater detail, the forces of these three models, representing, respectively, the institutional formation of the church, the powerful but artificial making of the fetish, and the nonproductive expenditure of the potlatch, shape very different understandings of the character of religion. Furthermore, the play of these three models in popular culture shows, again, that the very term *religion*, including its definition, application, and extension, does not, in fact, belong solely to academics but is constantly at stake in the interchanges of cultural discourses and practices.

THE CHURCH OF BASEBALL

Buck O'Neil went on to clarify why baseball is a religion to him: because it is an enduring institution that is governed by established rules. "If you go by the rules," he explains, "it is right." Baseball is a religion, according to O'Neil, because "it taught [him] and it teaches everyone else to live by the rules, to abide by the rules."[14] This definition of religion as rule-governed behavior, however, is not sufficiently comprehensive or detailed to capture what Ken Burns presents as the religious character of baseball. The "church of baseball" involves much more than merely a rule book. It is a religious institution that maintains the continuity, uniformity, sacred space, and sacred time of American life. As the "faith of fifty million people," baseball does everything that we conventionally understand to be done by the institution of the church.[15]

First, through the forces of tradition, heritage, and collective memory, baseball ensures a sense of continuity in the midst of a constantly changing America. As Donald Hall suggests, "Baseball, because of its continuity over the space of America and the time of America, is a place where memory gathers."[16] Certainly, this emphasis on collective memory dominates Burns's documentary on baseball. But it also seems to characterize the religious character of the sport in American culture. Like a church, Major League Baseball institutionalizes a sacred memory of the past that informs the present.

Second, baseball supports a sense of uniformity, a sense of belonging to a vast, extended American family that attends the same church. As journalist Thomas

Boswell reports in his detailed discussion of the church of baseball, his mother was devoted to baseball because "it made her feel like she was in church." Like her church, Boswell explains, baseball provided his mother with "a place where she could—by sharing a fabric of beliefs, symbols, and mutual agreements with those around her—feel calm and whole."[17] Boswell draws out a series of analogies between baseball and his mother's church: both feature organs; both encourage hand clapping to their hymns; both have distinctive vestments; and in both, everyone is equal before God. Although his analogy between the base paths of a diamond and the Christian cross seems a bit strained, the rest of the essay provides sufficient justification for Boswell's assertion that his mother regarded her attendance of baseball games and church as roughly equivalent.

Third, the religion of baseball represents the sacred space of home. In this respect, baseball is a religion of the domestic, of the familiar, and even of the obvious. As Boswell explains, "Baseball is a religion that worships the obvious and gives thanks that things are exactly as they seem. Instead of celebrating mysteries, baseball rejoices in the absence of mysteries and trusts that, if we watch what is laid before our eyes, down to the last detail, we will cultivate the gift of seeing things as they really are." The vision of reality that baseball affords, therefore, is a kind of normality, the ordinary viewed through a prism that only enhances its familiarity. While many religions point to a perfect world beyond this world, Boswell observes, baseball creates a "perfect universe in microcosm within the real world."[18] By producing such a ritualized space within the world, baseball domesticates the sacred and gives it a home.

Fourth, the religion of baseball represents the sacred time of ritual. "Everything is high-polish ritual and full-dress procession," Boswell notes. The entire proceedings of the game are coordinated through a ritualization of time. But baseball also affords those extraordinary moments of ecstasy and enthusiasm, revelation and inspiration, that seem to stand outside the ordinary temporal flow. According to Boswell, his mother experienced such moments as "ritual epiphany" in church. "Basically," he reports, "that's how she felt about baseball, too."[19] Through ritual and revelation, baseball provides an experience of sacred time that liberates its devotees from time's constraints.

In these terms, therefore, baseball is a church, a "community of believers." Certainly, the church of baseball is confronted by the presence of unbelievers within the larger society. Thomas Boswell also reports that his father failed to find his rightful place among the faithful in the church of baseball. "The appeal of baseball mystified him," Boswell explains, "just as all religions confound the innocent bewildered atheist." Like any church, however, baseball has its committed faithful, its true believers. The opening speech of Annie Savoy in the film *Bull Durham* (1989) can be invoked as a passionate statement of religious devotion to baseball. "I believe in the church of baseball," she declares. She testifies that she has experimented with all other forms of religious worship, including the worship of Buddha, Allah, Brahma, Vishnu, Siva, trees, mushrooms, and Isadora Duncan, but those religions did not satisfy. Even the worship of Jesus, she confesses, did not work out, because the Christian religion involves too much guilt. The religion of baseball, however, promises a freedom beyond guilt. Although she observes the analogy between baseball and the Christian church, which is supported by the curious equivalence between 108 beads on the rosary and 108 stitches on a baseball, Annie proclaims baseball as a church in its own right. "I've tried them all, I really have," she concludes, "and the only church that truly feeds the soul, day in, day out, is the church of baseball."[20]

"What nonsense!" an unbeliever might understandably conclude in response to all of this testimony about the church of baseball. Baseball is not a religion. It is recreation; it is entertainment; and it is big business supported by the monopoly granted to Major League Baseball. All this religious language merely mystifies the genuine character of the sport in American society.

For all the apparent mystification, strained analogies, and improbable statements of faith, however, the depiction of baseball as a church is highly significant in attempts to locate religion in American popular culture. In earlier anthropological accounts, especially those produced by the anthropologist-from-Mars school of cultural anthropology that gave us the "Nacirema" (*American* spelled backward) tribe, baseball registers as magic rather than religion.[21] For example, a frequently anthologized article, "Baseball Magic," records the techniques employed by baseball players to manipulate unseen forces and control events.[22] They use various kinds of amulets for good luck and engage in specific practices such as never stepping on the foul line and always spitting before entering the batter's box, which appear to be, in Freudian terms, "what are called obsessive acts in neurotics." In their magical practices, baseball players display an obsession with "little preoccupations, performances, restrictions and arrangements in certain activities of everyday life which have to be carried out always in the same or in a methodically varied way."[23] Although Freud held that such obsessive acts characterize the practice of both ritual and magic, George Gmelch, the author of "Baseball Magic," implicitly upholds the familiar analytical distinction between the two. Instead of interpreting baseball as religion, he highlights its superstitious practices as magic.

Gmelch's account of baseball as magic raises two theoretical problems. First, by so characterizing baseball, Gmelch pushes us back to the basic opposition between "religion" and "superstition," which has been crucial to the very definition of religion in Western culture. As we recall, the linguist Émile Benveniste observed that "the notion of 'religion' requires, so to speak, by opposition, that of 'superstition.'"[24] The ancient Latin term *religio*, indicating an authentic, careful, and faithful way of acting, was defined by its opposite *superstitio*, a kind of conduct allegedly based on ignorance, fear, or fraud. In these terms, *we* have religion; *they* have superstition. Only rarely has the oppositional character inherent in the notion of "religion" been recognized. Thomas Hobbes, for example, observed that the "fear of things invisible is the natural seed of that, which everyone in himself calleth religion; and in them that worship or fear that power otherwise than they do, superstition."[25] Baseball magic, in this view, is not religion. It is a repertoire of superstitious beliefs and practices that stand as the defining opposites of authentic religious practices. From the perspective of the anthropologist, who stands outside and observes, baseball magic is clearly something very strange that they do; it is not our religion.

Second, by focusing on baseball magic, Gmelch recalls the tension between the individual and society that has characterized academic reflections on the difference between magic and religion. In Émile Durkheim's classic formulation, magic is essentially individualistic and potentially antisocial. Unlike religious ritual, which affirms and reinforces the social solidarity of a community, magic manipulates unseen forces in the service of self-interest. As Durkheim insisted, there can be no "church of magic."[26] Accordingly, if baseball is magic, there can be no "church of baseball."

Ken Burns intervenes in these theoretical problems by reversing their terms. Adopting a functional definition of religion, he documents the ways in which baseball operates like a church, by meeting personal needs and reinforcing social integration. In fact, his implicit theoretical model of religion seems to be informed by the kind of functional assumptions found in J. Milton Yinger's definition of a universal church as "a religious structure that is relatively successful in supporting the integration of society, while at the same time satisfying, by its pattern of beliefs and observances, many of the personality needs of individuals on all levels of society."[27] Like a church, with its orthodoxy and heresies, its canonical myths and professions of faith, its rites of communion and excommunication, baseball appears in these terms as the functional religion of America.

Of course, this consideration of the church of baseball is positioned in a historical moment of great public disillusionment with the professional game. Feeling betrayed by both greedy players and arrogant owners, many devotees have become apostates of the religion of baseball. In this context the phrase "church of baseball" shifts from metaphor to irony, signaling the transformation of collective memory from commemoration of an enduring tradition to nostalgia for a lost world. From this vantage point, the continuity and uniformity of the baseball tradition, the sacred time and sacred space of the baseball religion, can only be re-created in memory.

THE FETISH OF COCA-COLA

A very different theoretical model of religion is developed in Mark Pendergrast's *For God, Country, and Coca-Cola.* Drawing upon the familiar definition of religion provided by Clifford Geertz, Pendergrast proposes that Coca-Cola is a religion because it is "a system of symbols which acts to establish powerful, pervasive, and long-lasting moods and motivations in men by formulating conceptions of a general order of existence and clothing these conceptions in such an aura of factuality that the moods and motivations seem uniquely realistic."[28] To his credit, Pendergrast does not force his history of Coca-Cola into the mold of Geertz's definition. Rather, he allows the major actors in the drama to evoke their religious moods and motivations in their own voices. Here are the most striking examples:

From the beginning, the beverage was enveloped in a sacred aura. Its inventor, John Pemberton, referred to one of Coca-Cola's original ingredients, cocaine (which remained in the mix from 1886 until 1902), as "the greatest blessing to the human family, Nature's (God's) best gift in medicine" (page 27). During the 1890s Coca-Cola emerged as a popular tonic in the soda fountains, which a contemporary commentator described as "temples resplendent in crystal marble and silver" (page 16). Eventually, however, the blessings of Coca-Cola moved out of the temple and into the world.

The beverage elicited distinctively religious responses from company executives, advertisers, bottlers, and distributors. Asa Candler, the Atlanta entrepreneur who started the Coca-Cola empire, was described by his son as regarding the drink with "an almost mystical faith" (page 68). Candler eventually "initiated" his son "into the mysteries of the secret flavoring formula" as if he were inducting him into the "Holy of Holies" (page 61). Robert Woodruff, who became president of the company in 1923, "demonstrated a devotion to Coca-Cola which approached idolatry" (page 160). Harrison Jones, the leading bottler of the 1920s, often referred to the beverage as "holy water" (page 146). Even the bottle itself was seen as a sacred object that could not be changed. At a 1936 bottlers convention Harrison Jones declared, "The Four Horsemen of the Apocalypse may charge over the earth and back again—and Coca-Cola will remain!" (page 178). Archie Lee, who assumed direction of Coke's advertising in the 1920s, complained that the "doctrines of our churches are meaningless words," speculating that "some great thinker may arise with a new religion" (page 147). Apparently, Lee, along with many other "Coca-Cola men," found that new religion in Coke.

Throughout the second half of the twentieth century the Coca-Cola religion inspired a missionary fervor. At the first international convention at Atlantic City in 1948 an executive prayed, "May Providence give us the faith . . . to serve those two billion customers who are only waiting for us to bring our product to them" (page 238). Another executive later said it has "entered the lives of more people than any other product or ideology, including the Christian religion" (page 406). As the advertising director in the early 1950s, Delony Sledge, proclaimed, "Our work is a religion rather than a business" (page 261). Obviously, the Coca-Cola Company has imagined its enterprise as a religious mission.

For the consumer, however, Coke has also assumed religious significance. In the jive vocabulary of the 1930s Coca-Cola was known as "heavenly dew" (page 178). But the religious significance of Coca-Cola extended far beyond the scope of such a playful invocation. It gave America its orthodox image of Santa Claus in 1931 by presenting a fat, bearded, jolly old character dressed up in Coca-Cola red; it became the most important icon of the American way of life for U.S. soldiers during World War II; it represented an extraordinary sacred time—the "pause that refreshes"—that was redeemed from the ordinary postwar routines of work and consumption; and from the 1960s it promised to build a better world in perfect harmony. An indication of the popular devotion to it was the public outcry at the changed formula of "New Coke" in 1985, which caused one executive to exclaim, "They talk as if Coca-Cola had just killed God" (page 364). In these profoundly religious terms, as editor William Allen White observed in 1938, Coca-Cola became a potent symbol of the "sublimated essence of America" (page 198).

The religion of Coca-Cola has pervaded American society and many more. Represented in over 185 countries—more countries, Pendergrast notes, than are included in the United Nations—the Coca-Cola Company has extended its religion all over the world. As former company president Roberto Goizueta put it, "Our success will largely depend on the degree to which we make it impossible for the consumer around the globe to escape Coca-Cola" (page 397). Suggesting the impossibility of escaping the religion of Coca-Cola, the 1980s film *The Gods Must Be Crazy* presented an absurd parable of its effect among a remote community of Bushmen in southern Africa. As Mark Pendergrast notes, the film opens as "the totemic bottle falls out of the sky onto the sands of the Kalahari Desert, where it completely transforms the lives of the innocent Bushmen as surely as Eve's apple in Eden" (page 406). Here we find Coke as a sacred sign, a sign subject to local misreading, perhaps, but nevertheless the fetish of a global religion, an icon of the West, a symbol that can mark an initiatory entry into modernity. Through massive global exchanges and specific local effects, the religion of Coca-Cola has placed its sacred fetish all over the world.

"What utter nonsense!" a skeptic might justifiably conclude after reviewing this alleged evidence for the existence of a religion of Coca-Cola. Coca-Cola is not a religion. It is a consumer product that has been successfully advertised, marketed, and distributed. In the best tradition of American advertising, the Coca-Cola Company has created the desire for a product that no one needs. Even if it has led to the "Cocacolonization" of the world, this manipulation of desire through effective advertising has nothing to do with religion.

In the study of popular culture, however, the religious character of advertising, consumerism, and commodity fetishism has often been noted. "That advertising may have become 'the new religion of modern capitalist society,'" Marshall W. Fishwick has recently observed, "has become one of the clichés of our time."[29] Advertising-as-religion has turned "the fetishism of commodities" into a way of life. In the symbolic system of modern capitalist society, which advertising animates, commodities are lively objects. Like the fetish, the commodity is an object of religious regard.

As a model for defining and locating religion, the fetish raises its own theoretical problems. In a series of articles, William Pietz has shown that in Western culture the term *fetish* has focused ongoing controversies over what counts as authentic *making*. From the Latin *facere*, "to make or to do," *fetish* has carried the semantic burden of indicating a making that is artificial, illicit, or evil, especially in the production of objects of uncertain meaning or unstable value. In this respect, the fetish is not an object; it is a subject of arguments about meaning and value in human relations.

As a modern dilemma the problem of the fetish arises in complex relations of encounter and exchange between "us" and "them." From one point of view, the fetish is something "they" make. Familiar with the notion of evil making—the *maleficium*—in black magic, Portuguese traders on the west coast of Africa in the seventeenth century found that Africans made *fetissos,* objects beyond rational comprehension or economic valuation. Likewise, from the viewpoint of generations of anthropologists, the fetish was an object that "they" make, a sign of their "primitive" uncertainty over meaning and inability to evaluate objects. From another point of view, Marx, Freud, and their intellectual descendants have seen the fetish as something "we" make—the desired object, the objectification of desire—something that is integral to the making of modern subjectivities and social relations.[30]

Drawing upon this ambivalent genealogy of the fetish in Western culture, anthropologist Michael Taussig has emphasized the importance of "state fetishism" in both making and masking the rationality and terror of the modern political order.[31] This recognition of the role of fetishism in the production and reinforcement of the state resonates with recent research on the making of those collective subjectivities—the imagined communities, the invented traditions, the political mythologies—that animate the modern world.[32] All of these things are made, not found, but they are made in the ways in which only the sacred or society can be produced.

Unlike the historical continuity and social solidarity represented by the church, therefore, instability is the inherent nature of a religion modeled around the fetish. As an object of indeterminate meaning and variable value, the fetish represents an unstable center for a shifting constellation of religious symbols. Although the fetishized object might inspire religious moods and motivations, it is constantly at risk of being unmasked as something made and therefore as an artificial focus for religious desire. The study of religion in popular culture is faced with the challenge of exploring and explicating the ways in which such "artificial" religious constructions can generate genuine enthusiasms and produce real effects in the world.

THE POTLATCH OF ROCK 'N' ROLL

As if it were not enough to bestow religious status on baseball and Coca-Cola, we now have to confront the possibility that rock 'n' roll should also count as religion. Certainly the relations between rock and religion have been ambivalent. As Jay R. Howard has observed, "Religion and rock music have long had a love/hate relationship."[33] On the one hand, rock has occasionally converged with religion. Rock music has sometimes embraced explicitly religious themes, serving as a vehicle for a diversity of religious interests that range from heavy-metal Satanism to contemporary Christian evangelism.[34] On the other hand, rock has often been the target of Christian crusades against the evils that allegedly threaten religion in American society. From this perspective, rock music appears to be the antithesis of religion, not merely an offensive art form, but a blasphemous, sacrilegious, and antireligious force in society.[35]

Perhaps less apparent than rock's ambivalent relationship with religion is its inherently religious character. How do we theorize rock 'n' roll as religion? Attempts have been made. For example, rock 'n' roll has given rise to "a religion without beliefs"; it has given scope for the emergence of a new kind of "divinely inspired shaman"; rock has revived nineteenth-century Romantic pantheism; rock music, concerts, and videos have provided occasions for what might be called, in Durkheimian terms, "ecstasy ritual"; and a new academic discipline, "theomusicology," has included rock 'n' roll in its mission "to examine secular music for its religiosity."[36] From various perspectives, therefore, rock 'n' roll has approximated some of the elementary forms of religious life.

In one of the most sustained and insightful analyses of the religious character of rock 'n' roll, Dave Marsh has undertaken a cultural analysis of the archetypal rock song "Louie, Louie" in order to explore the secret of its meaning, power, and rhythm, the "sacred *duh duh duh. duh duh.*"[37] Marsh issues a daunting assessment of all previous attempts to address his topic. The "academic study of the magic and majesty of *duh duh duh. duh duh,*" as Marsh puts it bluntly, "sucks." To avoid this condemnation, we must proceed not with caution but with the recklessness that the song requires. Like its African American composer, Richard Berry, who first recorded "Louie, Louie" as a calypso tune in 1956, we must say, "Me gotta go now," and see where that going takes us.

In following the sacred rhythm of "Louie, Louie," especially as it was incarnated by the Kingsmen in 1963, Dave Marsh dismisses previous attempts to explain the secret of the song's appeal either as the result of effective marketing or as the effect of the intentional mystification produced by its unintelligible lyrics.

As an example of the first explanation, Marsh cites the commentary of Geoffrey Stokes, who authored the section on the 1960s in *Rock of Ages: The Rolling Stone History of Rock and Roll*. "It's almost embarrassing to speak of 'significance' in any discussion of 'Louie Louie,'" Stokes claimed, "for the song surely resists learned exegesis."[38] Its success, he maintained, can be attributed only to aggressive marketing and efficient distribution.

To illustrate the second explanation, Marsh invokes the analysis of Robert B. Ray, professor of film studies at the University of Florida, who has earned his rock credentials by serving as songwriter and singer for the band the Vulgar Boatmen. According to Ray, the Kingsmen's rendering of "Louie, Louie" revealed that they had "intuited a classic strategy of all intellectual vanguards: the use of tantalizing mystification." Like Jacques Lacan and Jacques Derrida, for example, the Kingsmen employed terms and phrases that "remained elusive, inchoate, quasi-oral charms."[39] The result—alluring but ultimately incoherent—was the strategic production of mystery.

In rejecting these economic and rhetorical explanations, Marsh advances an analysis of the secret of "Louie, Louie" in explicitly religious terms, uncovering layers of religious significance that are all associated with the gift. Although his discussion is inspired by the dramatic prelude to the instrumental break—"Let's give it to 'em, right now!"—it is directly related to the power of giving and receiving in the history of religions.

The song might be regarded as if it were a divine gift. As Marsh's colleague Greil Marcus puts it, by the 1980s "the tune was all pervasive, like a law of nature or an act of God." Marsh plays on this theme: if the song was a gift from God or the gods, he observes, "he, she, or they chose a vehicle cut from strange cloth, indeed—*deus ex cartoona*."[40] However, the sacred gift of "Louie, Louie," the hierophany of incoherence, three chords, and a cloud of dust, cannot be accounted for in the conventional terms of any orthodox theology. Accordingly, Marsh turns to a passage in the Gnostic Gospel of Thomas that seems to capture the "holy heartbeat" of "Louie, Louie": "Jesus said, 'If you bring forth what is within you, what you bring forth will save you. If you do not bring forth what is within you, what you do not bring forth will destroy you.'" Bringing forth all that is within them, the gnostic celebrants of "Louie, Louie" are saved, if not "eternally," as Marsh clarifies, then at least temporarily during the liberating moment in which they participate in the rhythm of the "sacred *duh duh duh. duh duh*" and the "magical incantation" of "Let's give it to 'em, right now!"[41]

Ultimately, however, the religious significance of the gift must be located in relations of exchange. Here a Native American ritual, the potlatch, provides a model for giving and receiving in which the gift assumes a sacred aura. From a Chinook term meaning simply "to give," the potlatch practiced by indigenous communities of the Pacific Northwest signifies the ritualized display, distribution, and sometimes destruction of valued objects at ceremonial occasions.[42]

Although potlatch has variously been interpreted in the ethnographic literature as religious ritual, as status competition, as a kind of banking system, and even as a periodic outburst of "unabashed megalomania," Marsh focuses on three aspects:

First, the gift is total. The potlatch demands giving "everything you had: your food, your clothing, your house, your name, your rank and title." As a ritual occasion for giving everything away, the potlatch demonstrates an "insane exuberance of generosity." Second, the gift is competitive. In ritual relations of exchange, tribes compete with each other to move to the "next higher plane of value." Third, the sacred secret of the gift is ultimately revealed in destruction. As the ritualized exchanges of ceremonial gift giving escalate in value, the supreme value of the gift is realized by destroying valued objects, so that, as Marsh concludes, "eventually a whole village might be burned to the ground in order that the rules of the ceremony could be properly honored."[43]

By odd coincidence, the Pacific Northwest was home to both the Native American societies that performed the potlatch and the rock 'n' roll bands of the early 1960s that played the song "Louie, Louie." In Marsh's account, both the potlatch and the song demonstrate the religious "secret" of the gift, especially as it was revealed in acts of conspicuous destruction, ritual acts that "violated every moral and legal tenet of non-Native American civilization, encumbered as it was with the even stranger socioreligious assumption that God most honored men by allowing them to accumulate possessions beyond all utility in this life, let alone the next."[44] In these "socioreligious" terms the "modern day electronic potlatch" of rock 'n' roll violates Euro-American religious commitments to capitalist production and accumulation, to property rights and propriety, by reviving the sacred secret of the gift.

In defense of the capitalist order, J. Edgar Hoover's FBI pursued a four-year investigation of "Louie, Louie" during the 1960s in search of evidence of subversion and obscenity in the song and its performers. As Marsh recalls, Hoover's mission "consisted precisely of visiting the plague of federal surveillance upon any revival of the potlatch mentality."[45] But "Louie, Louie" survived this state-sponsored inquisition. Defying all attempts to suppress it, the song remains the archetype of the sacred gift at the religious heart of the potlatch of rock 'n' roll.

"What utter, absolute, and perverse nonsense!" anyone might conclude after being subjected to this tortuous exposition of the religion of rock music. Rock 'n' roll is not religion. Besides its major role in the entertainment industry, rock is a cultural medium in which all the "anarchistic, nihilistic impulses of perverse modernism have been grafted onto popular music." As a result, it is not a religion; it is a "cult of obscenity, brutality, and sonic abuse."[46]

The model of the potlatch, however, refocuses the definition of religion. As exemplified most clearly by rituals of giving and receiving, religion is a repertoire of cultural practices and performances, of human relations and exchanges, in which people conduct symbolic negotiations over material objects and material negotiations over sacred symbols. If this theoretical model of religion as symbolic, material practice seems to blur the boundaries separating religious, social, and economic activity, then that is a function of the gift itself, which, as Marcel Mauss insists in his classic treatment, is a "total" social phenomenon, one in which "all kinds of institutions find simultaneous expression: religious, legal, moral, and economic."[47] According to Mauss, the potlatch, as ritual event, social contest, and economic exchange, displays the complex symbolic and material interests that are inevitably interwoven in religion. Similar interests, as Dave Marsh and Greil Marcus argue, can be located in rock 'n' roll.

In the performance of the potlatch, Mauss observes, the contested nature of symbolic and material negotiations becomes particularly apparent; the "agonistic character of the prestation," he notes, "is pronounced."[48] If contests over the ownership of sacred symbols characterize the potlatch, what is the contest that is conducted in the potlatch of rock 'n' roll? It is not merely the competition among musical groups, a competition waged in the "battle of the bands," which Marsh identifies as an important element of the history of "Louie, Louie." It is a contest with a distinctively religious character. In broad agreement with rock critics Marsh and Marcus, anthropologist Victor Turner proposes that rock 'n' roll is engaged in a contest over something as basic as what it means to be a human being in a human society. "Rock is clearly a cultural expression and instrumentality of that style of *communitas*," Turner suggests, "which has arisen as the antithesis of the 'square,' 'organization man' type of bureaucratic social structure of mid-twentieth-century America."[49] By this account, rock 'n' roll, as antistructure to the dominant American social structure, achieves the human solidarity, mutuality, and spontaneity that Turner captures in the term *communitas*. It happens in religious ritual; it happens in rock 'n' roll.

This agonistic character of the potlatch of rock 'n' roll, however, is evident not only in America. As Greil Marcus has proposed, the potlatch might unlock the "secret history of the twentieth century."[50] Constructing a disconnected narrative that links Dada, surrealism, litterists, situationists, and performance art, Marcus rewrites the cultural history of the twentieth century from the vantage point of the punk rock that was epitomized in 1976 by the Sex Pistols. Surprisingly, perhaps, that revised history depends heavily upon a sociology of religion that is implicitly rooted in the foundational work of Émile Durkheim and extended by Marcel Mauss's seminal essay on the gift; but it is a left-hand sociology of religion that takes an unexpected turn through the world of the French social critic, surrealist, and student of religion Georges Bataille.

In his 1933 essay "The Notion of Expenditure," Bataille takes up the topic of the potlatch to draw a distinction between two kinds of economic activity: production and expenditure. While production represents "the minimum necessary for the continuation of life," expenditure is premised on excess and extravagance, on loss and destruction, or, in a word, on the gift. This alternative economic activity "is represented by so-called unproductive expenditures: luxury, mourning, war, cults, the construction of sumptuary monuments, spectacles, arts, perverse sexual activity (i.e., deflected from genital finality)—all these represent activities which, at least in primitive circumstances, have no end beyond themselves." While production is directed toward goals of subsistence, gain, and accumulation, expenditure is devoted to achieving dramatic, spectacular loss. In expenditure, according to Bataille, "the accent is placed on a loss that must be as great as possible in order for the activity to take on its true meaning."[51] In the performance of the potlatch, especially when gift giving escalates to the destruction of property, Bataille finds a model of expenditure that informs his entire theory of religion.

As exemplified by the potlatch, religion intersects with rock 'n' roll because they are both cultural practices of expenditure. The gift, as in "Let's give it to 'em, right now," reopens the complex ritual negotiations over meaning and power, over place and position, over contested issues of value in modern American society. In this context, religion in American popular culture is not the church; nor is it a symbolic system revolving around a fetish. Beyond the constraints of any institution or the play of any desire, religion is defined by the practices, performances, relations, and exchanges that rise and fall and rise again through the ritualized giving and receiving of the gift.

RELIGION IN AMERICAN POPULAR CULTURE

So now where are we? If we have not found religion to reside in baseball, Coca-Cola, and rock 'n' roll after this long journey through their religious contours and contents, we are still left with the question: Where is religion in American popular culture? How do we answer that question? Where do we look? If we were to rely only on the standard academic definitions of religion, those definitions that have tried to identify the essence of religion, we would certainly be informed by the wisdom of classic scholarship, but we would also still be lost.

We might follow E. B. Tylor's classic definition of religion as beliefs and practices relating to spiritual, supernatural, or superhuman beings.[52] Certainly, the assumption that religion is about belief in supernatural beings also appears in the discourse of popular culture. For example, an extraordinary athlete can easily become regarded as a superhuman being. Michael Jordan's return to basketball in 1995 was portrayed in precisely superhuman terms as his "second coming." Jordan complained, "When it is perceived as religion, that's when I'm embarrassed by it." Although *Sports Illustrated* recorded Jordan's embarrassment over this religious regard for him as superhuman, it also added that this reservation was expressed by "the holy Bull himself" about "the attention his second coming has attracted." Adding to the embarrassment, the same article quoted Brad Riggert, head of merchandising at Chicago's United Center, who celebrated Jordan's return by declaring, "The god of merchandising broke all our records for sales."[53] This perception of Michael Jordan as a superhuman being—the holy Bull, the god of merchandising—should satisfy Tylor's minimal definition of religion.

We might follow Émile Durkheim's classic definition of religion as beliefs and practices that revolve around a sacred focus that serves to unify a community.[54] According to this definition, religion depends on beliefs and practices that identify and maintain a distinction between the sacred and its opposite, the profane—a distinction that has also appeared in the discourse of American popular culture. For example, during the long and difficult development of a crucial new software product, Microsoft hired a project manager who undertook the task with religious conviction. According to the unofficial historian of this project, that manager "divided the world into Us and Them. This opposition echoed the profound distinction between sacred and profane: We are clean; they are dirty. We are the chosen people; they are the scorned. We will succeed; they will fail."[55] By this account, the cutting edge of religion—the radical rift between the sacred and the profane—appears at the cutting edge of American technology.

Like church, fetish, and potlatch, these classic definitions of religion—belief in supernatural beings, distinction between sacred and profane—are at play in American culture. As a result, religion is revealed, once again, not only as a cluster concept or a fuzzy set but also as a figure of speech that is subject to journalistic license, rhetorical excess, and intellectual sleight of hand.[56] For the study of religion, however, this realization bears an important lesson: the entire history of academic effort in defining religion has been subject to precisely such vagaries of metaphorical play.

The study of religion and religious diversity can be seen to have originated during the eras of exploration and colonization, with Europeans' surprising discovery of people who were presumed to lack any trace of religion. Gradually, however, European observers found ways to recognize—by comparison, by analogy, and by metaphoric transference from the familiar to the strange—the religious character of beliefs and practices among people all over the world. This discovery did not depend on intellectual innovations in defining the essence of religion; it depended on localized European initiatives that extended familiar metaphors—those that were already associated with religion, such as the belief in God, rites of worship, and the maintenance of moral order—to the strange beliefs and practices of other human populations.[57] In the study of religion in American popular culture, I suggest, we are confronted with the same dilemma of mediating between the familiar and the strange.

The models of religion that we have considered allow some of the strangely religious forms of popular culture—baseball, Coca-Cola, and rock 'n' roll—to become refamiliarized as if they were religion. The religious models allow these cultural forms to appear as the church, the fetish, and the sacred gift of the ritual potlatch in American popular culture. Why not? Why should these cultural forms not be regarded as religion?

The determination of what counts as religion is not the sole preserve of academics. The very term *religion* is contested and at stake in the discourses and practices of popular culture. Recall, for instance, the disdain expressed by the critic who dismissed rock 'n' roll as a "cult of obscenity, brutality, and sonic abuse." In this formulation the term *cult* signifies the absence of religion. "Cult," in this regard, is the opposite of "religion." The usage of the term *cult*, however it might be intended, inevitably resonates with the discourse of an extensive and pervasive anticult campaign that has endeavored to deny the status of "religion" to a variety of new religious movements by labeling them as entrepreneurial businesses, politically subversive movements, or coercive, mind-controlling, and brainwashing cults. In that context, if we should ever speak about the "cult" of baseball, Coca-Cola, or rock 'n' roll, we could be certain about one thing: we would not be speaking about religion.

The very definition of religion, therefore, continues to be contested in American popular culture. However, the examples we have considered—baseball, Coca-Cola, and rock 'n' roll—seem to encompass a wildly diverse but somehow representative range of possibilities for what might count as religion. They evoke familiar metaphors—the religious institution of the church, the religious desires attached to the fetish, and the religious exchanges surrounding the sacred gift—that resonate with other discourses, practices, experiences, and social formations that we are prepared to include within the ambit of religion. Why do they not count as religion? From the church of baseball, through the fetish of Coca-Cola, to the sacred and sanctifying gift giving of the potlatch of rock 'n' roll, the discourses and practices of popular culture raise problems of definition and analysis for the study of religion. In different ways, these three terms—*church, fetish,* and *potlatch*—signify both the problem of defining religion and the complex presence of religion in American popular culture.

CHAPTER THREE · Plastic Religion

In his classic textbook, *Social Psychology*, published in 1908, Edward Alsworth Ross proposed that some religions are capable of changing, adapting easily to new situations and circumstances. Unlike the great monotheisms of Judaism, Christianity, and Islam, which have each developed fixed dogmas and rituals forming a structure that is rigid, resistant to change—a "solid system," according to Ross—some religions are "plastic," demonstrating a flexibility, a fluidity, a capacity to be molded into different forms.[1] Plastic religion, according to Ross, is able to survive profound social changes by transforming itself into something new.

During the 1960s, psychologist Robert Jay Lifton coined the phrase "protean style" for such plastic transformations in religious identity. With the breakdown of stable social structures and the decay of authoritative belief systems, many Americans developed a protean style of continuous psychological experimentation with the self.[2] Like the ancient Greek god Proteus, the shape-shifting sea god, who was constantly transforming from wild boar to wild dragon, from fire to flood, modern Americans experimented with changing, even multiplying, their identities in an unstable social environment. According to Lifton, the emergence of new religious movements, the so-called cults, mirrored the psychological symptoms of these protean identity shifts and multiplications.

Raising the stakes in these plastic, protean transformations of the self, cultural analysts at the beginning of the twenty-first century looked to advances in the computer, information technology, digital media, the Internet, and virtual reality as signs of a new posthuman identity. In the Human Genome Project, carbon-based life forms such as human beings were translated into the silicon-based bits and bytes of the new information technology. By rendering human life into information, the province of a new technology, the Human Genome Project blurred conventional distinctions among animals, humans, and machines. Bringing God into the mix, as President Bill Clinton did when he observed that sequencing the human genome enabled us to learn God's language, only further mixed and merged conventional religious classifications.

Like plastic or protean religion, virtual religion signifies a transformative capacity for unlimited shape shifting. In all these cases, we find one underlying substance—plastic or silicon—taking many different forms. At the nexus of these transformations, the human is also plastic, protean, or virtual, not a fixed identity, but an ongoing experiment in the making.

Representing this creative capacity, *plastic* also signifies the cheap, the tawdry, and the ephemeral. In addition to being almost infinitely malleable, plastic is almost immediately disposable. Most of the productions of popular culture seem to have this temporary, disposable quality. Popular films, television shows, music, and Internet sites have a short life. They pass quickly in and out of the brief collective attention span of popular culture. Even enduring artifacts, such as the recent "classic" rock of the 1970s and the instant "classic" Disney animation of the 1990s, have enjoyed a brief longevity. For the most part, the artifacts of popular culture seem to be produced only to be thrown away, to be dumped on the cultural trash heap with all other material plastic.

Like material plastic in another way, however, the disposable products of popular culture might not be biodegradable, because their traces linger in the ongoing, recurring patterns and processes of cultural production, circulation, and consumption. By pointing to enduring patterns and processes, I am not alluding to the physical substance of plastic, of which the basic media of popular culture are made. Of course, celluloid film is plastic. Records, tapes, and CDs are plastic. From outer case to silicon base, the computer is plastic. The underlying, enduring material plastic of popular culture is obvious. But can we also detect plastic forms and functions that survive the disposability of popular culture?

The term *religion* directs our focus to less obvious features of popular culture that might endure the passing, changing flow of style, taste, attention, and memory. As exemplars of the three forms of religion considered in the previous chapter—the mobilization of a community of sacred allegiance, the focus on a sacred object, and the ritualization of sacred exchange—baseball, Coca-Cola, and rock 'n' roll might never die, but they might. They definitely will change. But the basic patterns and processes of religious sociality, materiality, and exchange will certainly persist as the formula for plastic religion.

In practice, these three aspects of religion might come together in a single cultural formation within American popular culture. Plastic itself can be transformed into a plastic religion in popular culture. A line of useful household products, Tupperware, has appeared as the basis for a sacred community, focused on a sacred object, in all of its protean transformations, an object that is used in rituals of sacred exchange. In Tupperware's production of useful consumer products and sale of those products through an innovative network of direct-sales marketing, the entire enterprise has displayed traces of religious symbols, myths, and rituals that have been evident to participants in the business as well as to journalists, commentators, and the leading historian of Tupperware, Alison J. Clarke, who has shown how plasticity became the basis for "a kind of religion," a plastic religion.

PLASTIC COMMUNITY

In 1942 the ambitious but frustrated inventor Earl Silas Tupper took the black industrial waste product of polyethylene slag and transformed it into what he called Poly-T: Material of the Future, the basic material for a range of household products he created as Tupperware. "Through an act of genius and alchemy," according to historian Alison J. Clarke, "Earl Tupper summoned forth a divine creation to benefit humanity."[3] How could simple storage containers, made out of plastic, evoke such religious sentiments? John Pemberton's claim regarding his invention, Coca-Cola, was similarly extravagant: "the greatest blessing to the human family, Nature's (God's) best gift in medicine."[4] In American popular culture, inventors have had a privileged place in the myths of origin that are told and retold about the beginning of important cultural formations. Ford's invention of the Model T, Disney's invention of the Magic Kingdom, Kroc's invention of the "sacrosanct" french fry, and many other myths of origin animate popular culture.

In such creation myths, the inventor faces the dual problem of producing and marketing an invention. On the production side, historian Clarke invokes the term *alchemy* to capture the mysterious transformation of base, worthless matter into an object of high value. Like turning lead into gold, turning polyethylene slag into Tupperware products is an alchemical, magical, or religious act of creating something out of nothing. As alchemist, the inventor mediates powerful transactions between spiritual and material realms. Standing at the intersection of divinity above and materiality below, the inventor presides over an alchemical transformation of the world.

This positive image of the alchemist, a protoscientist officiating over the spiritual marriage of heaven and earth, has to be juxtaposed with the more negative stereotype of the alchemist as a pseudoscientist, a fake, a fraud, a charlatan. The alchemical dream of turning lead into gold is a chemical impossibility, a superstitious regard for the miracle of matter in the attempt to transform matter into miracles.

On the marketing side as well, the invention is given a religious significance—a divine blessing to the human family, a divine creation to benefit humanity; it needs only to be made available to people so that they will realize its extraordinary value in their lives. As a pure product of religious creation, the invention should actually sell itself, taking on a life of it own by extending its divine influence in being of service to others.

Unfortunately, Earl Tupper's invention did not sell. Having envisioned the total Tupperization of the American home, Tupper was frustrated by the lack of popular interest in his products. In department stores, catalogs, and direct marketing, Tupperware products failed to interest consumers. Although he was the originator of a "divine creation," Tupper found no devotees of his products.

In the early 1950s, however, an unemployed, divorced woman, Brownie Wise, initiated the Tupperware Party, an invention more important in the history of Tupperware than the production of Poly-T, because it created a community of sacred allegiance. The Tupperware Party was a radical innovation in direct marketing. But it was also an improvisation on basic patterns and processes in the production of sacred space and time. Essentially, Brownie Wise built a sacred, though diffused, sense of Tupperware community by mobilizing religious resources for sacralizing the home.

Previously, direct sales had been the province of the traveling salesman, a stranger, as Clarke observes, who was generally distrusted because of "his dislocation from the most sacred of all American institutions—the home."[5] Although the home must seem at first glance to be the most ordinary of places, it became enveloped in a sacred aura during the nineteenth-century emergence of an American "cult of domesticity." In 1869 the sisters Catharine Beecher and Harriet Beecher Stowe described "the American woman's home" as a sacred domestic space in which "a small church, a school-house, and a comfortable family dwelling may be all united in one building." Combining religious worship, education, and nurture, the Christian home, in these terms, was the sacred center for a Christian family, a Christian neighborhood, and ultimately a Christian ministry "training our whole race for heaven."[6]

While anchoring the intimate religious values of gender, sexuality, marriage, and child rearing, this sacred home was increasingly experienced during the first half of the twentieth century as threatened by social and economic changes in American society. During the 1950s, as historian David Watt has observed, "evangelical leaders frequently asserted that making sure America's homes were strong was the most important task facing the American people—more important than fighting poverty, or crime, or Communism."[7]

When Brownie Wise developed the Tupperware Party, she intentionally sought to strengthen that most sacred institution, the American home. No traveling salesman, dislocated from his own home and intruding into a woman's, thereby representing a potentially dangerous, defiling influence, would carry the Tupperware line of plastic products. Instead, the homemaker, by holding a Tupperware party, would control entry into her home, reinforcing its sanctity as an inviolable, essentially sacred place.

Within that domestic sacred space, the Tupperware Party marks a sacred time for what sociologist Dorothy Preven has called "religious-like rituals." As a ritualized activity, the Tupperware Party requires a meticulous management of objects, people, and place. In this domestic ritual, chairs are carefully arranged so that "guests face the product as if on an altar." While participants face the Tupperware altar, hosts present the plastic items with "religious zeal," trying to "invest their bowls with qualities demanding 'reverence,' 'awe,' and 'respect.'"[8] In these religious terms, the sale of Tupperware has created a small-scale, local (even if temporary) community of sacred allegiance through these practices of ritual attention and reverence.

According to Preven, these rituals use "religious revival techniques," not to convert sinners to a gospel of salvation, but to indoctrinate guests and hosts into the ideology of a home-party sales organization. Skeptics have argued that the Tupperware Party is actually a commercial transaction masquerading as a social event, thereby launching "a sneak attack of crass commerce on the sanctity of the home."[9]

Listening to the testimony of one participant in these rituals, Terri Lynn Main, pastor of Emergence Ministries, who described herself as an initiate into the mysteries of Tupperware in the 1990s, we learn that the plastic rituals of the Tupperware Party serve specific functions—as a rite of passage into American womanhood, as a ceremony of solidarity, as a ritual enhancing social, economic, and symbolic status—that have been important for women in modern American suburban life. "A bridal shower, a baby shower, a makeup party, a Tupperware party," Main concluded, "these are all the rituals of being a woman."[10] As Main found, under the leadership of Brownie Wise, the Tupperware Party emerged as a ritual for creating a sacred plastic community of women.

PLASTIC FETISH

Like any religion, this plastic religion of Tupperware has formed a sacred community, with its myth of origin, its sacred space, and its sacred time of ritual. In the hands of Brownie Wise, that social network was built around a sacred object, the black polyethylene slag, Poly-T: Material of the Future, that served as the basis of Earl Tupper's original act of creation. However, the sacred status of this material object depended upon the viability of this social network for its transmission. As the cultural analyst Régis Debray has observed, the material organization of a community always precedes the organization of the matter that enables the transmission of its culture.[11] In the plastic culture of Tupperware, the Tupperware Party provided the organizational base for transmitting a religious devotion to the plastic fetish. Once these "religious-like" communities had been formed, the sacred object, Poly-T, could become the focal point, not only for religious attention, but also for the transmission of a certain kind of plastic religious culture throughout America and eventually throughout the world.

Having created a viable social network for Tupperware, Brownie Wise reported in 1954 that she had preserved a lump of the original black polyethylene slag, which she affectionately referred to as Poly, and had insured it for fifty thousand dollars. Taking this black lump of plastic to Tupperware sales rallies, Brownie Wise invited dealers "to shut their eyes, rub their hands on Poly, wish, and work like the devil, then they [were] bound to succeed."[12] By establishing physical contact with the sacred object, Tupperware representatives could embody its plastic power for success, or so they were promised.

In this promise, Brownie Wise echoed the widespread belief in the power of positive thinking, especially as exemplified in the 1950s by Norman Vincent Peale's maxim "Faith made them champions," which pervaded the worldview of American popular culture.[13] Many believed that "Think and grow rich" was the formula for success in a land of unlimited opportunity. Faith, belief, and positive thinking, however, had to be attached to a material object. Although this faith evoked a kind of spirituality, it was a material spirituality, specifically anchored in selling a consumer product.

Nevertheless, this plastic faith involved more than just a fetishism of commodities, attributing life to objects, mystifying the real relations of value in a capitalist economy. Rubbing their hands on Poly, Tupperware dealers certainly understood that they were participating in a business that made money out of plastic. But they also wished to enhance the spiritual quality of life for themselves and their families by embracing a "gospel of prosperity" based on a merger of faith, family, and business. In American business, a variety of religio-economic corporations—Amway, Mary Kay Cosmetics, Herbalife, Shaklee, and many others—have adopted this gospel of prosperity into their commercial enterprises.[14] By serving God and working like the devil, participants in these business ventures have served themselves and their families to the material and spiritual benefits of the American dream.

Self-realization, however, also requires being of service to others. Focusing on Poly as a sacred object, Tupperware dealers could imagine that they were engaged in both personal fulfillment and public service. As a journalist reported, "Seeing every day the results of their work in other people's happiness, they find in their activity a kind of religion."[15] This plastic religion was experienced as a religion of service, extending the blessings of Tupperware to others. Like the "great mandate" of the Christian New Testament, urging Christians to extend their gospel to all the nations of the world, the mandate of Tupperware was to distribute its products, all ultimately derived from the original plastic fetish, to as many people as possible in order to increase their happiness, well-being, and prosperity.

Tupperware was certainly not alone among American direct-sale corporations in promoting this mandate to serve. Edward Fuller, founder of the Fuller Brush Company, maintained that his company's "ultimate goal is not to make money, but to secure the future of many persons, the nation under which they prosper, and the world at large."[16] Similarly, the Tupperware Corporation, regarding its products as divine gifts created to benefit humanity, imagined that the proliferation of its plastic was an extension of human happiness.

As the business expanded, Brownie Wise used Poly to situate Tupperware within a broader religious sense of territory by establishing a headquarters and identifying it as the sacred center of this plastic empire. Built in 1954 on a thousand acres in Orlando, Florida, Tupperware's headquarters became a sacred mecca, a pilgrimage site for Tupperware dealers. Reinforcing the importance of the sacred object, Brownie Wise sanctified a small body of water there, Poly Pond, by throwing a handful of polyethylene pellets into it. Dealers came to be baptized by touching the water of the "sacred Poly Pond" at Tupperware headquarters. As Brownie Wise declared in 1955, "The very ground here is consecrated to a program of furthering the interests of you in the Tupperware family." By ritually deploying a sacred object, casting plastic upon the waters, Brownie Wise ceremoniously consecrated that sacred ground in Orlando.[17]

PLASTIC EXCHANGE

Although Tupperware was a commercial enterprise, a business venture clearly committed to maximizing profits, it also incorporated traditional forms of gift giving. The Tupperware Party in private homes regularly featured gifts, small tokens of appreciation given to guests at those parties. Every guest received a plastic gift, which, even though an enticement to purchase more products, nevertheless, involved her in ceremonial gift giving, ritualized relations of exchange.

This ritual exchange was also formally established as a central feature of activity at corporate headquarters in Orlando. Tupperware dealers, the "high priestesses" of the regular rituals in private homes, could go on pilgrimage once a year to Tupperware headquarters to participate in a gift-giving ritual. At the Tupperware mecca in 1954, for example, Brownie Wise gathered her dealers to "dig for gold." Having buried a plethora of valuable objects in the consecrated grounds, she urged the dealers to dig for their gifts. As one journalist reported, "Six hundred erect shovels, set in the sacred Tupperware grounds, awaited the eager gold diggers."[18] By going to the sacred center, these devotees of Tupperware could participate in the sacred ritual of the gift.

In such ritualized display and extravagant expenditure, Brownie Wise reinforced the power of Tupperware, not according to conventional economic indicators, but through symbols, myths, and rituals of religion. As Alison Clarke has observed, Tupperware developed a corporate culture that "bolstered concepts of religiosity, ritual, love, kinship, and informal economy." While doing business, Tupperware "relied on systems of barter, reciprocity, and displays of ritual, mysticism, and gift giving." A crucial ingredient in the success of Tupperware, therefore, was the company's adaptation of rituals of sacred exchange in its business practice.[19]

"Tupperware—Everywhere," was Brownie Wise's slogan for her network of home parties. By the end of the 1950s, however, the inventor Earl Tupper had forced Tupperware's organizational, cultural, inspirational, and religious mobilizer out of the business, reportedly because he was outraged by her proposal that the company open up a new product line—a Tupperware dog dish. Regarding this suggestion as a heresy, a blasphemous denigration of his gift to humanity by its extension to animals, Tupper effectively excommunicated Wise, removing all images of her from Tupperware headquarters. Tupper's attempt to maintain the "orthodoxy" of his plastic empire suggests that he continued to view his product with religious regard. Of course, he also knew that Tupperware was a business. A few months after excommunicating Brownie Wise, Tupper sold the enterprise to the Rexall Drug and Chemical Company. While Tupper retired from the world, buying a remote island off the coast of Central America, his company, under new ownership, dramatically expanded into a vast global network.

By the end of the twentieth century, American popular culture was global. In the case of Tupperware, for example, a company that has been described as "all-American as the stars and stripes," 85 percent of its sales came from outside the United States. Similarly, other major transnational corporations—for instance, Coca-Cola, McDonald's, and Disney—carried American popular culture around the globe. New relations of exchange, often invested with potent religious imagery, have animated this global expansion. Not only signifying transnational modes of economic production, circulation, and consumption, globalization has also entailed dramatic cultural transformations.

As anthropologist Arjun Appadurai has proposed, *globalization* is a term in our intellectual armory that might advance our ongoing struggles to analyze the shifting cultural terrain of a changing world. At the very least, globalization signals our growing awareness that things have changed in the world's landscapes of human, technological, financial, ideological, and media geography. In charting this new human geography without fixed borders, our attention is directed toward global fluidity, fluctuation, circulation, and dispersion of people, machinery, capital, ideas, and images. Appadurai has identified these global flows as the fluid movement of people through new ethnoscapes, of machinery through new technoscapes, of capital through new financescapes, of ideas of political solidarity through new ideoscapes, and of mass-media-generated images of human possibility through new mediascapes.[20] Globalization, in these terms, is fluid, protean, and plastic.

In trying to make sense out of new global markets for products, ideas, and images of human possibility, some analysts have turned to the virus as a model for cultural transmission. Following the lead of evolutionary biologist Richard Dawkins, who transposed the biological gene into a new term, *meme,* for a cultural unit that is transmitted like a virus, these market analysts have argued that the global diffusion of cultural forms, styles, and products is basically contagious, caught like a virus, transmitted by contact. According to Seth Godin, former executive of the Internet search engine Yahoo, this viral transmission of culture, which is carried by human contact and intercourse, by gossip and word of mouth, means that "our future will resemble one vast global Tupperware party."[21] Despite the success of Tupperware in the proliferation of its products, Brownie Wise might be surprised by the corporation's significance as a model for global culture.

All of this global exchange, of course, is not really a party. Exchange is constrained by the realities of a global political economy in which many people—perhaps most people—cannot actually play. However, the aura of religion surrounding a global business enterprise like Tupperware creates the impression that everyone can be included. As a religious convert, initiate, or devotee, anyone can engage in its patterns and processes of forming a sacred community, focusing on a sacred object, or participating in rituals of sacred exchange. These recurring forms and functions of religion, as I have suggested, characterized the emergence of Tupperware not only as a successful business but also as a kind of religion that effectively captured the materiality and spirituality of plastic.

THE AGE OF PLASTIC

Looking back at the twentieth century, historians in the future could very well find that the entire world was living in the Age of Plastic. In the early decades of the century, *plastic* was used to signify the opposite of fixed, permanent, or rigid. In the academic work of the pioneering American sociologist Edward Alsworth Ross, whose observations about plastic religion we have already encountered, everything in human society could be classified as either rigid or plastic. Every social institution—religious, scientific, legal, and so on—had its rigid and plastic sides. As Ross maintained in *Social Psychology,* the rigid aspects of a society are always at risk, only waiting for destruction, because the rigid "admits only of the replacement of the old by the new." By contrast, the plastic features of social institutions are able to survive change. "Advance on the plastic side," Ross explained, "is much easier than on the rigid side." Instead of risking the fate of being entirely replaced by the new, the plastic side of any social institution "admits of accumulation by the union of the new with the old."[22]

While this American sociologist was calculating the stress relations between the rigid and the plastic in society, the French philosopher Henri Bergson undertook a sociological investigation of laughter. He was interested in the ways in which laugher works "to readapt the individual into the whole," and he employed a structural opposition between the rigid and the plastic similar to Ross's in finding that the function of laughter "is to convert rigidity into plasticity."[23]

During the Age of Plastic, plasticity might have remained merely a rhetorical opposition to rigidity in cultural analysis if not for the dramatic transformations in the imagination of matter that attended the chemical engineering of polyethylene. This breakthrough in scientific imagination, intervention, and ingenuity transformed plasticity into plastic, the polyethylene substance of material plasticity. In regard to the Age of Plastic, we must forgive any historian the rhetorical extravagance of invoking divinity or alchemy when talking about a development in plasticity as important as Tupperware.

One of the leading scholars of plastic signs, the semiologist Roland Barthes, realized that plasticity signified everything important about the imagination of matter in the twentieth century. According to Barthes, the production of plastic is an alchemical transformation that mediates exchanges not only between base matter and gold but also between human beings and God. As Barthes described these alchemical transactions, "At one end, raw, telluric matter, at the other, the finished human object; and between these two extremes, nothing; nothing but a transit, hardly watched over by an attendant in a cloth cap, half-god, half-robot."[24] Half God, half robot; part divine, part machine; something superhuman, but also something subhuman—the scientist overseeing the alchemical transformation of earth into plastic was positioned, according to Barthes, at the intersection of these supreme, absolute extremes—divinity above, machines below—which framed the meaning and power of the modern world.

In this way of imagining matter, plastic seemed to represent a midpoint, a nexus, or an *axis mundi* in creative exchanges, in the sudden, unobserved, and perhaps imperceptible transitions conducted among the more than human, the human, and the less than human. In a plastic age celebrating its alchemy, plasticity seemed to define the contours of a religious world. Plasticity, however, pertains to more than that which is fluid. Plastic signified not only the alchemical transactions between different levels of reality but also a basic underlying uniformity—a substantial uniformity of materiality. Continuous with the past, uniform in the present, the underlying substance of plastic has always been the same because, however it might be molded, plastic has always been plastic.

Recognizing that homogeneity of plastic, Barthes declared, "The hierarchy of substances is abolished: a single one replaces them all: the whole world *can* be plasticized, and even life itself; we are told, they are beginning to make plastic aortas." Replaced, in principle, by plastic, human life becomes equivalent with all other values. In this plastic imagination of matter, with the abolition of any differentiation of material substances, everything is plastic, even life itself.[25]

At the end of the twentieth century, cultural analysts continued to use the idea of plasticity in a symbolic sense to denote fluidity, freedom, independence, detachment, and transformation. Anthony Giddens, for example, identified "plastic sexuality" as intimacy that is free of both the needs of biological reproduction and the bonds of social obligation. "Plastic sexuality," according to Giddens, "can be molded as a trait of personality that is intrinsically bound up with the self."[26] In the case of Tupperware, plasticity even became the basis for a business enterprise, with its sacred object, its sacred rituals, and its myths of redemption through faith, positive thinking, and hard work all operating as "a kind of religion."[27] Of course, all over the world, many bad things were also said about plastic: Sampling the cuisine at a McDonald's in India, one customer, Malvi Patel, reported, "I find it all a little plastic tasting." Responding to the incursions of Disney into Europe, the French reportedly reacted against "American imperialism—plastics at its worst."[28]

BEYOND PLASTIC

In American popular culture, plasticity has characterized a certain disposition toward the body, a tendency to regard the human body as a malleable, moldable substance that can be shaped into different forms. Body building, body piercing, and weight-loss programs designed for "losing one's way to salvation" have molded the body according to the demands of a plastic religion that is simultaneously spiritual and physical.[29] Taking this plastic, protean style to an extreme, New Age shamans have claimed to be able to transform their bodies, shape shifting from humans into animals and back again. As the shaman John Perkins has explained, "Most of the work I do could be classified under something called shape shifting."[30] Committed to changing the shape of personal consciousness and social institutions, Perkins also claims to be able to transform physically, at the cellular level, into an animal body, shape shifting, for example, into a jaguar or a dolphin. Between the animal and the divine, these forms of plastic religion advance experiments in human plasticity.

By the beginning of the twenty-first century, however, plastic was being replaced by silicon, with computers, information technology, and virtual reality providing emergent symbolism for the human problems and prospects that Roland Barthes had found in plastic. If Barthes was worried that everything, including life itself, was becoming plasticized, he would certainly be impressed by the ways in which carbon-based life has been translated into the silicon-based language of information technology.

In the Human Genome Project, the fundamental building blocks of life, the chromosomes of human DNA, have been mapped and sequenced as a computer-generated code. The underlying substance of humanity, according to this project, is information. All of the multiple, multiplying forms of biological life, whether human or otherwise, are derived from the information that is stored and transmitted in the genetic code. By gaining access to that information, by cracking the genetic code, scientists have acquired knowledge that will enable them to intervene directly in the production of human life.

This Frankenstein scenario, in which a mad scientist creates a human machine, is a recurring myth in American popular culture, providing the basic plotline for countless films, television shows, science-fiction novels, and comic books. Although the mapping and sequencing of the human genome has renewed public interest in Frankenstein's creation, the prospect of creating living organisms by genetic engineering has been a long-standing concern in America. In 1963, for example, an editorial in the *New York Times* warned that Americans were not ready for this new scientific power to manufacture life. "The danger exists that scientists will make at least some of these God-like powers available to us in the next few years," the editor warned, "well before society—on present evidence—is likely to be even remotely prepared for the ethical and other dilemmas with which we shall be faced."[31] How do we prepare for the advent of these God-like powers, whether they are available to us or used on us? Evidently, preparation involves rethinking what it means to be a human being.

Like Barthes's characterization of the production of plastic as a transaction among gods, machines, and humans, the Human Genome Project has involved transgressions of conventional religious classifications of persons. Scientists, politicians, and publicists have used highly charged religious symbols in their rhetoric, employing ultimately religious language in attempts to popularize scientific discovery for a broader audience.

On June 26, 2000, when the sequencing of the human genome was announced, U.S. president Bill Clinton declared, "Today, we are learning the language in which God created life." While an American politician might be predisposed to intoning such religious rhetoric in seeking broad national support, a scientist is certainly courting religious controversy by invoking God in talking about a scientific discovery. Director of the Human Genome Project, Francis Collins, personally a devout Christian, entered such a contested public terrain by resorting to religious language when he asserted, "We have caught the first glimpse of our own instruction book, previously known only to God."[32] Learning God's language, reading God's book—these religious claims announced a religious investment in the new knowledge and power of the human genome. Rhetorically, politicians and scientists, as in the case of Clinton and Collins, have blurred any distinctions that might be made among the spheres of political power, scientific knowledge, and religious faith by asserting religious significance for scientific discovery.

Scientists have made other extraordinary claims about genes, genomes, and genetic engineering. Genes are gods, according to John Avise, supernatural beings in their own right, exercising godlike powers over the course of nature and human lives. Transmitted through continuous, although mutating, genetic lineages over millions of years, genes have achieved a kind of immortality, revealing themselves as the "genetic gods" of all life.[33] At the same time, genes are animal life, a genetic inheritance that humans share with other animal species. "About 99 percent of our genes are identical to the corresponding set in chimpanzees," Edward O. Wilson has observed, "so that the remaining 1 percent accounts for all the differences between us."[34] Between gods and animals, the human soul, the essence of human identity, has also been rhetorically transformed into genetic information. As Dorothy Nelkin and Susan Lindee have observed, "DNA has taken on the social and cultural functions of the soul. It is the essential entity—the location of the true self—in the narratives of biological determinism."[35]

Negotiating these classifications of gods, animals, and humans, some scientists have seen godlike powers operating in the genetic engineering of humans as if they were machines. In this new world, deification is promised for both the scientific agents and the human subjects of genetic engineering. Scientists become gods by entering God's domain, as Clinton, Collins, and molecular biologist Lee Silver described in regard to the new genetics. "Although all other intrusions into the body may work around the edges, genetic engineering, it seems, impinges on the essence of life itself—the soul," Silver observed. "And the soul is clearly in God's domain."[36] Taking this scientific entry into God's territory further, the physicist Richard Seed, an advocate of human cloning, found in genetic engineering the ultimate mystical union of human beings with God. "God intended for man to become one with God," Seed revealed. "Cloning and the reprogramming of DNA is the first serious step in becoming one with God."[37]

Human subjects of genetic engineering, benefiting from the godlike powers of scientists, also become gods. "I predict that human destiny is to elevate itself to the status of a god and beyond," declared John H. Campbell, director of the Center for the Study of Evolution and Human Origins at the University of California,

Los Angeles. In his manifesto for human divinity, "The Moral Imperative of Our Future Evolution," Campbell promised that genetic engineering will produce a godlike human race. In coming generations, he stated, "our descendants will match more closely our images of minor gods, if not Jupiter himself, than humans." This dramatic transformation from humanity to divinity, according to Campbell, will be achieved when we are "able to redesign our biological selves at will."[38]

Although earlier generations of scientific reformers saw the possibility of intervening in human evolution, especially through the selective breeding programs of eugenics, Campbell's vision of a humanity evolving from animals to gods was stimulated by the new discoveries of human genetics that had opened new possibilities of editing the human genome. No longer confined to science fiction, such as the classic vision of human engineering in Aldous Huxley's *Brave New World*, scientific interventions to modify the species have been facilitated by deciphering the human genome.

A scientist such as Campbell might be regarded as a prophet of a scientific religion, promising human deification through genetic engineering, just as the human genome has appeared in popular culture as a "cultural icon" for the hopes and fears of a changing humanity. In some cases, DNA, genes, and the human genome have become symbols with a distinctively religious character in American popular culture. For example, Campbell's essay on our future evolution, with its promise of human deification, was promoted on the Internet by a new religious organization, the Church of Prometheus, which advocated an evolutionary scientific religion. Other new religions in cyberspace, such as the Church of Virus, claimed religious significance for evolution, including the new evolutionary potential for manufacturing a divine humanity.

During 2000 a group of performance artists, the Critical Art Ensemble, toured the United States and other countries as a new religion, the Cult of the New Eve. Members of the ensemble had expertise in different fields—art, technology, radical politics, and critical theory. In this particular tour, they showed that they were also religious artists, creating within the medium of religious classifications and orientations.

The Cult of the New Eve announced nothing less than the remaking of the world in the light of the Human Genome Project. With the advent of this new religion, all previous religious worldviews, with their various myths of human origin and destiny, were declared dead; they had been replaced by transcendent knowledge and power that was independent of either God or nature. No faith was required, no belief was necessary, and no miracles were expected, because the miraculous would soon be an ordinary occurrence through the science of genetic engineering. "We control our own destinies," the Cult of the New Eve declared. "All the promises that religions have made but failed to keep are now ours to fulfill."[39]

According to the teachings of the cult, the New Eve was the woman who had provided the blood samples for the Human Genome Project. Since her DNA was the original source for mapping and sequencing the human genome, which represented the basis for all future engineering of human life, this woman was the true Eve, the original source of humanity in this Second Genesis. Although the Human Genome Project derived DNA samples from multiple donors, whose anonymity has been maintained, the Cult of the New Eve insisted that one woman, living in the city of Buffalo, New York, was the only donor whose samples were actually used. Dedicated to protecting her identity, the cult nevertheless embarked on a letter-writing campaign to convince the mayor of Buffalo that his city should be renamed New Eden and a statue should be erected there in honor of the New Eve. Attacking all imposters, such as the biblical Eve, the goddess Eve, and the science-fiction android Eve, the cult celebrated the Eve of the Human Genome Project as the sacred mother of a new humanity. In the future, all humans, since they shared the same mother in this Second Genesis, would be united "not through a shared spirit, but through shared molecules." In its vision for a genetically engineered future, the Cult of the New Eve promised "the elimination of disease, the conquest of death, earthly paradise" (in Buffalo, New York, the New Eden), "and universal connectedness," all achieved through the knowledge of the human genome and the power of genetic engineering.

As children of the New Eve, members of the public had to be prepared for their role in the future. For religious guidance, they could refer to words of inspiration, some of which I have already cited, from John H. Campbell, E. O. Wilson, Lee Silver, Richard Seed, and other leaders within the inner circle of genetic wisdom. Awaiting deification, they could read the signs of genetic transformation—the cloned sheep, the glowing mice, the artificial goat fetus, and other triumphs of genetic science—in the assurance that humanity was being similarly transformed into something new. In the Second Genesis, everything was possible, even the transformation of human possibility. "Thanks to the New Eve," the cult affirmed, "we now have the knowledge to grow the Tree of Life. We can shape the body so that it is the most perfect phenomenon on the planet." Better than protein, plastic, or even silicon, the new moldable, shapable humanity promised the ultimate human perfection: no limits.

RELIGIOUS LIMITS

Whatever else religion might be about, it is about limits. Religious classifications (e.g., of gods, humans, animals, machines) and orientations in time and space are enabling, empowering a human identity, but also limiting, establishing boundaries around what it means to be human in a human place. Of course, religious limits are also constantly tested and contested through ongoing negotiations over the meaning of being human. As we have seen, from Tupperware to the Human Genome Project, plastic religion has generated religious classifications and orientations in American popular culture.

In plastic classifications, a human is a being situated between the superhuman and the subhuman, at a nexus between godlike powers and animals, machines, or objects. The inventor Earl Tupper, drawing on superhuman power for his divine creation, was reportedly shocked when Brownie Wise proposed desecrating Tupperware by giving it to dogs. In stark contrast with Tupper's and other scientists' aspirations to a superhuman status for humankind, the sociobiologist Edward O. Wilson saw the Human Genome Project establishing a common, underlying identification of humans with animals at the genetic level. The constant testing of these basic classifications renders human identity a plastic identity.

In the world of Tupperware, Brownie Wise defended the sanctity of the home, but she also found new ways to intervene in gendered identity, reinforcing conventional family values, perhaps, but also empowering women with new economic and social status. Like other constructions of human identity, gender displays a certain plasticity. As we have seen, Terri Lynn Main, pastor of Emergence Ministries, recounted her initiation into the Tupperware Party as an important rite of passage into American womanhood. Like other women's rituals, such as the bridal shower, this plastic ritual has reinforced conventional gender roles for women in America. For Main, however, participating in this American ritualization of female identity was particularly meaningful because she had been born in a male body. Growing up as a boy, dreaming of being a woman, she understood the Tupperware Party as the "grand ritual of womanhood." Now, as a woman, she led a Christian ministry "dedicated to serving the spiritual and physical needs of the transgendered community."[40] Having demonstrated the plasticity of gender in her own life, Main was reshaping the religious resources of both Christianity and Tupperware in ways that affirmed the viability of transgendered and transsexual forms of human identity.

Main argued that changing gender, moving from cross-dressing to cross-living, was just like correcting a birth defect, thereby reengineering genetic inheritance. Genetic engineering promises to correct all birth defects along with its promise to deify humans, making them immortal. As the biologist Michael Rose proposed, genetic science has already achieved the capability of repairing cells. Soon, scientists will identify "genes conferring immortality." Echoing the promise made by the first-century Christian apostle Paul, who advised early Christian communities that many among them would not die before the coming apocalypse made them immortal, Michael Rose declared on the basis of new developments in genetic science, "I believe there are already immortal people."[41] In plastic religion, therefore, people can change—from male to female, from mortal to immortal—in the plasticity of human identity.

New ways of changing identity also merge with the production of multiple identities. As we recall, the Human Genome Project has inspired new ways of imagining human beings as simultaneously divine and animal, as both godlike and apelike. Sharing 99 percent of their genetic blueprint with chimpanzees, human beings, who hold the godlike power of creating life, are still basically animals. While scientists were busy mapping and sequencing the human genome, securing their transcendent knowledge of the fundamental underlying code of humanity, the Walt Disney Company was producing films dealing with the interface between human beings and apes. As the Human Genome Project rushed to completion, Disney released four films that featured the ape-man—*George of the Jungle* (1997), *Jungle to Jungle* (1997), *Mighty Joe Young* (1998), and *Tarzan* (1999). As Eleanor Byrne and Martin McQuillan observed, these Disney films dealt directly with "the meeting between the 'savage' and the civilized, the animal and the human."[42] They mediated popular concerns about what it might mean to be a human being, between apes and gods, at the end of the twentieth century.

Other popular films, of course, mediated popular concerns about the interface between humans and machines. As Richard Dawkins argued in *The Selfish Gene*, human beings are essentially "robot vehicles" programmed to perpetuate their genetic information.[43] Along similar lines, the emergent sciences of cybernetics, artificial intelligence, and virtual reality rendered both human beings and computational machines into information technology. Popular films such as *The Matrix* (1998) explored this interface between humans and machines, enveloping both in the same web of virtual signification and human significance.

Both genetic engineering and information technology are reportedly creating a new posthuman identity. Francis Fukuyama, who already declared the end of history, worries that new developments in genetic science are ushering in a posthuman future.[44] Katherine Hayles, informed by a close reading of scientific research in cybernetics, artificial intelligence, and information technology, has charted the ways in which humanity has already been rendered posthuman.[45] These lines of cultural analysis, weaving together biological life and mechanical information, mirror the new developments in genetics, genomics, and computer science.

Even in a plastic religion, identity must still be located in place. In the human geography of religion, religious orientation requires a sacred center, a fixed axis in a turning, changing, and plastic world. As we have seen, the plastic religion of Tupperware was centered in the Tupperware mecca of Orlando, Florida, while the proposed center of the genetic religion of the Cult of the New Eve was the "New Eden" of Buffalo, New York. These sacred centers, in both cases, were intentionally conceived as new Edens, as new Meccas, or as new Jerusalems for religious attention, ritual pilgrimage, and ceremonial commemoration. In developing religious strategies of spatial orientation, these plastic religions suggested that even a plastic, changing, and multiple religious identity needs a fixed center in the religious geography of the world.

Or maybe not: Although the Tupperware Corporation, under the visionary leadership of Brownie Wise, identified its sacred center as the Tupperware mecca in Orlando, Florida, with its sacred relic of polyethylene, its sanctified waters, and its consecrated grounds, the religious work of this plastic religion was actually decentralized in and through the recurring ritual of the Tupperware Party, which was conducted in private homes, officiated by ordinary women, throughout America and eventually throughout the entire world. Likewise, although the Cult of the New Eve identified Buffalo, New York, as the sacred center of a genetic religion, the religious potential for testing human identity, between gods and animals, is actually radically decentralized, because the human genome is carried in every living human body. These plastic religions, therefore, ultimately reside in homes and bodies: home is where the heart is; the body is where the heart is—home and body are the heart of the matter, even in these plastic religions of human possibility.

In this chapter, I want to test the sense of touch as an avenue for entering the embodied, visceral, and material field of American religion and popular culture. According to our experts in such matters, the psychology of the human sense of touch includes three things: the sensitivity of the skin along the entire cutaneous field of the body; the sensations involved in the kinesthetic movement of the body; and haptics, the perceptual information gained through the physical manipulation of objects in the body's environment.[1] During the 1980s, under the leadership of the sociologist Robert Bellah, a team of researchers investigated the religious sentiments, the "habits of the heart," that facilitate social cohesion in America.[2] In American religion and popular culture, I suggest, the habits of the heart are also haptics of the heart, the religious tactility of the body.

Haptics refers to the work of the hands—handling, caressing, grasping, manipulating, hitting, and so on—as instruments of knowledge. Not limited to the hands, however, haptics also includes the work of the elbows and shoulders, the feet and toes, the lips and tongue, and all of the other extensions of the body, and, as far as I can tell, it also includes the kind of acute awareness of the environment that can be gained only by bumping into sharp and solid objects in the dark. All these aspects of the sense of touch—the cutaneous, the kinesthetic, and the haptic—provide an extremely wide perceptual field (perhaps as extensive as the body itself), which is useful for the study of religion and popular culture. Heat and cold, pleasure and pain, pressure and release, the wet and the dry, the rough and the smooth, and all the movements and manipulations of physical embodiment are encompassed in the sense of touch.

How can we narrow this perceptual field? After briefly touching on the denigration of tactility in Western thought, I will point to the contributions of two theorists, Emmanuel Levinas and Walter Benjamin, in recovering the sense of touch, whether the intimate caress or the violent shock, as a way of knowing and being in the world. The heart of my discussion, however, is devoted to tracking modes of religious tactility in modern American religion and popular culture. By paying attention to sensory media and metaphors and particularly to tactile practices, postures, and pressures, I hope to suggest some basic features of religious tactility that are not necessarily seen or heard but nevertheless pervade contemporary religion and culture. Schematically, I proceed from cutaneous binding and burning, through kinesthetic moving, to haptic handling in order to enter this field of tactile meaning and power. I want to point to the presence of a tactile politics of perception that might help us to understand one of the most vexed questions of critical theory: How do we account for the intersections of human subjectivity with social collectivity?

CARESS AND SHOCK

A long tradition of Western philosophical reflection on the senses has identified touch as the lowest sense, the most animal, servile, and unconscious of the resources of the human sensorium. The sense of touch, as Aristotle insisted, is metaphysically and morally inferior to all other senses.[3] Despite their regard of touch as the lowest of the senses, ancient Greek philosophers of perception nevertheless tended to explain the higher senses of sight and hearing in terms of tactility. Vision was thought to work like touch—the arm of vision, the stick of vision—to establish immediate and continuous contact. Hearing was explained as the result of a blow that strikes the air, travels over a distance, and impacts the ear. On the basis of ancient Greek science of the senses, therefore, both sight and hearing—sight as tactile contact, hearing as tactile concussion—can be glossed as species of a more fundamental tactility on which all sense perception depends.[4]

In the formation of Greco-Roman Christian religious discourse, this underlying tactility of perception was never explicitly developed as a theme. Certainly, the New Testament displayed an ambivalence about touch. The apostle Thomas, the patron saint of Christian tactility, is presented in the Gospel of John as demonstrating that touching is believing (John 20:24–29), and Mary, the patron saint of a kind of antitactility is told not to touch the resurrected Jesus (John 20:17). More than a contradiction, this calculus of touching and not touching has been central to the practice of Christianity.

Laying on hands, anointing with oils, washing feet, holy kissing, swearing oaths on the Bible, taking up snakes, and so on, are all forms of religious tactility that both signify and enact a direct, powerful, and even intimate contact with the sacred. At the same time, the sacred is inevitably surrounded by prohibitions on illicit contact, with those restrictions implicitly or explicitly backed up by force or its threat, as in the case of the Israelites before Mount Sinai, who were warned that "whosoever touches the mount shall surely be put to death" (Exod. 19:12). For early Christian theorists, this dialectic of touch was generally submerged in the transcendent demands of sight and hearing. Adopting the Greek hierarchy of the senses, Augustine of Hippo, for example, might have employed the tactile metaphor "embrace of truth," but he was clear that "the objects that we touch, taste, and smell are less like truth than the things we see and hear."[5] By paying attention to the sense of touch, however, religious discourse and practice can be situated in this dialectic of contact and concussion, embracing and striking, that defines the basic character of religious tactility.

During the twentieth century, two theorists of tactility, Emmanuel Levinas and Walter Benjamin, expanded our understanding of contact and concussion— the intimate caress, the violent shock—in the perceptual dynamics of the sense of touch. Both explicitly addressed the tactility of religion. Levinas was a theorist of the embrace, finding in the sense of touch the underlying unity of the senses and the basic engagement of the self with the world. Levinas proposed that the flesh implicates the self in a world of contact, proximity, and intimacy. In this approach, the world is experienced because it is intimately touched, a process that renders tactility more than merely a sense. As a metaphor for embracing the world of experience as a whole, touch represented for Levinas the basis for all sensory experience. According to Levinas, "One sees and hears like one touches."[6]

This insistence on the tactile basis of the senses has at least two implications. First, sensory perception entails an intimate tactile embrace of the world that is performed not only by grasping objects but also, most important, by caressing the other. As Levinas observed: "The caress is a mode of the subject's being, where the subject who is in contact with another goes beyond this contact. . . . The seeking of the caress constitutes its essence by the fact that the caress does not know what it seeks. This 'not knowing,' this fundamental disorder, is the essential."[7] This unconscious tactility of the caress, embracing the fundamental disorder of "not knowing," goes beyond conscious sensory contact, which Levinas located in the visual domain of light, to open the self to an intimate, self-involving engagement with the world.

Second, for the study of religion, the primacy of touch entails a shift in analysis from religious belief or doctrine to religious action or practice. According to Levinas, touch provides the phenomenological ground for religious ritual, a ground laid by a kind of doing that precedes the auditory reception of ethical commands or the visual contemplation of doctrinal propositions.[8] Like the caress, we might assume, religious ritual also does not know what it seeks. With no practical objective, no instrumental goal, no usefulness whatsoever in the world, this type of activity provides the religious equivalent of the intimate embrace, which suggested for Levinas both the essential character and the fundamental disorder of tactility. The work of Levinas, therefore, developed one side of the dialectic of touch, the side of immediate contact and intimate embrace, however unconscious or unknowing, as a way of situating human subjectivity in the world.

Walter Benjamin was a theorist of the shock, finding in tactile concussion both the underlying unity of the senses and the basic organization of art, religion, and politics in modernity. As developed in Benjamin's influential essay "The Work of Art in the Age of Mechanical Reproduction," the sense of touch has been reorganized by recent technological developments (chromolithography, photography, and cinematography) that have given aesthetics a new tactile character. What Benjamin called the "tactile appropriation" of aesthetic objects has at least three significant implications for a consideration of the role of tactility in modern religion.

First, artworks of mechanical reproduction assume their tactile character by striking the audience, by producing what Benjamin called "shock effects." From Dada to cinema, Benjamin found that aesthetics has become "an instrument of ballistics," with images and words, styles and techniques, deployed in ways that "hit the spectator like a bullet . . . thus acquiring a tactile quality."[9] What Benjamin called the "shock effect of the film" has nothing to do with subject matter. Rather, the basic techniques used in the production and reproduction of film—cutting, panning, zooming, and so on—produce shocks by striking and distracting the audience in ways that create an essentially tactile aesthetic experience.

Second, by identifying the characteristically modern aesthetic experience as tactile, Benjamin developed a basic analytical opposition between visual concentration and tactile distraction. Like the experience of motion pictures, the experience of moving through a modern city is guided not by visual contemplation but by a tactile appropriation that is "accomplished not so much by attention as by habit." The challenges of negotiating a modern city, Benjamin observed, "cannot be solved by optical means, that is, by contemplation alone. They are mastered gradually by habit, under the guidance of tactile appropriation."[10] As the "polar opposite" of visual attention, habitual distraction represents the characteristically tactile mode of human sense perception that came to prominence under the historical conditions of modernity.

Third, with the historical shift from visual attention to the tactile distractions of the arts of mechanical reproduction, the work of art has been alienated from its traditional location. Tradition, as that which is "handed down," anchors objects in place, signifying precisely where and when they might be touched, thereby certifying the "aura" of their originality and authenticity. With the effects of mechanical reproduction, however, art has undergone "a tremendous shattering of tradition." Previously grounded in ritual, the work of art has been liberated from tradition, only to be recaptured, however, by another social formation. "Instead of being based on ritual," Benjamin observed, "it begins to be based on another practice—politics."[11] What kind of a politics of perception, we might ask, operates in the tactility—the intimate caresses, the violent shocks—of contemporary American religion and popular culture?

BINDING

If we give credence to etymology—and if we accept that *religio* has its root in *religare*, "to bind"—then we have a tactile basis for the very notion of religion.[12] From its ancient origins, according to this rendering, religion has been about binding relations, either among humans or between humans and gods, relations that have constituted the fabrics and textures, the links and connections, the contracts and covenants of religion. In this respect, although religious discourse might very well point beyond all that can be seen, heard, smelled, tasted, or touched, it points with a hand that is religiously bound. Tactility, in this view, is the fundamental bond of religion.

For the history of religion in America, however, we need to pay attention to a more contingent and complex sense of the religious dynamics of "binding" in the intercultural "contact zones" of colonialism, in the bondage of slavery, or in the compelling terms and conditions of a new covenant. Rhetorically, the seventeenth-century Puritan settlers in North America proceeded hand in hand with their God. Invoking the paradigmatic biblical narrative of oppression and resistance, in all its symbolic tactility, John Winthrop insisted that his Puritans had been liberated from the "spiritual bondage of Egypt," led across the sea by God's "own immediate good hand," to undertake in America the "great work in hand."[13]

While this tactile imagery culminated in the central symbol of covenant, the sacred bond between God and a "peculiar people," it carried at least three implications that are worth noting. First, the tactile bond of the covenant was a bondage not only of pleasure but also of pain. As Increase Mather put it, the covenant entailed "sanctified afflictions," the painful suffering that Mather understood to be both punitive and purifying.[14]

Second, the bond of the covenant entailed violence against the indigenous inhabitants of America, a violence represented in explicitly tactile terms by the Puritan poet Michael Wigglesworth, who celebrated God's "furious flail" and "fatal broom" that had been deployed against Native Americans "to make my people elbow room."[15] In these potently tactile terms, the covenant disclosed the inherent violence of tactility as concussion, as the blow that was struck by the violent hand of God in the forceful extension of body space—the elbow room—within a territory.

Third, the covenant community was consolidated by economic relations that were represented (and mystified) as a process of gift giving, from hand to hand, that fulfilled the religious bond with God precisely because of the inherent inequalities of wealth, status, and power on which those covenantal relations depended. In the Puritan covenant, God's gifts had to be handled by an elite class of middlemen in the exchange relations between God and the world. As John Winthrop declared in his sermon on charity, God was glorified more "in dispensing his gifts to man by man, than if he did it by his own immediate hand."[16]

During the first half of the 1990s, President Bill Clinton invoked the powerful imagery of the covenant with his central political slogan, New Covenant. Although we have probably forgotten the initiative this slogan invoked, distracted by the later preoccupation with a different register of tactility that was found in the insistent investigation into precisely when and where the president might have touched a White House intern, it was enshrined in 1992 in the very title of the national platform of the Democratic Party, "A New Covenant with the American People," a covenant that promised to repair "the damaged bond" between Americans and their government. In his acceptance speech for the Democratic candidacy, Clinton countered the vision of his political opponent, explicitly deriding "the vision thing" of George Bush, with the tactile symbolism of the covenant, stressing in particular the relations of giving and receiving. "I call this approach a New

Covenant," Clinton proclaimed, "a solemn agreement between the people and the government, based not simply on what each of us can take, but on what all of us must give to our nation."[17]

In his defining terms of this covenant, Clinton declared, "Opportunity and responsibility go hand-in-hand."[18] Opening and enclosing, empowering and constraining, liberating and binding—the terms and conditions of the New Covenant were certainly vague yet somehow compelling in their inherent tactility. Here was a "political theology," as one analyst has observed, that merged "the stern rhetoric of conservatism with the generosity of liberalism."[19] Yet this slogan and its rhetorical elaboration could hardly be called a theology, political or otherwise, since the basic tactility of the New Covenant pointed to binding relations that could only be sensed. As Levinas might have observed, this covenant was a binding tactility that "does not know what it seeks." It was guided not by the light of vision but by the "not knowing" of the caress, the embrace, the intimate relations of exchange that bind self and other as "us." By invoking the bond of the gift, the new opportunities for receiving and the new responsibilities for giving, hand in hand, this New Covenant rhetorically configured an America bound together by a compact in which, as Clinton declared in that same acceptance speech, "there is no them; there is only us."[20]

After 1995, perhaps partly in response to the vigorous publicity attending the Republicans' Contract with America, Clinton dropped the New Covenant slogan for representing the bond that unifies America. Increasingly, he began to use the phrase "a bridge to the twenty-first century" to capture the common interests that should be shared by Americans in embracing a global future. Toward the end of his administration, however, Clinton was also distracted by impeachment, a term that incidentally is derived not from an etymology of verbal accusation but from the tactile root *impedicare*—to fetter, to snare, to tie the feet together, in other words, to bind—which suggests, at the very least, that not all bonds create an "us" in which there is no "them" to be excluded.

BURNING

While tactile metaphors can represent religious bonds, indicating the adhesive character of religion as unified systems of beliefs and practices that unite all those who adhere to them into one single moral community, to follow the classic Durkheimian formula, such binding social adhesion is only one feature of religious tactility. In addition to the apparently stable terms of religious adherence, a different aspect of tactility, its thermal register, generates heat. As an important dimension of Rudolf Otto's classical formulation of the *mysterium tremendum,* heat is found in the religious energy or urgency of "vitality, passion, emotional temper, will, force, movement, excitement, activity, impetus," culminating in the "consuming fire" of mystical experience.[21]

As registers of religious temperature, religious discourse and practice have often had recourse to a fire that gives off much more heat than light. In his own classic formula, John Wesley characterized his conversion of 1738 as an experience of the "heart strangely warmed." On the basis of that experience of religious heat, Wesley stated a strategic disinterest in the formal "systems of beliefs and practices" that seemed to him to divide more often than they unite. "Is thy heart herein as my heart?" was the only religious question he professed to find relevant. "If it be," Wesley proposed, "give me thy hand."[22] Hand in hand, in this case, signifies not a binding social covenant but an interpersonal exchange of divine heat. In American history, an acutely developed tactile sense of sacred energy has often been invoked as a defining feature of religion and politics. During the revolutionary era, for example, Thomas Jefferson reported that a national holiday of humiliation, fasting, and prayer could produce a tangible effect "like a shock of electricity."[23] During the era of the Civil War, to cite another example at random, Horace Bushnell characterized Americans in his Yale graduation address of 1865 as "souls alive all through in fires of high devotion."[24] Accordingly, religion has been a matter not only of binding relations but also of burning energy—the warmth, the electricity, the sacred fires—that can be perceived and engaged only by a spiritual sense of touch.

A distinctively tactile ritual of the "sacred fire," firewalking, gained a considerable following in the United States by the end of the 1990s. Some organizations developed an explicitly religious understanding of firewalking. The Fire Tribe of Sundoor, for example, pointed to the universal religious significance of fire. "Because of its integral role in the survival of the human species," Sundoor declared, "fire has had aspects of religious significance to all the peoples of the Earth." Similarly, an organization known as Wings of Fire proclaimed that "firewalking, next to prayer, is one of the oldest transformational tools the world has ever known," a religious method used for "ritual purification, healing and worship." In the United States, however, the ritual of firewalking was employed as a method of empowerment, as "people choose to walk on fire to overcome fear and beliefs that limit their lives." By transcending limiting beliefs, such as the belief that fire burns, Wings of Fire promised that "a whole New World of opportunities and possibilities [would] become reality, because, we say to ourselves, 'I WALK ON FIRE, I CAN DO ANYTHING I CHOOSE.' "[25]

Skeptical observers, of course, could provide reasonable scientific explanations: that hardwood, charcoal, and even volcanic rock are poor conductors of heat, and that the soles of human feet, especially sweaty soles, are good insulators.[26] Nevertheless, even the science editor of *National Geographic*, Rick Gore, found his own experience of firewalking to be liberating and empowering. As he was promised, Gore experienced firewalking as a technique for overcoming fear. "Whenever fears surge up," he reported, "I recall the fire walk." Concluding his May 1998 account, Gore testified, "I have learned now to embrace the fire."[27]

What does it mean to embrace the fire? Gore reported that one of the leaders of his firewalk, the fortuitously named Heather Ash, explained that the "fire is a teacher," pointing to two basic teachings of the fire that we might gloss here as democracy and opportunity. First, the ritual of firewalking, "an ancient practice in many cultures," was democratized in the United States. "Historically," Heather Ash said, "this opportunity was given only to medicine men, priests, and shamans." However, in the United States, the ritual was available to anyone, no longer the preserve of a ritual elite. Therefore, firewalking was not only democratized but has also had its own further democratizing effect in providing broad access to spiritual power.

Second, the opportunity to participate in the ritual also expands opportunities in life. According to Heather Ash, the fire "teaches you to overcome your fears and do what you thought was impossible," thus expanding personal opportunities for love, health, success, wealth, and general prosperity. By walking on fire, in Ash's view, anyone can achieve what Otto called "vitality, passion, emotional temper, will, force, movement, excitement, activity, impetus." According to Rick Gore, the teachings of the fire generate "an energy that seemed almost religious." Before taking his twelve steps across the burning coals, Gore was given one last instruction. "Always respect the fire," he was told. "Otherwise, you're going to get burned."[28]

The ritual of firewalking must certainly appear as a fringe phenomenon in American religion, a marginal, New Age, self-help, human-potential, or quasi-religious enterprise that mixes a tactile spirituality with promises of tangible prosperity, attracting, as the Sundoor reported, both "individuals seeking to deepen their spiritual connection and empower themselves" and "corporate executives wanting to give their companies the leading edge."[29] As a teacher, however, the fire conveys lessons—democracy, opportunity, and respect—that are central to an American imaginary, an imagined sense of America that during the twentieth century came to be most tangibly signified by the flag of the United States. In the 1990s, the supreme act of disrespect to the flag—burning—became the focus of legal controversy, state legislation, and proposed amendments to the U.S. Constitution.

At first glance, this juxtaposition—firewalking and flag burning—must seem arbitrary, especially in a review of religion and tactility, since burning a flag involves a visual display of flames, light, and color, an act that has been interpreted by the U.S. Supreme Court as the functional equivalent of free speech protected under the First Amendment. Seeing and hearing, therefore, seem to be the relevant senses at stake in the controversy over desecrating the flag by burning. However, a visit to a Web site's Flag Burning Page, especially the Flag Flames Page, demonstrates that Americans can have a tactile, tangible, and visceral identification with the flag.

On the Flag Flames Page, one correspondent, identified as "Pissed Off American," experiences flag desecration as a personal assault, as a kind of ordeal by fire that touches him directly. "When people burn the flag, it's like touching my ass with a lit match," he reports. "I don't like people touching my ass." In another testimony to the visceral connection between flag and body, Craig Preston asserts that "you can burn my flag when you rip it off of my smouldering rotting corpse." Ultimately, the flag as a tangible sign symbolizes all the dead bodies of those who have sacrificed for America. According to another correspondent, identified as "someone.who.cares," burning a flag is an act "desecrating the symbol of our nation, the one that my fellow servicemen have given their lives for in the past," a sentiment echoed in many speeches in the *Congressional Record* in support of legislation against flag burning, confirming Jean Bethke Elshtain's observation, in another context, that the modern nation has been built on mounds of bodies, a corporeal mound, we might add, with a flag at its summit.[30] Like the lessons of the fire, the lessons of the flag, especially when desecrated by burning, highlight issues of democracy, opportunity, and respect in a visceral engagement with America.

MOVING

In the kinesthetic movements of the body, tactile information is acquired. For the study of religion, kinesthesia calls attention to embodied movements—kneeling, standing, prostrating, walking, climbing, dancing, and so on—not only as types of ritual performance, but also as paths of knowledge. As a significant feature of the American imaginary, mobility has been a distinctively tactile way of knowing the world, especially in the moving body's mediation by machines that have extended the speed, rhythm, and scope of its motion, from the bicycle to the space shuttle.

The religious aura carried by machines of mobility is certainly striking. The "bicycle craze" of the 1890s celebrated the emergence of the first mass-produced machine that was not a tool but a recreational vehicle. Linking recreation with religion, Henry Ford declared the Model T automobile "more than a car; it was a calling," a mission to extend to every American "the blessings of hours of pleasure in God's great open spaces." According to historian James J. Flink, the American "cult of the automobile" promised that every American could achieve the blessings of "mass personal automobility." In even more extravagant terms, historian Joseph J. Corn has argued that the "winged gospel" of air travel was embraced by Americans as "an instrument of reform, regeneration, and salvation, a substitute for politics, revolution, or even religion." More recently, space travel, whether undertaken by NASA astronauts or by alien abductees, has assumed a religious aura in transcending spatial limits through the extraordinary movement of the body out of this world.[31]

What sort of tactile knowledge is gained through all this mobility? In a discussion of "democratic social space," literary critic Philip Fisher has outlined the basic features of an American imagination of space: it is uniform, open, and familiar. In its fundamental uniformity, democratic space is defined by grids and plots, by cells and atoms, which are in principle interchangeable units of space, "identical from place to place." Open and unbounded, this democratic space allows for free movement, a freedom of entry and exit, of immigration, emigration, and internal mobility, which might alter the space's shape and size but has no effect on its essential uniformity.

Moving through the uniformity of democratic social space, Americans can experience a certain familiarity, a tangible sense of any place as recognizable, intelligible, transparent, and comfortable. According to Fisher, "It is this feeling of familiarity that lets us move from point to point without much effort," engaging even new places on familiar terms as if their "novelty has no strangeness." In the uniformity, openness, and familiarity of democratic social space, "it feels 'like' home everywhere." As a result, Fisher has argued, democratic social space allows for no outsiders, no critical observers, no oppositional positions external to the fabric of society.[32] In democratic social space, to recall Clinton's campaign promise, "there is no them; there is only us."

Someone, however, must be watching this American space. According to Joseph

Firmage, the former "Silicon Valley mogul" and now purveyor of "the Truth," aliens from outer space have long adopted that "observer position," watching the earth from a distance. Firmage has promised that these alien observers will soon "touch down." In response to this contact, he advises, all we need to do is "have the wisdom and courage to warrant an opportunity to touch heaven."[33] By anticipating this tactile exchange—touching down, touching heaven—Firmage has joined many enthusiasts of the extraterrestrial, not only those who report sightings of UFOs, but also those who claim tangible contact, the "close encounters of the fourth kind," including cases of physical abduction by aliens from outer space.

As an extraordinary kind of embodied mobility, alien abduction has been defined as the "forced removal of a person from his or her physical location to another place. It may include an altered state of awareness for the purpose of physical, surgical, or psychological procedures performed by non-humans. After the abduction, the person is returned to his or her physical location and frequently has little or no recollection of the experience."[34] Most abductees have no memory of the experience, so a Web site, the Official Alien Abduction Test Site, provides a helpful questionnaire with fifty-two indicators to help to determine "are you an alien abductee?" One of the indications that you are, of course, is that you do not remember. Those who pass the test are entitled to send in $4.95 for an "official alien abduction certificate," which is intended as proof for their families, friends, and coworkers that they have been moved by aliens.[35]

While some enthusiasts, such as Joseph Firmage, find these extraterrestrial interventions to be a sign of hope, even a promise of salvation in the tactile contact, encounter, and exchange between worlds, other abductees, perhaps most, have characterized their experience of alien abduction as a violation of their humanity. Katharina Wilson, for example, author of *The Alien Jigsaw*, who has claimed to have experienced many alien abductions, finally came to the conclusion in 1996 that "the aliens have taken much more from [her] than they have given." In her many encounters with the alien "greys," "tans," and "hybrids," Wilson endured "*painful* psychological and physiological experiments" that forced her "to exist in a perpetual state of duress."[36]

By manipulating the body, instilling fear, and causing pain, Wilson reported, aliens from outer space enforce their will over human beings, using their instruments of manipulation to produce their own desired results, operating, in this respect, like organized religion. "It is ironic that organized religion," she reflected, "has become similar to the way the aliens behave."[37] In both alien abductions and organized religion, Wilson found a kind of kinesthetic tactility that is fundamentally antihuman—

not moving but being moved, not touching but being touched, not manipulating but being manipulated—in its transformation of human beings into objects. In these terms, alien abduction might represent the ultimate violation of the human right to freedom of movement in democratic social space.

HANDLING

In contrast with kinesthetic movement, haptic manipulation involves the sense of touch when engaged in handling the environment and acquiring sensory information by moving and manipulating objects. In a reversal of roles, as in the case of alien abduction, Americans often have imagined that they themselves are moved and manipulated by hidden hands—the "invisible hand" of the market, the unseen touch of contagion—resulting in the risk of their most basic goals of health, wealth, and prosperity. In the tactile imagery of an economic reasoning that has become common sense, reality is moved and manipulated by tactile forces that cannot be seen. According to the online Guide to Economic Reasoning, "Economic reality is controlled by three invisible forces—the invisible hand (the price mechanism), the invisible handshake (social and historical forces), and the invisible foot (political and legal forces)." Although these three invisible forces—the hand, the handshake, and the foot—are supposedly responsible for the "smooth" allocation of capital, they often send the economy on a "rough" ride.[38]

Like the capitalist economy, the microscopic realm of the body is also imagined to be driven by invisible tactile forces, by invisible contacts at the cellular level. "Cells interact by touch," as Bateson and Goldsby have observed, "you might even say embrace."[39] Invisible to the naked eye, healthy cellular embraces maintain the immune system, which ensures the safety and security of the body, guaranteeing the body's sanctity, in Jacques Derrida's terms, as the "safe and sound."[40] In violating that sanctity, however, the invading cells of a virus enter into illicit embraces, grasping and bonding with the cells of the immune system.

As cultural analyst Marita Sturken has noted, this religious imagery of illicit contact is frequently evoked in popular scientific literature depicting HIV and AIDS. "HIV is seen to enter the immune system's most sacred space and to rescript its genetic memory," Sturken has observed. "HIV is constantly described as entering the 'innermost sanctum' of the cell and the 'sacrosanct environment' of the body."[41] In these highly charged religious terms, the body is configured as a sacred space at constant risk of desecration by the unseen contact, the secret touch, the illicit embrace of intruders that enter its innermost sanctum only to violate.

From the world of the global economy to the world of the physical body, how do people handle living in a realm that is manipulated by invisible tactile forces? As anthropologists Jean Comaroff and John L. Comaroff have argued, we are witnessing a dramatic global increase in "occult economies," which involve the essentially magical manipulation of secret means for gaining health and prosperity.[42] For the purposes of analyzing religion and tactility, we might want to recognize many of these magical or ritual techniques as forms of haptic manipulation, touching directly, so to speak, the secret, hidden, and invisible forces that animate both the physical body and the capitalist economy.

With respect to the physical body, which has come to be dominated by the "gaze" of modern scientific medical practice, alternative forms of healing often make use of touch, from the techniques of chiropractic (literally, healing "done by the hands"), to dramatic rituals of faith healing by "laying on hands," to recent innovations in pastoral counseling that employ what one advocate has called "healing touch, the church's forgotten language."[43] In all of these instances, the touch involves not only hands on the physical body but also manipulation of the unseen forces that are imagined to be responsible for health and well-being. In the case of chiropractic, that force is the innate intelligence of the body; in faith healing, the Holy Spirit; in pastoral counseling, faith, hope, and love.

Although these forms of "body work" usually depend on establishing direct physical contact, the haptic manipulation of unseen forces can also be accomplished at a distance, as demonstrated by the charismatic faith healer Ernest Angely, who used to end his televised faith-healing services by putting his open palm up to the camera, thus projecting the image of an enormous hand into America's living rooms, so that his viewers could bring their afflicted body parts into contact with the screen. In the hands of Angely, television truly became a tactile medium, a medium for establishing a kind of physical contact that manipulated unseen powers of healing.

During the golden age of TV evangelism, television also became a religious medium for economic exchange, with incessant appeals for funds to support the television ministries becoming an integral part of the message, often accompanied by promises of miraculous financial returns for the donor. In a characteristic sermon of the 1980s, for example, the Reverend Jerry Falwell identified four kinds of giving—systematic, spontaneous, sacrificial, and spiritual—with the ultimate form of giving, the spiritual, defined as the act of pledging money to the ministry of Christ, specifically money that viewers did not already possess but were willing to pledge in the faith that Jesus would provide it. Of course, all major credit cards were accepted.

In this haptic manipulation of money, with its implicitly tactile reference to the hand-to-hand exchange of giving and receiving, spiritual gifts can be explicitly identified as material. In the ministry of Reverend Ike, who proclaimed a distinctive gospel of money, this equation of the spiritual and material was the whole point: "I am telling you, get out of the ghetto and get into the get-mo. Get some money, honey. You and me, we are not interested in a harp tomorrow, we are interested in a dollar today. We want it NOW. We want it in a big sack or a box or a railroad car but we WANT it. Stick with me. Nothing for free. Want to shake that money tree." Clearly, the rhetoric of Reverend Ike's gospel of money sent potently tactile signals—the binding promise of "stick with me"; the burning desire to "get-mo"; the kinesthetic movement out of the ghetto; and the haptic shaking of the "money tree"—signals that we have considered here as basic features of religious tactility. In practical terms, all Reverend Ike asked was that people tithe 10 percent of their monthly income to him. In return, they could expect a miraculous tenfold increase in their wealth, a dollar in the hand that was far better than any promise of a harp in the future. "I say LACK OF money is the root of all evil," Reverend Ike declared. "The best thing you can do for poor folks is not be one of them."[44] By handling the invisible forces that produce wealth—by shaking hands with the "invisible hand"—poor people could hope to eradicate the root of all evil in their own lives. As an "occult economy," this gospel of prosperity provides religious techniques of haptic manipulation for handling the world.

RELIGION UNDER PRESSURE

As Walter Benjamin proposed, the challenges faced by human beings at the turning points of history cannot be solved solely by visual contemplation. Guided by what Benjamin called tactile appropriation, people gradually and perhaps unconsciously adjust to new situations by habit. In adjusting to the new era of sensory challenges presented by electronic media—the shocks to sensibility, the bombardment of sensory stimuli, the risk of sensory overload, and so on—new strategies of engagement have emerged to deal with what Benjamin identified as the most characteristic sensory condition of modernity, distraction.

The discovery of a new and apparently pervasive medical condition, attention deficit disorder, seems to confirm this insight. Identified by one author as "an increasingly common brain imbalance," this disease "causes acute restlessness and a propensity toward boredom and distraction."[45] Apparently, one of the diagnostic signs of this disorder is that the person is unaware of suffering from distraction.

In this respect, the disease is like alien abduction—a disturbance, dislocation, or disorientation that touches people unawares. We are unaware of our experience, in both these cases, not because we made no effort to pay attention but because we were fundamentally distracted.

In religious ritual, where attention to detail is required, distraction can often pose a serious problem. According to the catechism of the Catholic Church, for example, distraction is a problem for the ritual of prayer. "The habitual difficulty in prayer," the catechism teaches, "is distraction." Not only disrupting the flow of words in verbal prayer or deflecting the concentration of the inner vision in contemplative prayer, distraction "can concern, more profoundly, him to whom we are praying." From God's perspective, "a distraction reveals to us what we are attached to," which suggests that a distracted person in prayer is touching the world rather than engaging with God through the spiritual senses of sight and sound. "Therein lies the battle," as the catechism concludes its advice on distraction, "the choice of which master to serve."[46] The medical diagnosis of a disease of distraction, therefore, strangely recalls a long history of religious valorization of strict, single-minded, and pure attention.

At the same time, the value of distraction has been recognized in modern medical practice as a nonpharmacological method of dealing with pain. According to one account, "Distraction is a strategy of focusing one's attention on stimuli other than pain or the accompanying negative emotions."[47] As a strategy for dealing with pain, even the ritual of prayer, which the Catholic catechism maintains is threatened by distraction, can itself be converted to medical use as an instrument not of attention but of distraction. From this perspective, distraction is a very good thing.

"The distracted person, too," Benjamin noted, "can form habits." In 1985 the sociologist Robert Bellah and his colleagues who produced *Habits of the Heart* proposed that the quality of American life depends on paying careful attention to the "face-to-face" relations of individuals in community. In the midst of so many distractions, however, how can individuals form habits that are not shaped under pressure? Risking an extremely broad generalization, we can conclude that the habits of the heart being formed under the conditions of modernity are the haptics of the heart, the strategies for handling distraction, pressure, and stress.

A quick trip through any bookstore, even by a distracted observer, reveals the wealth of advice for handling stress. Selecting at random, we could read any number of the following titles: *Dealing with Stress, a Biblical Approach; Heavenly Ways to Handle Stress; Healthy and Holy under Stress; Too Blessed to Be Stressed; How to*

Make Work, Stress, and Drudgery a Means to Your Sanctity; Prayerstarters to Help You Handle Stress; What Would Jesus Do to Rise above Stress? Or, if we really want to gain a perspective on life that might reverse the pressures of stress, we could read the book *Stressed Is Desserts Spelled Backwards.* Without reading any of these religious texts, however, we can conclude only that they are directed at a world under pressure, stressed out, struggling to cope with the tactile conditions of a modernity that Benjamin called distraction.

Distracted, we also struggle with the invisible hands, the secret embraces, the shocking disclosures, and what Jean Baudrillard has called the "strike of events."[48] As students of culture and religion, however, our task is not to cope but to make sense, to make sense out of the myriad discourses and practices that operate at the intersections of human subjectivity and social relations. Without drawing a map or advancing an argument, I have only touched upon some of the features of religion and tactility in contemporary American culture. Rhetorically, through an apparently random series of unexpected juxtapositions and free associations, I have tried to give a particularly tactile account of religion and the sense of touch, although I realize that my presentation has tended more toward the "shock effect" than the caress. Nevertheless, I do think that attention to tactility—even distracted attention—can illuminate the shifting terrain of religion and American popular culture in modernity.

First, religious tactility is binding. As historian of religions Bruce Lincoln has observed, the study of religion is constantly confronted with the challenge of making sense of the discourses and forces through which any first-person plural— any "us"—is constructed.[49] Obviously, religious traditions generate symbolic terms and conditions for constructing a religious body—the body of Christ in Pauline Christianity, the body of Purusha in Vedic Hinduism, and so on—that is also a simultaneously unified and differentiated social body. Under the sign of the first-person plural, the integrated social body is inevitably diversified into the head, hands, thighs, and feet. In the rhetoric of President Bill Clinton, an American first-person plural is motivated through tactile symbolism in which there is no head or feet but only hands: there is no "them" above or below the "us" who stand together hand in hand in an egalitarian relationship and exchange goods hand to hand in a reciprocal relationship.

Although we might dismiss this imagery as merely political rhetoric, let alone as disingenuous political posturing, the potency of tactile metaphors has evidently been an important feature of real embodiment in the world. Any line separating real embodiment from "mere" metaphor has always been blurred. As a significant constellation of the "metaphors we live by," tactility—even metaphoric, symbolic, or virtual tactility—has produced real effects in the real world.[50]

In Clinton's tactile rhetoric of a visceral, tangible bond that forges an "us" with which there is no "them," the categorical differences of race, class, and gender were obviously elided. To refer here only to gender, we need to ask: In what ways has religious tactility been gendered, especially when an "us" is constituted as a social body in which males are the head and hands and females are the thighs and feet? Arguing that women generally prefer touch to sight, Luce Irigaray risked reinforcing this male hierarchy of the body in order to recover and valorize a tactile sensibility.[51] A more nuanced analysis of tactility, however, might disclose a variety of female subject positions in the tactile religious experience of women, from Heather Ash's celebration of the empowering energy and unbounded freedom of the sacred fire to Katharina Wilson's disempowering abduction and captive manipulation at the hands of alien forces, whether extraterrestrials or organized religion.

At the same time, we have to suspect that a particular kind of gendered tactility persists in rendering the haptic dynamics of the unseen forces of modernity in peculiar ways so that the "male" political economy, with its masterful invisible hands and handshakes, is implicitly distinguished from the "female" passivity, vulnerability, and risk of violation by illicit embraces of cellular microbiology. In constructing an "us" with which there is no "them," the religious tactility of binding generates both sacred bonds and bondage.

Second, religious tactility is burning. As energy, enthusiasm, or vital force, religion has often been portrayed as the heat that fuses subjectivity with collectivity. In Durkheim's terms, religion, particularly religious ritual, generates the boiling, bubbling energy of the "collective effervescence" in which individuals effectively melt into the social group. As we have seen, the modern, mass-marketed ritual of firewalking has represented a particularly tactile medium for melting not only into the exclusive community of experienced, initiated firewalkers but also into an imaginary American collectivity of democracy, opportunity, and respect, a collectivity also represented by the flag of the United States, especially when that material symbol has been at risk of desecration by burning.

In such a "hot" culture, the only thermal register we can expect in the United States is one turned up to high. But why has all of this burning energy of sacred fires, electricity, or even individual hearts strangely warmed been consistently interpreted by Americans in such cold, pedantic, and doctrinaire terms? Whether defending the flag from fire at the center or developing an alternative ritual of fire at the periphery, the American testimonials considered here seem to be struggling to translate heat into light but failing to capture the burning intensity of heat in words.

Third, religious tactility is moving. It is kinesthetic motion. According to a modern ideology of progress, the movement of humanity, culture, and religion is inexorably forward, aided by better, faster machines from the bicycle to the space shuttle, in order to achieve a transcendence of space and time. Ironically, this transcendence has been accomplished in large part through scientific discoveries of distinctively tactile limits that restrict motion—gravity, inertia, and resistance.

But then modernity, for all its straightforward, developmental thrust toward progress, has also been a fertile field for the flowering of irony. For example, the modern world is supposedly a domain of visibility, constituted by the hegemony of the gaze, governed by panoptic surveillance, and ruled by the "scopic regimes of modernity."[52] Under the predominance of vision, all modern individuals are required to pay attention. But modernity is also tactility, distraction, and pressure. By paying so much attention to the dominance of sight in Western culture, we forget that our principal theorists of modernity, Marx and Freud, were also theorists of tactility—capitalist oppression, psychological repression—in touch with resistance. As we have seen, religious tactility might move, but its motions are inevitably under pressure.

This contradiction (with all its attendant irony) between a prevailing visual modernity and the acutely tactile sensibility of the major theorists of modernity's engines demands further exploration. In his critical analysis of the modern capitalist political economy, Marx proposed that "the forming of the five senses is a labour of the entire history of the world down to the present."[53] Turning Hegel on his head, of course, meant turning inside out the Western hierarchy of the senses that Hegel had inherited. In that Marxist turning of the senses, with its anticipation of a materialist apocalyptic inversion of the senses in which the first would finally be last and the last would be first, seeing and hearing could never compete for authenticity with tasting, smelling, or touching, or, above all, with working in the sensory economy of knowledge and power.

Freud's discovery of the unconscious, with its multiple repressions, developed an entirely different hermeneutics, energetics, and economy of the senses that nevertheless also wrestled with the problem of motion. How can we possibly move forward when we are bound—by completely unconscious primal repression, by the semiconscious repression that Freud called "after-pressure," by the driving fixations of cathexis that bind desire to objects, and even by "the uncanny" (often religiously portrayed as the holy, the sacred, or supernatural power), which Freud analyzed casually as "something repressed which recurs," as "something which is familiar and old-established in the mind and which has become alienated from it only through the process of repression?"[54] If modernity is about freedom of movement, its tactile mobility is clearly negotiated in relation to powerful forces of resistance, repression, and oppression.

Fourth, religious tactility is ultimately the capacity to handle the challenges of living in the world, especially the challenges posed by what cannot be seen or heard. Under pressure, people deploy religious resources under difficult conditions. Adapting the distinction between strategies and tactics that Michel de Certeau proposed, we might understand religious strategies as exercises within the domain of power, as transparent uses of religion for the legitimization or reinforcement of a political order that is "bound by its very visibility." We might regard religious tactics as oppositional maneuvers, as tactile maneuvers in the dark, so to speak, that defy, subvert, or otherwise interfere with an established domain of visibility by engaging in "the very transformation of touch into response, a 're-turning' of the surprise expected without being foreseen."[55] In an analysis of the intersections between the individual and the collective, this distinction between strategies and tactics—between the strategic domain of visibility and the tactical terrain of touch, response, twists, turns, and surprises that defy any hegemony of vision—leads back to what I have been calling a haptic engagement with culture and religion.

By adopting such a tactile engagement with contemporary American religion and culture, we might begin to make sense of a religious sensibility that reveals America, wherever it might be, in Walt Whitman's terms, as "a kosmos, disorderly, fleshy and sensual."[56] In its contacts and concussions, its caresses and shocks, its binding, burning, moving, and handling, America has remained a problem that confronts us—or distracts us—in its irrecoverable tactility, in its capacity to be in touch with the lowest sense, the most animal, servile, and unconscious of the resources of the human sensorium. The habits of the heart, in this reconstitution of American culture and religion, are haptics of the heart, the tactile strategies and tactics of binding, burning, moving, and handling that animate being religious in America, in modernity, in the world.

CHAPTER FIVE

Sacrificial Religion

On November 18, 1978, over nine hundred Americans living in the cooperative agricultural community known as Jonestown entered into a collective murder-suicide. Founded by the charismatic communist religious leader Jim Jones, who had led many members of his Peoples Temple into exile in the jungles of Guyana, Jonestown was a community that felt besieged. They feared attack by the U.S. government, the media, and former members, who called themselves "Concerned Relatives" but were perceived by the community as traitors. When a U.S. congressional delegation, accompanied by media and former members, entered Jonestown, an extraordinary explosion of violence, murder, and suicide was set off. Residents of the Jonestown community chose to kill themselves rather than submit to their enemies. Many, perhaps most, of the adult participants understood the Jonestown mass suicide as a redemptive act. They thought this single superhuman act of self-sacrifice would redeem a fully human identity from the dehumanizing pull of an evil capitalist world.

Even the killing of infants and children was interpreted as redemptive. Jim Jones insisted that truly loving people would kill their children before allowing them to be taken back to America to be tortured, brainwashed, or even killed by a society he regarded as fascist. That sentiment was echoed by a member of the community; surrounded by the bodies of the children who were in fact sacrificed, he said: "I'd rather see them lay like that than to see them have to die like the Jews did." Death in Jonestown promised to redeem those children from a dehumanized life and death in America. If Americans captured the children, this particular speaker concluded, "they're gonna just let them grow up and be dummies, just like they want them to be, and not grow up to be a *person* like the one and only Jim Jones." Sacrificial death, he believed, promised the redemption of an authentic human identity.[1]

Most Americans found the deaths at Jonestown unthinkable. If considered at all, the mass murder-suicide registered as something so obviously outside the mainstream of American cultural life that it stood as a boundary against which core American values could be defined. Yet, from 1980 to 1988 the symbolic center of the American public order was occupied by a political figure who, on numerous occasions, idealized the ideology of redemptive sacrifice. A speech to the National Association of Evangelicals in Orlando, Florida, on March 8, 1983, provides only one striking example. In that speech, Ronald Reagan related the following anecdote: A certain prominent young man in Hollywood stood up in a public gathering and said there was nothing in the world that he loved more than his daughters. Reagan recalled how he had worried at that moment that this man did not have his priorities straight. He said to himself: "Oh, no, don't. You can't—don't say that." Then, however, the father set Reagan's mind at ease by concluding that it was precisely because he loved his daughters that he was willing to sacrifice them in the interest of a higher good. According to Reagan, the father had declared, "I would rather see my little girls die now, still believing in God, than have them grow up under communism and one day die no longer believing in God."[2]

Here, of course, is a curious parallel: Jones wanted children to die to save them from capitalism, while Ronald Reagan wanted children to die to save them from communism. Each leader—one on the periphery of American public life, the other at its center—employed the powerful ideology of redemptive sacrifice in order to justify mass death. Furthermore, both Reagan and Jones fashioned potent ideologies of sacrifice out of the same political and symbolic economy of the cold war conflict between capitalism and communism. Those ideologies call for a comparative analysis to reveal the contrasting, yet strangely similar, strategies for negotiating redemption through sacrifice.

When news of the Jonestown mass murder-suicide broke, Ronald Reagan was in Bonn on a tour of European capitals. Reporters asked for his reaction to the event. "I'll try not to be happy in saying this," Reagan remarked. "[Jones] supported a number of political figures but seemed to be more involved with the Democratic Party. I haven't seen anyone in the Republican Party having been helped by him or seeking his help."[3] Reagan did seem to derive some pleasure from associating Jonestown with the Democrats and distancing himself and his political party. Such distancing was characteristic of the general trend in reactions to Jonestown, which enveloped the movement and its sudden demise in layers of denial. This strategic distancing also obscured the latent ideology of redemptive sacrifice that existed at the very center of the American public order at the same time as it was enacted by a movement on the periphery of American society. In an important sense, Reagan's presidency was dedicated to revitalizing the sacrificial center of American society.

Jones's ideology of redemptive sacrifice was intentionally decentering: he argued that the Jonestown deaths would have a performative impact on America that would shake the country's faith in its own centered order, an order that Jones characterized as racist, capitalist, fascist, and oppressive. On the last night in Jonestown, Jones declared, "We win when we go down." What did Jones think they would win?

Here, I can only summarize my findings. First, Jones thought he and his followers would win their ongoing battle against outside enemies—the U.S. government, the media, and traitors who called themselves Concerned Relatives—through an act of suicide, for which those enemies would bear the guilt. Second, he thought they would win glory for their sacred cause through an act that would demonstrate both the purity of their commitment to socialism—Divine Socialism, God, Almighty Socialism—and the ultimate seriousness of their protest against a world dominated, defiled, and dehumanized by capitalism. Third—and this relates to Jones's distinction between revolutionary suicide and self-destructive suicide—he thought they would win a fully human identity by redeeming themselves from a dehumanized life and death in America through a single superhuman act.

Ronald Reagan also spoke of winning through sacrifice. America had won and would continue to win in the struggle for freedom, only because America's sons and daughters would pay the highest price, give the greatest gift, make the supreme sacrifice. Although this patriotic rhetorical formula must seem familiar, I think Reagan's revitalization of the sacrificial center of America bears further examination. Reagan understood sacrifice in terms of three overlapping symbolic registers: the metaphysical truth of the human soul, the kinship bonds of the family, and the supreme expenditure of human life in an American political economy of the sacred. When Reagan's rhetoric of redemptive sacrifice is juxtaposed with Jim Jones's sacrificial ideology, new significance to the phrase "Win one for the Gipper" becomes apparent. Since I have already reconstructed the worldview of Jim Jones elsewhere, I will devote the first part of this chapter to a recollection of the sacrificial metaphysics of Ronald Reagan.

SACRIFICIAL TRUTH

Many have attempted to explain the power of Reagan's presidential rhetoric. He used compelling tropes, such as "path" and "disease/healing" metaphors. He made frequent anecdotal use of synecdoche to reduce a complex whole (often mistakenly) to some (often fictitious) part. He used the imagery and illusion of the movies, made more powerful because, as Michael Rogin has noted, "during Reagan's lifetime the locus of sacred value shifted from church not to the state but to Hollywood." Reagan symbolically substituted familiar imagery drawn from home, family, and neighborhood for situations of public or global scope. He consistently dissolved existing lateral, binary oppositions—"neither east nor west," "neither left nor right"—and proclaimed in their stead a centered verticality of good above and evil below. Finally, and most important, Reagan penetrated, appropriated, and exploited the American civic ceremonial rhetoric of death.[4]

Rhetorical analysis of the speeches of the "Great Communicator" could endlessly explore the strategies he used in turning speech into "symbolic capital" for the implementation of public policy programs. Yet, none of his strategies was more potent than the ideological rhetoric of death, martyrdom, and redemptive sacrifice. I want to isolate that complex of rhetorical imagery through which Reagan revitalized the ideology of redemptive sacrifice. Consistently throughout his political career, Reagan reiterated a metaphysical code that reinforced what he claimed as the profound sacrificial truth at the heart of America.

An examination of Reagan's speeches from 1964 to 1989 reveals a recurring metaphysical claim: human beings have souls because they are capable of sacrificing their bodies. Sometimes Reagan seemed to imply that only Americans have souls to be revealed through sacrifice. At other times, he seemed to intend a more epistemological shading to this claim by suggesting that human beings demonstrate the knowledge that they have souls whenever they are willing to sacrifice their bodies. In any event, the sacrifice of the body, the physical, or the material was defined by Ronald Reagan as redemptive, because it alone discloses what he referred to as the "profound truth" of the soul.

In his March 1983 address to the National Association of Evangelicals, Reagan concluded his anecdote about the young father who was willing to sacrifice his daughters to save them from communism by describing the response of the "tremendous gathering" that had heard those words in California during the cold war 1950s. "There were thousands of young people in that audience," Reagan recalled. "They came to their feet with shouts of joy. They had instantly recognized the profound truth in what he had said, *with regard to the physical and the soul and what was truly important.*"[5] In other words, the joyous revelation beheld by that shouting audience was the profound truth that Americans have souls, and know they have souls, because they are willing and able to sacrifice the physical. Sacrifice not only demonstrates the American soul, however; it also promises to redeem that soul from the communist fate, which is worse than death. Redemptive sacrifice, in Reagan's view, is the "profound truth" at the heart of America.

This profound truth was not merely cooked up for Reagan's evangelical audience. It was part of a sacrificial ideology that ran throughout his speeches. In his commencement address at Notre Dame on May 17, 1981, for example, Reagan meditated on the theme of redemptive sacrifice that was embodied in his movie role as George Gipp in *Knute Rockne, All American* (1940), "a sports legend so national in scope, it was almost mystical." George Gipp stood as the central cinematic *figura* of redemptive sacrifice in the worldview of Ronald Reagan. Immediately following his invocation of the sacrificial power of the Gipper, however, Reagan used a citation from William Faulkner to reinforce his central metaphysical claim that humans have souls that are revealed in the act of sacrifice. "He is immortal," Reagan quoted Faulkner, "because he alone among creatures . . . has a soul, capable of compassion and sacrifice and endurance." In conclusion, Reagan drew out the mystical, national implications of this sacrificial ideology by describing America as that "giant country prepared to make so many sacrifices."[6]

Reagan employed the Faulkner quotation on numerous occasions. For example, in his address to the Irish parliament on June 4, 1984, he led up to Faulkner by first citing a statement apparently made by the leader of the Polish Solidarity movement. "As Lech Walesa said: 'Our souls contain exactly the contrary of what [the Soviet leadership] wanted. They wanted us not to believe in God, and our churches are full. They wanted us to be materialistic and incapable of sacrifice.'" Walesa's equation of soul and sacrifice was too similar to Faulkner's formulation of the profound sacrificial truth for Reagan to resist invoking it: "He is immortal because, alone among creatures, he has a soul, a spirit capable of compassion and sacrifice and endurance."[7] Apparently, Reagan's own profound sacrificial truth allowed for the possibility of American souls and some Polish souls but not communist souls. The communists did not know the difference between the spiritual and the physical, lost as they were in the Marxist faith of materialism.

Clearly, an ideology of redemptive sacrifice was integral to Ronald Reagan's presidential worldview. Yet, such an ideology was already present at the beginning of his career in electoral politics. In his October 27, 1964, television address on behalf of Barry Goldwater, the basic elements of this sacrificial ideology were already firmly in place. Reagan used domestic imagery to describe differences between Democrats and Republicans as a "family fight" that should be resolved so that Americans could unite against a common enemy, "the most dangerous enemy ever known to man." He collapsed binary oppositions, dissolving them into vertical, centering imagery, by declaring that "there is no left or right, only up or down, up to the maximum of individual freedom consistent with law and order, or down to the ant heap of totalitarianism." Finally, he intensified his rhetoric, raising the stakes to the highest degree possible, by insisting that America was in danger of having to face "the final ultimatum."

Confronted with that ultimatum—which Reagan repeatedly formulated as "surrender or die"—Americans had the civil-religious obligation to merge with a redemptive history of martyrdom. They must sacrifice all in order to win everything by following the example of Moses, Jesus, American revolutionary patriots, and all the martyrs of history into sacrificial death. As Reagan told his television audience:

> The English commentator Kenneth Tynan has put it that he would rather live on his knees than die on his feet. Some of our own have said, "Better Red than dead." If we are to believe that nothing is worth the dying, when did this begin? Should Moses have told the children of Israel to live in slavery rather than dare the wilderness? Should Christ have refused the cross? Should the patriots at Concord Bridge have refused to fire the shot heard round the world? Are we to believe that all the martyrs of history died in vain?

Reagan closed this speech, as he often would his presidential speeches, by invoking children and even the unborn: "Let our children and our children's children say of us we justified our brief moment here. We did all that could be done."[8] Justification would come from doing all that could be done—giving all, risking all, sacrificing all—like those martyrs who set the sacrificial example for America: the children of Israel, the son of God, and the original patriotic sons of the fatherland.

As president, Reagan seemed to derive his greatest power from presiding over civic rituals of sacrificial death, not only through patriotic speechmaking, but also through rituals at monuments, cemeteries, funerals, and memorials for America's sacrificed dead. His inaugural and State of the Union addresses were ceremonial tributes to martial sacrifice, most obviously evoked in his 1981 inaugural citation of the sacrificial dedication of Martin Treptow, who was killed in World War I. Treptow had written in his diary, "I will work, I will save, I will sacrifice."[9]

Reagan consistently portrayed the significance of civil-religious monuments as symbols of sacrificial death. In 1982, he described his emotions at seeing *The Spirit of American Youth Rising from the Waves*, the statue commemorating American deaths during the Normandy landing in World War II, by saying that its symbolic significance transcends words. "Its image of sacrifice," Reagan told the United Nations General Assembly, "is almost too powerful to describe."[10] Even the Statue of Liberty was a monument to sacrificial death in Reagan's ideology of redemptive sacrifice. With French president Mitterand by his side on July 3, 1986, Reagan explained that the Statue of Liberty stands as "a reminder since the days of Lafayette of our mutual struggles and sacrifices for freedom." He continued, "Call it mysticism if you will," but it was sacrificial death that provided "the common thread that binds us to those Quakers *[sic]* on the tiny deck of the *Arbella*," those sacrificial founders who risked all and sacrificed all for the shining American city on a hill.[11]

Obviously, cemeteries provided Reagan ample opportunity to meditate on sacrificial death, from his first inaugural meditations on Arlington National Cemetery, where the white markers "add up to only a tiny fraction of the price that has been paid for our freedom," to his 1985 visit to Bergen Belsen. There he explained, "Everywhere here are memories [that] take us where God intended His children to go—toward learning, toward healing, and, above all, toward redemption."[12]

Reagan's sacrificial ideology was so pervasive, in fact, that it even transformed accidental deaths into redemptive sacrifices. Speaking at a memorial service for the seven *Challenger* astronauts on January 31, 1986, he explained that their "brave sacrifice" had once again revealed the "profound truth" of the uniquely American soul that can be disclosed only through sacrificial death. From their sacrifice, the souls of the living derive both revitalizing energy and valuable instruction in profound sacrificial truth. "The sacrifice of your loved ones," Reagan told the mourners, "has stirred the soul of our nation and through the pain our hearts have opened to a profound truth: . . . We learned again that this America, which Abraham Lincoln called the last, best hope of man on Earth, was built on heroism and noble sacrifice."[13] When thirty-seven sailors aboard the *U.S.S. Stark* were accidentally killed by a misguided Iraqi missile in May 1987, Reagan once again presided over a civic ritual that revealed the profound sacrificial truth. "These men made themselves immortal," Reagan declared, "by dying for something immortal."[14]

Examples of Reagan's sacrificial ideology could certainly be multiplied. All suggest that he served not merely as president but also as psychopomp, as guide for the soul, presiding over American ceremonies of sacrificial death. In a frequently cited 1985 interview with François Mitterand, Marguerite Duras suggested that Reagan was "the incarnation of a kind of primal, almost archaic power." Mitterand agreed. But if Reagan did, in fact, incarnate any such primal power, it resulted not from his ability to govern "less with his intellect than with common sense," as Duras concluded, but from his appropriation of the primal power of sacrificial death.[15]

That primal, sacrificial power, however, was certainly displaced in modern social, political, and economic contexts, particularly when Reagan frequently identified the sacrificial heroism of America's martyred dead with the everyday heroism of factory workers, farmers, entrepreneurs, taxpayers, and all others who made "voluntary gifts" of their lives and labor as a sacrificial offering to America.[16] As historian of religions David Carrasco has observed, a modern American society is "not a sacrifice society or a massacre society but a mass sacrifice society."[17] The United States does not perform regular sacrificial rituals, let alone religious ceremonies of human sacrifice as the Aztecs did, nor does it openly pursue or condone the massacre of civilians, although correlations between sacrifice and warfare have often been drawn. In Reagan's sacrificial ideology, however, sacrifice reveals the soul of Americans in every aspect of public and private life, not only on the battlefield. His was an ideology of redemptive sacrifice for a modern "mass sacrifice society."

But perhaps *modern* is not the correct adjective in this case. Ronald Reagan may have been the first postmodern president—artist of simulation, idol of consumption. In fact, one analyst of postmodernism could think of no better example of Baudrillard's notion of simulation than the Reagan presidency.[18] Clearly, Reagan drew much of his power from the theatrical simulation of film. In a revealing remark, Reagan disclosed the secret of his artful simulation as president. "The only way to look natural on a stage," Reagan explained, "is to hold your hands and arms in a way that does not feel natural. . . . What you have to do is just let your arms hang by your side straight down. Then you curl your fingers so that they just cup your thumb. It feels uncomfortable, but you look relaxed and at ease."[19]

Reagan's body language of simulation was both signal and symptom of a profound shift in the symbolism of the sacred in a postmodern world of imagery consumption, "from church to Hollywood," in Michael Rogin's phrase, but then, finally, to the state during the Reagan presidency. In a sense, film acts as a ritualized medium, fulfilling most of the requirements of Jonathan Z. Smith's explanation of ritual as "the creation of a controlled environment where the variables (i.e., the accidents) of ordinary life may be displaced"—on the cutting-room floor; through the rehearsals and retakes; under the director's supervision; in the preservation and permanence of the image—"performing the way things ought to be in conscious tension to the way things are in such a way that this ritualized perfection is recollected in the ordinary, uncontrolled, course of things."[20]

When Reagan recollected the ritualized perfection he had achieved in film, he recalled perfect patterns of redemptive sacrifice. In the photographs that illustrate Reagan's 1965 autobiography, as Michael Rogin has noted, the "stills evoke redemptive suffering."[21] Rogin has argued that Reagan simulated the sacrificial victim, from his film roles to his presidential office, from the redemptive sacrifice of George Gipp to his symbolic death and rebirth resulting from the 1981 assassination attempt, ironically perpetrated by a man acting out a part in the simulated world of film, from which Reagan derived so much of his power. In the simulations of film and political office, Reagan embodied a primal power—like the shaman, like the martyr, like the sacred king—to transform sacrificial suffering and death into life, healing, and redemption.

However, Reagan also simulated the sacrificer, the ceremonial officiant of American sacrificial death. As civil theologian of redemptive sacrifice, Reagan over and over again reinforced the "profound truth" of the American soul that could be disclosed only through sacrificial death. On Memorial Day, 1982, Reagan laid a wreath at the Tomb of the Unknown Soldier. As he was leaving, walking out through the honor guard, he was overheard muttering to himself, "My God, why would anyone want to send these kids off to die?"[22] He should not have had to ask. The year before, he had provided ample justification in his commencement address at Notre Dame, spelling out the profound truth of redemptive sacrifice: humans are immortal because they have souls that are revealed and redeemed through sacrificial death. Reagan quoted Winston Churchill to his audience: in such death, "we learn we are spirits, not animals, and that something is going on in space and time, and beyond space and time, which, whether we like it or not, spells duty."[23] Spirits and animals, space and time, transcendence and duty—these elements hint at processes of classification and orientation that operated in Reagan's civil-religious worldview.

Reagan's rhetoric empowered that worldview by claiming and revitalizing its sacrificial center: the American family. In his final State of the Union address, as in his 1964 speech for Goldwater, Reagan collapsed lateral, binary oppositions—neither east nor west; neither left nor right; neither Republican nor Democrat—into a single center: "There are no Republicans, no Democrats, just Americans," whose center is the family. At that single center, Reagan called for a revitalization of "civic ritual." Addressing the children of America, Reagan insisted that civic ritual must begin around the family dinner table. Collapsing public and private space, Reagan left America with the suggestion that civic sacrificial ritual must begin at home and that it must begin with the children of every American family.

SACRIFICIAL FAMILY

To summarize, Reagan and Jones both recommended a similar profound sacrificial truth: the human spirit is disclosed, liberated, or redeemed in sacrificial death. In the rhetoric of Reagan and Jones, *sacrifice* was a highly charged figure of speech that intensely manipulated the diverse and complex elements of their respective worldviews. Jim Jones manipulated the ideology of redemptive sacrifice to create a meaningful context at Jonestown, in which the only way to recover a human identity in a dehumanizing world was through the self-sacrifice of revolutionary suicide. In this view, redemptive sacrifice marks the line of classification that distinguishes human from subhuman. "Dying comes to all," Jones told the residents of Jonestown. "Why not make it for a revolutionary purpose, [a] beautiful goal, something that makes us above the animals?"[24]

Dying for America, in Reagan's terms, also marks classifications of persons: spiritual and material, human and animal. Not all sacrifice demonstrates a human spirit. Terrorists such as the Beirut truck bomber who killed 241 Marines along with himself might sacrifice their lives for a cause, but according to Reagan's report to the United Nations General Assembly, such a sacrifice is "a despicable act of barbarism by some who are unfit to associate with humankind."[25]

More than simply a truism of modern political violence—one person's freedom fighter is another's terrorist—Reagan's ideology of redemptive sacrifice was a strategic device for manipulating elements of his worldview. In this case, that strategy involved transforming a classification of persons that distinguishes between human and animal into a global distinction between us and them.

At the center of the sacrificial discourse of Jim Jones and Ronald Reagan stood the *figura* of the child. An odd fictive doubling, a self-absorbed mirroring process in relation to children seemed to preoccupy both of them. Jones symbolized the integrated, nonracial character of his community in and through the figure of his adopted "rainbow family." In sermons, Jones often warned enemies of the community, "No one messes with the Jones family." To the end, he fought child custody battles because, he argued, if one child were taken, the community would be destroyed.

The child who played the central role in the demise of the Jonestown community—John Victor Stoen—was the focus of an ongoing child custody dispute. Arguably not Jones's biological offspring, John Victor Stoen was nonetheless generally acknowledged by the Jonestown community as Jones's son. When questioned on this point, Jones would insist that the child was his because they looked alike. For whatever other reasons Jones may have had, that child played a special role in the life and death of Jonestown because he mirrored Jim Jones. The child who looked like Jones, who embodied the present community and its promise as a whole, was sacrificed on the last night of Jonestown in order that he and the entire community be saved from a capitalist fate worse than death.

If John Victor Stoen was the center point around which Jonestown's sacrificial death turned, the central child in Ronald Reagan's symbolic universe was the young Reagan himself. The ironies of Reagan's personal domestic life have often been noted: not only was he the first divorced president in American history, but also he was a father who seemed to have ambivalent and somewhat strained relations with his own children. Yet, when asked how he felt watching his old movies, Reagan consistently quipped, "It's like seeing the son I never had." Immortalized through the medium of film, that son—particularly the young George Gipp, who appeared for all of fifteen minutes in *Knute Rockne*—was an emblem of redemptive sacrifice, the young Reagan sacrificed, yet immortalized on film, so that the old Reagan could live.

Most of Reagan's major political speeches began and ended with references to children. Reagan invoked American children—"our children and our children's children"—as the ultimate source of support for his public policy programs. Children also played a crucial role in the discourse of Jim Jones, a role most dramatically played out on the last night of Jonestown as the children of the community were the first to be "redeemed" in that final mass sacrifice. How do we account for the significance of children in these ideologies of redemptive sacrifice?

Research on biopolitics has suggested that patriotic rhetoric and sentiment, particularly the disposition toward self-sacrifice on behalf of a collectivity, might be sustained by socialized perceptions of kinship.[26] In the ideologies of Jim Jones and Ronald Reagan, however, kinship symbolism places children in two roles: first, the child represents a reciprocal relation between part and whole in the symbolism of the family; and, second, the child represents the highest price that can possibly be paid in a symbolism of the economy. In both symbolic roles, within the private intimacy of the family or the public values of the economy, the child provides a key to the sacrificial ideologies of Jones and Reagan.

Jones and Reagan both used kinship terminology, particularly the terms *children* and *family*, to invest a sense of familiarity in their political projects. But they also used this familiarity, based on a sense of kinship, to establish a relationship between individuals and a larger social enterprise, whether that enterprise was Jones's Divine Socialism or Reagan's America. Their language of kinship created a powerful symbolic relationship in which every part, whether follower or citizen, was integrated into the whole and the whole was fully embodied in each of its parts. In their language of kinship, they assumed that each child, although only a part of a family, nevertheless represented the whole family. At the same time, each family, which was a full, complete social unit, was fully embodied in each and every child. Their frequent use of images of kinship, therefore, was not really about raising children or instilling family values. It was directed toward establishing a reciprocal relationship between individual parts and a social whole in which the whole was embodied in each part and each part represented the whole. In other words, they spoke about kinship, saying that the child lives for the family and the family lives in each child, to establish terms for integrating individuals into their political projects.

For Jones and Reagan, this understanding of "family" was crucial to their understanding of life: each part must live for the whole; the whole must enhance the lives of every part. However, the supreme value of this relationship between children and family, this reciprocity between part and whole, was ultimately realized in sacrificial death.

The sacrificial character of this part-to-whole relationship is probably best revealed in the way Jones consistently described the sacrificial construction of the Jonestown community: each part was ready to die on behalf of the whole; the whole was ready to die on behalf of any one part. The result of this reciprocal relation between part and whole provided a definition of community that drew a highly charged boundary around a group, which in turn revealed its integration in its dedication to die for the socialist cause—one for all and all for one.[27]

Likewise, Reagan's ideology of redemptive sacrifice depended on a similar relation of part to whole in his recurring symbolism of the kinship that bound all Americans. When Reagan referred to civic rituals practiced around the family dinner table, he was talking not about kinship but about the intersection of public and private domains, the interpenetration of individual part and collective whole, on which his ideology of redemptive sacrifice was based.

It is important at this point to remember that an ideology of redemptive sacrifice is not necessarily equivalent to sacrificial ritual, however much residual, perhaps even archaic, elements of ritual might persist in the symbolic construction of that ideology. In the ideologies of Jones and Reagan, redemptive sacrifice is ritual only by analogy. Nevertheless, reflection on ritual sacrifice clarifies something important about their ideologies that might otherwise not be apparent.

Recent analysis of sacrificial ritual as symbolic action in the interest of what might be called *sacrificial totalization* is helpful in understanding the strategic invocation of redemptive sacrifice by Jones and Reagan. By "sacrificial totalization" I mean the way in which sacrifice, as anthropologist Valerio Valeri observed, accomplishes "a passage from incompleteness to completeness," drawing ritual closure around sacrificers, participants, recipients, and victims, with the sacrificial act standing like a period in a sentence, giving closure to some coherent, unified, meaningful whole.[28]

In the ideologies of Jim Jones and Ronald Reagan, sacrifice is that act that totalizes all the elements of a worldview into a meaningful and powerful whole. All of their descriptions of redemptive sacrifice evoked this sacrificial totalization. Sacrificial death is the highest, the greatest, the supreme, the last, the final, the ultimate act; it is the full measure, the complete devotion, the totalizing act that absorbs the sacrificed part into the organic whole of the community. The discourse of redemptive sacrifice reveals a "passage from incompleteness to completeness" that can be actualized only in death. Although not ritual as such, redemptive sacrifice promises a ritualized perfection that brings the integration of parts and whole—a reciprocal identification of parts and whole that both Jones and Reagan symbolized in the kinship terminology of family—into their supreme, ultimate totalization. In fact, in their view, sacrifice alone instantiates the whole—whether Jonestown or America—as a whole, as a sacrificial totalization in which the family is dedicated to sacrificial death on behalf of the children and the children on behalf of the family.

In both cases, however, this symbolism of kinship reciprocity disguises asymmetrical relations of power. First, the family implies not only a pattern of reciprocity but also a pattern of inclusion and exclusion, a pattern best revealed in Jones's and Reagan's reflections on nuclear war. Jones and Reagan saw the largest arena of sacrificial totalization in the prospect of nuclear destruction. The nuclear family dominated their imaginations when they pictured the ultimate redemptive sacrifice, a nuclear apocalypse, out of which each saw his own family emerging as the redeemed remnant.

Jones welcomed nuclear war as a sacrificial purification, a cataclysmic cleansing that would rid the world of capitalists. "I'd be glad to be blown away," Jones declared in one sermon, "just to see them blown away." Such a war would achieve victory for socialist nations that love and protect their people by providing them underground shelters, radiation shields, and radiation counteractive medications. In most of his speeches and sermons on the topic, however, Jones assured his audience that they would be perfectly protected in the event of a nuclear war. Particularly at Jonestown, which Jones described as a nuclear-free "zone of protection," the "Jones family" was safe from nuclear war.[29]

Reagan seemed to share something of this anxiety about providing his family a zone of protection from nuclear war. Whatever its practical implications, Reagan's Strategic Defense Initiative (SDI) was promoted in domestic symbols of protection: the roof, the umbrella, the child safe from danger through the clever initiative of the "smart daddy."[30] In the event of a nuclear war, Reagan's SDI promised that the American family would be the surviving, redeemed remnant of a nuclear holocaust.

Survival, not death, was the goal of these nuclear fantasies, whether attributed to the paranormal power of Divine Socialism or the technological magic of SDI. To survive the sacrificial totalization of the world in nuclear war, however, a person had to be in the zone of protection that would save a redeemed remnant. The symbolism of family, therefore, represents not only an integrated pattern of reciprocity but also an asymmetrical pattern of inclusion and exclusion.

In addition to exclusion, however, the symbolism of family also contains an asymmetrical pattern of domination and subordination. In other words, kinship reciprocity disguises asymmetrical relations of power in the symbolic construction of sacrificial totalization. I think it is safe to say that no such thing as a "whole" exists outside its symbolic, ideological, or sacrificial construction. Throughout American history, "America" has been constructed by means of strategic totalizations in which special, local, regional, often privileged, exclusive interests have made some claim on the country as a whole. Often, in order to endow themselves with national place and power, local interests have tied themselves to totalizing strategies by reference to the primordial, the transcendent, the ultimate, or what Reagan called the mystical. By symbolizing the whole of America in its totality as a single entity in time (from primordial origin to eschatological rendezvous with destiny) and space (located in a land, as Reagan often claimed, hidden by God between two oceans to be discovered by "a people of a special kind"),[31] American interpretive strategies have underwritten fundamental claims to privileged ownership of the country.

In struggles over the ownership of America, religion might be regarded as the cultural process of stealing sacred symbols, back and forth.[32] This suggestion that religion is a cultural struggle over the always contested ownership of symbols might seem to be a notion appropriate only to social relations organized around capitalist modes of production. However, claims to ownership of sacred symbols—often privileged, exclusive claims—seem to belong to a perennial process in the history of religions. As Jonathan Z. Smith once noted in passing, "Where we have good ethnography, it's always clear that myth and ritual are owned by certain subsets within the collective."[33] In negotiations over the ownership of sacred symbols, sacrifice has often represented the greatest gift, the highest price, the final offer, the last move, the total strategy designed to bring a complete closure to the process of negotiation. In their negotiations over sacred symbols, Jones and Reagan used the child to symbolize not only a relationship between part and whole but also the highest price that could possibly be paid to close the negotiations.

Ironically, negotiations inevitably are reopened after every act of sacrificial closure. As Reagan noted when invoking America's sacrificial dead, they represent only a small part of the price that has been paid; others paid in the past, and more will continue to pay in the future. In Reagan's sacrificial ideology, Americans have to continue paying because they live in a state of indebtedness that no payment can cancel. Even when Americans make the supreme sacrifice, no price paid can finally close the sacrificial account.

On the last night of Jonestown, Jim Jones tried to transfer the sacrificial debt to the enemies of Jonestown, particularly the Concerned Relatives that Jones and his community regarded as traitors. "They will pay for this," Jones declared. Those enemies would have to carry the debt; the people of Jonestown had made their final payment by giving the greatest gift. Nevertheless, in the aftermath, negotiations over the meaning of Jonestown were immediately reopened in the media, government, and popular reactions to the event. Among other things, those reactions tried to renegotiate the meaning of Jonestown by transferring the debt of guilt for its demise back to Jim Jones and his community. If the people of Jonestown carry that debt, then Americans owe them nothing.

All of this suggests that the kinship symbolism of redemptive sacrifice, by which Jones and Reagan inscribed a reciprocal relationship between part and whole into the social order, is also a political economy of the sacred, in which expenditure—the price, the gift, the offering—represents a negotiated claim on the ownership of sacred symbols. Therefore, a basic contradiction resides at the heart of the ideology of redemptive sacrifice: the contradiction between kinship reciprocity and economic competition. Kinship reciprocity represents the completeness of an integrated whole—a totalization, a closure—that is constructed in the sacrificial ideology and demonstrated in the sacrificial act. But, at the same time, the ideology of redemptive sacrifice defines a site of competition over symbolic resources that might appear to be totalized in the sacrificial act but that, by their very nature as fluid, mobile, and contested symbols, nevertheless resist every act of totalization. Although inscribed in a symbolic discourse of kinship reciprocity, the ideology of redemptive sacrifice is also embedded in a symbolic economy that permeated the religious worldviews of Jim Jones and Ronald Reagan.

SACRIFICIAL EXPENDITURE

The religious worldviews of Reagan and Jones were both embedded in the political economy of the cold war 1950s. For both, religion was aligned with a particular economic system, but each constructed his worldview on different sides of the geopolitical line that divided capitalism from communism in the international arena. According to François Mitterand, Reagan had "two religions: free enterprise and God."[34] Jones went further, although not much further, in building his religious worldview around the apotheosis of an economic system. His theological formula might be expressed this way: No transcendent, personal God exists (a God whom Jones often ridiculed as the Sky God, Unknown God, Mythological God, Spook, or Buzzard), but a genuine God exists that is love, that is "from each according to his ability to each according to his need," that is the practical and paranormal power of Divine Socialism. In his creative biblical remythologizations, Jones traced the origin of the worldview of the Peoples Temple back to the primordium of the Garden of Eden. The Garden was not, however, a primordial paradise but a primordial prison, from which Lucifer, the first revolutionary socialist, rescued Adam and Eve by revealing to them the liberating truth: "Ye shall be as gods" in a socialist freedom from capitalist oppression.[35]

On this mythological point regarding the primordial origin of Marxism, Jones and Reagan were in general agreement. In his 1983 address to the National Association of Evangelicals, Reagan referred approvingly to the definition of Marxism-Leninism as the world's second oldest faith (a definition provided by that notorious authority on communism Whittaker Chambers), which was "first proclaimed in the Garden of Eden with the words of temptation, 'Ye shall be as gods.'"[36] If communism is the second oldest faith, presumably Reagan's religious mixture of free enterprise and God laid claim to being the oldest. When Reagan concluded that speech, as he often did, by misusing Thomas Paine's revolutionary call to "begin the world over again," one rendering of that new beginning might have been a mythic return to the primordial Garden before the communist evil was introduced into the world.

Obviously, both Jones and Reagan defined the conflict between capitalism and communism as a religious war, a contest between two religions or faiths—rather than between two socioeconomic systems—that represented the opposite poles of good and evil in the world. In addition to those obvious Manichean oppositions, however, both worldviews were constructed in such a way as to advance the apotheosis of productive economic activity, although one divinized a capitalist organization of the modes of production while the other divinized a communist one. These symbolic relations of production in the worldviews of Jones and Reagan were ironic, however. Jones built a financial base for his movement largely by exploiting the American system of welfare capitalism.[37] Reagan, as Michael Rogin has pointed out, was not the hero of economic production, which he idealized in his political rhetoric, but an idol of consumption, a figure suited to a postmodern society of simulation, a *simulacrum* in a political economy based on the circulation of signs.[38]

In the economic analysis of Georges Bataille, we recall his simple, but useful, distinction between two basic kinds of economic activity, production and expenditure. In contrast to the productive activity of a rational economy, expenditure, in Bataille's notion, fits these ideologies of redemptive sacrifice. As an unproductive expenditure, redemptive sacrifice represents "a *loss* that must be as great as possible in order for that activity to take on its true meaning."[39] In the ideologies of Jones and Reagan, Jonestown and America were premised precisely on such foundations of expenditure. Reagan's America and Jones's Peoples Temple Cooperative Agricultural Project were defined in the idiom of expenditure, in terms of a sacrificial loss that must be as great as possible in order for persons and places to assume their true meaning.

Bataille described expenditure as disinterested economic action, as an end in itself. In their ideologies of redemptive sacrifice, however, Jones and Reagan saw sacrificial expenditure as a supremely interested action. Sacrifice redeems—literally "buys back"—something. Here is a fundamental difference in their strategies of redemptive sacrifice, a difference derived from their respective locations in the same symbolic and political economy. To state this difference simply: while Reagan tried to negotiate a sacrificial redemption *of* America, Jones struggled to negotiate a sacrificial redemption *from* America.

Reagan advocated sacrificial expenditure in order to buy back America. As supreme sacrificer, Reagan claimed symbolic ownership of a nation—its people, land, origin, and destiny—by officiating over the sacrificial ceremonies of its greatest expenditure. Reagan's was an ideology of "supply side" sacrifice. Recalling the observation of political analyst Jean Bethke Elshtain, we find again that "the nation-state, including our own, rests on mounds of bodies."[40] Reagan claimed, as his symbolic capital, ownership of the almost unlimited supply of bodies on which America has been built. Since it takes symbolic capital to make symbolic capital, Reagan found ways to accrue interest on America's sacrificial dead, by insisting that those sacrifices, each representing the greatest gift, the highest price, the supreme sacrifice, place all Americans in a perpetual state of indebtedness. Americans can be redeemed from debt only by making further voluntary sacrifices.

In his address to the United Nations General Assembly in September 1984, Reagan invoked the "favorite expression of another great spiritualist," Ignatius Loyola: "All is gift."[41] Regarding a state of perpetual sacrificial indebtedness, however, Reagan's theory of the gift requires ongoing sacrifices in order to make payments on the debt incurred by the gift.[42] Each payment expands the symbolic capital base, but, ironically, he deemed the expansion necessary in order to maintain, preserve, protect, and keep America in its divinely ordained place in the world. In a word, Reagan's ideology of redemptive sacrifice was locative; it required sacrificial expenditure in the interest of maintaining, reinforcing, and renewing the present social order. Perceiving that order as threatened, Reagan presided over ceremonies of sacrificial expenditure in order to negotiate a redemption of America.

Jim Jones, however, negotiated a sacrificial redemption from America. Lacking the millions of living bodies and the countless souls of America's sacrificial dead that Ronald Reagan claimed as his symbolic capital, Jones had fewer than a thousand bodies with which to negotiate redemption. These were "bodies of power and action," as Jones defined them, which were worth something in the revolutionary struggle against American capitalist and racist oppression.[43] The supreme worth of those bodies was put on the line in one final act to close the negotiations, the act of revolutionary suicide. In the worldview of Jim Jones, the Peoples Temple, and Jonestown, all was not gift; all was theft. Jones's followers experienced themselves as dispossessed in America, perceiving themselves as subclassified on the basis of social class, race, gender, age, or poverty in ways that deprived them of their fundamental humanity. Sacrificial expenditure, therefore, was enacted not to maintain the social order but to escape it and, in the process, to shake, subvert, or even invert the prevailing order that dominated America. In a word, then, Jones's ideology of redemptive sacrifice was utopian, involving a sacrificial expenditure that would buy back human beings from a dehumanizing American social order.[44]

What did it mean to Reagan to win such negotiations? At Notre Dame in 1981, Reagan warned that the phrase "Win one for the Gipper" should not be "spoken in a humorous vein." If the Gipper's name is not to be taken in vain, under what conditions might it be invoked? Reagan invoked the Gipper's name to mark significant occasions of ceremonial expenditure in three areas of American public life: sports, electoral politics, and military sacrifice. "Do it for the Gipper," Reagan instructed the U.S. Olympic athletes in 1984. "Win those races for the Gipper," was how Reagan exhorted the American electorate to vote Republican.

In his address at Notre Dame, Reagan revealed the mystical secret behind "Win one for the Gipper" in the power of martial sacrifice to unify Americans in common cause against a common enemy, just as the sacrificial death of George Gipp enabled a team torn by dissension and factionalism to join together in a common cause and attain the unattainable.[45] In this last context, the sacrificial totalization of America in the name of the Gipper was a strategy for winning a unified American society to be owned and operated as a whole by Ronald Reagan through the power invested in him by all of America's sacrificial dead.

Or, perhaps, Reagan was not in fact the owner and operator of that sacrificial totalization but only a *simulacrum* for those who did "buy back" America under his administration. Reagan served as an image for those who wanted to redeem America not all the way back to the primordium but only to the 1950s, that "golden age" when Americans were willing to "pay the price in blood" to fight communism. This golden age was imagined to be a time of unified, total American consensus on "the moral and political dimension for the sake of which sacrifices could be intelligently demanded by the government and willingly made by the people."[46]

Unlike the nation-state, however, Jonestown did not rest on mounds of bodies; it was buried under them. "We win when we go down," Jones declared on the last sacrificial night of Jonestown. Yet, revolutionary suicide did not bring closure to the negotiations over the meaning and power of American society, in the interest of which those sacrificial deaths were enacted. Instead, the bodies of Jonestown were turned into different kinds of symbolic capital, by public exorcism, strategic distancing, and ritual exclusion. Although the Jonestown dead tried to negotiate a human identity through the supreme expenditure of sacrificial death, the American public did not acknowledge them as fully human.

Clearly, Ronald Reagan constructed his worldview on one side of the highly charged geopolitical and racial lines that constituted the framework of American civil religion, at least since the 1950s.[47] Not only calling America back to a golden age of anticommunism, Reagan invoked the sacred time of his own childhood, as he described that time in a 1980 debate with Jimmy Carter, when "this country didn't even know it had a racial problem."[48] The Peoples Temple of Jim Jones stood on the other side of those lines, a self-proclaimed black, communist, revolutionary movement dedicated to a sacrificial liberation from the very America that Reagan tried to reinforce by revitalizing its symbolic, ceremonial, sacrificial center. In the end, Reagan looked a lot like Jim Jones, inverted mirror images, perhaps, one at the center, the other at the periphery of American society, but both reflecting an ideology that negotiates redemption through the supreme expenditure.

More generally, both operated in a political economy of the sacred, in which classification and orientation, person and place, are intensely negotiated. The highest stakes in those religious negotiations over person and place are signified by blood. Human identity is ultimately paid for in blood—in the blood demanded, blood taken, and blood spilled out on the altar of the land by the state, as well as in the blood willingly expended in protest (perhaps futile, symbolic protest) against dehumanization and displacement by the social, economic, and political order of the state. Although engaged in different strategic projects, the sacrificial negotiations conducted by Jim Jones and Ronald Reagan were enacted in the same American political economy of the sacred in which person, place, and power can be negotiated through inherently violent acts of human expenditure.

In the 1930s, political scientist Harold Lasswell observed, "For better or worse we are embedded in historical configurations which are characterized by the existence of a large number of comprehensive symbols in the name of which people die or kill."[49] One of our tasks must certainly be the analysis of those potent historical configurations of violent symbols. In the American historical record, Jim Jones has represented a bizarre, aberrant intersection of religion, politics, and violence; he is often compared to Kurtz in Joseph Conrad's *Heart of Darkness*—"The horror." From our discussion of redemptive sacrifice in the ideologies of Jim Jones and Ronald Reagan, however, we might conclude that it was Reagan, not Jones, who most successfully captured the heart of darkness at the heart of America by reclaiming and revitalizing its ceremonial, sacrificial center. At the very least, we can conclude that what seemed to be only out on the periphery was also at the center, that the sacrificial symbols in the name of which people die and kill were not only running wild through the jungles but were also securely established in the nation's capital.

Act Now, Inc., an online religious supplies store for evangelical Christians, provides "Money Tracts," fake U.S. currency that contains a message: the offer of personal salvation through faith in Jesus Christ. When carefully folded, this religious tract looks like a real dollar bill, which can be left in public places—on sidewalks, in restrooms, at bus stations—for people to pick up, surprised to find some cash, then even more surprised to find a different kind of promissory note, the promise of salvation.[1]

According to the sociologist Max Weber, "Money is the most abstract and 'impersonal' element that exists in human life."[2] Unlike the personal, tangible sense of kinship developed within religious communities, the contractual relations operating in the modern world of money work against any religious ethics of human reciprocity, mutuality, and solidarity. As Weber observed, there appears to be an inherent conflict between money and religion, between the competition of the market and the cooperation of the religious community in seeking salvation. "Ultimately," he found, "no genuine religion of salvation has overcome the tension between their religiosity and a rational economy."

Although the tension between other-worldly religion and this-worldly money might be impossible to resolve, Weber identified two ways of dealing with the dilemma, a religious ethics of self-discipline, which he called the Protestant ethic, and a religious mysticism of self-sacrifice, the "'mystic's benevolence' which does not inquire into the man to whom and for whom it sacrifices." As a mystical detachment, this benevolence is "an objectless devotion to anybody, not for man's sake but purely for devotion's sake." Both religious strategies, the self-disciplinary and the self-sacrificial, are religious dispositions that focus thought, desire, and action on life in this world. Both hold implications for engaging the world of money. While the religious ethics of self-discipline leads to accumulating money, the religious mysticism of self-sacrificial benevolence leads to giving it away.

As suggested by the evangelical Money Tracts, however, there are more religious uses for money than merely getting or giving it. Money can be used ritually to mark holy days, birthdays, rites of passage, and other religious occasions. Also, besides helping to mark religious life, money can assume a religious life of its own. In a popular religious practice among peasants of Colombia, money could be baptized secretly during an infant's baptism, a practice widely believed to cause money to multiply, thus giving it a life of its own. Unfortunately, since the money, instead of the infant, received the benefit of the baptism, such a ritual substitution of money for a human life was also believed to have the consequence of condemning the child's soul to hell.[3] Another perspective on money with religious significance is the widespread conviction among participants in New Age spirituality that "money is just spiritual energy," a life force readily available.[4]

According to its textbook definition, money is a medium of exchange, a unit of accounting, and a store of value. But money is also a symbolic system. Mirroring Clifford Geertz's definition of religion, money is a system of symbols that generates powerful moods and motivations, desire and agency, and clothes those human dispositions in an aura of factuality that makes them seem ultimately real. Although the modern West supposedly arose out of a broadly Christian heritage in Europe, the modern Western individual has thoroughly ignored the biblical warning of the Christian New Testament that "the love of money is the root of all evil" (1 Tim. 6:10). Everybody loves money. Not merely operating as a useful medium of exchange, unit of accounting, or store of value, money is an object of passionate desire. Money is at the center of a moral economy, a material spirituality, an almost religious mystery.

Occasionally, the love of money is invested with an explicitly religious meaning, as in the case of the popular television evangelist Reverend Ike, considered in chapter 4, who built his ministry on the principle that "the lack of money is the root of all evil." More cynically, the Church of the Profit$ proudly claims to be the only honest church in America, because it openly acknowledges that it is in the business of religion only for the money. Certainly, in the United States, the gospel of money seems fitting. After all, the U.S. one dollar bill displays sacred symbols—an ancient Egyptian pyramid with the all-seeing divine eye, the American eagle of war and peace—and religious slogans, "In God We Trust," *"Annuit Cœptis"* (God has favored our beginnings), and *"Novus Ordo Seclorum"* (a new order of the ages). Religious meanings, hopes, and dreams are directly invested in American money.

In his classic text on "primitive" religion, *The Elementary Forms of the Religious Life*, Émile Durkheim identified blood as the basic currency of ritual. Basing his analysis on reports of Australian Aboriginal religion, which he assumed to be elementary, not because it was the earliest, but because it was the simplest, Durkheim found that "blood itself is a sacred liquid that is reserved exclusively for pious use." Among the indigenous people of Australia, "there is no religious ceremony in which blood does not have some role to play." Finding in Australian totemism the social basis for religion and the religious basis for society, Durkheim concluded that both religion and society are underwritten by "the mystical and sacred quality of the blood."[5]

Blood is sacred. Money is sacred. In this chapter, I want to explore elementary forms of blood and money as media of exchange, accounting, and value in a political economy of the sacred. By "elementary" I do not mean the earliest or the simplest—not E. B. Tylor's primitive, not Émile Durkheim's primitive—but something like GAAP, generally accepted accounting principles, within which the sacred might be negotiated. As noted in chapter 1, by "political economy of the sacred" I refer to three religious processes: the means, modes, and forces in the production of the sacred; the religious work, labor, or industry of transforming scarcity into sacred surplus; and the ongoing struggles over the ownership of sacred symbols.

Instead of taking Australian Aborigines as my data, I will cite evidence involving inhabitants of the United States of America. Blood and money are central to the meaning of America in the world. America is produced as a meaningful, powerful, and even sacred place not only within the territorial limits of the United States but also through interpretive efforts outside the United States. Beginning with a distinctive South African interpretation of the meaning of America, I will examine calculations of blood and money in America, in the secret conspiracies that allegedly run the world, and in the new visions of global order emanating from America.

GANGSTERS

In June 1999 a prominent gangster in Cape Town, South Africa, Junaid "Yengo" Josephs, a leader of the Dixie Boys, was found dead, his body stuffed into a shopping cart, his hand holding an American flag.[6] What did that flag signify? According to the popular press, the flag signaled that a rival gang—the Americans—had effectively claimed responsibility for the killing. In the impoverished Coloured townships of the Cape Flats, the Americans were the dominant criminal gang. Calling their territory "America," the gang invoked a divine right of possession over that turf by rendering their name an acronym from All Mighty Equal Rights Is Coming and Not Standing, which signaled the redemptive promise and liberating potential of America. Proudly displaying the flag of the United States, the Americans interpreted the Stars and Stripes as a sacred icon that reveals the truth of money. According to the Americans, the U.S. flag represents bank notes stained in blood. More specifically, the six white stripes on the flag signify the clean work—not wage labor, but organized criminal activity—that generates money, and the seven red stripes designate the dirty work of blood, the violence that is required to support the clean work of making money. In this rendering, the U.S. flag represents the secret truth of blood and money.

Besides appropriating the U.S. flag, the Americans adopted the symbols of the bald eagle and the Statue of Liberty as well as the motto of the United States, which was altered slightly to read, "In God we trust, in money we believe." Gang initiations employed these symbols of blood and money in rituals performed at the "White House."[7] In the case of Junaid Josephs, planting the American flag evoked this thick, complex mixture of symbols, myths, and rituals to assert not only responsibility for the killing but also the sacred truth of blood and money.

Rival gangs also developed sacred symbols, myths, and rituals. While the Dixie Boys evoked imagery of the American South, another gang, the JFKs—whose acronym is rendered from any of several names: Junky Funky Kids, Join the Force of Killers, and Justice, Freedom, and Kindness—maintained that they were enemies of the Americans gang because an American had killed their first president, John Frank Kennedy. The most powerful rival of the Americans, the Hard Livings gang, adopted the British flag, called themselves the Chosen Ones, and countered the Americans' emphasis on the sacred mystery of money with their own motto, "Rather wisdom than gold." In these symbolic maneuvers, Cape gangs fought over local position and power as if they were operating as global superpowers.

As products of advanced urban marginalization, growing alienation, impoverishment, moral despair, and criminal activity on the periphery of urban life, the Cape gangs are also exemplars of advanced urban globalization to the extent that their local success depended, and indeed still depends, on participating in the global network of narco-capitalism by dealing in illegal drugs. Entangled with both local conflicts and global market forces, the Cape gangs have deployed highly charged symbolic discourses and practices that evoke the sacred. As an attempt to resolve gang conflicts, a new consortium, the Firm, was established to coordinate the drug trade on a sound business basis, although the consortium's name could be considered an acronym of For It Requires Money, which might still be read as reasserting the secret, sacred truth of blood and money.

During the second half of the 1990s, religion featured prominently in this political economy of blood and money in Cape Town. By operating in the idiom of highly charged symbols, myths, and rituals, the Americans and other Cape gangs seemed to be doing a kind of religious work. Recognizing the importance of ritual in the lives of gangsters, criminologist Don Pinnock argued for the creation of alternative rites of passage. Pinnock enlisted the assistance of Ian Player, a leader in ecotourism and wilderness adventures, and Credo Mutwa, a Zulu traditional ritual specialist, or *sangoma*, in forming a nongovernmental organization, Usiko (meaning "rituals"), with the mission "to make better, richer, more ritual-filled, gang-like groups."[8]

At the same time, the Cape gangs were subject to the interventions of more conventional and easily recognizable religious interests. While the organization known as People against Gangsterism and Drugs (PAGAD), with its resurgent Muslim leadership, was allegedly killing the leaders of the Americans, the Hard Livings, and other gangs, Christian evangelical organizations, many with their roots in the United States, such as the Rhema Church, the Shekinah Tabernacle, and the Lighthouse Mission, were busy trying to convert gangsters to Christianity. In this conflict, Muslim and Christian contingents in Cape Town were turning gangsters, including the Americans, into cultural capital for their own local projects, whether by converting them or killing them. Whether "born again" or dead, gangsters were being appropriated by competing religious groups within the same political economy of the sacred in Cape Town.[9]

BLOOD AND MONEY

Although I began in Cape Town, South Africa, this strange story of blood and money can also be located in the United States. The color symbolism of the flag of the United States, which the Americans gang rendered as red blood and white money, poses a profound interpretive problem, because, as the House of Representatives publication *Our Flag* observed in 1989, "The colors red, white, and blue did not have meanings for the Stars and Stripes when it was adopted in

1777."[10] By contrast, the colors of the Seal of the United States were explicitly explained by the secretary of the Continental Congress, Charles Thompson, in terms of the abstract virtues of white purity and innocence, red hardness and valor, and blue vigilance, perseverance, and justice.[11] Although these associations could be applied by extension to the flag, the flag's colors actually had no official, formal, or fixed meanings. Of course, this did not stop American patriots from discerning in the red and white stripes what Julia Ward Howe called "a holy lesson" in a flag that was "red with the blood of freemen and white with the fear of the foe."[12] The Americans gang in Cape Town simply added money to this holy mix of blood, terror, and violence.

In the patriotic rhetoric of American religious nationalism, however, blood and money have often been fused. In the text of the American's Creed, adopted by Congress in 1918, for example, we find a confession of faith in the nation "for whom American patriots sacrificed their lives and fortunes," that is, their blood and money.[13] The rhetorical figure "blood and treasure" has consistently recurred in American political discourse, employed variously to signify a payment, a waste, and a debt.

First, as scarce resources but symbolic surpluses, blood and treasure have signified the necessary payment that authorizes, legitimizes, and even underwrites some claim on America, such as Thomas Paine's 1776 assertion in *Common Sense* that their "expense of blood and treasure" had certified the American colonists' claim on the continent.[14] In such a calculation, blood and money feature in a productive economy, an economy of value in which settlement of account, entitlement to property, and legitimate ownership of resources are adjudicated. As the highest price, payment in blood can be regarded as money, settling the account in transactions within a productive political economy of the sacred. Payment of blood and money, therefore, can be invoked to underwrite privileged claims on the ownership of the sacred.

Second, in reference to an excessive expenditure, the phrase "blood and treasure" has had a more critical function, as when Frederick Douglass pointed to post–Civil War Reconstruction in America as "a scandalous and shocking waste of blood and treasure."[15] In this critical use of the phrase, the waste of human and material resources calls for a different kind of accountability. Condemning European wars for "squandering of the people's blood and treasure," Karl Marx proposed an alternative method of accounting value, labor value, in developing a critical analysis of political economy.[16] Celebrating excess, sacrificial blood, and an economy of expenditure, Georges Bataille, as we have seen, also advanced an alternative method of accounting value, in which loss must be as great as possible to establish the secret, sacred truth of surplus.[17] Both condemnation and celebration of the waste of blood and money, however, advance critiques of the accounting, entitlement, and ownership claims of the sacred within a capitalist economy of the sacred.

Third, as a debt, the cumulative sacrifice of lives and fortunes, of blood and money, has been invoked to reinforce a binding obligation to the past, as when the U.S. House of Representatives Committee on the Judiciary, considering articles of impeachment against President Bill Clinton, was informed on September 11, 1998, by its chairman, Henry Hyde: "Let us conduct ourselves and this inquiry in such a way as to vindicate the sacrifices of blood and treasure that have been made across the centuries to create and defend that last best hope of humanity on earth, the United States of America."[18] In between profit and loss, debt weaves together the political economy of the sacred through its mysterious capacity to be simultaneously a liability and an asset, a binding obligation and a source of empowerment. In the case of Henry Hyde, for example, acknowledging a debt was also gaining a line of credit in the American political economy of the sacred.

In this long history of American political rhetoric, which I have only been able to sketch here, blood and money often seem to be interchangeable terms in a symbolic economy. A randomly selected recent example spells out this calculus of blood and money in striking clarity; the religious gun enthusiasts Jews for the Preservation of Firearms Ownership, Inc., based in Hartford, Wisconsin, explain that freedom requires ongoing payments in blood and money. "Freedom is not free," the JPFO explains. "There are two forms of payment: cash and blood. Some of each usually is needed. In part, cash and blood may be substituted for each other. Generally, the more cash that is available, the less blood need be shed."[19]

Although rarely calculated so bluntly, this interchange between blood and money is central to any nationalist rhetoric of redemptive sacrifice. The role of blood in this nationalist equation is obvious. Blood symbolizes continuity with the past and uniformity in the present—a continuity with ancestors who "have shed it in a certain way," a uniformity with contemporaries who are "of the same blood."[20] Not constituted on the basis of kinship, that bloody continuity and uniformity can be constructed only through killing and being killed.

As Carolyn Marvin and David Ingle have recently observed, religious nationalisms "organize killing energy by committing devotees to sacrifice themselves to the group."[21] Metaphorically, the blood of redemptive sacrifice is often represented as if it were money—the highest price—that an individual can pay to ensure the ongoing survival of the collectivity. By the 1990s, however, these calculations of

blood and money had spilled over from nationalism to a new globalism. In the calculations of Arthur Schlesinger Jr., for example, "We are not going to achieve a
new world order without paying for it in blood as well as in words and money."[22]

But how does money actually operate in this political economy of the sacred? In
a conventional sense, money is defined as a medium of exchange, a unit of accounting, and a store of value. From classical to neoliberal economics, the origin of
money has been located in relations of exchange, working on Adam Smith's
assumption of the basic human propensity to "truck, barter, and exchange." Alternative theories, however, have linked the origin and development of money directly
with blood sacrifice. In his 1843 essay, "Über das Geldwessen," for example, the
"Communist Rabbi," Moses Hess, argued that the capitalist monetary system
evolved from earlier sacrificial systems. "Hess linked money and sacrifice, the consumption of flesh and blood," as Paul Morris has recalled. "He described money 'as
social blood' and cautioned that 'we,' workers and capitalists, 'are the victims who
suck our own blood, consume our own flesh.'"[23] Outlining a history of religion,
blood, and money, Hess identified a three-stage progression, from the ancient
Israelite sacrificial system of substitute blood, through the Christian eucharistic system of symbolic blood, to the modern capitalist system, in which actual blood is
drained from oppressed humanity by the "modern Jewish-Christian shopkeeper."

In a more circumspect fashion, the classicist Bernhard Laum proposed in his
1924 study, *Heiliges Geld,* that the ritual killing of cattle, not exchange, provided
the basis for the emergence of money as a unit of accounting. In ritual sacrifice,
the apportionment and distribution of roasted cuts of meat—a system of accounting—prefigured metallic currency's symbolic representation of degrees of value.
Reportedly, Laum was so disappointed by the lack of enthusiasm for his theory of
the sacrificial origin of money that he left the study of classics and became an
economist.[24]

Nevertheless, other theorists have sensed a possible basic homology between
blood sacrifice and money, especially if, as Adorno and Horkheimer proposed,
economic exchange is "the secular form of sacrifice," and sacrifice is "the magical
pattern of rational exchange."[25] William Pietz, for example, has developed this
theme in several essays that suggest a structural analogy between money and
sacrifice—in the origin of calculating the monetary value of a human life and in
colonial discourses about human sacrifice and monetary debt.[26]

For purposes of analysis, I find the analogy between money and blood sacrifice
more compelling than the analogy between money and God, even though the image
of money as deity has been advanced in familiar figures of speech, such as Shake-

speare's "visible god," Luther's "God of this world," and Marx's assertion that "money is the god among commodities."[27] In relation to transcendent, supernatural, ultimate, or imperishable qualities, this analogy between God and money lurks behind recent critiques of the "religion of the market" and the "market as God."[28] Certainly, this analogy between God and money has had a certain purchase for those suffering under the harsh, inscrutable judgments of a wrathful deity. In South Africa, for example, President Thabo Mbeki deployed the analogy between God and money in urging South Africans to reject "the notion of 'the market' as the modern god."[29]

Nevertheless, I would like to suggest that the analogy between money and God only further mystifies the workings of money. Money is not an object, let alone the supreme object of devotion, in a "religion of the market"; rather, money is a system of symbols. Within the social order of capitalism, that system of symbols is represented by what one economist has called "the Sacred Accounting formula: ASSETS = LIABILITY + EQUITY."[30] As William Pietz has reminded us, the key term in this equation is *liability*, that accounting term with the remarkable capacity to appear as a credit on one side of the ledger and as a debt on the other side. "It is capitalized debt (those liabilities that are another's assets)," Pietz observes, "that knits together various monetized obligations in a general system of social reproduction."[31]

At the heart of the sacred accounting formula, therefore, is a liability with a double life, both credit and debt, that makes money. Like money, ritual sacrifice, according to anthropologist Luc de Heusch, is driven by debt, even by a debt that cannot be paid, since the ultimate payment would be one's own life. As de Heusch observed, "The most perfect sacrificial debt is that which a man must pay with his own blood in order to continue to exist."[32] In sacrificial ritual, the victim stands as a substitute in a chain of substitutions in which different aspects of the ritual— having, being, dividing, and consuming—merge into a single transaction. Accordingly, sacrifice might be understood as ritualized refinancing of debt, both a recognition of liability and an extension of credit, in a political economy of the sacred in which blood is money and money is blood. How debt can also be credit is the sacred secret of blood and money in a capitalist economy.

SACRED SECRETS

Let us admit: the sacred is a strange, yet familiar, contradiction. In its contradictory constitution, the sacred is set apart but central; separate but integral; radically different but fundamentally the same in grounding the social solidarity of a human community. Over, under, and all the way through, the sacred operates—as the sacred canopy, the sacred cement, and the sacred ground—in forging a necessary impossibility, in facilitating the myriad intersections between human subjectivity and social collectivity. As an authentic forgery, the sacred stands as the extraordinary that frames the ordinary, the forbidden that authorizes the permissible, the alien that underwrites affiliation, and the limit that invites transgression. The sacred has been enlisted as a sign to stand for multiple, multiplying oppositions (inside and outside, center and periphery, domination and subordination, purity and pollution, and so on) that are all necessary, all impossible, but also all consistently, perhaps inevitably, sacralized in negotiations over the meaning and power of being human. Although the sacred might very well be set apart, it is set apart at the core of the human enterprise, at the heart of the matter.

In regard to what Arnold van Gennep called the "pivoting of the sacred," anything can be sacralized through the work of religious interpretation, ritualization, and negotiation. In the essay "Materialism and Idealism in American Life," published in 1934, George Santayana indicated the extraordinarily wide sweep of what might be regarded as sacred in the United States. "To the good American many subjects are sacred: sex is sacred, women are sacred, children are sacred, business is sacred, America is sacred, Masonic lodges and college clubs are sacred." According to Santayana, the sacralization of these many subjects has been necessary for the American to maintain faith in an entire way of life. "If he did not regard all these things as sacred," Santayana concluded, "he might come to doubt sometimes if they were wholly good."[33]

By the end of the twentieth century, an American subculture of conspiracy theorists was convinced that the sacred institutions of Masonic lodges and college clubs, the last two items on Santayana's list, were not wholly good. According to these theorists, secret societies, from Europe's Freemasons to Yale's Skull and Bones Society, with their sacred oaths, blood rituals, and blood money, were operating behind the scenes to control the world.

According to *Newsweek*, during the 1990s, 75 percent of Americans believed that the government was involved in conspiracy. As conspiracy theories multiplied in America, "conspiracism," *Newsweek* found, became "a kind of para-religion."[34] Among the many webs of conspiracy in this para-religion, I will focus here on only two, the secret Society of the Elect and the secret Skull and Bones Society, since both have been featured in conspiratorial accounts of the blood and money that supposedly rule the world, and both have allegedly produced American presidents.

In one popular scenario, the new world order was the design of British imperialist, politician, and mining magnate Cecil Rhodes. While accumulating his vast fortune in South Africa, Rhodes proposed in 1890 to start a movement driven by a secret society, the Society of the Elect, which in one hundred years would culminate in the emergence of a single, English-speaking world government. If, as his biographer Sarah Millin observed, "the government of the world was Rhodes' simple desire," then the Society of the Elect would fulfill that desire for world government by secretly manipulating blood and money.[35]

With respect to blood, the Society of the Elect was behind the wars of the twentieth century, responsible for seducing the United States into shedding American blood on foreign battlefields of Europe. A member of the Society of the Elect, Lord Esher, negotiated the entry of the United States into World War I, urging "the importance upon the morale of the French army and the French people of cementing the Alliance by shedding American blood at the earliest possible moment. If many lives have to be sacrificed, the influence on the American people can only be beneficent."[36]

With respect to money, besides drawing financial benefit from war, the Society of the Elect used its financial resources to secretly train generations of young people in the image of Cecil Rhodes. According to this conspiracy theory, the Rhodes scholarships were designed to reproduce the secret leadership of the Society of the Elect. In a letter of 1890, Rhodes had suggested that recipients of the scholarships should not only be capable of high academic achievement and athletic prowess but should also display character traits of "smugness, brutality, unctuous rectitude, and tact." In his analysis of these traits in a frequently reproduced article of 1995, "Reviewing the Rhodes Legacy," conspiracy theorist William F. Jasper referred to *Webster's Dictionary* to clarify the meaning of *unctuousness:* "oily in speech or manner; plastic; moldable; characterized by a smug, smooth pretense of spiritual feeling, fervor, or earnestness, as in seeking to persuade." Looking to the White House, Jasper insisted that *unctuousness* perfectly characterized that Rhodes scholar President Bill Clinton, earning him the nickname "Slick Willy," defining his "special Rhodesian quality," and making him "Cecil Rhodes' man for all seasons."[37] From Cecil Rhodes to Rhodes scholar Clinton, the secret Society of the Elect had come very close to realizing its hundred-year plan to rule the world.

More so than the conspiracy theorist's tenuous connection of Clinton to Cecil Rhodes, the initiation of George Bush Sr. and George W. Bush into the Skull and Bones Society at Yale University signaled their secure place at the center of the secret, sacred rites of blood and money in the new world order. Reports about the ritual of initiation into the society—symbolic death by placement in a coffin, symbolic rebirth through a name change, ceremonial robes, and a sacred bone—suggest that the Skull and Bones Society has certainly operated as a "richer, more ritual-filled, gang-like group." With the presidential candidacy of George W. Bush, conspiracy theorists showed renewed interest in the Skull and Bones Society, although Bush does not appear to have been a particularly cunning conspirator, since reportedly, during his initiation, he could not think of an initiatory name for himself, so he was given the name "Temporary," which apparently stuck with him permanently within the society.[38] Nevertheless, even "Temporary" could be located in the enduring lineages of blood and money that purportedly drive the global order.

Although the election of George W. Bush suggested to some pundits a "Bush dynasty," conspiracy theorists traced the Bush "bloodlines"—most extravagantly in the case of New Age conspiracy theorist David Icke—back through the House of Windsor, the Merovingians, the pharaohs of ancient Egypt, and ultimately to extraterrestrial reptilians, the "serpent race" that came from outer space to interbreed with humans. According to Icke, these reptilian-human hybrids produced aristocratic bloodlines that flowed into the royalty of Europe as well as into all the presidents of the United States. "The Rothschilds, Rockefellers, the British royal family, and the ruling political and economic families of the US and the rest of the world," Icke has insisted, "come from these SAME bloodlines."

With their hybrid DNA, they are able to change, to "shape shift," between human and reptilian forms. On the basis of his research, Icke stated, "Former US president, George Bush, is mentioned more than any other person in my experience in relation to shape-shifting." In one of his books, *The Biggest Secret*, Icke cites numerous eyewitness accounts of George Bush appearing as a serpent. To maintain his human form, Bush, like all other shape-shifting reptilians, must regularly drink the blood of human beings for the energy it contains, in order "to maintain their DNA codes in their 'human' expression." Icke explained, "That is why people like George Bush are exposed in my books as reptilian shape-shifters who take part in human sacrifice and blood drinking." According to Icke, the election of George W. Bush merely continued this lineage of power and money, human sacrifice and blood drinking. "Presidents are not EL-ected by ballot," Icke observed, "they are SEL-ected by blood."[39]

Although Icke assured his readers that he was only laying out the facts, promising "the truth shall set you free," it is tempting to interpret his account of hybridity, shape shifting, human sacrifice, and blood drinking as an allegory about money. During the early eighteenth century in Europe, as historian Gábor Klaniczay has argued, fear of the evil, disruptive power of witches was gradually displaced by the fear of vampires, those shape-shifting, blood-sucking aliens, during a historical transition from landed wealth to stock exchanges, in which credit and debt took on new meanings in an emerging capitalist society.[40] At the end of the twentieth century, Icke's extraterrestrial blood-drinking reptiles seemed to configure another dramatic transformation in the history and geography of money that is changing both America and the larger world.

In reconstructions of the history of money, Michael Polanyi's three-stage account of the development of economic exchange—reciprocity, redistribution, and market exchange—has had an enduring effect on anthropology, history, and the study of religion. From a variety of perspectives, cultural analysts at the end of the twentieth century argued that global capitalism had entered a new era of money, a fourth stage, although there was widespread disagreement about how we should now understand money. It is a question of life and death. According to some analysts, money is dead. Its demise occurred in 1971 when the Nixon administration delinked the currency from the gold standard.[41] U.S. money was now formally recognized as fiat money, that is, as money with value based on faith. Pointedly, many critics have compared the death of money, despite the pious invocation of God on U.S. currency, with the death of God. Like the death of God, the apparent separation of money from any stable, material reference point represents a crisis of value. "The de-linking of the financial system from active production and from any material monetary base," as geographer David Harvey has observed, "calls into question the reliability of the basic mechanism whereby value is supposed to be represented."[42] If money has died, however, it has had a particularly lively afterlife, taking on a new life of its own by reproducing itself in global markets. As sign value, money represents money representing money. According to Jean Baudrillard, in the life of this virtual money, fractal money, or viral money, "value radiates in all directions, occupying all interstices, without reference to anything whatever, by virtue of pure contingency."[43] Money is not dead after all, only crazy, only what political economist Susan Strange has called "mad money."[44]

However we might understand this most recent transformation in the history of money, it has coincided with a dramatic change in the geography of money, in which currency domains are no longer defined by territorial frontiers.[45] In the global flow of money within "financescapes," in Arjun Appadurai's term, capital has transcended the spatial limits of nations, states, and territories. Appearing, in this respect, as extraterrestrial, shape-shifting, and fluid, money circulates as the mysterious lifeblood animating the global order.

According to conspiracy evangelist Texe Marrs, pastor of Living Truth Ministries in Austin, Texas, the election of George W. Bush occurred during a period of intense conflict between old money, the secret society finances of the Rothschilds, Rockefellers, and other "blood dynasties," and the new money of companies listed on the NASDAQ stock exchange. In other words, the ostensible conflict involved a battle between the blood money of ancient conspiratorial bloodlines, allegedly driven by the Illuminati, the Masons, the Society of the Elect, the Skull and Bones Society, or some other secret society, and the new bloodless money of advanced information technology, the Internet, and e-commerce.[46]

At the approach of the new millennium, Texe Marrs and David Icke issued a warning that former president George Bush and other Illuminati were planning to convene at the Great Pyramid of Cheops to perform a ritual, a black mass of human sacrifice and blood drinking, which would revitalize the power of the old, secret, blood money that rules the world. According to a December 1999 story in *U.S. News and World Report,* Icke and Marrs hoped to expose and prevent the performance of this evil ritual of money and blood by arriving at the pyramid with an indigenous South African ritual specialist, the Zulu shaman Credo Mutwa, and the self-confessed former "human sacrificer" for the Illuminati, Arizona Wilder.[47] These conspiracy theorists insisted that human sacrifice is the central ritual of blood and money that empowers the new world order. Human sacrifice appears as the ritual in which local blood is captured, consecrated, and consumed all over the world by the forces of global money.

GLOBAL MONEY, LOCAL BLOOD

During 1998 two global leaders came from the Americas to South Africa, Bill Clinton and Fidel Castro. In their speeches before the South African parliament, Clinton and Castro reminded us that the ongoing exchanges of the Atlantic world continue to be represented in strikingly different ways. According to President Clinton in his address of March 26, 1998, the United States and South Africa share a common purpose, which he traced back to "the principles that are enshrined in our [U.S.] Constitution," and a common future leading "out of the darkness and into the glorious light." Situating international relations between the United States and South Africa within the narrative structure framed by that inspiring past and bright future, Clinton employed a single recurring metaphor—the partnership—to represent the current realities of the global economy. "As the new South Africa emerges," Clinton said, "we seek a genuine partnership based on mutual respect and mutual reward." As partners, the two countries would not always agree about everything, he advised, since disagreements arise even in the most intimate "family partnerships." Nevertheless, Clinton proposed that the United States and South Africa can "build together new partnerships" that will benefit everyone in a global economy, partnerships based on mutual recognition and reciprocity. According to President Clinton, the global economy should be understood as a partnership.[48]

By contrast, when Fidel Castro addressed the South African parliament on September 4, 1998, he employed a different metaphor—the casino—to represent the reality of the global economy. The world, according to Castro, "has become an enormous gambling house." With $1.5 trillion at play in world markets every day, Castro observed, the global casino is a confidence game underwritten by the "eternal deceit" of the international financial, banking, and trade arrangements through which "money has become a fiction." Based on deception and illusion, like an alchemist's dream of turning base matter into gold, the global gambling house has stripped values of any real material basis. Like any casino, this global game is rigged so that only the house wins. "Sooner or later," Castro noted, "the world will have to pay the price."[49]

So what is the global economy, a partnership or a casino? Here is my unscientific, unofficial scorecard, which might reflect a widely shared South African perspective on the question. During the two speeches, which were roughly of equal length, Bill Clinton was interrupted by the applause of South African parliamentarians nine times, whereas Fidel Castro was interrupted by their applause thirty-eight times, with at least five of those interruptions accompanied by appreciative laughter and another five by enthusiastic interjections of "Yes, yes!" On the basis of these raw statistics, we can only conclude that South African parliamentarians generally found Fidel Castro's view of the world more convincing than Bill Clinton's. In support of this finding, I invoke one further piece of evidence: at the end of President Clinton's speech, the assembly did not erupt into chanting "Bill! Bill! Bill!" but the conclusion of Castro's speech was marked by a majority of parliamentarians chanting "Fidel! Fidel! Fidel!"

Both Bill Clinton and Fidel Castro, I submit, were doing not only political but also religious work by maneuvering within the symbolism of blood and money in the political economy of the sacred. In the case of Bill Clinton, his powerful imagery of a common past and a shared future moving "out of the darkness and into the glorious light" (echoing 1 Peter 2:9) evoked a religious redemption that resonates with crucial moments in South African religious history. In the religious relations between America and South Africa, it recalls key transatlantic exchanges: the impact of the early nineteenth-century Ethiopian movement, with its "highway across the Atlantic," which brought Bishop Henry McNeal Turner of the

African Methodist Episcopal Church from America to South Africa and South African religious leaders to the United States; the development of Zionist Christian churches in South Africa, which by the end of the twentieth century accounted for the religious affiliation of over 30 percent of the South African population in over five thousand denominations and can be traced back to exchanges with American missionaries from Zion City, Illinois; and the memory of the largest mass movement in South Africa during the 1920s and 1930s, the "American" movement, which promised millenarian redemption with the imminent advent of liberating black Americans. Clinton's redemptive promise, "out of the darkness and into the light," even recalls the origin of the African National Congress in 1912, since many of its original leaders went to America, such as ANC president A. B. Xuma, and felt that "it was really just like going to heaven."[50]

During the 1950s, while Nelson Mandela warned against American imperialism, African intellectuals were drawn to the imagery of American films, automobiles, and gangsters. As author Zakes Mda has recalled, in the vibrant African township of Sophiatown "gangsters driving long American cars ruled the roost." According to Mda, during that decade "Sophiatown ushered in the worshipping of all the negative aspects of US culture prevalent today." With their aspirations shaped by American gangster movies, Sophiatown intellectuals were effectively, Mda alleged, "the pioneers of US cultural imperialism."[51] Fifty years later, in the townships of Cape Town, the Muslim leadership of PAGAD was fighting against American imperialism, globally by orchestrating demonstrations against the United States, such as the burning of U.S. flags when President Bill Clinton visited Cape Town in 1998, and locally in opposing gangs, especially the Americans. In contrast to the gangsters' understanding of the U.S. flag as blood and money, President Clinton insisted that the United States stands for an economy of reciprocity, an economy of the gift, an economy of mutuality, mutual recognition, and mutual reward.

Just as South African parliamentarians, for the most part, found President Clinton's promise of economic reciprocity through a transatlantic partnership to be an unconvincing account of the global economy, so has most of the world. As Jonathan Kirshner has argued in his study of *Currency and Coercion: The Political Economy of Economic Power,* money is not only a medium of exchange, a unit of accounting, and a store of value; it is also an instrument of power in the strategic or subversive disruption of economic systems, the establishment of regimes of monetary dependence, and the ongoing interventions in currency manipulation.[52]

In this view, currency and coercion, money and blood, constitute a terrain of competition, conflict, and violence rather than the mutual reciprocity of Clinton's partnership. In the political economy of the sacred, money comes to life to reveal the secret, sacred truth of currency and coercion. During the 1940s, for example, Sergei Mikhalkov, coauthor of the Soviet national anthem, composed a poem, "The Ruble and the Dollar," in which he made these currencies come to life. When the "pompous American Dollar" met the humble Ruble, the Dollar declared, "Humanity trembles before me! All doors are open to me, all borders! I can buy anything, whatever I want." In reply, the Ruble retorted, "I know who you are, and what you've been around the world. You merely show up in a country and want and death follow in your footsteps."[53]

Similarly, the new South African government has found great difficulty in imagining any kind of reciprocity between its currency, the rand, and the dollar. At a conference in 1999, South African president Thabo Mbeki reported that global missionaries of the dollar (President Bill Clinton, the World Bank, and the International Monetary Fund) had come to him and asked him to recite what he referred to as the "new catechism" (democracy, human rights, market economy, free trade, relaxed exchange controls, and open boundaries for the flow of global capital) as a "prayer of hope for the future that will only produce enormous poverty."[54] In this recognition, Thabo Mbeki indicated that the structural adjustments demanded by the high priesthood of global money are a kind of religious work, a "catechism," a "prayer," and perhaps even a human sacrifice to the "god of the market," which promises to produce only more poverty, want, and death.

In the case of Fidel Castro, his depiction of the global economy as a casino resonated with most South African parliamentarians because they, too, feel compelled to play in a game that is fixed so that only the house, the global regime of blood and money, can possibly win. Also evoked here were deep alliances based on the struggle against apartheid, alliances between South Africa and Cuba that have been more profound and enduring than relations with the United States. Castro's metaphor of the global casino also resonated with academic analysis of the global economy. For example, according to political economist Susan Strange, the global economy is determined not by substantial assets but by speculative risks, as is suggested by the evocative title of her book *Casino Capitalism*.[55] In proposing that money has become a fiction, Castro echoed the findings of cultural analysts such as Marc Shell, who has observed that money, especially paper money, is essentially and only a fiction, "a symbol that claims to stand for something else or to be something else."[56]

By invoking the imagery of alchemy, however, Fidel Castro most directly entered the domain of religion. As noted in chapter 4, Jean and John Comaroff have argued that the global economy at the end of the twentieth century was driven not only by production, exchange, and consumption but also by an "occult economy," a millennial capitalism "in its messianic, salvific, even magical manifestations." From junk bonds to pyramid schemes, from cargo movements to the gospel of prosperity, a Christian gospel that "evokes not a Jesus who saves, but one who pays dividends," the global economy has generated an occult economy that might be regarded as its shadow but also as its substance, especially if, as Castro proposed, the object of the global casino involves the alchemical dream of miraculously turning worthless matter into material wealth.[57]

SEPTEMBER 11

In the wake of September 11, the potent symbolism of blood and money was revitalized in the United States. "Donate blood and money" was the urgent appeal echoing throughout the country. Occasionally, other suggestions were made in addition to that appeal. For example, the Ontario Consultants on Religious Tolerance proposed, besides giving blood and money, "approach the leaders of the religious education section of your place of worship and suggest that they add a course about other religions to their curriculum."[58] Generally, however, donating blood and money was the primary symbolic means that enabled ordinary Americans to invest their personal subjectivity in the national collectivity.

Although we can only speculate on motives, most Americans who donated blood and money did not regard their gifts as a payment in a productive economy based on maximizing profit and minimizing loss. Rather, they regarded their donations as a sacrifice, a payment on a sacrificial debt that can never be paid off in one's lifetime because the ultimate payment is one's own life. Acknowledging the sacrifices of victims and heroes, Americans could participate in this political economy of the sacred, refinancing their personal debt by donating blood and money to the nation.

Within the three months following September 11, Americans donated $1.4 billion and hundreds of thousands of units of blood. Most of those donations of blood and money were managed by the Red Cross, which came under intense criticism at the end of 2001 for wasting all this blood and treasure. The money was not getting to the families of victims, and a large quantity of the blood, with its shelf life of forty-two days, had to be destroyed. Conspiracy theorists, of course, already believed that the Red Cross was not to be trusted with blood and money. In the essay "The American Red Double-cross," conspiracy theorist Len Horowitz traced the roots of the charitable organization back through the Rockefellers to the Freemasons, the Rosicrucians, and the Illuminati. As an integral part of the secret conspiracy of blood and money ruling the world, the Rockefeller Red Cross now planned "to eradicate half of the planet's current population." America's war on terrorism, Horowitz warned, was the first stage of implementing this plan. Believing in the existence of this conspiracy, he "found it nauseating that Americans so readily gave their blood and money to the Rockefeller's Red Cross." More than merely wasting their blood and treasure, Horowitz warned, Americans who donated to the Red Cross were collaborating in their own destruction.[59]

While Americans were trying to pay a debt that cannot be paid, President George W. Bush transformed that debt into a line of credit, invoking the sacrifices of victims and heroes to underwrite U.S. foreign and domestic policy. Here also conspiracy theorists were hard at work trying to expose the complicity of the Bush administration in the events of September 11 as a conspiracy of blood and money. Conspiracy theorist Mike Ruppert observed that the Bush administration had re-written the national motto to read "IN GOD (GOLD, OIL, DRUGS) WE TRUST."[60] Like the Americans gang in Cape Town, conspiracy theorists imagined that American military force, the currency of blood, was being used to sustain the commerce, legal or illegal, of making money.

During the war in Afghanistan, beginning October 2001, which was transacted with global money and local blood, people on the Afghan-Pakistan border in February 2002 received a strange gift from the United States. According to the Reuters report:

> US aircraft over southern Afghanistan have scattered $100 bills tucked into envelopes bearing a picture of President George W. Bush, witnesses said on Thursday. Some of the envelopes were carried by the wind and fluttered to earth over the Pakistan border town of Chaman, sending people scrambling for the cash. "C-130 planes dropped white-colored paper envelopes with a photo of President Bush and two bills of $100 each," said Abdul Hadi, a resi-dent of Chaman on the border with southern Afghanistan. "They are actually dropping these over areas across the border but a few were carried away by the wind to this side," Hadi said. "People pushed and fought with each other to get their hands on the envelopes." The envelopes bore no message, the wit-nesses said.[61]

Unlike the evangelical Money Tracts, with their hidden message of salvation, these envelopes bore no message, except for the text of money, not as a medium of exchange, a unit of accounting, or a store of value, but as the nexus of a symbolic system of meaning and power. Perhaps this American money, falling from the sky, contained an implicit message of salvation that the United States hoped would be intuited by Afghanis. However, as witnesses reported, the blank envelopes were perceived to bear no message at all.

"Americans are rich in possessions," George W. Bush observed in a campaign speech in November 1999. "We are also rich in a sense of the sacred." As we have seen, America's sense of the sacred has been heavily invested in money. Signifying a sacred entitlement, a debt to the past, and a credit for the future, U.S. currency has been widely regarded as a divine trust. This monetary trust is a sacred bond that unifies Americans. After all, as Bush reminded all Americans in October 2000, "it's your money. You paid for it."

Following September 11, George W. Bush declared a war on terrorism, a war of blood and money that involves seizing terrorist assets. "Money is the lifeblood of terrorist operations," Bush explained on September 24, 2001. "Today we're asking the world to stop payment." In this formulation, perhaps unintentionally, Bush paraphrased the eighteenth-century satirist Jonathan Swift, who had observed, "Money is the lifeblood of the nation." Whether working for or against the nation, blood and money, as elementary forms of religious life, continue to represent key terms in negotiating personal subjectivity, social collectivity, and global extensions of the meaning and power of America in the world.

CHAPTER SEVEN · Global Religion

"So you've decided to go global!" begins *Kiss, Bow, or Shake Hands: How to Do Business in Sixty Countries*, a popular manual for doing cross-cultural business. In his preface to the manual, Hans Koehler, director of the Wharton Export Network, clearly explains that *global* in this instance pertains to doing international business. "Globalization, by definition, requires you to deal with, sell to, and/or buy from people in other countries." Entering the global marketplace, trading with foreign partners, negotiating with foreign competitors, or managing foreign workers requires a basic knowledge about foreign cultures. "Multicultural awareness," Koehler notes, "is a vital component of any global marketing strategy," providing "the knowledge a U.S. executive needs in order to operate overseas."[1]

To achieve multicultural awareness, the U.S. executive will need to learn something about foreign history and geography, languages and customs, business practices and negotiating techniques, cultural orientations and cognitive styles. Successful global executives might even have to know something about foreign religions in order to avoid potentially costly mistakes, such as the one reportedly made by the Thom McAn Company. When it attempted to market its shoes in Bangladesh, the company finally learned that its nearly illegible logo, printed inside every shoe it manufactures, resembles the Arabic script for Allah, which offended Muslims, who objected to desecrating the name of God by walking on it.[2]

Among all of these areas of specialized knowledge, the form of multicultural awareness that one can gain most readily and immediately is appropriate physical gestures within different cultures. A vast literature in the field of international business communication recommends careful attention to local body languages. Addressed primarily to American entrepreneurs, or more specifically to Euro-American entrepreneurs who have little or no experience of cultural diversity within their own country, this literature warns, for example, against kissing in China to avoid being mistaken for a cannibal; it recommends bowing frequently in Japan to show respect; and it advises mastering the distinctive African handshake, a "handshake with a twist," when doing business in Africa.

Unveiling the mystery of the African handshake, an Internet guide for doing business in South Africa instructs: "Use the traditional Western-style handshake, and then without letting go of the person's hand, slide your hand around the other person's thumb, then go back to the original Western position. After a few tries, you'll get it right."[3] It is hard to imagine that anyone could get it right on the basis of these instructions, especially if "you'll get it right" implies that all the communication skills necessary to do business will have been acquired.

Although most advice related to multicultural awareness is designed to help American entrepreneurs establish rapport and avoid embarrassment when dealing with foreign people, this attention to body language often reinforces the notion of fundamental cultural differences between Americans and the rest of the world. In the analysis of body language, cultural kinesics, or the "nonverbal channel of communication," the science of international business communication portrays a pervasive exceptionalism among Americans, both in body language and perspective.

In a review of kinesics and cross-cultural understanding, for example, one author reproduces an inventory of "postures used to signify humility" in certain cultures, but those postures are actually gestures of defeat, submission to a conqueror. For instance, the Chinese join hands over their heads and bow, signifying "I submit with tired hands." Turks and Persians bow and extend their right arm, moving it down, up, and down again, signifying "I lift the earth off the ground and place it on my head as a sign of submission to you." The African Batokas throw themselves onto their backs, roll from side to side, and slap the outside of their thighs, signifying, "You need not subdue me. I am subdued already." Although these signs of submission might be useful to know in global business negotiations, the point of drawing up such an inventory of kinesics is to illustrate American exceptionalism. As the author of the review observes, these postures "would either embarrass or disgust most Americans, who are not readily inclined to show humility in any guise."[4]

In the science of international business communication, Edward T. Hall and

Geert Hofstede are generally recognized as founders and guiding spirits, even though they have produced very different works. For Edward T. Hall, author of an evocative series of books on gestures, time, space, and other forms of "silent language," culture is primarily a matter of context and style. Distinguishing between high-context and low-context cultures, and differentiating between implicit and explicit styles of communication within cultures, Hall seemed less interested in drawing comparisons among cultures than in exploring the dynamic relationship between background context and foreground communication in any cultural exchange.[5]

By contrast, Geert Hofstede developed a science of comparing cultures that was specifically designed to serve the purposes of doing cross-cultural business. As Hofstede asserted in the title of one essay, "the business of international business is culture."[6] What did Hofstede understand by *culture*? Basically, he operated on the assumption that *culture* is a generic term for all the many cultures but that each culture can be reduced to a mentality, the "software of the mind," that establishes distinctive ways of processing information. Drawing on a database generated from 116,000 questionnaires, distributed in 1968 and 1972 to IBM employees in forty countries, Hofstede distilled four (and, later, five) indicators of cultural differentiation in the ways in which people do business.[7]

Marking out cultural differences as if they could be plotted against a fixed set of binary oppositions in ways of thinking—that is, in cultural mentalities or mental software programs—Hofstede tracked the oppositions between individualism and collectivism, egalitarianism and hierarchy, masculinity and femininity, and risk taking and risk avoidance. Later, bringing China, or at least Hong Kong, into his database, Hofstede added a fifth opposition: the difference between short-term and long-term orientations, involving observations about the "Confucian dynamics" of upholding cultural obligations of virtue over the long term as opposed to getting to the truth of the matter in business dealings in the short term.

Unavoidably, these oppositions, designed to be useful when doing business in a foreign culture, reflect the cultural interests of American business. It is easy to suspect that all of these oppositions can be distilled into a fundamental distinction between us and them, especially if *we* can appear as individualists in an egalitarian business environment that is nevertheless masculine in its strength and willing to take risks, while *they* register as collectivist, traditionally hierarchical, essentially feminine, and fearful of taking the kind of risks necessary for gaining profits quickly in the short term.

While Hofstede's findings have been open to debate, they have generally set the parameters for cultural analysis in doing cross-cultural business. From prestigious business schools to consultants advertising on the Internet, those focused on international business communication have generally followed the lead of Geert Hofstede in translating the complex, bewildering, and perhaps indeterminate diversity of cultural contexts and styles of communication into simple indicators of opposition.

In a representative text for intercultural business communication, the author identifies ten ways that culture affects negotiation. At the end of a long discussion of cultural variables in doing cross-cultural business, we end up with a basic opposition between two types of culture, Type A and Type B. In business negotiations, Type A cultures seek a contract rather than a relationship; they prefer informal rather than formal interaction; they value time instead of disregarding it; their style is emotionally expressive rather than emotionally restrained; they make specific rather than general agreements; they build agreements from the bottom up rather than from the top down; they negotiate through teams organized around one leader rather than around an implicit group consensus; and they are willing to take risks rather than avoid them. Although the author warns that no culture fits entirely within either Type A or Type B, it is difficult not to conclude that this analysis of international business communication has merely reproduced some of the fundamental cultural stereotypes that Americans hold about others, especially when the author concludes that "Americans may tend to be type A and Japanese type B."[8]

All of this knowledge about local body languages, mentalities, and cultures is supposed to be useful for doing global business. But what is globalization in this context? Is it a new description of a changing culture or a new and rapidly changing culture of description? On the one hand, as Arjun Appadurai proposed, globalization represents a new fluidity in the transnational movement, the global "flows" of people, machines, money, ideas of human solidarity, and images of human possibility.[9] Here globalization appears as a descriptive account of homogeneity and difference, continuity and disjuncture, within the shifting landscapes of the world.

On the other hand, in the literature of international business communication, globalization appears less as a descriptive account of the world than as a mythic narrative, a sacred charter, or a religious mandate for transcending borders and opening new markets all over the world.[10] During the 1990s, according to cultural analyst Thomas Frank, global business interests opened up a new ideological space, "one market under God," which excluded "dumb heathens" who were "unanointed in the ecstatic religion of instant and infinitely increasing wealth," as Mike Davis observed in a review of Frank's book.[11]

Playfully, but pointedly, these invocations of religion suggest that doing cross-cultural business draws upon sacred symbols, myths, and rituals that operate just as religion does. Recently, analysts of successful global businesses—Coca-Cola, McDonald's, Disney, and others—have specifically used the term *religion* in attempting to capture the meaning and power of these multinational corporations, suggesting that they have assumed symbolic, mythic, and ritualized forms that approximate the forms and functions of world religions. In the context of vast global exchanges and profound local effects, how should we understand these "religious" factors and forces in doing cross-cultural business?

COCACOLONIZATION

As the supreme icon of American cultural imperialism, Coca-Cola has often been portrayed in religious terms. For instance, in the words of Delony Sledge, the company's advertising director in the early 1950s, the Coca-Cola Company has operated as if its "work is a religion rather than a business."[12] What kind of religion is this? As I have argued, the religion of Coca-Cola revolves around a sacred object, the fetish of Coca-Cola, which is both a desired object and the objectification of desire. "Coca-Cola is the holy grail," as one company executive observed. "Wherever I go, when people find out I work for Coke, it's like being a representative from the Vatican, like you've touched God. I'm always amazed. There's such reverence toward the product."[13] In these potent images of the holy vessel that held the blood of Jesus and the enduring tradition of the universal church, this Coca-Cola executive represented his product as an icon of religious desire.

The Coca-Cola Company has produced a massive network of global exchanges and local effects that must be regarded as significant forces in any notion of globalization. While the vast exchanges that have established and empowered the Coca-Cola empire are obvious, some of the local effects can be surprising. Coca-Cola is not only transnational; it is also translational. Coca-Cola trades on the translation of information, imagery, and desire among vastly different cultural contexts all over the world.

In the company's fashioning of this worldwide enterprise, foreign governments, trade restrictions, access to supplies, and local competition have often presented problems, but so has cultural translation. Not only signifying "the global high-sign," Coca-Cola has sometimes generated a chaos of signification in its attempts at global translation. For example, the Chinese characters that most closely reproduce the sound of "Coca-Cola" apparently translate as "bite the wax tadpole." In Dutch, "Refresh Yourself with Coca-Cola" translates directly as "Wash Your Hands with Coca-Cola." French-speakers misheard the French version of the song "Have a Coke and a Smile" as "Have a Coke and a Mouse," while Spanish-speakers in Cuba reportedly misread the sky-writing for "Tome Coca-Cola" (drink Coca-Cola) as "Teme Coca-Cola" (fear Coca-Cola). However, not all mistranslations of Coca-Cola involve such blatant misunderstanding. Apparently, Spanish-speakers in Latin America had good reasons to fear Coca-Cola. In 1978, Guatemalan union organizer Israel Marquez informed the company at its annual meeting that its alleged complicity in state-sponsored terrorism against labor unions had resulted in a serious image problem. "Coca-Cola's image in Guatemala could not be worse," Marquez asserted. "There, murder is called 'Coca-Cola.'"[14]

As a global religious mission, Coca-Cola enters new frontiers, new "contact zones," and is encountered locally as a problem not only of translation but also of power relations. In the 1980 South African film *The Gods Must Be Crazy*, director Jamie Uys created an absurd allegory for such a local engagement with the "holy grail" of Coca-Cola. Over the Kalahari Desert of Botswana, a Coca-Cola bottle is thrown carelessly from an airplane, falls out of the sky, and lands in a Bushman community. The people there perceive this mysterious object as "one of the strangest and most beautiful things they have seen" and gradually find uses for it in their hunting and food preparation and even as a musical instrument in religious ritual. In becoming a focus of desire, this object also becomes a flash point for competition, dissension, and conflict among individuals in the community, creating a situation that is similar in some respects to the cycle of violence analyzed by René Girard, a cycle of reciprocal revenge that can be stopped only by identifying a sacrificial victim, a scapegoat, to be expelled from the community.[15] In this case, one of the Bushmen identifies the single source of violence as the Coca-Cola bottle. Setting out from the camp, he decides to travel to the end of the earth to return this mysterious object to the gods. On that sacred journey, however, the Bushman is delayed in modern Johannesburg and initiated into the sordid mysteries of modernity.[16]

Although this allegory was not produced by the Coca-Cola Company, it nevertheless reinforces the myth of Coca-Cola as the supreme icon of modernity. John Tomlinson, author of *Cultural Imperialism*, has suggested that if goods are actually desired by people rather than imposed on them by force, then their entry into global markets should be regarded not as cultural imperialism but as "the spread of modernity."[17] Certainly, this benign reading of the role of a desired commodity—especially the supreme commodity that nobody needs but everyone desires, the sacred beverage, bottle, and icon of Coca-Cola—misrepresents the power relations in which the translation of desire is precisely what is at stake. Like the Bible, the cross, and European styles of housing, clothing, and weapons in other colonial situations of Christian missionary intervention, Coca-Cola marks fundamental oppositions, signifying the slash between primitive and civilized, traditional and modern, communist and capitalist.

In a range of popular imagery, the sacred object of Coca-Cola stands at the frontier of competing religions in a global contact zone. For example, a widely reproduced photographic image from Saudi Arabia shows Muslims bowing in prayer; they are facing Mecca but also inadvertently bowing before a bright red soft-drink vending machine, in what the photograph confuses as a posture of religious submission before the sacred logo of Coca-Cola. Visiting the World of Coca-Cola in Atlanta, a group of Tibetan Buddhist monks, wearing robes, were photographed one by one, sticking their heads through a cardboard cutout of a waiter pouring a glass of Coca-Cola. They enjoyed making such "modern discoveries," a translator explained.[18] Arabian Muslims bowing in a blind devotion that made them oblivious to the modernity that was overwhelming them, Tibetan Buddhists encountering that same bewildering modernity with wide-eyed surprise—these images, in different ways, reinforce stereotypes that have elevated Coca-Cola to the position of a crucial sacred object in a frontier zone of interreligious relations.

Following the collapse of the Soviet Union, Coca-Cola operated as a sacred icon not only of modernity but also of a kind of religious initiation into global markets that promised to transform people from "primitive" communism to "modern" capitalism. As the anthropologist Alaina Lemon has observed, "News photos titillate by juxtaposing supposed opposites: for example, fur-hatted soldiers drink Coca-Cola on Red Square." Although Russians had long been familiar with the beverage, Coca-Cola was mobilized to signify both the opposition between communism and capitalism and Russia's recent conversion from one to the other. Lemon, recalling a long history of images of "first contact" between European missionaries and startled natives, concluded that newspapers show photos such as the Coke-drinking soldiers to "amuse and astound with images of Russians shaking the invisible hand."[19]

As Constance Classen has observed, Coca-Cola operates in a global symbolic economy of "surreal consumerism," in which products "are touted by their advertisers as an eruption of the extraordinary into the everyday."[20] Obviously, Coca-Cola, as the "pause that refreshes," is marketed similarly, as a surrealistic transformation of the ordinary into the extraordinary. If consumer products signify such a conflation of the extraordinary and the ordinary, thereby representing a kind of hierophany, or manifestation of the sacred, reflective consumers will inevitably ask, "Where do these things come from?" During her fieldwork in northwestern Argentina, Classen asked people how they felt about drinking a product such as Coca-Cola, which comes from America and bears the weight of American cultural imperialism. She was surprised to find that people generally assumed that Coca-Cola was indigenous; living with the product and its imagery all their lives, people understood Coke as a local product. As Classen recounted, "A woman from a Northwestern town asks when I bring up the subject of Coke's status as an import: 'But isn't Coca-Cola Argentine?'"[21]

This assumption that Coca-Cola is actually a local product recalls the surrealist story written by Leonora Carrington involving a vision of the Mexico of the future, in which people value "bottles of the rare old Indian drink called coca-cola."[22] All over the world, indigenous people have found ways to integrate alien commodities into local culture. Without ignoring the coercive force of cultural imperialism, we can still recognize the creativity of these local translations of global signs into indigenous meanings. Local problems of translation, which are beyond the control of corporate headquarters in the United States, are not always experienced as global extensions of America.

MCDONALDIZATION

In his popular analysis of modernization, sociologist George Ritzer coined the term *McDonaldization* to represent "the process by which the principles of the fast-food restaurant are coming to dominate more and more sectors of American society as well as of the rest of the world."[23] Updating the classic work of Max Weber, who argued that the principles of bureaucratic rationalization, organization, management, and control are the hallmarks of modernization, Ritzer proposed that the fast-food restaurant has extended the scope of those same principles throughout every aspect of personal and social life. Concentrating on McDonald's as the chief model, the ideal type, or the paradigm for this process, Ritzer identified four principles of rationalization: efficiency, calculability, predictability, and control over labor by replacing human with nonhuman technology. Not merely selling burgers, fries, and milkshakes, McDonald's, in Ritzer's view, is actively advancing these principles of rationalization in America and the larger world.

As Ritzer recognized, a social force with such awesome and pervasive power seems to function like a global religion. Certainly, Ray Kroc employed religious language. "The french fry would become almost sacrosanct for me," Kroc reported, "its preparation, a ritual to be followed religiously."[24] But McDonald's did more than generate a sacrosanct object. "To many people throughout the world," as George Ritzer has observed, "McDonald's has become a sacred institution." As evidence, Ritzer cited a newspaper account of the opening of McDonald's in Moscow: "as if it were the Cathedral in Chartres." Reportedly, a Moscow worker described McDonald's as a place to experience "celestial joy."[25] What kind of religion is this? Anchored in a sacred institution, a "cathedral of consumption," McDonaldization might be regarded as a powerful sectarian movement within a broader "consumer religion."[26]

In that consumer religion, with its places of pilgrimage, times of ritualized gift giving, and sacrosanct objects of desire, McDonald's fast-food restaurant could be regarded as a sect in the political economy of the sacred, competing for a religious market share with other sacred institutions that celebrate the spiritual ecstasy of consumerism, such as the shopping mall. According to Ritzer, however, the "sacred institution" of McDonald's has established a religion that is based not on spiritual ecstasy, despite the Russian worker's claims about experiencing celestial joy, but on spiritual discipline, a kind of inner-worldly asceticism that regulates desire according to the requirements of bureaucratic rationalization. Unlike the religion of Cocacolonization, with its cross-cultural translation of desire for the sacred object, the religion of McDonaldization represents a cross-cultural rationalization of desire and a desire for rationalization. Embedded in the sacred institution of McDonald's, but extending through all social institutions, McDonaldization is the religious rationality of modern institutionalized life.

Following Weber's dark vision, Ritzer warned about the "iron cage" of rationality, the confining, oppressive structures of bureaucratic rationalization "in which people cannot always behave as human beings—where people are dehumanized."[27] In response to the human irrationality of modern rationalization, people can reclaim their humanity through local acts of resistance to the global religion of McDonaldization. Increasingly, such resistance has become organized. Since the mid-1980s, UN World Food Day, October 16, has been celebrated as Worldwide Anti-McDonald's Day. The fifteenth annual Anti-McDonald's Day in

1999 was marked by 425 local protests in twenty-three countries. Generally, protests against globalization, especially against the orchestration of the global economy by the International Monetary Fund and the World Bank, have found McDonald's a useful target for opposition.

According to some cultural analysts, however, the activity of consumption, even the act of eating a Big Mac, can be an occasion for consumers to mobilize alternative meanings that should also count as acts of resistance to the "iron cage" of McDonaldization. In his semiotic reading of eating at McDonald's, for example, John S. Caputo proposed that consumers are buying not a rationality but a story, a myth, a sacred narrative of "family, food, and fun," in which they can participate in personal and meaningful ways. Nevertheless, Caputo also recognized that this story has a distinctively American flavor. The myth of McDonald's is basically the story of "American culture and consensus—the myth of freedom and equality in which anyone can and does go and eat at McDonald's."[28]

In his argument with Ritzer, Caputo emphasized the importance of *mythos* over *logos,* the meaning of consumption over the machinery of production, and the creativity of human imagination over the routinization of dehumanizing bureaucratic rationalization. Still, given the central role that America plays in both the sociological and the semiotic accounts, how do we understand the global transmission of McDonald's into more than a hundred different countries and their different languages, different cultural orientations, and perhaps even different cognitive styles? By 1996, McDonald's had surpassed Coca-Cola in global brand-name recognition. How has that brand actually been recognized, consumed, and assimilated in different cultural contexts? As Caputo asked, "How could McDonald's sell a hamburger to the Japanese whose diet consisted primarily of fish and rice?"[29] Anticipating that problem, the founder of McDonald's in Japan, Den Fujita, had an answer. McDonald's promised to effect a dramatic human transformation. "The reason Japanese people are so short and have yellow skins is that they have eaten nothing but fish and rice for two thousand years," Den Fujita reportedly maintained. "If we eat McDonald's hamburgers and potatoes for a thousand years, we will become taller, our skin will become white and our hair blond."[30]

Arguably, this promise of human transformation from the image of a traditional Japanese to a modern Euro-American places Den Fujita as an inside agent of alien American imperialism. "Unlike more traditional conquerors," as Ronald Steel has observed, Americans "are not content merely to subdue others. We insist that they be like us."[31] By this account, Den Fujita was doing the job of American conquerors better than they could ever have done it themselves. McDonald's establishment in Japan, however, did not signify an American conquest, the submission of the Japanese to an alien and globalizing force, not even the pervasive force of rationalization that Ritzer called McDonaldization. Rather, McDonald's emerged as a site of local negotiations over food and foodways, eating and etiquette, age groups and family values, sociality and society. As a result of these ongoing negotiations, as James L. Watson has observed, "the Big Mac, fries, and Coke do not represent something foreign. McDonald's is, quite simply, 'local' cuisine."[32]

Although McDonaldization represents a universalizing rationality of efficiency, calculability, predictability, and control, McDonald's restaurants have had to adapt to local situations and circumstances. Adapting to local tastes, rather than simply imposing a global, homogenized "convergence of taste," McDonald's has produced such culturally specific variations as McSpaghetti in the Philippines, McLaks (grilled salmon burger) in Norway, McHuevo (hamburger with a poached egg on top) in Uruguay, and MacChao (Chinese fried rice) in Japan. Like Coca-Cola, McDonald's has also been actively engaged in interreligious relations, especially when the menu set by its headquarters in the heartland of America (at Hamburger University, Oak Brook, Illinois) conflicts with religious customs, ethics, or laws governing diet.

More intimately than Coca-Cola, however, McDonald's enters into the foodways of the world. The occasional conflicts involved have been intensely negotiated because of foodways' intimate relationships to religion, although eventually McDonald's has consistently shown a willingness to adapt to local religious requirements. After considerable controversy, McDonald's in Israel agreed to provide hamburgers without cheese at several outlets, to avoid violating Jewish dietary law. In Malaysia, Singapore, and other countries with a large Muslim presence, McDonald's submitted to inspection by Muslim clerics to ensure the ritual cleanliness and absence of pork in the preparation and presentation of meat. In opening new franchises in India, again after considerable controversy, McDonald's introduced a range of new products—mutton-based Maharaja Macs for Hindus, who do not eat beef, Vegetable McNuggets and the potato-based McAloo Tikki burger for Hindus who do not eat meat at all—to accommodate religious restrictions on food, even though Hindu fundamentalists of the Bharatiya Janata Party (BJP) campaigned against McDonald's on religious grounds nonetheless.

In all of these corporate negotiations over the religious significance of food, McDonald's demonstrated an impressive responsiveness to local traditions. Of course, McDonald's was in a strong position to make these local accommodations, because it had reportedly mastered the art of producing french fries that are religiously neutral, making them a dietary constant that is embraced globally by all religions, "ever-present," as James Watson has observed, "and consumed with great gusto by Muslims, Jews, Christians, Buddhists, and Hindus."[33]

As defined by George Ritzer, McDonaldization represents a globalizing steamroller in which the American mastery of the rational arts of efficiency, calculability, predictability, and control subjects people in America and the rest of the world to a regime of rationalization that is basically dehumanizing. Certainly, the critical perspective advanced by Ritzer echoes the dehumanizing conditions of colonial situations, except that the imperial, colonizing power, in this case, is ideologically legitimated not by God, country, or manifest destiny but by a Big Mac, fries, and a Coke. As in the case of Coca-Cola, however, McDonald's meaning and power have been appropriated by consumers all over the world as local productions, as if the corporation were a local, indigenous institution. Reversing the thrust in the classic colonial narratives of "first contact" between Europeans and startled natives, many stories have been told about a child coming from some other part of the world to the United States and expressing astonishment to find a McDonald's restaurant. "Look!" exclaimed the son of a Japanese executive visiting America. "They even have McDonald's in the United States!"[34]

DISNEYIZATION

While *McDonaldization* has emerged as a technical term for bureaucratic rationalization, a contrasting but complementary term, *Disneyization,* has been advanced to capture the importance of managing, engineering, and molding the human imagination. As defined by sociologist Alan Bryman, *Disneyization* refers to "the process by which *the principles* of the Disney theme parks are coming to dominate more and more sectors of American society as well as the rest of the world."[35] Those principles—theming; dedifferentiation of consumption; multisector merchandising; and emotional labor—undergird the "imagineering" of cross-cultural business most clearly exemplified by the Walt Disney Company but increasingly informing the way business is conducted in general.

Taking Disneyland as a paradigm, businesses imagineer by applying the principle of theming to create imaginary worlds that evoke a thematic coherence through architecture, landscaping, costuming, and other theatrical effects to establish a focused, integrated experience. In the process, the activity of consumption is dedifferentiated from entertainment, dissolving the distinction between shopping and playing, so that, as Umberto Eco observed, "you buy obsessively, believing that you are still playing."[36] Reinforcing this coherence of imagination and integration of experience, the merchandising of products depends on associating goods with logos, with powerful images, such as the Disney characters who sell films, which sell videos, which sell theme parks, which sell consumer products, which sell films, producing "an endless round of self-referential co-advertisements."[37]

In the end, Disneyization is a system of emotional labor that is empowered not only through the emotional investments made by consumers but also in the management of emotions by workers at the point of production. As workers, or "cast members" in Disney-speak, perform their scripted interactions with the public— the "friendly smile," the "friendly phrases"—they master a kind of emotional labor that conveys the impression that work is not work but play.[38]

In cross-cultural communication, of course, the body language of the "friendly smile" is not always appreciated as a valid form of emotional labor. Although McDonald's also sells a smile with its products, the corporation discovered that throughout most of East Asia, where sales people and service personnel are expected to adopt an expression of seriousness, the friendly smile is generally not trusted. For the opening of the first McDonald's in Moscow, where a visible smile can be interpreted as a personal challenge, a McDonald's representative stood outside to explain the meaning of the emotional labor at work in the fast-food restaurant: "The employees inside will smile at you. This does not mean that they are laughing at you. We smile because we are happy to serve you."[39]

Selling a "Coke and a smile," the Coca-Cola Company also operates in the field of emotional labor, participating in the imaginary merger of work, play, and consumption. The Walt Disney Company, however, has set the global standards for imagining happiness, especially through its "classic" animated films and its theme parks, each proclaimed as the "happiest place on earth," where employees and consumers, cast members and guests, both engage in the emotional labor necessary for the success of Disneyization.

It is a cliché of cultural criticism that Disney animated films have been doing a kind of political work. In their classic salvo against American cultural imperialism, *How to Read Donald Duck*, Ariel Dorfman and Armand Mattelart exposed the imperialist ideology encoded in Disney comics and animation, most notoriously in the animated feature *The Three Caballeros* (1945), which explicitly represented and implicitly targeted Latin America.[40] Coinciding with the escalation of the Vietnam War, Disney's *Jungle Book* (1967) altered the geography of Kipling's colonial India—Baloo was transferred from Great Britain to the United States, Maugli was not an Indian but a "jungle boy"—in ways that have led many critics to read the film as a political allegory for the United States' "civilizing" mission in the "primitive" jungles of Vietnam. After a long dormant period, Disney animation revived in the Eisner era, with the production of a series of extremely popular and financially successful films during the 1990s, which also have been analyzed as doing a kind of political work.

According to Eleanor Byrne and Martin McQuillan in *Deconstructing Disney*, these films can be read as a strange merger of U.S. and Disney foreign policy. In their deconstructive reading, *The Little Mermaid* (1989) is a story about people of the sea and people of the land, a mermaid who desires human commodities but incurs a debt that must be paid in order for her to join the humans and gain access to human goods, thus constituting a political allegory for the fall of the Berlin Wall, the collapse of communism, and the indebtedness of Eastern Europe to the West. In contrast to this allegory of debt, *Beauty and the Beast* (1991) is a story about the gift, focusing on the value of hospitality, thereby serving as both legitimization of and invitation to the new Disney theme park and hotels outside Paris.

Pursuing a global expansion of this Disney politics, *Aladdin* (1992) advances the same U.S. interests in the Arab world as those that drove the Gulf War, with the genie representing American military advisers. Moving into Africa, *The Lion King* (1994) presents a neoliberal vision of human harmony in response to the demise of apartheid in South Africa. Returning to Europe, *The Hunchback of Notre Dame* (1996) deals with themes that recall reports of "ethnic cleansing" and calls for "humanitarian intervention," which justified U.S. policy in Bosnia. Finally, extending the scope of the Disney political imagination to the Far East, *Mulan* (1998) responds to the Tiananmen Square massacre by opening relations with China and also anticipating the establishment of a "major Disney attraction," as Michael Eisner proposed in 1999, "in the world's most populous nation."[41]

As cultivated by the Walt Disney Company, therefore, the emotional labor invested in Disneyization has sustained a kind of political work, the production and reinforcement of a political imagination that had become increasingly global in scope by the end of the twentieth century. Was this political imagination also a kind of religious imagination? Certainly, in calling for a boycott of Disney films, theme parks, and products, the Southern Baptist Convention regarded the Walt Disney Company not only as detracting from religion, allegedly promoting "immoral ideologies," but also as advancing an alternative religion, a pagan religion, through its animated features in the New Age harmonial spirituality of the "circle of life" in the *Lion King* or the earth-based indigenous spirituality of *Pocahontas*.[42]

In *Pocahontas* (1995), the American centerpiece of the Disney decade of global expansion—a film that also coincided with the company's plans for a new theme park, the aborted Walt Disney's America in Virginia—we find a key moment suggesting that the religious work of Disney animation is the adjudication of human identity and difference. In the scene in which Ratcliff and Pohattan prepare for battle, the leaders stand on either side of the colonial divide between civilization and savagery. Bursting into song, they represent each other. Ratcliff sings, "Here's what you get when races are diverse. Their skins are hellish red, they're only good when dead." In turn Pohattan responds by singing, "This is what we feared, the paleface is a demon. The only thing they feel at all is greed." Instead of resolving this counterpoint in a critique of colonial greed, racism, and violence, however, the film dissolves the differences between European invaders and indigenous Americans by having Ratcliff and Pohattan harmonize on the refrain, "They're savages, savages, barely even human."

In this harmony of mutual denial, the audience can only conclude that there was a basic equivalence—mistakes on both sides, misunderstanding on both sides, failure on both sides to recognize the humanity of the other—in intercultural relations between Europeans and Native Americans. Effectively erasing the asymmetries of power, let alone the violence of colonization, this equivalence leaves simply a human identity, an identity that might be called the human neutral, which stands as a generalized, even universalized, basis for dealing with difference.

Throughout the animated films of the 1990s, Disney worked on elaborating this universal construction of human identity. In *The Little Mermaid,* where human beings walk on two legs, but the sea-people have no legs, we learn that a sea-person can become a human being by paying a debt. In *Beauty and the Beast,* where human beings walk on two legs, but the Beast walks on four legs, we learn that a beast can become human by extending the gift of hospitality. Having sorted out these basic human relations of reciprocity and exchange, the gift and the debt, Disney animation proceeded to broaden its scope by adjudicating human identity and difference in the Muslim world, the African world, and the Asian world. Certainly, these films engaged difference in ways that reproduced stereotypes, risking the reinforcement of religious, cultural, and racial prejudices, but they consistently reinforced a human identity, the human neutral, as an identity defined by its capacity for transcending all differences. If religion is about human identity and difference, human formation and orientation, then Disney animation during the 1990s was definitely engaged in a kind of religious work.

The theme parks provide a more obvious point of reference for assessing the religious work of Disney. As many cultural analysts have observed, these alternative worlds—Disneyland in Anaheim, Disney World in Orlando, EuroDisney outside Paris, and Disneyland in Tokyo—have become sacred places of pilgrimage in American and global popular culture. In addition to operating as sacred sites within global tourism, the Disney parks also represent a sacred time, a transcendence of the ordinary time of the present. Passing through the gates, visitors are informed, "Here you leave today, and enter the world of yesterday, tomorrow, and fantasy."[43] As Walt Disney revealed in 1955, the Disney version of time is both American and global, preserving the American past of yesterday in the interest of a global future for tomorrow, dramatizing the "truths that have created America" so that they might be "a source of courage and inspiration to all the world."[44]

Critics have argued that the "truths" distilled from the American past and enshrined at Disney theme parks—the complete domination of nature, the unlimited faith in technology, and the uncritical acceptance of the free enterprise system—have not always been a source of hope for the rest of the world. Nevertheless, the Disney theme parks can respond to such criticism by performatively demonstrating that the company knows the world better than the world knows itself. In its theme parks, Disney shows that it has located the center of the world—Main Street—and has understood the world's past, present, and future. The company shows that its understanding can encompass all the people of the world, in all of their diversity, because, as the song says, "it's a small world after all."

In an analysis of the cross-cultural religious business of the Walt Disney Company, the success of Tokyo Disneyland provides an important test case for theories of globalization and cultural imperialism. Clearly, Tokyo Disneyland is American. "We really tried to avoid creating a Japanese version of Disneyland," spokesperson Toshiharu Akiba recalled. "We wanted the Japanese visitors to feel they were taking a foreign vacation."[45] Nevertheless, Tokyo Disneyland is a particular kind of "America"—a foreign America that is owned and operated by the Japanese. The success of Tokyo Disneyland has depended entirely on detailed local negotiations over the processes that we have been considering in reviewing the global dynamics of cross-cultural business—translation, rationalization, and imagination. These dynamics can be suggested only briefly here.

First, the challenge of translation involved not only the task of rendering the English scripts for popular rides into Japanese but also the challenge of mediating the intercultural dynamics of body language. Although the "friendly smile" might fail to translate easily into Japanese, the high-pitched voice of Mickey Mouse curiously resonates with the conventional "service voice" expected from women waiting on customers in department stores.[46]

Second, the principles of bureaucratic rationalization—efficiency, calculability, predictability, and control—exemplified by American management were quickly taken out of the hands of Disney managers from America and mobilized by Japanese managers of Tokyo Disneyland. As sociologist and former Disney cast member John van Maanen observed, "The Japanese have intensified the orderly nature of Disneyland. If Disneyland is clean, Tokyo Disneyland is impeccably clean; if Disneyland is efficient, Tokyo Disneyland puts the original to shame by being absurdly efficient."[47]

Finally, with respect to imagination, especially the temporal imagineering of the past, future, and fantasy, Tokyo Disneyland has incorporated important features of the Disney orientation in time, the future of Tomorrowland and the fantasy of Fantasyland, but it has fundamentally recast the past. Although its landscape includes modified versions of Adventureland and Frontierland (Westernland), Tokyo Disneyland has replaced Main Street, USA, with the World Bazaar, which is similarly situated as an avenue of shops leading from the park's entrance, but it suggests a past different from a small-town American past, a past that might lead to a different future.

One former attraction that was unique to Tokyo Disneyland, called Meet the World, involved an act of Disney imagineering in presenting a thoroughly Japanese reworking of the past. Featuring the traditional White Crane as a guide to the past and introducing two cartoon children to their legacy, Meet the World developed a Disneyized version of Japanese history that showed the Japanese people arising from the primordial waters, forming an island nation, and meeting the other people of the world, from the Chinese (though not the Koreans) to the Americans. All the gains and losses entailed in those encounters were presented in ways that prepared everyone to sing "We Meet the World with Love."[48]

GLOBALIZATION

In the shifting terrain that we call globalization, cross-cultural business has been conducted by multinational corporations that operate like religions in providing a material basis for organizing the meaning of matter, especially for focusing on the problems of the translation, rationalization, and imagination of matter in a new political economy of the sacred. Through vast global exchanges, these material signs of the sacred—the sacred object of Cocacolonized desire, the sacred institution of McDonaldized rationality, and the sacred, wonderful world of Disneyized imagineering—have produced profound local effects. They have marked out new sites of struggle, contact zones, or contested frontiers for renegotiating what it means to be a human person in a human place.

As a transnational mode of economic production, which is increasingly decentered and decentralized, globalization has defied earlier understandings of relations between center and periphery. But it has also altered conventional notions of production and consumption. In globalization, production takes place in multiple sites; consumption takes on multiple meanings.

Like the globalizing production of economic values, the production, consumption, and circulation of religious values have also undergone this decentering, decentralizing process through large-scale global exchanges with profound local effects. Through the globalization of Christianity, especially in its evangelical and Pentecostal forms, its religious beliefs, practices, experiences, and forms of social organization have had a dramatic impact on local Christian communities all over the world. The globalization of Islam, sustained by radio, television, and Internet communications, emanating for the most part from Saudi Arabia, has also led to transformations around the world. If for a moment we take Coca-Cola, McDonald's, and Disney seriously as transnational religions, we can see the missions they represent as the religious challenges of globalization.

Translation, as we have seen, has represented Coca-Cola's central problem, the problem of transposing, transferring, or transforming desire, the desire for a product that no one needs. Lamin Sanneh, a scholar of Christian and Muslim missions in Africa, has identified translation as the crucial dynamic in the conversion of Africans to Christianity or Islam.[49] In principle, translation can be a two-way street, a reciprocal process, in which it is not necessarily the foreign imposition of an alien language on unwilling subjects. In earlier generations of missionary propaganda, historians of Christian missions often referred to the "planting" of Christianity in foreign lands. Now, following Lamin Sanneh, they talk about the give and take of translation in the process of conversion. Similarly, under globalizing conditions, the translation of desire for a consumer product such as Coca-Cola appears as an exchange between local interests and a global commodity.

Rationalization, as supremely exemplified in the bureaucratic efficiency, calculability, predictability, and control of McDonald's, bears all the hallmarks of modernization. Earlier generations of social theorists, like earlier generations of Christian missionary historians, imagined that this modernization could simply be "planted" all over the world. The "sacred institution" of Western modernization, which George Ritzer identified as McDonaldization, promised to extend itself, perhaps not organically like a living plant, but mechanically like a machine, inexorably steamrolling across the world, flattening everything in its path into its uniform pattern. Uniformity, however, is not always the result, since people find different ways to engage with food, family, and fun. Also, another result, widespread resistance to McDonald's, which places living human bodies in front of the steamroller, has emerged as a popular form of engagement with globalization.

Imagination, as engineered by the Walt Disney Company, has also been a significant feature of globalization, especially with this imagineering's production of new images of human possibility, including the possibility of achieving the universal human neutral and new ideals of human solidarity, located in the "happiest place on earth," the wonderful worlds of Disney. Still, as the imaginative work in and around Tokyo Disneyland suggests, human identity, time, and space can undergo a Disneyization of the imagination in local terms. By producing an America that is more "American" than America, Tokyo Disneyland has engaged in precisely such a local, Japanese imagineering of America.

As all of these global processes indicate, corporate headquarters in the United States do not necessarily control these intercultural negotiations over the sacred. Indigenous versions of global signification are constantly being developed through local appropriations of Coca-Cola, McDonald's, Disney, and other transnational forces emanating from America. Many analysts have used the term *religion* for these global exchanges and local appropriations. If religion is about human identity and orientation, about what it is to be a human person in a human place, even if that place is undergoing dramatic globalizing changes, then cross-cultural business has been doing a kind of religious work through the symbolic, material negotiations over the ownership of the sacred terms and conditions of being human in a human place.

America's most original contributions to popular music—jazz, blues, rock, rap, and hip-hop—originated in Africa. But what does it mean to say that these musical forms came from Africa? In reconstructing the transatlantic exchange between Africa and the Americas, scholars have engaged in a longstanding argument about continuity and change, some finding African cultural "survivals" in African American culture, others finding only African cultural loss under conditions of enslavement in America.[1]

Following the rhythm, mapping the beat, musicologists have identified a dynamic continuity between traditional African religious ritual and popular American musical forms. Robert Palmer, in a history of rock 'n' roll, observed that African ritual is based on the conviction that "certain rhythm patterns or sequences serve as conduits for spiritual energies, linking individual human consciousness with the gods." In African traditional religion, as well as in African religions in the Americas, such as Vodou, Santeria, and Candomblé, this rhythmic access to sacred power is central to religious life. According to Palmer, the same rhythmic pattern pulses through rock 'n' roll, establishing a continuity with Africa in which "the fundamental riffs, licks, bass figures, and drum rhythms that make rock and roll *rock* can ultimately be traced to African music of a primarily spiritual or ritual nature."[2] In this genealogy of popular American music, rhythm reveals an original source in African religion.

The transatlantic religious exchange between Africa and America concerned the sociologist, historian, and political activist W. E. B. Du Bois. In his classic 1903 text, *The Souls of Black Folk,* Du Bois insisted that the religious life of African Americans did not begin in America; it was built on "definite historical foundations," the religious heritage of Africa. Characterizing indigenous African religion as "nature worship," with its incantations, sacrifices, and attention to good and evil spiritual influences, Du Bois invoked the displaced African priest as both the guardian of African religious tradition and the mediator of religious change under slavery in America. As a result of European colonization, passage to the Americas, and enslavement there, African social formations were destroyed, "yet some traces were retained of the former group life," Du Bois observed, "and the chief remaining institution was the Priest or Medicine-man."[3]

With the destruction of established African social relations of kinship and political sovereignty, which originally bore their own religious significance in Africa, the African priest represented a relatively mobile, transportable focus of religious life. Assuming multiple roles as bard, physician, judge, and priest in the Americas, the African ritual specialist "early appeared on the plantation and found his function as the healer of the sick, the interpreter of the Unknown, the comforter of the sorrowing, the supernatural avenger of wrong, and the one who rudely but picturesquely expressed the longing, disappointment, and resentment of a stolen and oppressed people."[4] In these evocative terms, Du Bois recalled the creativity of the African priest, who deployed indigenous African religious resources under radically altered conditions.

Although the religion of the African priest came to be known by different names, such as "voodooism" or "obi-worship," Du Bois provocatively proposed that another name eventually adopted in America for indigenous African religion is "Christianity." Within the limits of the slave system but also within the space opened by the African priest, "rose the Negro preacher, and under him the first Afro-American institution, the Negro Church." According to Du Bois, this church, in the first instance, was not Christian but African, since it placed only a "veneer of Christianity" on the ongoing adaptation of indigenous African beliefs and practices under slavery. Suggesting that the Christianization of indigenous African religion should be regarded as a gradual process of religious transformation, Du Bois observed that "after the lapse of many generations the Negro church became Christian." In reviewing the "faith of the fathers" in *The Souls of Black Folk,* Du Bois sought to establish a basic continuity in religious life from Africa to African America. The "study of Negro religion," he insisted, had to track a transatlantic process of religious development carefully, "through its gradual changes from the heathenism of the Gold Coast to the institutional Negro Church in Chicago," which began with indigenous African religion.[5]

In both religion and popular culture, however, more dynamic, ongoing transatlantic exchanges have occurred between the two continents than might be suggested by this historical trajectory from ancient origins in Africa to modern developments in America. While Du Bois was analyzing the religious significance of Africa for African Americans in a series of books between 1903 and 1949, Africans were finding new ways to imagine the religious significance of America in Africa. During the 1920s and 1930s, the largest mass movement in central and southern Africa, the "American" movement, was based on the premise that salvation was coming from America. As an apocalyptic, millenarian movement, the American movement anticipated an imminent, sudden, and dramatic redemption of Africans from the oppressive conditions of European colonization through the supernatural advent of liberating Americans. Although this apocalypse failed to materialize, the vision of redemption permeated southern Africans' popular imagination of America.

In South Africa, after 1948, Africans suffered under the racist system of apartheid. As institutionalized racism, apartheid excluded Africans, the majority population, from citizenship and ensured that they were vulnerable to exploitation as labor. As the struggle against apartheid developed in the 1950s, the African National Congress, under the leadership of Nelson Mandela, found that the United States had emerged as the most important, and most dangerous, imperial power in the world, because it came to Africa "elaborately disguised" through diplomacy and foreign aid as well as through religion and popular culture. In 1990, after spending twenty-seven years as a political prisoner, Mandela was released and later visited the United States that same year, demonstrating the ongoing salience of transatlantic exchanges in religion and popular culture between Africa and America. Not merely a place of ancient origin, Africa is also present in America, just as America is a presence felt throughout Africa.

AFRICA IN AMERICA

During the long course of his life, W. E. B. Du Bois took up the challenge of providing a general historical overview of Africa and the African diaspora in five books: *The Negro* (1915); *Africa: Its Place in Modern History* (1930); *Black Folk: Then and Now* (1939); *The World and Africa* (1947); and *Africa: An Essay toward a History of the Continent of Africa and Its Inhabitants* (1963). Although Du Bois's wide reading enabled him to synthesize a diverse range of historical and ethno-graphic sources, his interest in writing these books was certainly not strictly his-torical. Instead, he engaged the African past as a basis for forging a Pan-African future. Having looked back in order to look forward, Du Bois concluded his ear-liest account of African history in *The Negro* with the promise that the "future world will, in all reasonable probability, be what colored men make it."[6]

As a significant part of African cultural heritage, the indigenous religious life of Africa featured in *The Negro*. In his discussion of African religion, Du Bois seemed concerned with three things: the meaning of the fetish, the belief in God, and the continuity between the indigenous religion of Africa and African American reli-gion across the Atlantic. Adopting a social evolutionary account of religious development, Du Bois maintained, "The religion of Africa is the universal ani-mism or fetishism of primitive peoples, rising to polytheism and approaching monotheism chiefly, but not wholly, as a result of Christian and Islamic missions."[7]

One of Du Bois's sources, *Fetichism in West Africa*, published in 1904 by the missionary Robert Hamill Nassau, had maintained that the fetish stood at the cen-ter of African religion, involving a superstitious regard for insignificant objects that wove witchcraft and sorcery into African thought, government, family, work, and daily life. According to Nassau, the fetish had practical effects, leading to can-nibalism, distrust, poisoning, secret societies, and depopulation, which effectively degraded Africans.[8] By contrast, Du Bois sought to rehabilitate the fetish. "It is not mere senseless degradation," he insisted. "It is a philosophy of life."[9] As the mate-rial focus of an indigenous African philosophy, the fetish, according to Du Bois, represented both a logical and a practical recognition of the dynamic forces of life, the positive and negative spiritual conditions within which Africans lived. Amplified by reports about the Ewe of West Africa and the Xhosa of South Africa, Du Bois's account of fetishism placed the fetish in a positive light. In recovering an African history of the fetish, Du Bois, in 1915, suggested that fetishism was not superstitious ignorance, fear, or fraud but a coherent material philosophy of the spiritual dynamics of life.

Reinterpreting the fetish, however, was not sufficient to demonstrate that indigenous Africans had their own religion. Africans' additional belief in God served this purpose. Du Bois found the Yoruba as his privileged example of Africans who not only believed in God but also made that divinity the foundation of organized political life and state building. In *The Negro*, however, Du Bois deferred to the testimony of European reporters to establish the indigenous African belief in God. "The African has a Great Over God," the explorer Mary

Kingsley observed.[10] No matter how superstitious Africans might be, the missionary Robert Hamill Nassau found, no one needed "to begin by telling them that there is a God."[11] Relying upon these reports, Du Bois was able to establish that belief in God was an indigenous feature of African religion that was not necessarily introduced by Muslim or Christian missions. Although he reviewed the importance of these missionizing religions in Africa, Du Bois appeared to regard them as a disruption of African life, noting, for example, that the modern slave trade coincided with "the greatest expansion of two of the world's most pretentious religions."[12] With the practical philosophy of the fetish and a belief in God, African religion had its own integrity.

Crossing the Atlantic, Du Bois argued in *The Negro* for a basic continuity between African indigenous religion and African American religion. In the African diaspora, the indigenous priest, responsible for religion and healing, carried that continuity. Unaffected by the plantation system, the African priest continued to function as "the interpreter of the supernatural, the comforter of the sorrowing, and as the one who expressed, rudely but picturesquely, the longing and disappointment and resentment of a stolen people." The Black Church, "the first distinctively Negro American social institution," emerged directly from these indigenous African religious resources. "It was not at first by any means a Christian church," Du Bois insisted, "but a mere adaptation of those rites of fetish which in America is termed obe worship, or 'voodooism.'" In his analysis of the fetish, the missionary Robert Hamill Nassau also proposed a direct continuity between Africa and America; however, he complained that the religion of the fetish, "the evil thing that the slave brought with him," had not only endured but actually grown under slavery. Again, rehabilitating the fetish, Du Bois proposed that fetishism marked the authentic religious inheritance from Africa. Although covered by a "veneer of Christianity," Du Bois argued, "the Negro church of to-day bases itself upon the sole surviving institution of the African fatherland," the indigenous religion of the fetish.[13]

Nearly twenty-five years later, Du Bois substantially revised and expanded his earlier account of African history for publication as *Black Folk: Then and Now*. With respect to African indigenous religion, his discussion in *Black Folk* remained largely unchanged from his treatment of fetishism and God in *The Negro*, except for one dramatic alteration. Removing the explorer Kingsley, the missionary Nassau, and their reports on West African beliefs in God, Du Bois introduced the Yoruba god, Shango. As Du Bois observed, Shango, the African god of thunder, "soars above the legend of Thor and Jahveh," thereby transcending the power of the European and Semitic gods of thunder. In an unreferenced quotation, which seems to appear from nowhere, Shango registers as a force: "He is the Hurler of thunderbolts, the Lord of the Storm, the God who burns down compounds and cities, the Render of trees and the Slayer of men; cruel and savage, yet splendid and beneficent in his unbridled action. For the floods which he pours from the lowering welkin give life to the soil that is parched and gladden the fields with fertility. And, therefore, mankind fear him, yet love him."[14]

By 1939, the authority of the European explorer and the Christian missionary had been replaced by the awesome indigenous power of Shango, the violent destroyer of cities and compounds, which are tempting to read as colonial cities and native compounds. More powerful than alien gods, Shango—the destroyer, the source of life—registers as the most important indigenous divinity of Africa.

Turning to America, Du Bois was much less confident in *Black Folk* about transatlantic religious continuity. In contrast with *The Negro*, where he had observed that slavery had not destroyed the religion of the fetish or the religious role of African priests, in *Black Folk* he stressed the radical disruption of kinship, community, and religion under slavery:

> The African family and clan life were disrupted in this transplantation; the communal life and free use of land were impossible; the power of the chief was transferred to the master, bereft of the usual blood ties and ancient reference. The African language survived only in occasional words and phrases. African religion, both fetish and Islam, was transformed. Fetish survived in certain rites and even here and there in blood sacrifice, carried out secretly and at night; but more often in open celebration which gradually became transmuted into Catholic and Protestant Christian rites. The slave preacher replaced the African medicine man and gradually, after a century or more, the Negro Church arose as the center and almost the only expression of Negro life in America.[15]

In this version, Du Bois charted the transatlantic crossing not as continuity but as change. The cumulative effect created by his key terms—*disruption, impossibility, transference, transformation, transmutation,* and *replacement*—is a sense of complete disjuncture between Africa and African America. Du Bois made no reference in *Black Folk* to the persistence of obeah or vodou in America. Traces of African heritage, he acknowledged, might be found in customs, literature, art, music, and dance, but further study would be required. He no longer seemed confident that the persistence of cultural resources, let alone religious resources, could be obviously established. In the case of the Black Church, which he had earlier identified as the "sole surviving institution of the African fatherland," we find an American institution that had become "almost the only expression of Negro life in America."[16] In his treatment of African religion in 1939, Du Bois highlighted destruction and discontinuity, the awesome destructive power of the Yoruba god, Shango, and the radical discontinuity between indigenous African religious life and slave religion, African American religion, or the Black Church in America.

In 1947, after two global wars, Du Bois returned to the challenge of writing a comprehensive history of Africa. In *The World and Africa*, he devoted less attention to religion than in the previous accounts. Nevertheless, Du Bois's interventions in the analysis of fetishism, divinity, and transatlantic connections are decisive and important for understanding African religion. Instead of rehabilitating the fetish, Du Bois in 1947 vigorously denounced fetishism as an account of African indigenous religion. Citing the German anthropologist Leo Frobenius, who observed, "I have seen in no part of Africa the Negroes worship a fetish," Du Bois rejected fetishism as a foreign, alien, and ultimately denigrating and dehumanizing characterization of African religion.[17]

As Frobenius had proposed, the very term *fetishism* was implicated in European representations of Africans as commodities for the slave trade. The market in African slaves, Frobenius argued, "exacted a justification; hence one made of the Negro a half-animal, an article of merchandise. And in the same way the notion of fetish (Portuguese *feticeiro*) was invented as a symbol of African religion." Insisting that he had never witnessed Africans worshiping a fetish, Frobenius observed that European discourse about African fetishism was an integral part of colonizing projects in subjugating, dehumanizing, and commodifying Africans. Under the sign of fetishism, he concluded, "the idea of the 'barbarous Negro' is a European invention."[18] By embracing and advancing this critique of fetishism, Du Bois recast African indigenous religion as a site of struggle over conflicting representations of materiality and humanity.

Although he referred briefly, in passing, to the fetish at one other point in *The World and Africa*, Du Bois basically erased his previous accounts of African fetishism. When he considered African indigenous religion as part of African history in 1947, he removed not only the European explorer and missionary but also the European category "fetishism," which had been deployed as an instrument of dehumanization and enslavement. Within the limited scope that he gave in this volume to reconstructing the indigenous religion of Africa, only Shango remains.

Revealing the source of his unreferenced citation in *Black Folk* as Leo Frobenius, Du Bois expanded on the divinity and power of the Yoruba god. In addition to his destructive force and creative capacity, Shango is the source of political power, authority, and sovereignty, father of royal rulers, whose "posterity still [has] the right to give the country its kings."[19] Having rejected the alien construction of fetishism, Du Bois celebrated the indigenous African religious resources supporting independent and autonomous political sovereignty.

In his African history of 1947, Du Bois seemed to have lost interest in the question of continuity or discontinuity with America. Instead, he devoted his attention to actively building a Pan-African solidarity. His reconstructions of African religion, however, were part of that transatlantic project, in unexpected ways. For example, the problem of African fetishism, which Du Bois wrestled with from 1915 to 1947, moving from imaginative rehabilitation in *The Negro* to critical rejection in *The World and Africa*, became a point of departure for the anticolonial work of Aimé Césaire, who drew inspiration for his *Discourse on Colonialism* from the same passage by Frobenius as the one Du Bois cited to reject fetishism, "the idea of the 'barbarous Negro' is a European invention."[20]

While Du Bois worked to mobilize Pan-African unity against the fetishism of European colonialism, eventually immigrating to West Africa, where he died in 1963, Africans in central and southern Africa developed new ways of imagining America as a religious promise of redemption from colonial oppression. In South Africa, the American movement swept through the Eastern Cape and Natal during the 1920s, promising its apocalyptic American redemption, which was captured in the rallying cry "Ama Melika ayeza"—the Americans are coming.

AMERICA IN AFRICA

During the 1920s, the myth of American redemption spread throughout central and southern Africa. The imminent advent of black American liberators was anticipated from the mining centers to the remote rural areas of the region. In the Congo (now the Democratic Republic of the Congo) many people expected that American liberators were about to sail in a huge battleship up the Congo River to deliver Africans from bondage and force whites to leave.[21] In Northern Rhodesia (now Zambia) believers in the American redemption anticipated the arrival of a mighty black American army. As one of the Zambian leaders announced in 1924, "America will be the chief of this country with the black people: the whites will go back to England. . . . These white people—the country is not theirs; when America comes you will see that America and we will own the country."[22] In Nyasaland (now Malawi) people awaited the arrival of American planes dropping bombs that would hit only white people. This expectation of airborne black American liberators was given voice in a popular song: "We're pleased that/We went to America/To learn the making of aeroplanes/So as to 'fix up' all foreigners."[23]

Elsewhere in central and southern Africa, the American liberators were expected to arrive on motorcycles, or to appear suddenly from under the ground, or to drop from the skies in balloons. In all these cases, America represented a utopian space of redemption, a sacred place inhabited by free black people, who could wield the power of the latest military technology and transcend spatial limits through the most modern modes of transportation to bring an apocalyptic salvation to Africa.

Several factors contributed to the formation of this redemptive image of America. First, the extensive American missionary activity of the prophetic Watchtower movement, an outgrowth of the Watch Tower Bible and Tract Society, which came to be known in the United States as the Jehovah's Witnesses, combined an apocalyptic expectation of the end of the world with a depiction of America as a land in which either all the people were black or all the people, regardless of race, lived in harmony.[24] In central Africa, the figure of John Chilembwe, who returned from three years of theological training in Virginia in 1900, also stimulated interest in America as a land of opportunity for Africans.[25]

Second, the prominent role of the United States in World War I linked America with images of advanced military technology, of which the airplanes, battleships, motorcycles, and machine guns would be used to liberate Africa. Like many other twentieth-century millenarian movements in Africa and elsewhere, this American movement looked not for salvation in the recovery of a precolonial past but for redemption in a capitalist future, symbolized by Westernized black Americans, the latest military technology, and the wealth controlled by whites. The future was America.

Third, the 1924 tour of the continent by the African-born American educator James K. Aggrey, sponsored by the Phelps-Stokes Fund, stimulated widespread expectations of the advent of Americans. As George Shepperson recounted, in Nyasaland "the image of America as a land peopled almost entirely with Negroes was also widespread amongst Africans," and the arrival of Aggrey "was seen by many as the prelude to an American Negro invasion, in which all wrongs would be righted and the Europeans driven out of the country."[26] Aggrey was met with a similar reception in South Africa. Although he intended to promote education on the Tuskegee model, Aggrey was received, as Edwin Smith noted, as "the herald of some invading band of Negroes—they (the Africans) thought all Americans were Negroes—who would drive the whites of South Africa into the sea."[27] People came to hear him in Umtata, hoping to learn about the coming of the Americans. Some expected that Aggrey, as harbinger of that arrival, would give away trade goods. These listeners were disappointed, according to one account, not only because Aggrey did not distribute wealth, but also because he failed to mention the American government.[28]

Finally, the promise of redemption associated with Marcus Garvey must have featured in the American myth. Reports of Garvey's "Black Star Line" might have inspired rumors of the arrival of Americans in modern forms of transport. In addition, however, stories circulated throughout central and southern Africa about a prophet named America, who was distinguished, like Garvey, by a gold tooth. In Zambia, a prolonged criminal investigation even resulted in 1929 in the arrest of a suspect for supposedly being this subversive prophet "America."[29]

In South Africa, an American redemption was anticipated after the 1906 Bambatha rebellion in Natal and Zululand. Rumors spread that heroes killed in the rebellion would rise from the dead, "assisted by 'black abelungu' (black Americans) with modern weapons."[30] In 1923 in the Eastern Cape, a woman by the name of Nonteto preached a message, under the aegis of Ethiopianism: "American Negroes are coming who will cut the throats of Europeans."[31] Diagnosed as suffering from manic-depressive psychosis, she was confined to a mental hospital. By the end of the 1920s, however, interest in America was so pervasive that it could not be restrained. A principal of a Pondoland teacher-training college observed in 1927 that "unsophisticated natives in these parts . . . regard the voice of America as that of a mighty race of black people overseas, dreaded by all European nations. . . . [Americans] manufacture for their own purposes engines, locomotives, ships, motor cars, aeroplanes, and mighty weapons of war. . . . today the word America *(iMelika)* is a household word symbolic of nothing else but Bantu National freedom and liberty."[32] This enthusiasm for American redemption was organized in South Africa by the enigmatic religious leader Wellington Buthelezi. Eventually picked up by the Industrial and Commercial Workers Union, the American myth inspired the largest mass religious movement to occur in South Africa during the 1920s.

Although born in Natal, Wellington Buthelezi claimed to have been born in Chicago and trained as a medical doctor in North America. In 1925 he initiated a religious movement based on the promise that black Americans were coming to

South Africa as powerful liberators. Buthelezi announced, "A new and powerful race of people is to come shortly out of the sea, and an end will be made of all tyranny and wrong."[33] According to him, this imminent redemption was coming from America. "The American negroes have decided to fight the Europeans and will help the local natives," Buthelezi taught, according to one account. "There are already three ships with ammunition on this side of the sea," and "balloons are also coming over."[34] Traveling around the region, he supported his prophetic message with the use of medicinal herbs, a battery to give patients electric shocks, and a crystal in which followers "would see numbers of aeroplanes and motor cars filled with negro troops sailing in the sky, awaiting the call to land."[35]

Buthelezi rapidly gained a large following that included local chiefs, headmen, ministers, and congregations of both independent and mission churches. In particular, he mobilized the rural poor and migrant laborers, who were most responsive to the prospect of liberation. Followers of this millenarian movement were known as Wellingtonites, or "Americans," but they were also known by a term that signified their preparation for an imminent apocalyptic war of liberation, Amafela Ndawonye, "those who are prepared to die together."[36] At Wellingtonite meetings, hymns, prayers, and sermons celebrated the coming salvation, which was expected soon, when black Americans in airplanes would fly over the country, dropping fire from the skies that would destroy all whites and all black nonbelievers. "The Americans are coming," became the rallying cry of Wellington Buthelezi's millenarian movement. With his followers already looking to the skies for signs of the American planes, he encouraged them further, "Now when these things begin to take place, look up and raise your heads, because your redemption is drawing near."[37]

Although local government authorities deported Wellington Buthelezi in March 1927, the American movement continued, with its promise of redemption taken up by other leaders, especially by representatives of the Industrial and Commercial Workers Union. Leaders of the movement advocated two ritualized means of preparation.

First, people had to purchase membership tickets in the Industrial and Commercial Workers Union (ICU). When the American liberators came, holders of the red ICU tickets would be spared from destruction. During 1927, the ICU membership ticket was transformed into a religious icon of salvation; substantiating this, a minister of the independent African Native Church told his followers, "You will die if you do not buy the ticket!" People had to obtain the ICU card to show to the "American angels" when they arrived. An ICU leader in Natal observed, "If you didn't possess that card to show to that angel you were lost." ICU tickets were purchased from activists in the mines, who "said that the Americans were coming and the people working on the mines were going to be released from labour." Although ticket holders were also instructed to stop paying taxes, adding practical interest to membership, the ticket itself became a religious symbol of redemption from the impending destruction of whites and white rule in South Africa.[38]

Second, people had to protect themselves through ritual acts of sacrifice, especially by killing their white animals and fowl. If they wanted to avoid being burned to death by the fires descending from the skies, believers in the American redemption had to eliminate animals associated with whites, in particular, pigs. The widespread, ritualized pig slaughters carried out by believers in the American movement during 1927 drew on a complex of religious symbolism that associated pigs with whites, not only because pigs had been introduced by Europeans into southern Africa, but also, and more important, because pig fat was associated with lightning, fire, and witchcraft. Although many people in the Eastern Cape believed that lard provided protection from lightning sent by witches, leaders of the American movement argued that pig fat would attract the lightning flames that would descend from the American planes. If the believers killed their pigs, then whites and nonbelievers would be the only ones left in South Africa still owning animals that would attract the flames of destruction from the skies.[39] Although the ritual killing of pigs drew on "traditional" religious resources, it was clearly linked with a "modern" means of fighting white political domination and economic exploitation, namely, the purchase of a membership ticket in a labor union. Furthermore, both the traditional and the modern aspects of the American movement were woven together by adopting a Christian expectation of a final cosmic battle, a kind of Armageddon, in which the forces of good would defeat evil and eliminate it from the world.

In the history of religions, millenarian movements have often been explained as responses to deprivation, natural disaster, or social disruption. During the 1920s in central and southern Africa, however, religious movements with apocalyptic expectations of sudden redemption responded to the more specific historical conditions of colonialism, capital penetration, labor exploitation, and white political domination. Although they occasionally drew on traditional symbolic resources, these millenarian movements were not regressions to the "primitive." Rather, they were modern innovations, promising an imminent, instant, collective, and this-worldly redemption.

As a sacred, redemptive space, America was at the symbolic center of those modern innovations. America stood as an organizing symbol around which other signs of modernity constellated. Modern transport, weapons, trade goods, wage labor, taxation, and colonial dispossession of the land were all incorporated into the American myth. Although a foreign sacred space, America nevertheless focused local reflections on power relations and local struggles over power in Africa. "Whatever its origin," as historian Karen Fields has observed, "a mythic vision of America's greatness was cultivated in Africa—as on other continents during this century—and it gave blacks and whites a luxuriant symbolic language in which to think about African liberation."[40] The apocalyptic myth of American redemption focused black hopes and white fears of dramatic social change. While magistrates and missionaries complained about "American agitators," many Africans looked to the skies for their liberation, waiting for the apocalyptic advent of the American utopia.

America, as we have seen, served as a symbolic device appropriated and mobilized by Africans for achieving an inversion of the prevailing organization of space, which had alienated, dehumanized, and displaced them within the South African political economy. Since Africans had been submerged by a reign of oppression that pervaded South African space, many aspired to a utopian liberation from place. America provided one compelling symbol of that utopian hope. A utopian orientation toward space, as Jonathan Z. Smith has suggested, can be contrasted with a locative worldview that emphasizes the maintenance of everyone and everything in their assigned places. A locative order is based on a stable, supposedly permanent center that anchors a fixed order "in which each being has its given place and role to fulfill." It depends on the ongoing reinforcement of order, hierarchy, and boundaries, requiring a high degree of conformity to place. It tends to feature prominently in the official ideology of any normative, imperial order.

By contrast, a utopian worldview tests boundaries and transcends limits. It involves an orientation in space "in which beings are called upon to challenge their limits, break them, or create new possibilities." Rather than the maintenance of place, the utopian worldview calls for liberation from place, often requiring the transgression or destruction of a prevailing social, symbolic, or spatial order, thus entailing an orientation in space in which "the categories of rebellion and freedom are to the fore."[41]

Smith has qualified this contrast by observing that the locative and the utopian are "coeval possibilities," simultaneously available options in any social world.

However, America's appearance to South Africa as sacred space suggests that the locative and utopian can be not merely "coeval" but can involve intimately related maneuvers in contests over local space. America appeared as utopian space precisely for Africans, who suffered under the imposed locative order inherited from conquest and colonialism. By producing America as a utopian space, people were responding to the specific historical conditions of domination. Displaced within a dominant locative order, Africans forged a new, utopian space that bore the name "America." They anticipated a radical transposition of space, an expectation that is commonplace within apocalyptic movements—the first would be last, the last would be first, the up would be down, the down would be up, the inside would be out, and the outside would be in. In that expectation, America represented the imminent reversal of the prevailing spatial order of domination and exclusion in South Africa.

The myth of American redemption in Africa bears certain resemblances to the millenarian "cargo" movements that swept through the Melanesian islands after World War II. Like the Wellingtonites' movement, some of these movements perceived America as the source of their salvation. Perhaps the most adamantly Americanist of these movements, the John Frum movement, began on the island of Tanna in the early 1940s. After the departure of U.S. troops in 1946, leaders of the movement predicted the imminent return of Americans by ship, submarine, or airplane to establish a new island utopia. The redemptive power of America has even been personified in the mysterious figure of John Frum, who embodies the American promise of salvation—John from America, the "King of America." "He teaches the good road," proclaims one John Frum hymn, "he points to the place, to America, to America."[42] Into the twenty-first century, John Frum movements have continued to propagate their "American dreams" of utopian redemption.

But the hope of American redemption also featured in other religious movements. On the Admiralty Islands, for example, Paliau Maloat, founder of Melanesia's first independent church, declared in 1946 that America would come soon, "to show us the road that would make us all right."[43] In the 1960s, similar movements in Melanesia continued to look to America, most notably the movement of the Remnant Church, on the Solomon Islands, which held that it shared an ancient, theocratic covenant with America, and a Tungak movement in New Hanover, in the Bismark Archipelago, which collected money in order to purchase American president Lyndon B. Johnson and have him shipped to New Hanover.[44]

However, the resemblance between the utopian movements in South Africa and those in Melanesia is more profound than merely the invocation of America. Most cargo movements, like the Wellingtonites, engaged in specific practical strategies that directly addressed the historical situation of colonial domination. These strategies were intentionally disruptive of basic colonial structures, designed "to challenge their limits, break them, or create new possibilities." If the dominant, locative order was based on the extraction of native labor, these movements called on their followers to refuse to work. If its political administration was based on centralized taxation, their followers were forbidden to pay taxes. If its rationale was capital accumulation, resistance was exercised through the ritualized destruction of symbols of wealth. In these terms, the locative and utopian orientations toward space were contested within specific historical conditions of oppression and resistance.

When African prophets in central and southern Africa during the 1920s predicted liberation from colonial domination in the name of America, colonial administrators labeled them crazy and tracked them down as criminals. However, in the course of events, these prophetic "Americanists" actually turned out to be right, because forty years later the European colonial administrators were gone, everywhere, that is, except in South Africa. There, oppression was only further entrenched, after 1948, under the racist system of domination and exclusion known as apartheid. If America symbolized a utopian space of liberation, Africans in South Africa remained waiting for America.

PILGRIMAGE TO THE CENTER

During 1990, two South African political leaders, African National Congress (ANC) president Nelson Mandela and state president F. W. de Klerk, journeyed to America. Both leaders addressed the issue of sanctions, that symbolic key to the international spatial dynamics that had come to characterize relations between the United States and South Africa during the 1980s. While Mandela pressed for sanctions that would further isolate the South African government, De Klerk sought an easing of sanctions that would lead to his nation's readmission to the international community. These two visits can be regarded as more than merely efforts to influence American foreign policy, however; they were also ritual pilgrimages to the sacred center of the world. By asserting their competing claims on the center of America, Mandela and De Klerk hoped to mobilize power back home in the political struggle over the future of South Africa. In this respect, their visits appeared as a ritual contest over America but were, at the same time, part of an ongoing local contest over power in South Africa.

When Nelson Mandela was released from prison on February 11, 1990, after serving nearly thirty years on charges of treason, his emergence was interpreted in dramatically apocalyptic terms by the Reverend Jesse Jackson, in South Africa for the occasion. Nelson Mandela, according to Jackson, "was a Christ-like figure" who had "suffered his way into power." Upon Nelson Mandela's release, Jackson continued, "now that the stone has been rolled away," the world beheld an apocalyptic "second coming."[45] Rather than sudden redemption, however, South Africa entered into a long, slow, and often violent process of negotiation. In symbolic terms, going to America was a significant maneuver in the contested negotiations over meaning and power in a "New South Africa."

In June 1990, all of America witnessed the "second coming" of Nelson Mandela during his two-week tour of eleven cities in the United States and Canada. Americans, and particularly African Americans, embraced Mandela's visit in highly charged religious terms. Nelson Mandela was publicly hailed as "the most sainted man of our time." New York mayor David Dinkins addressed him as "a modern day Moses." The Reverend Jim Holley, pastor of the Little Rock Baptist Church, identified him as an African pope, because, as Holley explained, "whatever the Pope means to Catholics, that's what Mandela means to us." His wife, Winnie Mandela, was also sacralized, described in one church service as Eve, Esther, and Ruth, "the perfect person God decided to make when He finished creation." Even *Time* magazine had to resort to religious imagery to make sense of the fervor of Mandela's reception in America. "On a more transcendent plane, where history is made and myths are forged," *Time* declared, "Mandela is a hero, a man, like those described by author Joseph Campbell, who has emerged from a symbolic grave 'reborn, made great and filled with creative power.'" In these potent symbolic terms, as *messiah, Moses, pope,* and *hero-with-a-thousand-faces,* Nelson Mandela was welcomed by America.[46]

Even beyond the extravagance of the rhetoric, the deep resonance of the Mandela tour with religious and political interests in America was obvious. In particular, many African Americans found the Mandela visit an opportunity to reassess their position in American society. At one ritual tribute to Mandela in New York City involving a reading of "praise songs" by thirty political poets, the organizer observed, "We're so troubled by racial conflict in New York that we desperately need some kind of Messiah."[47] In this search for local salvation, South Africa, which had stood for so long as a symbol of racist evil, was ironically transposed into a sacred place, the distant birthplace (and rebirthplace) of an African savior.

At the same time, however, Mandela's visit produced several significant spatial effects that promised to alter the position of African Americans in America. First, every place Mandela visited became, even if only temporarily, a sacred place, a shrine for American pilgrims. As one commentator observed, "Like pilgrims contemplating a joyous vision, millions of black Americans are trying to gauge the long-term effects of Mr. Mandela's visit to the United States."[48]

Second, among the potential long-term effects, Mandela's visit raised the possibility of reviving the social activism and aspirations of the civil rights movement. Benjamin F. Chavis Jr., executive director of the Commission for Racial Justice of the United Church of Christ, announced this promise specifically in terms of the creation of a new sacred space for African Americans in America: "I think you're going to see a lot of African-Americans break out of the cycle of hopelessness we've had. We have a new Jerusalem. We have to keep that flame alive, and thank God Mandela has lit a flame that was extinguished in the 1960s." Third, the visit promised to relocate African Americans, and their interests and concerns, from the periphery to the center of American life. "Whatever its international implications," the *New York Times* observed, "the Mandela visit locally has become perhaps the largest and most vivid symbol of the fact that after years on the edges of New York city power and politics, the black community has arrived."[49]

In these ways the visit of Nelson Mandela held the potential to transform spatial relations for Americans. New sacred places, even a "New Jerusalem," along with new representations of the position of African Americans in the United States and the world, suddenly seemed possible, all because of the visit of a man, who, in the words of the Reverend Joseph Lowery, president of the Southern Christian Leadership Conference, "gives flesh to the struggle against apartheid in South Africa—and against the apartheid mentality in South Georgia and America."[50]

For Mandela and the ANC, however, the American tour had specific goals of local, South African significance. Certainly, forging ties with America was important as one of those goals, especially in establishing alternative connections that bypassed the official foreign relations between the United States and South Africa. Indeed, Mandela met with "official" America. After conferring with President George Bush and Secretary of State James Baker, Mandela addressed a joint session of the U.S. Congress. That event reinforced Mandela's standing as an international statesman back in South Africa. However, his connections with the "other" America during his trip established symbolic links, which probably held greater significance for his goals specific to South Africa. In addition to participating in all the public celebrations, ticker-tape parades, and church services, Mandela went on a special pilgrimage to Atlanta, to the graveside of Martin Luther King Jr., where he placed a wreath decorated in the ANC colors, black, green, and gold. In this ritual act, Mandela reaffirmed connections between the liberation struggle in South Africa and the civil rights movement in the United States. But the most dramatic, and publicized, attempt to forge connections with America occurred in New York, at Yankee Stadium, when Mandela, in a baseball cap, announced his identification with all the people of America. "You know who I am," he declared. "I am a Yankee!"[51]

Besides establishing symbolic links with America, Mandela pursued two other goals of local, South African import during his visit; in addition to pressing for sanctions against the government of South Africa, he raised funds. These practical, political goals tended to be controversial in America. His fundraising attempts were frustrated by contentious questions that arose regarding the ANC and such issues as its alliance with the South African Communist Party, its socialist economic policies, and its armed struggle, as well as the issue of Mandela's defense of Arafat, Gadhafi, and Castro as "brothers in the struggle." But even some who celebrated Mandela as an African messiah showed resentment about his fundraising by pointing to the commodification of his charisma during the American tour. As Rashida Ismaili complained, "Every little inch of the man's flesh and every second of his time is being equated with a certain amount of money—the tip of his nose is worth $100, one minute is worth $1000. He has been commodified to such an extent that he no longer has meaning." On the issue of sanctions, Mandela appealed to Americans to maintain the spatial and spiritual isolation of the South African regime from the international community. On this issue as well, however, many Americans observed an incongruity between Mandela's charisma and his political agenda. Mandela's call for sanctions, according to one commentator, was "as if the Second Coming were devoted to pressing Rome for the recall of Pontius Pilate." Mandela, however, had come not to save America but to sanction the South African government.[52]

Although the sanctions campaign of the 1980s continued to hold local significance in South Africa, Americans by 1990 were starting to lose interest, and sanctions against the South African government were beginning to ease. In part, the easing was related to the public relations efforts of the South African president, F. W. de Klerk, during his own pilgrimage to America in September 1990. De Klerk's visit was not marked by parades, church services, ceremonies at American shrines, or any other form of public celebration. Rather, De Klerk went straight to the "official" America, on pilgrimage exclusively to the symbolic heart of the locative world order, the White House. Despite its limited scope, that visit was sufficient to produce significant effects on the South African periphery. As one popular South African newspaper reported, De Klerk's visit to the political center of the world signaled the return of South Africa to the international community. More than that, however, De Klerk's visit to the White House symbolized a mythic journey to the sacred center of the world. "If Washington is the world's informal capital and the United States' president its most powerful man," this newspaper report observed, "the Oval Office in the White House must surely be a very important place."[53] With meticulous attention to spatial symbolism, this report described the Oval Office as the central point from which ripples of power seem to radiate across the entire world, like the circles that radiate from a rock thrown into a lake.

Standing at the sacred center of the world, surrounded by the flags of the fifty states, the United States, and South Africa, De Klerk participated in one ceremonial act, a photo session with George Bush, posed under the portrait of George Washington. According to the South African press, however, that simple ritual held profound significance for South Africa: "That president F. W. de Klerk met his counterpart, George Bush, in that office last September symbolized the promise of South Africa's eventual return to the global community."

This conclusion expressed two assumptions. First, it asserted that F. W. de Klerk was the "counterpart" of George Bush, implying that De Klerk was the equivalent of the "most powerful man" in the world. In local South African contests over power, De Klerk, rather than Mandela, according to this account, derived greater empowerment from his pilgrimage to America. Second, it revealed that America continued to operate as a sacred space that held the promise of redemption. Obviously, Mandela and De Klerk sought to empower different kinds of redemption, one seeking liberation from local oppression, the other seeking inclusion in the international community. Although they employed many other strategies toward those ends, both advanced their claims on power during 1990 by means of a journey to America, a pilgrimage from the periphery to the locative center of the world order.

Rituals of pilgrimage enact a symbolic transformation of ordinary space. By going to what anthropologist Victor Turner called the "center out there," pilgrims renegotiate ordinary relations between that center and periphery of their worlds. Similarly, during 1990, Mandela and De Klerk tried to renegotiate international relations between the South African periphery and the American center by ritual means. Characteristically, pilgrims abandon their conventional roles on the journey to adopt, in Victor and Edith Turner's terms, "an alternative mode of social being." They enter a special world of pure potential, unbound by the familiar temporal and spatial limits of their social worlds. In America, as we have seen, Mandela became an African "messiah," and De Klerk became the "counterpart" of the most powerful man in the world. They adopted new roles for America but also for their own society, which was undergoing a violent transition toward a new South Africa. Accordingly, the full significance of their travels was realized, as in any pilgrimage, only when they returned, bearing signs of new power derived from the sacred center, to what the Turners described as the pilgrim's "warm and admiring welcome at home."[54]

Back home in South Africa, the meaning and power of America as the locative center of a world order continued to be contested on the periphery. As negotiations over a political settlement dragged on, it was difficult to assess what had been gained by going on pilgrimage to America. Mandela had raised funds; De Klerk had succeeded in gaining support for lifting sanctions. Nevertheless, neither could claim clear victory in the symbolic appropriation of America as sacred space. In part, their failure to register a convincing claim on America resulted from the fact that the United States, although apparently the center of the world, does not itself revolve around a single center. The United States is composed of multiple centers—from the White House to the grave of Martin Luther King Jr., from Wall Street to Yankee Stadium, from the John F. Kennedy Library in Boston to Harlem's Africa Square—each accessed by different pilgrimage routes. Pilgrimage to the American center, therefore, revealed a center that is fragmented and dispersed.

Accordingly, the meaning and power of America are also contested at the center, as Mandela's visit especially showed by refocusing, however briefly, the endemic conflicts between an official America and an other America that imagined American society, in the mirror of South Africa, as a space of oppression. As we have seen, many African Americans responded to Mandela's visit as an occasion for reminding America of its own "apartheid mentality." Of course, this vision of America in the mirror of South Africa was not new. In 1960 Martin Luther King Jr. revealed that he had "taken a particular interest in the problems in South Africa because of the similarities between the situation there and our own situation in the United States."[55] Increasingly, during the 1960s, King emphasized the inherent connection between racist oppression at home and abroad, identifying the central role in that oppression as played by "the greatest purveyor of violence in the world today—my own government."[56] Thirty years later, these similarities and connections between America and South Africa remained salient, with many African Americans continuing to experience the United States as a locative order that dominated and oppressed people both at its center and at its periphery.[57]

Many people in South Africa shared that impression. However, because America was a contested space, echoes of an American utopia reverberated. In their analysis of ritual pilgrimage, Victor and Edith Turner suggested that pilgrims acquire a new sense of possibility, gaining new insight into "what may be," by going to a sacred center. Perhaps Nelson Mandela beheld such a vision on his return to America in 1993. On January 20, 1993, while F. W. de Klerk remained in South Africa, Mandela was in Washington, DC, for the inauguration of President Bill Clinton. Invited by the Congressional Black Caucus, Mandela sat with his hosts in the stands. As a South African newspaper reported, Mandela's presence, in dramatic contrast to his reception in 1990, "passed almost unnoticed." Nevertheless, Mandela's second visit held a symbolic significance for South Africa that was even greater than the first. At Clinton's inauguration, while "witnessing the ritual," this report speculated, Mandela must have had a new vision of "what may be" for South Africa, for "he surely must have been impressed by the ease by which such enormous power is transferred."[58] Whatever it meant to Americans, this ritual of power, from the vantage point of the periphery, symbolized the possibility that a similar transfer might one day occur in South Africa.

TRANSATLANTIC TRANSFERS

Reviewing these transatlantic exchanges between Africa and America, we can clearly see that we are not dealing merely with African cultural origins and African American cultural survivals. Throughout the twentieth century, the ongoing exchanges between Africa and America produced different forms of intercultural subjectivity and collectivity within religion and popular culture. So, we need new stories about the religious, cultural, and transatlantic horizons of those exchanges.

In Africa, the political philosopher Achille Mbembe has highlighted this need for new narratives. "At the intersection of religious practices and the interrogation of human tragedy," Mbembe has observed, "a distinctively African philosophy has emerged."[59] But that African philosophy of tragedy, with its roots in slavery, colonization, and apartheid, has engaged religion in different ways. On the one hand, we have stories of primordial nativism; on the other hand, we have stories of radical nationalism; rejecting each other, both have failed to provide convincing mythic narratives for charting an African future.

Against the radical nationalist dismissals of the viability of indigenous religion for any revolutionary postcolonial projects, nativist positions, with their "re-enchantment of tradition," have sought to recover the authentic precolonial religious resources of Africa as a foundation for the future. However, both political alternatives, radical and nativist, have had to maneuver within rapidly changing, globalizing conditions, which have transformed religion, even indigenous religion, within new political economies of the sacred.

In the name of an African Renaissance, with its promise of revitalizing an indigenous African heritage, formerly radical political interests can align with the global financial structures of the World Bank, the International Monetary Fund, the European Union, and the United States.[60] At the same time, a devoted African nativist such as Credo Mutwa, the self-proclaimed Zulu witchdoctor, later *sangoma*, and now shaman, can establish transatlantic continuity as featured artist on the Web site TheAfrican.Com, "the website of the African diaspora," for his depiction of the site's patron, the Yoruba god, Shango, thereby achieving global presence and power in the Atlantic world.[61]

As Achille Mbembe has suggested, indigenous African religion, which has not been adequately captured either by radical dismissals or by nativist reconstructions, has to be regarded as a mode of self-creation, through practice, through style, and through writing. In writing about the history of Africa, W. E. B. Du Bois was engaged in precisely such a struggle of self-formation, but he was also trying to make sense out of a political project, initially located in the United States but increasingly global in scope, which linked Africa and America.

Transatlantic exchanges, African style, have often been represented with medical metaphors that reflect the dominant colonizing discourse of the United States, according to which, African culture entered America through contagious transmission, through its "infectious rhythm."[62] As we have seen, however, the African and American transatlantic exchanges in religion and popular culture were not contagion but negotiation, the ongoing, living struggle to be human in relation to Africa, America, and the vast creative space of continuing interchanges between the two.

CHAPTER NINE · Shamanic Religion

During 2002, the Dream Change Coalition, an organization specializing in shamanic tourism, advertised an "unprecedented rare opportunity" to visit Credo Mutwa, the famous Zulu visionary, healer, and ritual specialist. For the price of $2,225, not including airfare, spiritual tourists could attend "Song of the Stars, a Weeklong Intensive with Zulu Shaman, Vusamazulu Credo Mutwa, in his home of South Africa." Not only advertised as the traditional "Keeper of Zulu Knowledge," Mutwa was also reputed to be an expert on heavenly knowledge, possessing detailed insight into aliens from outer space. As the publicity announced, Credo Mutwa "imparts knowledge from the stars, previously only divulged to initiates after many years of strenuous testing, now to be shared with a few who are called to him before he departs this life on Earth."[1] Now, from the local Zulu to the universal extraterrestrial, all his knowledge was openly available to enthusiasts of New Age spirituality.

The Dream Change Coalition was an initiative in New Age spirituality founded by the shaman Jim Perkins, previously discussed as an expert in the shamanic arts of plastic, protean shape shifting. On the visit to Credo Mutwa in South Africa, spiritual tourists from the United States would be led by Dr. Eve Bruce, a medical doctor specializing, incidentally, in plastic and reconstructive surgery, who also presented herself as a shaman, for instance, in her book *Shaman M.D.*[2] Thus, the Dream Change Coalition, itself evoking the protean style of plastic, shape-shifting religion, anchored its spiritual tourism in the reputed authenticity of an indigenous shaman, such as the South African Credo Mutwa.

Defenders of the integrity of indigenous religion have derided New Age shamans, as well as their indigenous collaborators, as "plastic shamans" or "plastic medicine men." The Web site Plastic-Shaman-Busters.com, for example, seeks to expose fraudulent claims to the religious authenticity of the shaman.[3] According to the classic definition proposed by historian of religions Åke Hultkrantz, a shaman is "a social functionary who, with the help of guardian spirits, attains ecstasy to create a rapport with the supernatural world on behalf of his [or her] group members."[4] As a social functionary, the shaman is defined not merely by extraordinary personal abilities to achieve ecstasy, communicate with spirits, and affect the healing of individuals but also by a public capacity to mediate between a transcendent reality and a particular social group. In many instances, the relevant social group for a shaman is constituted by kinship, since shamans often serve as hereditary ritual specialists for their clans. But broader social relations within a territory might also determine the constitution of a shaman's community. Operating as an inspirational mediator on behalf of a community, the shaman necessarily performs a range of political, social, and economic roles, which tend to be overlooked when the focus is on religious experience.

For many scholars in the academic study of religion, following Mircea Eliade's classic text *Shamanism*, the shaman exemplifies premodern religious experience cultivated by "archaic techniques of ecstasy," a spirituality that has been irrecoverably lost in modernity.[5] For enthusiasts of New Age spirituality, including selfproclaimed "white shamans" in the United States, the shaman exemplifies postmodern religious experience, available to anyone, anywhere.[6] By signing up for guided shamanic tours, which take spiritual tourists to meet with shamans in Siberia, Africa, and the Amazon, anyone can be initiated into the wild spirituality of the shaman. As a result, premodern religious resources have assumed a postmodern character—plastic, protean, and even virtual—in this new global shamanism.

During the 1960s, shamanism was popularized by the writings of Carlos Castaneda, whose accounts of the Yaqui shaman don Juan Matus, even if they were entirely fictional, described the spiritual insights and techniques of Native American shamanism. In his first book, *The Teachings of Don Juan*, Castaneda focused on the use of peyote and other drugs that formed the shaman's spiritual pharmacopoeia for inducing ecstasy.[7] Spilling over into popular culture, the shaman's "techniques of ecstasy," especially intensity, trance, and intoxication, served as models and metaphors for new developments in rock 'n' roll. Jim Morrison, lead singer of the Doors, was not merely a popular entertainer. He was the Lizard King, the electric shaman, opening the doors of perception. "The shaman," as Morrison related, "was a man who would intoxicate himself. See, he was probably already an unusual individual. And, he would put himself into a trance by dancing, whirling around, drinking, taking drugs—however. Then, he would go on a mental travel and describe his journey to the rest of the tribe."[8] The features of shamanic ecstasy—intoxication, trance, and mental travel—are more than 1960s countercultural productions. They run deep in mainstream American popular culture, especially considering that the prevailing symbolism of Santa Claus may be rooted not only in Coca-Cola advertising but also in the religious practices of Siberian shamans. These shamans achieved ecstasy by using a hallucinogenic mushroom, the red and white fly agaric, and, with their reindeer, flew around the world or into heavenly or subterranean worlds. Even the reindeer became intoxicated by drinking human urine bearing traces of the mushroom. Although St. Nicholas, the Christian saint of merchants, was also incorporated into this popular tradition, the Siberian shaman, with the symbolism of the red and white fly agaric mushroom, spiritual travel, and even flying reindeer, suggests the defining features of Santa Claus.[9]

A ZULU SHAMAN IN AMERICA

The Zulu shaman Vusamazulu Credo Mutwa has gained a small following in the United States. Mutwa's attraction, many of his supporters would argue, is not religious, since he is not associated with any organized, institutionalized religion, but spiritual, involving an authentic spirituality that merges indigenous wisdom with healing power. Spiritual healing, drawing on techniques ranging from mental visualization to alternative medicine, has been a central preoccupation of the New Age.

Credo Mutwa first appeared in the United States as a spiritual healer. Under the editorship of Bradford P. Keeney, who has been described as a psychologist, medicine man, and shaman, a book on the healing wisdom of Credo Mutwa was published in the United States in the series Profiles in Healing.[10] Keeney apparently recommended the South African shaman to the attention of the directors of the Ringing Rocks Foundation, which was established in Philadelphia in 1995 with the mission "to explore, document, and preserve indigenous cultures and their healing practices." As its first project, the foundation decided to sponsor Credo Mutwa with a lifetime stipend to "allow this treasure to live out his days free to create as he chooses." Recognizing him as the high sanusi of the Zulu, the foundation bestowed another title upon Credo Mutwa, Ringing Rocks Foundation's "Distinguished Artist and Teacher of African Traditional Culture."

The foundation planned to give Mutwa space on its Web site to transmit his indigenous knowledge to others. The directors of the foundation intended the site to present a retrospective profile of Mutwa's long career of establishing cultural villages in South Africa. "We hope to spend time with him at each of the sites he has built," they stated, "recording through pictures and his own words the background for his cultural and healing villages."[11] Although he had no secure place in South Africa, the Ringing Rocks Foundation in the United States promised to provide Credo Mutwa with a healing center in cyberspace.

In keeping with the eclecticism of New Age spirituality, the African healing practiced by Credo Mutwa has often been equated with the healing systems of other indigenous cultures. Increasingly, he operated at the intersection of African and Native American traditions. In 1997, for example, Mutwa and Roy Little Sun, a Native American healer who had been born in Indonesia as Roy Steevenz but was reportedly adopted by the Hopi, performed a ceremony entitled Healing the African Wound. At the Wonderboom, the "Tree of Life," in Pretoria, South Africa, these healers took two feathers, one from an American golden eagle, representing the sky, the other from an African guinea fowl, representing the earth, and tied them together in a "medicine bundle" to signify the healing of Africa through the sacred union of earth and sky.

Unfortunately, since this ritual artifact included the feather of an endangered species, the healing feathers were confiscated by U.S. customs officials at the Atlanta airport when Roy Little Sun returned to America. Although his campaign to recover the feathers, including appeals to President Bill Clinton, failed to secure their return, Roy Little Sun returned to South Africa for another ceremony in 2000 to reaffirm the healing connection between the indigenous peoples of America and Africa.[12]

The indigenous authenticity represented by this fusion of African and Native American spirituality has also been attractive to some white South Africans. During 2001, for example, a New Age event in the Eastern Cape of South Africa was advertised as "A Tribal Gathering," not a gathering of indigenous African tribes, but a festival attracting primarily white South African enthusiasts of Native American spirituality. Living in a tepee circle, participants at this gathering would celebrate Mother Earth, enter a sweat lodge, and perform the ceremonies of the medicine wheel. Promising that African ritual specialists, *sangomas*, from the local village would also visit the gathering, the advertising for the event certified the merger of African and Native American spirituality by featuring a photograph of Credo Mutwa at the medicine wheel.[13]

In the United States, New Age enthusiasts have tended to assume the basic equivalence of all indigenous spirituality. For example, the Heart Healing Center in Denver, Colorado, hosted the conference "Indigenous Earth Healers" in 2001. At this gathering of indigenous healers from all over the world, Africa was represented by the high sanusi of the Zulu, Credo Mutwa. Unable to attend in person, Mutwa was replaced on the program by his student C. J. Hood, a "white Zulu" from Port Elizabeth in the Eastern Cape, who played a videotaped message by Credo Mutwa and performed a traditional Zulu dance. Praising his Zulu teacher, Hood declared, "Credo Mutwa will go down in history as a man who was able to bridge a gap between white and black South Africans and start a healing process." By invoking the indigenous authenticity of the Zulu healer, Hood was able to find a New Age audience in the United States for his message, as reported in the *Wellness eJournal:* "Respect all that is around us, accept all cultures as they are, and go back to our traditions."[14]

As these examples suggest, during the 1990s Credo Mutwa developed a certain profile in the United States as an indigenous shaman. Whether speaking for himself or represented by others, Mutwa signified an indigenous authenticity that resonated with Native American and New Age spirituality. In the popular media of his native South Africa, however, Mutwa has often "been called an old fraud, a charlatan," as journalist Angela Johnson observed.[15] Journalist Hazel Friedman, alluding to Mutwa's complicity with apartheid, the apartheid regime of the National Party, and apartheid structures of South African Bantustans, reported that he has been widely regarded as "a charlatan and opportunist who consorted with the enemy."[16]

In fact, when Mutwa has not been entirely ignored by the South African popular media, he has primarily appeared in stories about his failed predictions as a false prophet who nevertheless continues to predict the future. But how does such a fake produce real effects in the real world? How has Credo Mutwa emerged globally, if not locally, as the supreme bearer of South African indigenous authenticity?

During the 1990s Mutwa was celebrated not only as a Zulu shaman but also as an environmentalist, healer, prophet, teacher, and authority on aliens from outer space. The new religious space opened up by the Internet was crucial to this development. On his own Web site, he appears in cyberspace as "Credo Mutwa, a Small Ray of Hope for Africa."[17] In contrast, on many other Web sites he appears as one of the world's most important shamans. In what follows, I review the historical production of this indigenous authenticity.

AFRICAN ORIGINS

Born in 1921 in the South African province of Natal, Credo Mutwa grew up in a household that was religiously divided between his father's Roman Catholicism and his mother's adherence to African traditional religion. In 1935 his father converted to Christian Science, the American church founded in the nineteenth century by Mary Baker Eddy, who understood God as "Divine Mind," responsible for healing the body, mind, and spirit. Undergoing a serious illness, Mutwa was forbidden conventional medicine in keeping with the Christian Science avoidance of modern medical practice. Instead, his father read to him from the book *Science and Health,* by the "American holy woman."[18] Rejecting his father's "holy woman," Mutwa turned to his mother's family during his crisis. Under their tutelage, he was taught that his illness was not an illusion, as the teachings of Christian Science held, but an entry into a new and special role within African indigenous religion. As Mutwa later recalled, his initiatory sickness signaled his calling to become a *sangoma,* an indigenous healer, diviner, and seer.

In 1954 Mutwa found employment in a curio shop in Johannesburg that specialized in providing African artifacts for the tourist market. Mutwa's employer, A. S. Watkinson, relied on him to authenticate these objects of African art. Besides developing detailed interpretations of the meaning of African artifacts, Mutwa emerged as a gifted and imaginative storyteller, recounting elaborate tales that he insisted were drawn from the authentic repository of Zulu tribal history, legends, customs, and religious beliefs. Sponsored by Watkinson and edited by A. S. Brink, an academic with the Institute for the Study of Man in Africa at the University of the Witwatersrand, a collection of Credo Mutwa's stories was published in 1964 under the title *Indaba, My Children.*

As editor Brink explained, the term *indaba* refers to a Zulu tribal council at which different views are presented "to have their authenticity or acceptability evaluated." Ostensibly, therefore, Mutwa's stories were presented to the reading public to test their authenticity. However, the historical and ethnographic record could provide no help in making such an assessment, because the wild, extravagant, and imaginative poetry and prose of these texts bear little if any relation to anything previously recorded in print about Zulu religion. Nevertheless, rendering his own judgment, Brink advised that these tales are authentic because they reveal the "strange workings of the mind of the African."[19] Three decades later, reviewing the British republication of *Indaba, My Children*, Randolph Vigne could only agree that the entire point of Mutwa's account of Zulu tradition seemed to be "to project an African culture wholly alien to and unassimilable with any other, least of all that of the Europe-descended millions who share South Africa."[20]

This construction of indigenous authenticity certainly fit with the tribalism promoted by apartheid during the 1950s and 1960s. Under the auspices of its policy of separate development, the ruling National Party tried to create new African nations, with their own traditions, histories, languages, cultures, and religions, which would reinforce the establishment of separate homelands, or Bantustans, that were geographically within the territory of South Africa but legally outside the Republic of South Africa. In the case of Zulu nationalism, the Department of Native Affairs, under the direction of apartheid ideologue H. F. Verwoerd and anthropologist W. M. Eiselen, sponsored the first Shaka Day in 1954 to celebrate Zulu tradition. They convinced the Zulu king Cyprian to dress up in a traditional costume of leather loin covering, leopard skin, feathers, and beads, which neither Cyprian nor his father, King Solomon, had ever worn. For this recovery of tradition, Verwoerd and Eiselen had to refer to an illustrated book about Africans that had been published in 1855.[21] In this context, indigenous authenticity was constructed as a tribal continuity with a traditional past that allegedly prevented Africans from integrating into modern South Africa.

Although Mutwa has claimed to have an "unashamedly unpoliticised conscience," his writings in the 1960s clearly reinforced apartheid, a political system that legally excluded all black Africans from citizenship within the Republic of South Africa but nonetheless incorporated them as exploitable labor.[22] Like the architects of apartheid in the National Party, Mutwa argued that apartheid was not racial discrimination but racial separation that was consistent with divine and natural law. "Discrimination is to distinguish and decide which is best," Mutwa wrote. "Apartheid is to distinguish without deciding which is best." Insisting that Africans in South Africa actually wanted apartheid and were not interested in equal rights, Mutwa declared, "Apartheid is the High Law of the Gods! It is the highest law of nature!" Racial integration, according to Mutwa, "is as abhorrent as extermination." Praising Verwoerd, who by then had become president of South Africa, Mutwa maintained, "White men of South Africa are only too right when they wish to preserve their pure-bred racial identity. And what is good enough for them is good enough for us, the Bantu. . . . Separate Development . . . is the clearest hope that the Bantu have thus far had." Under apartheid, Verwoerd's National Party promised to protect independent African homelands from "Communists or militant Bantu rebellion-mongers" such as the African National Congress.[23]

Into the 1980s, Mutwa continued to lend his support to the apartheid regime, even writing the foreword to a book published in 1989, arguing that the United States should not impose sanctions on South Africa. Instead, the United States should embrace South Africa and consider making the country its fifty-first state. As he had argued in the 1960s, Mutwa insisted that such protection would save Africans from communists, militants, and rebels such as "the ANC terrorists."[24] Under the apartheid regime of the 1960s and the neo-apartheid regime of the 1980s, Credo Mutwa's only concern was that Africans should be free to preserve their distinctive tribal customs and their traditional way of life.

In his publications of the 1960s, Credo Mutwa declared himself the guardian of Zulu tribal tradition. Referring to himself as a Zulu witchdoctor, he related a bewildering array of traditional tales, which he himself characterized as "a strange mixture of truth and nonsense," showing a remarkable facility for literary invention. Mutwa's presentation drew its authority from a careful balance of transparency and secrecy. On the one hand, he claimed that he was relating common African folk traditions, the familiar "stories that old men and old women tell to boys and girls seated with open mouths around the spark-wreathed fire in the center of the villages in the dark forests and on the aloe-scented plains of Africa."[25] If this assertion were true, then the authenticity of these stories could presumably be confirmed by every African man, woman, and child.

On the other hand, Mutwa also claimed to be relating secrets that were revealed only during the initiation of a witchdoctor. "If ever you pass what you are about to be told today on to the ears of the aliens," his instructor had warned him during his own initiation, "a curse shall fall upon you." By publishing these stories, including a word-for-word account of all the secrets conveyed during his initiation, Mutwa had clearly broken his sacred tribal oath of secrecy. As he put it, he had made a "terrible choice to betray my High Oath as a Chosen One."[26] Although this betrayal apparently violated the source of his authority, Mutwa nevertheless asserted his role as traitor, as if it underwrote the authenticity of his accounts of Zulu folk religion.[27]

CULTURE AND NATURE

During the 1970s, Credo Mutwa was employed by the South African National Parks Board as the attendant of a traditional African tourist village he had created in the black township of Soweto, outside Johannesburg. Designed for the entertainment of foreign visitors, this display of "authentic" African religion, culture, and traditions was generally ignored by Africans. Above the entrance, Mutwa inscribed the warning: "ALL LIARS, ATHEISTS, SKEPTICS AND FOOLS MUST PLEASE KEEP OUT!" As American journalist Joseph Lelyveld observed, anyone who passed through the entrance found "a shrine that seemed to derive its inspiration partly from the cult of the avenging Hindu goddess Kali and partly from Disney World."[28] Struck by the eclectic and idiosyncratic symbolism on display, Lelyveld called into question the authenticity of this tourist attraction.

Like his writings, Mutwa's African village in Soweto evoked the strangeness of Africa. During the black-consciousness uprising of 1976, African students attacked Mutwa's shrine, burning its huts, carvings, and other artifacts, because they saw his tourist village as promoting the tribalism of apartheid and separate development. Although Mutwa eventually had to abandon his shrine and leave Soweto in 1978, the Credo Mutwa Village remained on the tourist itinerary into the 1990s, with its burned and blackened features, as one tourist agency declared, "lending the village an eerie atmosphere."[29]

During the 1980s, Mutwa established a larger and more ambitious tourist attraction within the South African Bantustan of Bophuthatswana, an African nation that was recognized by the apartheid regime in South Africa but not by any other nation in the world. At Lotlamoreng Dam Cultural Park, beginning in 1983, Mutwa supervised the construction of small adobe villages, each representing the traditional culture of one of South Africa's tribal African peoples, among them the Tswana, Zulu, Ndebele, Xhosa, and southern Sotho groups. Around these displays, Mutwa erected clay statues of African deities, most prominently a twenty-foot-tall African goddess. Praising Lucas Mangope, the president of Bophuthatswana, Mutwa declared, "Anyone who gives me the opportunity to rebuild the African past knows what he is doing."[30] Following the first democratic elections of 1994 and the reincorporation of Bophuthatswana into South Africa, the cultural park was deemed to belong to the National Parks Board, and Mutwa was expelled. By August 1995, as anthropologists Jean and John Comaroff found, the cultural village had become an informal settlement whose people lived in and around the various tribal displays.[31]

Moving to the Eastern Cape, Credo Mutwa was employed by the Shamwari Game Reserve, near Port Elizabeth, where he sold African artifacts such as sacred necklaces, headdresses, icons, and implements used in rituals. "In the Zulu tradition," according to the publicity for the reserve, "each of these artifacts must be kept alive by being used in a sacred way on a regular basis."[32] Accordingly, Mutwa was charged with the responsibility of performing the rituals that would keep these objects alive for the tourist market. In addition to authenticating African artifacts, Mutwa presided over the creation of a traditional African arts and culture village, Khaya Lendaba, the "Place of Enlightening Talk," next to the Shamwari Born Free Conservation and Education Center. Once the cultural village was built, however, Mutwa was forced to leave.

Although he left under uncertain circumstances, the merger of culture and nature at Shamwari defined a new role for Mutwa as an indigenous environmentalist. In August 1997, Mutwa received the Audi Terra Nova Award for his contribution to wildlife conservation at the Shamwari Game Reserve. The patron of the award, the conservationist Ian Player, identified Mutwa as the "sole surviving Sanusi, the highest grade of spiritual healer."[33] Mutwa then lent his support to various environmental causes. In 1997, he spoke at the Sixth International Whale and Dolphin Conference, sponsored by the International Cetacean Education Research Centre, in Queensland, Australia, relating traditions about the special relationship between Africans and whales and dolphins.[34] In 1999, he spoke at the Living Lakes Conference, sponsored by the U.S. Forest Service at the Mono Lake Visitor's Center, in Lee Vining, California, recounting indigenous African traditions about sacred lakes.[35] Proponents of animal rights found an indigenous African defender of animals in Mutwa. Speaking of an apartheid-like separation between human beings and animals, he observed, "Apartheid is dead, but 'separatism' is alive and well."[36] Environmentalists, conservationists, and animal-rights activists alike found Mutwa's aura of authenticity useful in the service of their causes.

At the heart of his claim to authenticity, Mutwa has insisted that he possesses specialized indigenous knowledge that can be used in healing, divination, education, and social transformation. However, as a prophet, seer, and master of African techniques of divination, Mutwa has remained a target of ridicule in the popular press. A feature discrediting the prophet seems to run at the beginning of every year. For instance, in January 2000 the *Sunday Times* observed, "Soothsayer Credo Mutwa got it wrong last year."[37] Nevertheless, Mutwa has lent his credibility to indigenous cures for AIDS, divination workshops, business training, educational programs, and even crime prevention, such as in the previously discussed organization of criminologist Don Pinnock, formed to rehabilitate gangsters by creating "richer, more ritual-filled gang-like groups."[38]

In all of these ventures, the indigenous authenticity of Credo Mutwa was appropriated to establish the validity of specific projects. Whatever its origins, Mutwa's authenticity became a valuable commodity in local and global projects for the construction of alternative realities.

During the 1990s, the new medium of the Internet changed the terrain for promoting cultural tourism. As previously noted, some of Mutwa's artwork, a depiction of the Yoruba god, Shango, decorated the Web site of TheAfrican.Com, which credited him as "His Holiness Credo Mutwa, Zulu Sanussi *[sic]* of South Africa."[39] This site is one indication that Mutwa's indigenous authenticity has become global on the Internet through his religious legitimization of an indigenous culture supposedly shared by Africans all over the world. Although he presided over a series of failed cultural villages in South Africa, Credo Mutwa has played an important role in a new global cultural village on the Internet.

ALIEN ENCOUNTERS

In his writings of the early 1960s, Mutwa referred to aliens and "the Strange Ones" who came from outside Africa. Beginning with the ancient Phoenicians, the Strange Ones arrived in unfamiliar ships from unknown lands across the sea, just as European colonizers later arrived to establish alien empires in Africa. In the postcolonial era, as Mutwa advised, Africans had to resist the "schemes of the Strange Ones," which included communism and parliamentary democracy—though apparently not the divine and natural law of apartheid—by maintaining indigenous African traditions.[40] In these terms, indigenous authenticity was established in opposition to the aliens and Strange Ones who came from other lands.

During the 1990s, however, Mutwa used the term *aliens* for beings from outer space, those extraterrestrials that supposedly feature prominently in African myths, legends, and traditions. According to Mutwa, Africans have long known about many species of extraterrestrials. Some are evil, bringing harm to human beings, such as the Muhondoruka, fifteen-foot-tall, cylindrical, columnlike creatures who cause violence, or the Mutende-ya-ngenge (also known as Sekgotswana and Puhwana), green creatures, with large heads, chalk-white faces, and large green eyes, who capture people, cut them up, and put them back together again. The most dangerous aliens, however, are the Mantindane, who are "star monkeys" and "tormenters"; the powerful extraterrestrial reptiles known as the Chitauri; and the Greys, the small servants of the Chitauri. The Chitauri's evil schemes to harm humanity include their support of institutionalized religions. "They like religious fanatics," he observed. "Ones who are burdened with too much religion are very popular with the Chitauri."[41] Working through institutionalized religions, the evil Chitauri seek to divide and conquer human beings.

In contrast to these dangerous aliens, other extraterrestrials are good. The

Mvonjina are three-foot-tall creatures, who look like a "caricature of a white person" and act as "a messenger of the gods" by bringing knowledge to humanity. Other races of beneficent extraterrestrials frequently appearing in Africa included the friendly Sikasa, the timid Mmkungateka, the beloved Nafu, and the apelike Mbembi. Besides trying to communicate with human beings, these aliens from outer space have often mated with African women. "There have been many women throughout Africa in various centuries who have attested to the fact that they have been fertilized by strange creatures from somewhere."[42] Although apartheid had criminalized interracial relations in South Africa, aliens from outer space were apparently engaging in interspecies sexual relations throughout Africa.

By his own account, Mutwa has experienced many encounters with extraterrestrial beings. As early as 1951, in what is now Botswana, he witnessed a falling star, a strange vehicle in the sky, and two alien creatures disappearing into the spaceship. In the bush where the spaceship had landed, these aliens left behind extraterrestrial rubbish. Along with the local people who witnessed this event, Mutwa made sure the rubbish was buried. "That is the African tradition," he explained.[43] He also encountered a variety of aliens from outer space in Kenya and what are now Zimbabwe and Zambia during his travels in the 1950s. In addition to seeing extraterrestrials, he claims to have eaten them, describing the smell and taste of their cooked flesh. According to Mutwa, the ritual consumption of extraterrestrial flesh has been common in Africa, sometimes causing severe illness, but other times resulting in mind-altering experiences of great beauty, harmony, and transcendence.

Visiting what is now Zimbabwe in 1959, Mutwa underwent his most dramatic encounter with extraterrestrials. While digging for medicinal herbs, he was suddenly confronted by five "little fellows," strange, unfamiliar beings, small dull-gray creatures with large heads but thin arms and legs, who captured him and took him to a metallic room shaped like a tunnel, where they probed and tested his body. The aliens then forced him to have sex with a female of their species, an experience that Mutwa reported as cold, clinical, and humiliating. "I felt like a victim at a sacrifice," he recalled.[44] After this ordeal, he was deposited back on Earth, with his clothing torn, only to discover that he had been missing for three days.

On the basis of these encounters, Credo Mutwa emerged as an authority on extraterrestrial beings. In a book on alien abductions, Professor John Mack of Harvard University devoted a chapter to Mutwa's meetings with beings from outer space. Although Mutwa recounted his humiliating treatment by his extraterrestrial tormenters, he stressed the positive potential of human exchanges with

aliens. "I just get furious," he declared, "because the people from the stars are trying to give us knowledge, but we are too stupid."[45] As confirmation of his global
recognition as an authority on aliens from other worlds, Mutwa was invited to
deliver the keynote address at the international Conference on Extraterrestrial
Intelligence in Australia during March 2001.

In establishing Mutwa as an African authority on extraterrestrials, David Icke,
the New Age conspiracy theorist, played a significant role. As discussed in chapter 6, Icke developed a distinctive blend of personal spirituality and political paranoia that he promoted through books, public lectures, and an elaborate Web site.
Although he seemed to embrace every conspiracy theory, Icke identified the central, secret conspiracy ruling the world as the work of shape-shifting reptilians
from outer space. These extraterrestrial reptiles interbred with human beings,
establishing a lineage that can be traced through the pharaohs of ancient Egypt,
the Merovingian dynasty of medieval Europe, the current British royal family, and
every president of the United States. Although they plot behind the scenes in the
secret society of the Illuminati, the aliens of these hybrid bloodlines are in prominent positions of royal, political, and economic power all over the world.
Occasionally shifting into their lizardlike form, they maintain a human appearance
by regularly drinking human blood, which they acquire by performing rituals of
human sacrifice.

In *The Biggest Secret*, which was dedicated to Credo Mutwa, David Icke invoked
the authority of the Zulu shaman to confirm this conspiracy theory about blood-
drinking, shape-shifting reptiles from outer space. Reportedly Mutwa declared,
"To know the Illuminati, Mr. David, you must study the reptile."[46] In a two-volume
video produced and distributed by Icke, *The Reptilian Agenda,* Mutwa confirmed
that extraterrestrials, the Chitauri, are a shape-shifting reptilian race that has controlled humanity for thousands of years. Icke and Mutwa also appeared together on
a popular American radio program, *Sightings,* to explain the alien reptile conspiracy. In his lectures in the United States, Icke insisted that Mutwa provided proof
for his conspiracy theory, as one observer noted, in the "pure voice of a primitive
belief system." In Mutwa, David Icke found indigenous authentication for an alien
conspiracy.[47]

FOLK RELIGION, FAKE RELIGION

In retracing his long journey from Zulu witchdoctor to New Age shaman, I have
highlighted Credo Mutwa's ongoing reinvention of himself in relation to different

appropriations of his authority. As we have seen, during the 1950s Mutwa was used to authenticate African artifacts for a curio shop in Johannesburg. Through his writings in the 1960s, his tourist attraction in Soweto in the 1970s, and his cultural village in Bophuthatswana in the 1980s, he was used to authenticate the racial, cultural, and religious separations of apartheid. During the 1990s, as he acquired the label "shaman" through the interventions of Bradford Keeney, Stephen Larsen, David Icke, and other exponents of New Age spirituality, Mutwa's authority was invoked to authenticate a diverse array of enterprises in saving the world from human exploitation, environmental degradation, epidemic illness, endemic ignorance, organized crime, and extraterrestrial conspiracy. In all of these projects, the indigenous authenticity of Mutwa added value, credibility, and force because he represented the "pure voice," untainted by modernity, of an unmediated access to primordial truth.

As I have tried to suggest, this assumption about Credo Mutwa's indigenous authenticity is problematic because of the very history through which that aura of authenticity has been produced. Unfamiliar with the details of that history, Mutwa's supporters in the United States have transformed his weaknesses into strengths. For example, Mutwa has been enthusiastically promoted by the African American feminist Luisah Teish, who has her own Web site, Jambalaya Spirit, celebrating feminist myths and rituals. According to Teish, Mutwa provides access to "authentic material from an elder, a wise man, a medicine man of the Zulu culture!"

Mutwa's authenticity is certified, in Teish's view, by the purity of his poetics and politics. In his storytelling, she observes, Mutwa conveys "real knowledge about South Africa that was not polluted by some anthropologist's opinion."[48] Of course, Mutwa's accounts of Zulu traditions and traditional symbols, myths, legends, rituals, and customs might be unpolluted by any anthropological opinion, bearing no relation to any historical or ethnographic account, because he invented them. Not only an inventive poet and narrator of fiction, Mutwa is an accomplished playwright, featuring in the history of black theater in South Africa.[49] Although Teish claimed that Mutwa's accounts are pure because they are untainted by anthropological interference, she might just as well have argued that his accounts are pure because they are purely fictional inventions.

At the same time, Teish praised Mutwa for the purity of his politics, locating him at the forefront of the struggle against apartheid, even suggesting that his indigenous African religious vision and mythology were necessary for "filling out and complementing Mandela's political journey."[50] But Mutwa's mythology cannot be seen as complementing Mandela's struggle for political liberation from apartheid oppression. Again, from the 1960s through the 1980s, Mutwa opposed Mandela's African National Congress as terrorists, communists, and "Bantu rebellion-mongers." By positioning Mandela and Mutwa as if they were complementary, Luisah Teish substantially misrepresented the history through which Mutwa's authenticity was produced as an adjunct of apartheid. Like other appropriations of his indigenous authenticity, this celebration of Mutwa's poetics and politics erased the entangled details of his history in the interest of isolating him as the living embodiment of an eternal, timeless African tradition.

These appropriations of Credo Mutwa raise important problems for any assessment of indigenous authenticity in religion and American popular culture. In conclusion, I highlight only two issues that require further reflection as we wrestle with the ordeal of adjudicating authenticity. Let us say, for the sake of argument, that Credo Mutwa is a fake, a fraud, a charlatan, as the South African media would have it, rather than the authentic voice of indigenous African religion, as he appears in cyberspace. Even if he is a fake, we are still faced with the problem of analyzing what Mutwa has really been doing in the field of indigenous African religion. Even a fake, as I will suggest in conclusion, can be doing something authentic.

First, even a fake religion can draw upon recurring, enduring motifs of indigenous religion. Although often assumed to be timeless, deriving its authenticity from the faithful repetition of discourses and practices that have persisted from time immemorial, indigenous religion, like any form of religious life, has reformers, reformulators, and innovators. Credo Mutwa, it might be argued, is precisely such an innovator in African religion. Like the eighteenth-century English poet William Blake, who adapted recurring pagan and Christian mythic motifs to create his own innovative, creative, and idiosyncratic religious mythology, Mutwa has drawn upon recurring patterns and processes of indigenous African religious life to produce an innovative mythology that ranges from the original earth goddess to the ultimate encounters of human beings with aliens from outer space.

Certainly, neither the goddess nor the extraterrestrials in this mythology simply preserve African indigenous religion. Instead, against the background of an indigenous religious landscape, these mythological inventions create new possibilities for African religion in the contemporary world. During the 1990s, widespread enthusiasm for these inventions was evident on the Internet. In cyberspace, any line that might divide folk religion from fake religion has been blurred. As a religious figure representing both indigenous authenticity and innovative applications, Credo Mutwa is perfectly suited, even if he is a fake, for playing a significant role in the emerging productions of different forms of folk religion on the Internet.

Second, even a fake religion can do real religious work by establishing the kinds of relations among superhuman beings, subhuman beings, and human beings that are worked out in any religion. In the case of Credo Mutwa, these classifications have been central to his ongoing creative work in redefining African indigenous religion. As a religious innovator, he has constantly called attention to the importance of these basic classifications, not by reifying them, but by emphasizing the creative exchanges among them.

Although the basic distinction among superhuman deities, subhuman animals, and human beings might seem stable, Mutwa has always worked to put those fundamental classifications at risk. Speaking at a whale and dolphin conference in 1997, for example, he urged his listeners to rethink these classifications. "Some time during the long journey of human history, there comes a time when human beings must stop thinking like animals, must stop thinking like perishable beings, must stop thinking out of greed, fear and ignorance. The time has come for all of us to think like Gods, to act like Gods, to speak like Gods, but to remain humanly humble."[51] Although he exhorted human beings to be like superhuman gods, Mutwa also insisted that representatives of Western civilization, who have consistently treated Africans as if they were a subhuman species (as he noted during the 1960s in *Indaba, My Children*), have falsely arrogated to themselves a supremely superhuman status. As Mutwa told Harvard researcher John Mack, "The entire Western civilization is based upon a blatant lie, the lie that we human beings are the cocks of the walk in the world, the lie that we human beings are the highest evolved forms in this world, and that we are alone and that beyond us there is nothing."[52]

Mutwa's reports about extraterrestrials, therefore, might be regarded as reinforcing this challenge to the "superhuman" status of Western human beings. Consistent with any measure of authenticity within religion, Mutwa was doing real religious work by mediating among superhuman, subhuman, and human beings in the world.

These classifications, like any religious classifications, represent religious mediations that can be situated in history. As I have tried to suggest, Mutwa's innovations in African folk religion can be located in a history that stretches over fifty years, from the enforced separations of apartheid to the fluid connections of the Internet. Briefly reviewing that history, I have tried to raise the problems involved in adjudicating the authenticity of this self-proclaimed representative of African indigenous religion.

If we assume that he is the real thing, we might conclude that Credo Mutwa is an exemplar of indigenous African folk religion in South Africa, which has been misappropriated by the global fake religion on the Internet. However, recalling that he has been generally dismissed within South Africa as a fake, a fraud, a charlatan, we must recognize that Mutwa has achieved a greater aura of authenticity in cyberspace than in Africa. At every stage in his personal history, Mutwa has found that his indigenous authenticity had to be certified by aliens, from apartheid ideologues to New Age conspiracy theorists, who have appropriated his aura of indigenous authenticity for their own projects. Throughout his long career, the line between folk religion and fake religion has been consistently blurred through this ongoing interchange between indigenous inventions and alien appropriations of authenticity. In the end, these exchanges suggest that Credo Mutwa has been most authentic when he has been used, claimed, or even abducted by aliens.

TRICKS OF THE TRADE

The shaman, as anthropologist Michael Taussig has argued, is not a fraud, skilled in deception. Rather, the shaman, working on behalf of a community, is skilled in the artful, careful revelation of deception. A shaman's art, in this respect, lies "not in skilled concealment but in the skilled revelation of skilled concealment." Part of the shaman's power, therefore, is derived from controlling what counts as authenticity.[53]

Notions of cultural authenticity, developed in eighteenth-century England, became fixated on originality, authorship, and copyright. Simultaneously cultural and legal, these indicators of authenticity could in principle be adjudicated in a court of law. Notorious cultural fakes, such as James McPherson's "translations" of the indigenous Scottish epics of Ossian, which were actually fabricated by McPherson himself, inspired the search for cultural, as well as legal, grounds for establishing authenticity and identifying the "crimes of writing."[54]

By the end of the twentieth century, however, under globalizing conditions, crime could be legitimate creativity, at least within the musical world of hip-hop, where creativity has sometimes involved sampling, arguably stealing, the copyrighted musical material of earlier artists.

Coming from the streets of New York City, emerging from the culture of criminal gangs, the founder of hip-hop in the late 1970s adopted the name Afrika Bambaataa and formed his musical group, the Zulu Nation. Stylistically, the Zulu Nation revitalized the rhythmic, percussive, and polyphonic heritage of an African original while sampling sounds from popular American music. In these musical negotiations, both original and derivative, Afrika Bambaataa initiated a new cultural contest over the ownership of the sacred riffs, licks, bass figures, and drum rhythms of Africa and America. Establishing his Zulu Nation on "Planet Rock," long before anyone had thought of Planet Hollywood, Afrika Bambaataa succeeded in fashioning an authentic African style that was also firmly located in America.

As Robin Sylvan has documented, hip-hop artists have attributed profound religious significance to this music. Finding God, finding community, and finding Africa in hip-hop, performers and audiences have regarded the music as an authentically religious art form.[55]

According to David Brooks, some white Americans have the luxury to search for religious authenticity in a Zulu shaman, in the Zulu Nation of hip-hop, or in the folk culture of indigenous people at home or abroad. Brooks identifies these Americans as bourgeois bohemians, the "Bobos in Paradise," who want to "get away from their affluent, ascending selves into a spiritually superior world." In that quest for authenticity, they value "People Who Really Know How to Live—people who make folk crafts, tell folk tales, do folk dances, listen to folk music."[56]

Within the United States, of course, Native Americans and African Americans have borne the burden of focus in such folkloric quests for authenticity, but only if they do not represent a real threat to Euro-American reality. Certainly, hip-hop artists, beginning with the Zulu Nation of Afrika Bambaataa, have been aware of the problem of indigenous authenticity in America. And certainly, they have refused to be harmless. They have refused to succumb to the fate of indigenous people, artists, and shamans appearing at tourist attractions all over the world, who have been rendered harmless as commodities for spiritual consumption.

In the United States, as the historian of religions Jim Perkinson has argued, the shaman has characteristically been portrayed as a person of color, whether African, Native American, or exotic; and black Americans, in this exchange, have generated the vital, vitalizing, and shamanic creativity of America. From African cave art to American inner-city graffiti, as Perkinson has suggested, shamanic impulses have operated in religion and American popular culture.[57] Like any writing on the wall, the authenticity of these cultural productions is just there, but also just there for appropriation.

CHAPTER TEN

· Virtual Religion

"So far as religion of the day is concerned," the great American inventor Thomas Edison declared, "it is a damned fake." Bluntly he insisted, "Religion is all bunk." Ironically, perhaps, for an inventor, Edison dismissed all religion as fake because he found that it is all invented. "All Bibles are man-made," he held, suggesting that the basis of religious authority in every religion is not divine intervention but human invention. In this skeptical dismissal, Edison placed religion in a difficult double bind: If a religion claims supernatural authority, it is lying; accordingly, its proponents are devious frauds. If a religion tells the truth by acknowledging it is man-made, then it is not a religion, so proponents who claim the status of religion for such an artifice are also devious frauds. Either way, religion is all bunk, all a damned fake.[1]

If all religion is fake, then the problem of distinguishing between religious authenticity and fakery is easily solved. No religion is authentic, unless by "authentic" we mean something like "really, truly, and genuinely fraudulent." Still, in the study of religion we occasionally have to confront outright frauds, religious fakes who deliberately deceive the public, a community, or a clientele with their religious claims, such as the alleged con artists of Greater Ministries International, the Baptist Foundation of Arizona, and IRM Corporation, with their Christian Ponzi and "affinity fraud" schemes, in some cases audited by the same accounting firm that reviewed the books at Enron, which by the end of 2001 had resulted in legal proceedings in twenty-seven U.S. states.[2] In such cases of religious fraud, the adjudication is easy: Take them to court, convict them, and lock them up.

Occasionally, however, we encounter religious frauds that are more difficult to adjudicate. During the eighteenth century in London, for example, the literary con man George Psalmanaazaar produced an entirely fake account of the society, culture, and religion of the island of Formosa. As anthropologist Rodney Needham argued, the temporary success of this fraud can be attributed to Psalmanaazaar's ability to make his fake account of the religion of Formosa look very much like a recognizable religion or at least one that would fit expectations of an "exotic" religion among his readers in England.[3] Such fraudulent productions of authenticity require a careful mediation between extraordinary accounts, which cannot be independently confirmed or disconfirmed, and ordinary expectations about the primitive, the savage, or the exotic. In this work of mediation, successful frauds in the study of religion have acted as intercultural brokers speaking in the name of silent partners who bear the burden of authenticity. Others of these intercultural mediations of authenticity have also taken some time and effort to be exposed as fraudulent, such as Eugen Herrigel's representations of the Zen master Kenzo Awa, or Carlos Castaneda's account of the Yaqui shaman don Juan Matus, or the English corset-maker Cyril Hoskin's promotion of himself as if he were the Tibetan Buddhist master Lobsang Rampa.[4] Although they still have defenders, careful research has exposed them as fakes.

In other cases, however, fraudulence or authenticity is very difficult to determine. If we critically review the exchanges between John Neihardt and Black Elk or between Marcel Griaule and Ogotemmeli, for example, we have to conclude that these accounts of indigenous religion were produced from specific intercultural mediations rather than through any extraordinary, unmediated access to authentic indigenous Sioux or Dogon religion.[5]

As these examples suggest, indigenous, popular, and folk religions have often borne the burden of authenticity. In the modern era, these "elementary forms of religious life" have carried an aura of authenticity because they evoke the organic religious life of a rural peasantry rather than the urban citizenry, the lower class rather than the elite, the ordinary people rather than the clergy. In the process of its production as a category, however, folk religion was appropriated, reproduced, and arguably reinvented by urban, literate elites within modern societies, to lend an aura of authenticity to emerging nationalisms. These "invented traditions" transformed folklore into what has been called *fakelore* in the service of various nationalist interests.[6] So, even fakelore or fake religion, although invented, mobilized, and deployed by frauds, can produce real effects in the real world.

Dilemmas posed by fake religion, I propose, go to the heart of whatever we might want to mean by religion. As we recall, the Latin term *religio,* whatever it meant, was inevitably defined in antiquity as the opposite of *superstitio,* which was understood as conduct based on ignorance, fear, and fraud.[7] Superstition, as fake religion, represented both the defining opposite and the defining limit of religious authenticity. This problem of the opposition between superstition and religion, between alleged fraud and assumed authenticity, has persisted in the constitution of what counts as religion in modernity.

As historian of religions Charles H. Long has observed, "The problematical status of religion itself as an authentic and even necessary mode of human experience and expression is an acute issue of the modern period."[8] Situated among different modern disputations, such as Christian interreligious polemic, European colonial denials of indigenous religion, and Enlightenment critiques of original religion, this crisis of authenticity has been central to the problem of religion in the modern world.

Pursuing the problem of religious authenticity, I want to highlight the productions of fake religion, focusing on the proliferation of invented religions, or "virtual religions," on the Internet. New religions in cyberspace, such as the Discordians, the Church of the SubGenius, the Wauists, the Church of the Covert Cosmos, the Church of Elvis, the Church of the Almighty Dollar, the Vendramists, and the Church of Virus, along with many other virtual religions, have indeed flourished. With over 150 virtual religions featured on their own Web sites, the formation of new religions has been an increasingly popular activity among Internet discussion groups; for instance, the Yahoo Groups devoted to "parody religions" expanded from about 120 in mid-2001 to over 400 by mid-2002. As indigenous religions of cyberspace, virtual religions defy conventional religious sanctions, colonial containments, and Enlightenment standards of clarity and discipline. Looking just like religions, these virtual religions on the Internet raise the problem of religious authenticity even when they are obviously fake, because they present themselves as real religions.

RELIGIOUS AUTHENTICITY

Establishing terms and conditions for religious authenticity, it might be assumed, is the prerogative of any religious community, defining orthodoxy against heresy, defending orthopraxy against invalid rites or deviant behavior. For example, eighth-century Roman Catholic attempts to define religious authenticity in Europe required ongoing struggles against alternative Christian claims, such as one by a

Christian leader in Francia, who purportedly had received a letter from Jesus, and claims arising from alternative religions such as Islam, whose prophet was represented in Christian polemic as an epileptic madman, a sexual deviant, and a political tyrant acting under the cover of religion.[9] In opposition to Islam, this allegation of fraud persisted, implicating the Prophet in the crime of "imposing a fake religion on mankind," as an eighteenth-century English author put it.[10] Whether directed against "internal" or "external" competition, these allegations of fraud certified authenticity by identifying alternatives and their proponents as fakes, charlatans, or imposters.

The European Enlightenment, with its demystifying rationality, dedicated to exposing concealment, took up the challenge of exposing the illusion, deception, and artifice of religion. Enlightened reason worked hard to expose fakes and imposters, forgeries and counterfeits, deceptions and delusions, hallucinations and illusions. As the historian of American religion Leigh Schmidt has observed, the effort to trace the origin of religion back to fraud provided the basic terms for the most popular theory of religion during the Enlightenment.[11] The fraud of priestcraft, by this account, produced religious illusions by playing on popular ignorance of scientific causation and fear of the unknown. Effectively, this argument recast the definition of religion by conflating it with the received definition of the opposite of religion, superstition, reducing both to ignorance, fear, and fraud.

During the eighteenth century, however, Enlightenment rationalists and Christian devotionalists seemed to agree on two criteria of authenticity: transparency and control. Obviously, rationalists exposed religious claims to the transparency of reason. On the devotional side, Jonathan Edwards's reflections on the exercises of religious affections, which were most evident in hearing mysterious voices and uttering strange sounds, posed the crucial problem of how to distinguish "counterfeit religion" from "true religion." Invoking the ideal of transparency, Edwards promised that "God will give much greater light to his people to distinguish between true religion and its counterfeits."[12] Authenticity, in this case, depended on an illuminated capacity for discerning genuine from artificial religion.

The second criterion of authenticity, control, resided in the disciplinary management of the senses. Here, hearing merged with tactility, a tactility in which hearing and speaking were subject to discipline as a measure of their authenticity. An entire Christian discipline for marking the dividing line between true and counterfeit religion could be derived from the implications of the discipline of the tongue set out in the New Testament Letter of James (1:26; 3:8). "Where the tongue is not governed," as Charles G. Finney sermonized in 1845, "there is and can be no true religion."[13] Certainly, the exuberance of evangelical revivals, which were "demonstrative and loud," raised questions about the governance of the tongue. Religion produced loud murmurs, sighs, moans, groans, cries, and shouts, the kinds of noise that Michel de Certeau identified as "sounds waiting for language," those "'obscene' citations of bodies," the unverbalizable "sounds of the body."[14]

Enlightenment rationalists and Christian devotionalists found common cause in the disciplinary management not only of speech but also of relatively uncontrolled bodily eruptions, the "unverbalizable" sounds of the body—belching, farting, sneezing, laughing, and so on—which provided grounds for determining authenticity. Norbert Elias, in his classic treatment of these matters in *The Civilizing Process*, proposed that authenticity required a certain degree of artifice when dealing with flatulence. "If it is possible to withdraw, it should be done alone," Erasmus of Rotterdam wrote in 1530. "But if not, in accordance with the ancient proverb, let a cough hide the sound." Two hundred years later, the disciplinary management of flatulence was all pretense and control, as La Salle instructed in 1729: "It is very impolite to emit wind from your body when in company, either from above or from below, even without noise; and it is shameful and indecent to do it in a way that can be heard by others." Authenticity, in this case, was based not on transparency but on a disciplinary control of embodied sounds.[15]

In the case of sneezing, we find a relatively uncontrolled bodily eruption that became subject to the disciplinary tests of authenticity implicit in the civilizing process during the modern era. In the "craze for sneezing" among the privileged classes of Europe and North America, which was aided and abetted by the use of snuff, sneezing became a status symbol, an important part of men's conversation, a sound that could be interpreted as a sign of disapproval, lack of interest, or boredom in upper-class rituals of speaking and listening. Something regarded as worthwhile was "not to be sneezed at." Moving from civilized affectation to primitive superstition, E. B. Tylor, the father of anthropology, portrayed the cultural significance of sneezing as a savage survival of the primitive doctrine of invading and pervading spirits he called animism. In his classic text of 1871, *Primitive Culture*, Tylor noted that the interpretation of sneezing among the Zulu, for example, recalled a primordial human soundscape in which "the explanation of sneezing had not yet been given over to physiology, but was still in the 'theological stage.'"[16]

Laughter is another sound that can register as a relatively uncontrolled bodily eruption, as something that both pietists and skeptics might try to control. While the Methodists were trying to restrain laughter, placing proscriptions upon "all lightness, jesting, and foolish talking," their evangelical camp meetings were erupting in holy laughter.[17] At the same time, while enlightened skeptics were developing a new seriousness, they were experimenting with the strange sounds that could be induced by nitrous oxide and hydrogen gas. In the disciplinary control of laughter, the devout and the skeptic could find common cause in identifying things that should not be heard. As a politics of authenticity, this embodied discipline might have prevented both "from grasping theoretically the nature of ambivalent festive laughter," but it nevertheless provided shared terms in which authenticity could be adjudicated through bodily control.[18]

A politics of authenticity based on visual transparency and embodied discipline excludes not only the ambivalence of festive laughter but also the laughter-inducing incongruity of irony and satire. Jonathan Swift, a satirist and student of religion, advanced a critique of both intellectual transparency and bodily control in his account of the religion of the Aeolians, as told in *A Tale of a Tub,* which transformed farting and belching into a hierophany.

In documenting the religion of the Aeolians, who are devoted to the deity of wind, Swift depicted a devotional religion of holy sound that resists any transparency of meaning. According to Aeolist doctrine, "words are but wind; and learning is nothing but words; *ergo* learning is nothing but wind."[19] For this reason, the holy teachings of the Aeolians are delivered not by words but by wind from the belly, by the eructation of belching and farting. "The wise Aeolists," as Swift recounts, "affirm the gift of belching to be the noblest act of a rational creature." Accordingly, "their belches were received as sacred."

A regular ritual reinforces the sacred meaning and power of wind. When the Aeolist priest enters a barrel, "a secret funnel is also conveyed from his posterior to the bottom of the barrel." Recalling the preoccupation with ventriloquism as the origin of religion in Enlightenment theories, Swift's account of this ritual satirized the devotional sounds and uncontrolled bodily eruptions of religious enthusiasm. "It is in this guise the sacred Aeolist delivers his oracular belches to his panting disciples; of whom some are greedily gaping after the sanctified breath, others are the while hymning out the praises of the winds; and, gently wafted to and fro by their own humming, do thus represent the soft breezes of their deities appeased." Swift's satire assumed the basic horizon but also challenged the basic principles of religious authenticity: transparency and control. Against the background of a religious authenticity that required transparent speech and bodily discipline, the Aeolians stood in dramatic contrast, by passing wind rather than speaking words and by farting openly rather than retiring secretly to ensure that such an indecent bodily eruption was not heard by others.

By inventing the religion of the Aeolians, Swift seemed to be anticipating the kinds of "fake" religions that would develop within the new medium of the Internet. Although the World Wide Web has provided new avenues of communication for conventional, recognized religions, it has also become an arena for the extraordinary proliferation of new, invented religions that challenge any assumptions about adjudicating authenticity by means of establishing standards of verbal transparency or embodied control. In some respects, these new Internet religions were anticipated by the anarchistic artistic movements of surrealism, Dada, and the Beat generation, including the public graffiti art of Jean-Michel Basquiat, who began his career in 1978 by inventing a religion devoted to the deity SAMO (from Same Ol' Shit) and tagging New York City with the religious promises that "SAMO SAVES IDIOTS" and "SAMO IS AN END TO MINDWASH."[20]

Virtual religions were also anticipated by invented religions in popular fiction, especially science fiction, where new religions, such as the Fordianism of Aldous Huxley's *Brave New World,* the Bokononism of Kurt Vonnegut's *Cat's Cradle,* and the Church of All Worlds of Robert A. Heinlein's *Stranger in a Strange Land,* were created to look just like conventional religions, but with the difference that they also advanced critical perspectives on modern religion and society.[21]

In some respects, by evoking alternative realities, virtual religions on the Internet also recall the 1960s experiments with mind-altering chemicals, those entheogens that produced "religious" experiences, which some dismissed as artificially induced. But as their advocate Walter Clark observed, "If this is a fake religion, then the fake is frequently better than the real thing."[22]

Surviving the 1960s, for some artists, meant creating new religions. Wavy Gravy created his Church of Fun; the San Francisco Mime Troupe initiated the annual St. Stupid's Day parades; and the Burning Man, an annual festival, was organized to provide an arena for new initiatives in religion. Dedicated to "the creative power of ritual," as organizer Larry Harvey explained, "Burning Man brings together art, performance, fire, and temporary community to create what has been called 'ritual without dogma.'"[23] At Burning Man festivals, temporary community often appears in new religions that celebrate the creative, uninhibited playfulness of ritual without dogma—religions such as the Church of St. John the Baptist of the Alien Artichoke, the Church of Naismith, the Alien Domination Gospel Mission, the Church of the Holy Electron, the Cult of Distraction, and the Dead Media Cargo Cult.

In some cases, these playful engagements with religion seem driven by serious intent, especially when intervening in the market economy, the dominant arena for adjudicating authenticity, by highlighting the commodification of religion and the religion of consumerism. At the Burning Man festival in 2001, for example, the commodification of religion was satirized at Enlightentrapment, where you could "choose a new religion (over 100 to choose from!!)," and at Kult Camp, "a post-Enlightenment response to the commodification of the spiritual experience by Old World religions and New Age groups," where religious consumers could buy into the In-n-Out Guru franchise, the fate-o-meter, the confessional, and the "chance to achieve Instant Endarkment." By 2001, however, one of the religious sites at the Burning Man festival, the Church of Holy Fucking Shit, had given up on religion. Renouncing the designation "church," the leaders of this camp decided that religion had been overwhelmed by Weberian rationalization, by the power of bureaucracy, science, and technology, so it no longer had any power. "It's not a church!" they declared. "Religion had its day, and fortunately for you, it's been replaced by bureaucracy and science in the Bureau of Holy Fucking Shit."

In cyberspace, invented religions have multiplied, often invoking similar religious commitments to surrealism, performance art, liberation from dogma, and implicit critiques of a modern world driven by market economy, consumerism, bureaucracy, science, and technology. Beyond censorship or discipline, virtual religions, even when obviously fake, have raised real dilemmas in negotiating the terms and conditions of religious authenticity.

VIRTUAL RELIGIONS ON THE INTERNET

Although they might develop and propagate apparently unbelievable religious propositions, some virtual religions on the Internet display characteristic features of historical religions, such as founders, beliefs, symbols, myths, and rituals that make them look like any other religion. "On the World Wide Web," as a representative of the ABM—the Anti-Bullshit Movement—put it, "a fake religion can look every bit as impressive as the Vatican."[24] As an entry into this wonderful world of impressive fakes, I want to identify briefly ten basic types of virtual religions that have appeared on the Internet.

BELIEF SYSTEMS

On the home page of the Abstract Ministry, we learn about the sacred texts, beliefs, rituals, and even sectarian divisions of an ancient religious tradition, Aramanism, which was founded in first-century Syria by Araman, prophet of the god Ikon. Having disappeared by the beginning of the fourth century, Aramanism revived and died again several times before it was finally established as the Abstract Ministry on the Internet, where reportedly "it has been growing ever since." Belief systems animating Internet religions are not always so complex. For example, the religion of Andersianism, one of the smallest but supposedly fastest-growing religions on earth, subscribes to one simple belief, "Anders is God." Although Anders is reportedly not a jealous god, he is beset by schismatics and heretics, such as the reformers in Presbyterian Andersianism and the opponents in the Arcane Order of the Coming of the One True Anders. But Andersianism seems most threatened by the alternative religion Asaism, which is exactly identical to the religion of Anders, a word-for-word reproduction, except for its central religious belief, "Asa is God." In the process of building a religious community around belief, we cannot help but suspect that these Internet religions are messing with the very notion of religious belief.[25]

If it were possible to trace a genealogy of virtual religions on the Internet, it would probably begin with Discordianism. According to the tradition recorded in multiple editions of the Principia Discordia, the Discordian religion began in 1957 when two friends, sipping coffee in a bowling alley in southern California, experienced a dramatic break in the time-space continuum, causing them to realize that chaos is the underlying principle of everything. This realization was reinforced by a vision of the ancient Greek goddess Eris, goddess of discord, conflict, and chaos, who revealed herself as the source not only of chaos but also of the "happy anarchy" of freedom, creativity, and laughter.

Discordian cabals spread across the United States during the 1980s, becoming part of the growing neopagan movement.[26] Committed to celebrating the liberating anarchy of Eris, Discordians are opposed to authoritarian social structures, especially the oppressive order imposed on the world by agents of the secret society the Illuminati. Discordians operate within a mythic horizon—the "hodgepodge" or "Sacred Chao"—in which liberating anarchy contends with oppressive order. In the midst of this conflict, enlightenment is possible through the body, by focusing on the pineal gland, but also through laughter.[27]

Flourishing on the Internet, Discordian sites multiplied to more than thirty by the beginning of the twenty-first century. Discordian offshoots also emerged, such as the Church of the SubGenius, under the divine leadership of J. R. "Bob" Dobbs, with its principled commitment to the doctrine of slack; the Otisians, the Illuminated Knights of Otis, devoted to Otis, the ancient Sumerian god or goddess (gender uncertain) who is worshiped in the Intergalactic House of Fruitcakes; and the Holy Church of Unified Borkism, devoted to the Swedish "Muppet chef extraordinaire," the Borkian lord and savior, and also dedicated to listening to loud music and poking fun at organized religion.

Like the Discordians, these offshoot religions have generated their own elaborate religious beliefs, symbols, myths, and traditions as the basis for relatively disorganized religious communities. In forming a sense of community, these religions often assert that everyone is already a member. In this respect, they are following the lead of the Universal Life Church, founded in 1959, a legally recognized religious body in the United States with the legal authority to ordain ministers, which also maintains that "everyone is already a member of the church and is just not aware of it as yet."[28]

More directly than the adherents of any other Internet religion, the Discordians have taken up the challenge of religious authenticity. Finding themselves classified by the Yahoo search engine under the category "Parody Religions," Discordians launched a massive e-mail campaign in May 2001 to get their religion reclassified. They inundated Yahoo with messages repeating their basic demand that either Discordianism must be removed from "Parody Religions" and listed with the "real" ones in the category "Religions and Faiths" or else all religions must be listed as "Parody Religions." As a model letter to Yahoo put the problem, "If Discordianism is a 'Parody,' then why aren't the alleged faiths of 'Christianity,' 'Judaism,' 'Islam,' or 'Hinduism'?" How would their members feel about being classified as a joke?

Observing that the pope would be outraged if Roman Catholicism were classified as a parody, this letter stipulated that Discordianism has billions of popes, since every person on the planet is a member, whether he or she knows it or not, and every member is a pope. "While it is true that many people do not choose to actively participate in the whoreship of Eris, Goddess of Discord and Confusion and Really Scwewy Stuff, these people are nonetheless members of the fastest growing religion in all creation (Discordianism grows at the exact same rate as the population, you see)." After three weeks of this campaign, the Discordians achieved a kind of victory with a shift from "Parody Religions" to "Entertainment—Religion—Humor," a category they found more acceptable because, as one Discordian observed, "Well, we are funny."[29]

ANTIBELIEF SYSTEMS

By contrast to these elaborated belief systems, many virtual religions on the Internet are explicitly formulated as antibelief systems, developing no doctrines, or explicitly renouncing all doctrines, or asserting that anything you believe, whatever it might be, is the "official" doctrine of their church. One might imagine that the Agnostic Church would undervalue religious beliefs, but the founder actually claims to have "VERY STRONG religious beliefs. They just happen to be of the agnostic persuasion." Other virtual religions similarly challenge religious belief by casting agnosticism as religion. In the "Religism" of the First Church of Rotate Your Envelope Stock, for example, the church's religious dogma features the teaching "Believe what you want; or don't." Members are encouraged to "fabricate a belief or non-belief system uniquely tailored to their own needs." As the church promises, "virtually any belief is allowed and encouraged." The Church of Bullshitology, a "religion based entirely on falsehood," is proclaimed as a "religion you can *not* believe in without going to hell."[30]

In some cases, virtual religions reject the validity of religious belief entirely. The Church of Nothing at All, for example, with a "congregation of none and no ordained priesthood," recommends a prayer to God: "Thou art a big fat zero and are not there at all. Amen." The Last-Chance Cathedral and Discount House of Worship addresses the question, "Is NOTHING sacred any more?" The answer, of course, is a resounding "NO." In other cases, the rejection of belief in any specific doctrines is worked out in impressive detail. In the religion of Wauism, for example, members are promised "a faith that works for you, Friendly Friend, instead of the other way around." Based on the study of religions and in-depth market research, Wauism promises a religion in which you can believe anything you want, eat whatever you want, and choose your own Supreme Being, with no sexual taboos, hazing rituals, or annual fees. Salvation is guaranteed. "All you have to do," Wauism urges, "is whatever you want," ending with the poignant promise: "Be a Wauist or don't be. You are still surrounded in a cone of love."[31]

In other cases, the dismissal of religious belief is radically simplified. Hauverism, for example, "is a religion consisting solely of the belief that only you exist." Because only you exist, anything you believe will be an accurate profile of the entire scope of religious doctrine in the religion of Hauverism. In the Church of the Covert Cosmos, religious belief is slightly enlarged to embrace only two core articles of faith: You exist. I exist. However, as the church acknowledges, since these tenets "don't make for a very rich body of dogma," members of the Church of the Covert Cosmos are invited to choose from a list of items they might also want to believe in, such as black holes, quarks, and neutrinos, which they can put together in a kind of "roll-your-own catechism." So, again, anything you believe is the doctrine of this church.[32]

PRACTICAL SYSTEMS

While discounting religious belief, virtual religions occasionally promote innovative religious practices, both ethical and ritual. The Church of Cyberosophy, for

example, requires no religious beliefs, but it does propound one ethical commandment, "Don't be such a jackass." The religious Web site No Sin provides ritual
confession, with guaranteed forgiveness, for anyone who feels he or she might
have violated any ethical commandment. Although the Church of the Covert
Cosmos has a minimalist set of religious beliefs, it has developed a ritual practice
that it regards as the central liturgy of the church. Instructions for celebrating the
liturgy are provided: Go outside. Incline your head backward and gaze up at the
firmament. Exclaim the ritual expression "Whooo-Whee!" loudly, if alone, but
quietly if anyone is nearby. Go back inside, making sure to look down, at this stage
in the ritual, to avoid tripping over the cat.[33]

The First Church of the Last Laugh, dedicated to St. Stupid, requires no religious beliefs but celebrates its annual holy day, St. Stupid's Day, which has been
observed every April 1 since 1978, by organizing festive ritual processions through
the streets of San Francisco. This church is proclaimed as the "world's fastest
growing snack religion, 150% less dogma, it's a Lite Religion, we practice what we
call enlightened religion biz only one day a year." During the St. Stupid's Day
parade of 2000, adherents of this enlightened religion biz marched in San Francisco, chanting, "We're here, we're stupid, we're not going away." The following
year, they chanted, "No more chanting. No more chanting." As the church observes, its ritualized stupidity preserves the original religion. Since religions are
based on guilt and fear, which are stupid, stupidity must have come first. The
annual St. Stupid's Day parade, in the view of the First Church of the Last Laugh,
practices the most basic religion of humanity.[34]

The Internet religions considered so far look just like religion, whether elaborating or discounting religious belief, whether emphasizing the myth of Eris in
Discordianism or the ritual of procession, chanting, and celebration on the holy
day of St. Stupid in the First Church of the Last Laugh. As the Discordians have
argued, they challenge any conventional system of distinguishing between real
religion and parody, joke, or fake religion. In other situations, virtual religions
have been explicitly formulated as satires of conventionally recognized religions,
with special attention to Christianity, New Age spirituality, and alternative religious movements.

CHRISTIANESQUE SYSTEMS

An entire genre of Christian or Christianesque satires has appeared on religious
sites on the Internet. While the First Church of Cyberspace asserts its legitimacy
as an "authentic" Christian ministry on the Internet, the only Christian church

existing solely in cyberspace, alternative constructions of Christianity appear in such sites as the Bastard Son of the Lord Home Page, Antichrist Bob's Family Fun Pages, and the home page devoted to the Christian wisdom, ethical guidance, and baking recipes of Betty Bowers, America's Best Christian.[35]

In some cases, alternative constructions of Christianity go beyond satire to appear as competing Christian claims. In the case of Web sites such as True Catholic or His Holiness Pope Gregory XVII, for example, elaborate alternative histories of the Roman Catholic Church are worked out to challenge the authority of the papacy. Similarly, the Landover Baptist Church, a satire on Baptists, has ended up in conflict with "real" Baptist ministries that object to its interventions. In these instances, "fake" Christian sites have emerged as real participants in genuine Christian controversies over religious legitimacy.[36]

Certainly, the most fervent Christian appeal on the Internet is made on the site DateJesus.com, where "Jesus seeks loving woman." Proclaimed as "the most extravagant personal ad in the history of civilization," this site features Jesus, with photograph, seeking "a woman who would rather have an authentic life instead of one guided by the pursuit of modern trends." On the Web site, women who might be in search of such Christian authenticity can learn more about how they can contact Jesus, date Jesus, and even bathe with Jesus. Endorsements are provided, indicating that Jesus has been successful in establishing such authenticity in the past. Like the Web site for "Liberated Christians" devoted to the Christian gospel of love, which endorses the enjoyment of multiple sexual partners, interpreted as polyamory, DateJesus.com represents a particular kind of religious interpretation of the meaning and power of Christianity, an interpretation underwritten in this case by the extraordinary claim that Jesus himself is looking for a loving woman to help him extend his gospel of love.[37]

NEW AGE SYSTEMS

Web sites devoted to satires of New Age, spiritual, or consciousness-raising movements run into a similar ambiguity: are they in opposition to, in counterpoint with, or in collaboration with such religious movements? Vendramism, for example, which is traced back to its founder, Sri Vendra Yallah, born in Madras, India, on December 25, 1874, develops into a path for achieving enlightenment, with slow and fast methods, but its spiritual techniques emerge in eating food, enjoying sex, smoking tobacco, and watching television. In a similar sacred transformation of normal pleasures, the religious movement of Alchodise, the Beer Church, and the Church of Our Lady of Malted Barley and Hops find enlightenment in alcohol, with special ritual attention to beer, which, as the religion of Alchodise proclaims, "is everlasting to everlasting, beer is eternal." At the same time, the religious movement of the Blaketashi Darwish, which weaves together the wisdom of Muslim Sufis and the English poet, artist, and visionary William Blake, seems seriously interested in exploring the spiritual resources that might arise from the conjunction of Islamic and British mysticism.[38]

The Center for Duck Studies, presenting an apparently absurd proposition for a religious movement, advocates "Duck Consciousness," facilitated by a quacked mantra, which must be regarded as a satire of New Age spirituality. However, Duck Consciousness advances wisdom that seems entirely consistent with certain forms of religion emerging both in New Age movements and on the Internet: "If you take the Duck seriously, then It is serious. If you take the Duck as a joke, It is a joke." Either way, "It remains the Duck."[39]

ANTICULT SYSTEMS

Ambiguity is removed on Web sites that promote new religious movements explicitly under the designation "cult." The intent of these sites is actually a certain kind of intervention in opposition to cultlike religious movements. However, unlike the conventional anticult sites that try to expose cults by citing allegations of brainwashing, corruption, and political subversion, these Internet religions attack religious movements by imaginatively creating cults—as if they were following the "Cult Construction Set," which enables you to build your own cult. On a number of sites, the Church of Scientology is explicitly attacked by being reconfigured as Diarrhetics; Clearity Is Confusion; Appliantology; Dianetech: Applied Spiritual Linguistic Technology; or Apelomatics: The Modern Pseudoscience of Mental Dentistry. Shifting from ridicule to exposure, the First Electronic Church of Scamizdat, which posted confidential Scientology documents on the Internet, was successfully sued by the Church of Scientology for violating copyright.[40]

More generally, new religious movements are attacked through the archetypal Internet cult, the Kick-Ass Post-Apocalyptic Doomsday Cult of Love. Under the leadership of the Honorable Reverend Sum Dum Guy, who is praised as a "Demented Psychopathic Megalomaniac," this new religious movement seeks "Toadies and Sheep" not only to join an "Extremist Revolutionary Religious Cult" but also to give up all their worldly possessions and submit with fanatical devotion to the leader's "perverted and deviant whims." In providing a profile of this cult, the Web site features photographs of the heavily armed followers and willing wives of the leader. While assuring prospective members that all the guns are legal, the site promises that the "Reverend's wives will do anything to get you to join the cult," but "once you are in and brainwashed they won't even give you the time of day." The children within the cult, pictured in karate uniforms and fighting poses, "are the cult's most valuable resources," but they are valuable only because they can be sold if the adult followers "really get hard up for money."[41]

Clearly, the Kick-Ass Post-Apocalyptic Doomsday Cult of Love is not a genuine religion. Its satirical intervention in the cult controversies, however, asserts a real position on the validity of new religious movements, a position underscored, but also complicated, by the site's coda: "We Love and bless all of the visitors to this site. Really, we mean it." Really, whatever this love and blessing might mean, the Doomsday Cult of Love is not a religion but a satire of religion that nevertheless does a kind of religious work, not only by imitating religion, but also by taking a stand in the representation of alternative, emergent, and new religious movements as dangerous cults.

ENTERTAINMENT SYSTEMS

By contrast to attempts at limiting what might count as religion, Internet religions have emerged to celebrate the entertainment industry of film, television, music, and sports as if these were truly religious enterprises. Of course, Elvis Presley, the King, reigns supreme as a divine being worshiped in the Church of Elvis; the First Church of Jesus Christ, Elvis; the First Presleyterian Church of Elvis the Divine; and the Elvisarian religion of Zaragrunudgeyon.[42] As might be expected, Star Trek and Star Wars, which also have a devoted following, have produced Internet religions: Star Trek, in the First Church of Shatnerology, with its own schismatic movement, the Second National Church of Shatnerology; and Star Wars, in the Jedi Religion, which actually succeeded in gaining recognition as a religion in the 2002 British census.[43]

Many other religions deifying or sanctifying popular culture have appeared on the Internet. Some religious sites sacralize the production of popular music, such as the Church of Rock, the First Church of Holy Rock and Roll, and the Church of Rock and Roll Online Chapel. Others focus religious attention on specific artists: the Church of AntiChrist Superstar, devoted to Marilyn Manson; the Temple of Bowie, devoted to David Bowie; and the Partridge Family Temple, which is an elaborate celebration of an entirely artificial, made-for-television musical group as if it were a real, genuine, and sacred focus of religious attention. In the Church of the Heavenly Wood, devotees can worship the creativity of the

B-filmmaker Ed Wood, and on the religious site Tiger Woods Is God, devotees can observe the sacred prowess of the ultimate golfer. By sacralizing the production of popular entertainment, these Internet religions demonstrate that popular culture can certainly appear as if it were religion.[44]

MARKET SYSTEMS

Since all of these forms of popular "religious" culture are driven by the supply and demand of the market, religion can also appear as if it were essentially about money, commodities, and consumerism. Frequently, Internet religions directly address the problem of the relationship between religion and money. While many ask for money, others celebrate, by way of satirical intervention, the capitalist economy of consumerism. The Holy Temple of Mass Consumption, the Shrine of Our Lady of Mass Consumption, and Jesus Christ Superstore, for example, are religious sites on the Internet that operate playfully but critically within a religious arena that has made religion a consumer product and consumerism a religion.

Adopting an adversarial position to the religion of the market, the Church of Stop Shopping, which opposes the seductions of consumerism, overtly assumes a religious stance against the religion of the market. The Church of Secularistic Holidayism, by contrast, suggests that moments of relief from the cycle of production and consumption is all that we have left of the sacred. Whether celebrating or opposing the religion of the market, however ironically they might construct their interventions, these religions seem to be suggesting that the market is the only religion worth considering as a religion.[45]

In the Church of the Almighty Dollar, a subsidiary of God, Inc., money is revealed not only as the object of worship, the ultimate value, but also as the basis for a religious system of meaning. According to the teachings of the Church of the Almighty Dollar, money is the medium of meaningful exchange between God and the world. Money is proof that God exists, a reminder that in God we trust, but also God's way of thinking about himself. As the ultimate reason for human existence, the underlying meaning and mystery of human life, money is God's way of making us feel good about ourselves and of showing others that he loves us, although money is also God's way of telling us to make more money. In the end, as the currency that redeems our souls, money is the religious bond between God and human beings in the world.

While the Church of the Almighty Dollar addresses the ways in which money has become a religion, another Internet church, the Church of the Profit$, attacks the ways in which religions, especially the ministries of television evangelists, often appear as money-making businesses. Objecting to such religious businesses, with their tax-exempt status, their distribution of literature in public schools, their support of Republicans, and their attempts to destroy the First Amendment separation of religion and state, the founder of the Church of the Profit$ established the only honest religion, dedicated, as he put it, to one simple truth: "You give me money, and I keep it." Although followers are expected to lead moral lives, if they sin, they have to pay, according to a fee schedule that covers sins from lying to impure acts. "To be forgiven," according to the Church of the Profit$, "you must do as is written in Matthew 22:10, 'Show me the money.'"[46]

As these two churches suggest, Internet religion operates in a terrain in which money is religion and religion is a money-making business. Certainly, these churches recall religious precedents, from Reverend Ike's gospel of money to televangelist appeals for donations, which have made a religion out of money and money out of religion, but these churches of money also capture an important feature of the relation between Internet religions and the market economy. Although new gods have appeared on the Internet, those deities are often revealed as products of corporations—God, Inc., God Co., Lord Co., Messiahs, Inc., and so on—as if God were now a subsidiary of a multinational conglomerate.

In the competitive market of Internet religion, these corporate gods have to compete for market share. The "Great God Contest," the ultimate test of divinity, has been set up for entering deities as if they were competing products in a consumer test of religious brands. Messiah Mickey, featured on his own religious site, has an advantage, of course, in being promoted not only by his devotees on the Internet but also by the Walt Disney Company. Likewise, the First Internet McChurch Tabernacle has the competitive advantage of being associated with McDonald's. "McChurch is a REAL religion," with easy-to-understand spiritual truths, supported by advertising slogans "that make McWorship as easy as picking up a burger and fries."[47]

An evil force such as Cthulu, a deity drawn from the horror fiction of H. P. Lovecraft, might be a more difficult god to market, but one of his sites has made a valiant attempt by supporting Cthulu's candidacy for president of the United States with the advertising slogan "If you are tired of voting for the lesser of two evils, why not vote for the greatest evil of them all?" Consistently, the theology of Internet religions, underwritten by corporate sponsorship, consumer choice, and market competition, is driven by the prevailing discourse of the late-capitalist market economy.[48]

OBJECT AND ANIMAL SYSTEMS

A remarkable number of Internet religions are devoted to material objects. Religious enthusiasts for objects have established the Church of the Avocado, the Church of the Big Plastic Fork, the Church of the Burnt Onion Ring, the Church of the Chainsaw, the Church of Ice Cream, the Church of the Twinkie, the Church of Volkswagenism, the First United Church of the Fisher-Price Record Player, and the shrine devoted to the Cult of the Potato.[49]

In addition to deifying material objects, Internet religions often identify animals as their focus of religious devotion. Among the religions deifying animals, we find the Church of the Bunny, the Church of the Gerbil, the Church of the Quivering Otter, the Kult of Hamstur, the Holy Church of Moo, the Holy Turtle's Internet Cathedral, the Holy Reformed Church of the Later Day Kangaroos, the Temple of the Sacred Cat, and the Virtual Church of the Blind Chihuahua.[50]

In most cases, these sites devoted to material objects or animals are just as thoughtful (or playful) about religion as the Discordians and other Internet religions. Nevertheless, by venerating objects and animals, they focus directly on materiality in a communication medium that is supposedly "virtual" rather than material. Challenging basic religious classifications—superhuman, subhuman, and human—these Internet religions also push religion in the direction of dealing with materiality.

SCIENTISTIC SYSTEMS

Within the division of labor established by modernity, the meaning of materiality is the province of science. While religion might deal with spirituality, materiality is covered by scientific inquiry, investigation, experimentation, and explanation. On the Internet, however, new scientific religions have emerged to deal with materiality in religious terms. Environmentalism has been invested with religious significance in the First Internet Church of All, but a kind of environmentalist religion is also proclaimed in the Church of Euthanasia, which advocates "Save the planet, kill yourself." The devotees of Lord Kelvin proclaim the scientific religion of physics, which observes the laws of thermodynamics, while proclaiming "Kelvin is Lord!!! All Praise the Lord Kelvin!! Only the One, True Lord Kelvin can Conserve you from Entropy!"[51]

The Church of Virus, however, which is dedicated to the truth of memes—a term coined by the evolutionary biologist Richard Dawkins in drawing an analogy between the propagation of genes through the gene pool and the cultural transmission of ideas—is entirely serious in advancing its religious claims about the ultimate significance of genetics, biological evolution, and the role of memes in the cultural evolution of humanity. The Church of Virus proclaims itself "a memetically engineered atheistic religion." Featuring Charles Darwin as its saint, having "illuminated" him through an induction into the church on February 12, 1996, the Church of Virus provides a lexicon of key terms in the science of memetics, terms familiar to scientific researchers working in the fields of evolutionary psychology or cognitive science. Other religions of biological, psychological, or technological evolution, such as Prometheism, Techanism, Technosophy, and the Church of the Almighty Revealed in Biotechnology, have also transformed any apparent opposition between religion and science into a religion of scientism.[52]

ADJUDICATING AUTHENTICITY

On the Web site of one Internet religion, the Holy Order of the Cheeseburger (HOC), the founder of this new religion makes a poignant confession. "I originally started this site to give people an alternative to crazy religions with an even crazier religion," he reports. "So, my journey began." Although that personal journey began with anarchistic humor about religion, providing a satirical alternative to conventional religions, it developed into a serious religious quest. "I have had a fun time with the HOC," he reflected, "but I have been getting more serious in my search for the one true religion."[53]

As a result of that search for the one authentic religion in the world, the founder of the HOC decided to shut down the fake religion he had created in the virtual world of the Internet. As a result of what he had learned through his personal search for the one true religion, he was no longer prepared to offer an invented religion as if it were true. "My search has yielded the following results," the founder of the order revealed. "Religion is bullshit!" Accordingly, removing himself from the business of religion, the founder of the Holy Order of the Cheeseburger advised any followers he might have had that they were now entirely on their own.[54]

Like Thomas Edison's assertion that religion is "all bunk," all "a damned fake," this confession settled the question of religious authenticity by judging religion essentially inauthentic. In making this judgment, however, Edison and the prophet of the Holy Order of the Cheeseburger must certainly have used different indicators of authenticity. Applying the conventional modern tests of authenticity, which have been shared by Enlightenment rationalists and Protestant pietists, Edison would have assumed that religion is bunk because it fails to meet the demands of visual transparency and bodily control, the transparency that led to the discovery of truth and the control of self-discipline and self-denial that led to the production of useful results in the world.

By stark contrast, Internet religions, including, we must assume, the religious quest of the founder of the Holy Order of the Cheeseburger, have sought authenticity not in transparency and control but in opacity and anarchy. Authenticity, in this sense, cannot be transparently discerned or disciplinarily managed from the outside, from some assumed center of knowledge and power; it can emerge only in the thick, rich, complex, and opaque discourses and practices that liberate the body—in the first instance, although the mind, spirit, or soul might also follow—from oppressive disciplinary regimens of control. Put differently, although Thomas Edison and the founder of the HOC agreed in dismissing the authenticity of religion, they disagreed over whether religion is bunk or bullshit, with bunk being a failure of transparency and control, and bullshit being an imposition of conventional transparency and authoritarian control that blocks embodied freedom.

The Discordians, in their campaign to redress the injustice of their classification as a "Parody Religion" by the search engine Yahoo, brought the question of authenticity into focus. As one Discordian appealed to Yahoo, "I ask that either you move us into the same category as the rest of the religions, or tell me what the criteria [are] to become a 'real' religion so that I might show how Discordianism meets [them]."[55] How would scholars of religion answer that question? What are the criteria for determining what should count as a real, genuine, or authentic religion? As I have suggested, the standard modern measures of establishing authenticity, visual transparency and disciplinary control, are directly challenged by the new religions emerging on the Internet. But these new religions also challenge other standards of authentication, such as historical methods of verification, morphological methods of comparison, psychological tests of sincerity, and philosophical assumptions—derived from what Theodor Adorno called the existentialist "jargon of authenticity"[56]—to assess existential identity, genuine commitment, and personal authenticity.

If asked about the historical reality of their religion, Discordians could point to Greco-Roman mythology. Undeniably, the Greek goddess Eris (Discordia to the Romans) is real; that is, she really featured in ancient religious texts, so her reality, as a focus of religious attention, can be historically corroborated. Similarly, other virtual religions employ historical reconstruction to create an aura of authenticity. For example, the histories of the ancient religion of Aramanism, the Hindu movement of Vendramism, and the "True Catholic" Church invoke historicity as a test of authenticity, even if those historical accounts are entirely fabricated.

Comparing their religion with the basic morphological patterns of other religions, Discordians cited the important role played by divine tricksters in the history of religions. "Many cultures have trickster deities, yet their religions aren't considered parodies," as one Discordian observed. "How do you think the Native Americans would react to your placing their religions in the 'Parody' section? You'd be up to your ass valves in lawsuits!"[57] Along similar lines, the morphology of religion, distilling basic patterns, structures, and elementary forms of religious life, provides the dominant standard of authenticity within the virtual religions of the Internet. In order to be a good fake, as Rodney Needham proposed, a fake religion must look exactly like a real religion. Basic forms of religion, such as myth, doctrine, ethics, ritual, personal experience, and social formation, represent the religious template not only for inventing new religions but also for asserting their authenticity.

Concerning the test of sincerity, Discordians insisted that their religion "is at least as serious as all the other major Religions (perhaps more so)." Although religious sincerity is difficult if not impossible to verify, as the U.S. Supreme Court found in trying to adjudicate the authenticity of the I AM movement during the 1940s, Discordians testified to their religious sincerity, which was central to their commitment to the "ha ha, only serious worldview."[58] Such a religious worldview, with its playful seriousness or serious playfulness, does not easily conform to conventional standards of sincerity. Naturally, serious critics have wanted to reassert seriousness, in opposition to playfulness, as the standard of authenticity. Ted Kaczynski, for example, in his Unabomber manifesto, questioned the sincerity of new pagan, environmentalist religions. In the defense of Nature against Technology, he observed, Nature could use religious support, but "it would be a mistake to concoct artificially a religion to fill this role." Asserting that "such an invented religion would be a failure," the Unabomber cited the pagan religion of the earth goddess Gaia. "Do its adherents REALLY believe in it or are they just play-acting?" he demanded, then pronounced, "If they are just play-acting their religion will be a flop in the end." In pursuing the war against technology, the Unabomber concluded that it is "best not to try to introduce religion into the conflict of nature vs. technology unless you REALLY believe in that religion yourself and find that it arouses a deep, strong, genuine response in many other people."[59] In contrast to a demand for personal sincerity and genuine response, virtual religions on the

Internet have not demonstrated the sincerity that would make them obvious allies for the Unabomber or any other political project.

In regard to existential identity as a measure of authenticity, Discordians have certainly displayed a playful fluidity in self-identification, signing themselves, for example, as Wonk, Maenad, Saint Mae, Prince Mu Chao, Lord Falgan, and Bishop Squarepeg Roundhole. Certainly, this ambiguity of identity is a feature of communication on the Internet. According to a Web site devoted to connecting buyers and sellers, What the Heck Is It.Com, authenticating anyone's identity in cyberspace is nearly impossible. "Because user identification on the Internet is difficult," this site advises, "whattheheckisit.com cannot and does not confirm that each user is who they claim to be."[60] However, the Discordians raise a profound question about human identity with their proposition that everyone is already a member of their religion by virtue of being human, although, in most cases, admittedly, they are completely unaware of their membership. On the basis of this expansive, inclusive construction of human identity, both personal identity and collective identity, Discordians could argue that any denigration of their religion is an act of discrimination against every person on the planet. An injury to Discordianism, in this expansive vision of collective human identity, is an injury to all. One Discordian tried to explain this to Yahoo by claiming that the search engine actually discriminated against its own membership by relegating Discordianism to the category of parody religions, because everyone, including those associated with Yahoo, is a member of Discordian religion.

Such an intervention in identity—claiming everyone as a member whether he or she knows it or not—has featured in other virtual religions on the Internet, as previously discussed. Apparently advancing a universal religious claim, this assertion radically personalizes religious identity, because anyone, wherever he or she might be, whatever he or she might believe, feel, do, or experience, is the author of authentic religion.

In this regard, we might recall the classic definition of religion provided by William James, who asked us to accept, "arbitrarily," that religion is "the feelings, acts, and experiences of individual men in their solitude, so far as they apprehend themselves to stand in relation to whatever they may consider the divine."[61] Certainly, James could not have anticipated the conditions in which men and women would find themselves a century later in the solitude of cyberspace, sitting alone before a computer, apprehending themselves in relation to the divinity of the ancient Greek goddess Eris or the divinity of the 1950s American image of the clean-cut, pipe-smoking, entrepreneurial salesman J. R. "Bob" Dobbs, who, despite the image, is committed to the doctrine of slack. James could never have anticipated the scope of a religious solitude in which people could find Mickey Mouse and McDonald's, Elvis Presley and Star Trek, money and consumerism, genetics and evolution, as authentic religious media through which they could stand in relation to whatever they may consider the divine. Certainly, churches of plastic forks or chainsaws, of gerbils, hamsters, or bunnies, would have been even more unthinkable.

By developing a psychological theory of religion, William James seemed to be asking for all of this. He focused on feelings. He located those feelings in solitude. And he seemed to place no limits on what might count as religion, since he included anything and everything that anyone might consider as divine. Accordingly, James might be regarded as the academic authority underwriting the authenticity of virtual religions on the Internet.

Of course, James was not asking for any of this. Although he allowed broad scope for what might count as the divine focus of religion, he substantially narrowed religion's psychological register by limiting religious thought and feeling to the serious and the solemn. Religion, as a way of thinking, according to James, "signifies always a *serious* state of mind." As a serious mentality, religion "says 'hush' to all vain chatter and smart wit"; it is "hostile to light irony." Emotionally, as James observed, "there must be something solemn, serious, and tender about any attitude which we denominate religious. If glad, it must not grin or snicker; if sad, it must not scream or curse. It is precisely as being *solemn* experiences that I wish to interest you in religious experiences." Clarifying his definition of religion as a response to whatever might be regarded as divine, James insisted that the "divine shall mean for us only such a primal reality as the individual feels impelled to respond to solemnly and gravely, and neither by a curse nor a jest."[62] Obviously, therefore, James would have had difficulty including the virtual religions of the Internet, with their jests and curses, their vain chatter, smart wit, and light irony, within the ambit of what should count as authentic religion.

Nevertheless, virtual religions at play on the Internet test any preconceptions we might have about religious authenticity. As we have seen, they raise, and defy, all the basic tests that might be applied in adjudicating the authenticity of a religion, such as historical genealogy, structural morphology, personal sincerity, and so on. Let us call them religions, since they are real fakes, acting just as religions do even if they are completely fake, because they are doing real religious work in a medium of communication in which anything, even religion, seems possible.

CHAPTER ELEVEN · Planet America

Animated by all the forces of globalization, with all their implicitly religious undercurrents, America has emerged as the center of the universe—the military, political, economic, social, cultural, and religious *axis mundi* of a globalizing world. The perception of American centrality is not a recent one. During the 1980s, when the apartheid regime in South Africa was trying to defend itself against international sanctions, which the United States had reluctantly agreed to impose also, two political consultants published a book, *South Africa: The 51st State*, appealing to the U.S. government not to sanction South Africa but to annex the country into the United States. "South Africa needs a saviour," this book declared, "and that saviour is the United States."[1]

In this appeal to annex South Africa, salvation meant incorporation into the political order of the United States. "We believe," the authors announced, "that only acceptance by the world's greatest democracy can solve one of the world's most complicated social problems." Not only would annexation save South Africa, but, the authors argued, it would also be beneficial to the United States in furthering its longstanding cultural tradition of drawing strength by absorbing other cultures. "The 'American-ness' of America," they observed, "comes from centuries of absorbing other cultures. . . . The waves of cultural immigration are over, and if new stimuli are to revitalise American-ness, Americans must look beyond their shores for them . . . *to the 51st State*."[2]

By assuming that America has constituted itself by absorbing other cultures, the authors presented an image of America as a centripetal force drawing the entire world into its vortex. In addition to imagining America as a centripetal center, the authors advanced two other spatial arguments to seal their case. First, they proposed that, in the modern "global village," with its rapid transportation and instant communication, the South Africa of the 1980s was actually closer to Washington, DC, than the California of a century earlier, considering the conditions that existed when it was admitted into the Union. Second, appealing to an American transcendence of space, the authors insisted that the proposal of statehood for South Africa was no more far-fetched than "the idea of putting Neil Armstrong on the moon." If Americans could plant their flag on the moon, the authors concluded, they could certainly plant it in South Africa.[3]

As I noted briefly in passing, this fervent appeal to the U.S. government to grant statehood to South Africa was endorsed by the Zulu shaman Credo Mutwa, who provided the foreword for the book. Incorporation into the United States of America would save the apartheid regime, which was widely characterized at the time as the "polecat of the world." So for some—global political consultants, indigenous religious specialists—America represented salvation in the political struggles of South Africa. However, American incorporation did not necessarily represent any hope for the liberation of the majority of South Africans from the political, social, and racial oppression they suffered under apartheid. Still, many people, even in their oppression, were drawn to the creativity of American popular culture.

This profound global ambivalence toward America, combining fascination with its popular culture and repulsion from its global politics, has appeared frequently in foreign accounts of American society. In 1996, the Spanish author Vicente Verdú published the book *El Planeta americano* (The American Planet), which evoked many of the criticisms of American popular culture that have been voiced by people all over the world while they have actively participated in its global productions. From the outside looking in, people complain about American popular culture much as they complain about the world. Simply, unavoidably, like the world, America is just there.

Besides being a critic of American popular culture, Verdú is also an astute observer of the religious dimensions and dynamics of popular culture, having published the book *Soccer: Myths, Rites, and Symbols*, about the religious character of the world's most popular sport. Analyzing America as an outsider, he focused on the religious nature of American popular, public, and political culture in *El Planeta americano*. Essentially, he highlighted two features of religion and American popular culture during the 1990s: diversity and unity. America, as a land of diversity, has achieved a kind of national unity through religious symbols, myths, and rituals that are produced and reproduced through the media of American popular culture.

In a land of ethnic, cultural, and religious diversity, Americans have cultivated a single-minded love for their country, which is generally regarded as "a beneficent deity," a national God, who "is revered with hymns and ceremonies in honor of the most insignificant occasions."[4] The slogan One Nation under God, from this perspective, is redundant, because the nation itself has actually become the beneficent deity of American religious devotion. Devotees of this national religion, however, do not seem to know, or even to care whether or not they know, the most basic elements of their patriotic faith. As many as 20 percent of Americans, for example, do not know how many stars appear on their national flag, the sacred stars and stripes of their country. Many Americans, according to Vicente Verdú, have no idea what they worship when they direct their devotion to the flag of the United States of America.

As we have seen, the U.S. flag has been subject to many interpretations, from that of the U.S. Congress, which also did not know precisely what the red, white, and blue actually signify, to that of the Americans criminal gang in Cape Town, South Africa, who insisted that they understood the secret, sacred significance of the red blood and white money depicted by the American flag.

National unity, however, has always obscured the complex, vibrant diversity of America. Over a hundred languages, cultures, and perhaps religions are represented among the children currently enrolled in American public schools. Absorbing all of this human diversity, as Verdú observed, "America combines everything on the globe to mythically create a new world, and becoming an American does not mean so much to acquire a nationality as to embrace a superior mythology."[5]

That American mythology, even if it does not require any knowledge of history or geography, pervades an American sense of being central to the human geography and historical destiny of the world. Nevertheless, religious communities, adhering to their own constructions of identity, time, and space, operate in America and within the scope of global Americanization. How, we might ask, do these religions continue to work under globalizing American conditions?

RELIGIONS AT WORK

Religious America, as historian of religions Diana Eck has documented in *A New Religious America,* is an America of many religions.[6] Clearly, religious diversity is a fact of life in America. Although it was never my intention to examine the multiple, complex relations between religious communities and popular culture, religions have nevertheless appeared in this book, often in strange situations and unexpected guises. Christianity, for example, which seems to permeate American popular culture, has appeared here only in the guises of Internet satires and Christian frauds, in Christian Science and Christian Gnostics, and in the conversion of Disney into a pagan religion by the Southern Baptist Convention and the conversion of indigenous African religion into Christianity by enslaved Africans in America.

Certainly, the Christian presence in American popular culture has been far more pervasive than these examples might suggest. A basic Christian religious vocabulary is familiar to most Americans, no matter what their religious affiliation, especially as Christian symbols have been mediated, dramatized, and popularized by film and television.

Judaism has appeared here briefly in two discussions. One involved negotiations over dietary requirements at McDonald's restaurants in the modern state of Israel, in which the corporation agreed to abide by the Jewish religious law of kashruth. The other noted the widespread impression that Jews have created and controlled the primary engine of American popular culture, the Hollywood film industry. As Tarek Atia insisted in his essay "Bruce Willis versus Bin Laden," it is the "Jews who invented and remain in charge of Hollywood."[7] Jewish involvement in Hollywood, however, has arguably been more important to the transformation of American Christianity than to the advancement of Judaism in America. Adapting an observation made by the novelist Philip Roth, we might say that next to the apostle Paul, the Hollywood songwriter Irving Berlin has been the most important Jew in the history of Christianity. Taking Jesus out of Christmas, his song "White Christmas" made the holy day about winter weather; taking Jesus out of Easter, his song "Easter Parade" made the holy day about spring fashions.[8] In American popular culture, these revisions of the religious significance of Christmas and Easter seemed to be welcomed by the American public.

Growing rapidly in the United States, Islam has altered sociologist Will Herberg's formula of the mid-1950s: that religious America is Protestant, Catholic, and Jew.[9] In this book, we have seen Muslims in Malaysia, Singapore, India, and elsewhere, like Jews in Israel, convincing the globalizing American enterprise of McDonald's to adapt to their religious dietary law, the observance of halal. However, we have also seen Muslims on the front lines of cultural conflict, objecting to Thom McAn's marketing of its shoes bearing a logo inscription that resembles the Arabic script for Allah, objecting to a Coca-Cola ad depicting them as if they were praying to one of its vending machines, and protesting the prejudicial stereotypes of Muslims in American movies.

Although American pundits try to render such conflicts as a clash of civilizations, the lines dividing these "civilizations" are not at all clear. While the globalizing of these intercultural, interreligious relations has been going on for a long time, not merely dating back to the U.S. promotion, training, and covert military support of fundamentalist Islamic freedom fighters in the 1980s, local interests are always at stake. In Cape Town, South Africa, for example, when the Muslim leadership of PAGAD declared war on Americans, its focus was the local criminal gang of that name. Elsewhere in the Muslim world, we might suspect, declaring war on the United States can also mean struggling against perceived local violations of religious integrity or political sovereignty.

Muslims in America, like Muslims elsewhere in the world, have been concerned that the symbolic resources of American popular culture have been deployed against them. In the early 1990s, political analyst Leon T. Hadar warned about precisely such a development, suggesting that the sudden, unexpected collapse of communism in the Soviet Union and Eastern Europe had caused America to look for an equivalent enemy, with global, monolithic, and absolutely evil proportions, to take the place of communism. Like the "Red Menace" of the cold war, the "Green Peril" of Islam was being represented in the information and entertainment media of American popular culture "as a cancer spreading around the globe, undermining the legitimacy of Western values and political systems."[10] The "cosmic importance of this confrontation," Hadar advised, would justify new military strategies, which would include, ironically, new Muslim allies, but it would also prepare the American public to accept the inevitability of a "never-ending struggle." According to Hadar, American popular culture has been crucial in this shift from the "Red Menace" to the "Green Peril," since the new villain has had to be "integrated into popular culture to mobilize public support for a new crusade."[11] As many Muslims argued, Hollywood films, such as The Siege, appeared to be mobilizing American public support against Islam.

In addition to these children of Abraham—the three faiths of Judaism, Christianity, and Islam—other religions have entered into negotiations with American popular culture. Here also I have given only the most superficial attention to Hindus, again contending with McDonald's over religious diet and securing new product lines in the Maharaja Mac, Vegetable McNuggets, and the McAloo Tikki Burger, and to Tibetan Buddhists visiting the World of Coca-Cola. Nevertheless, images of Asian religions have been significant in American popular culture. As

Jane Naomi Iwamura has shown, the Oriental monk has featured prominently in film and television, from D. W. Griffith's portrayal of a Buddhist monk in *Broken Blossoms* (1919) to the Tibetan Buddhist dramas *Little Buddha* (1993), *Kundun* (1997), and *Seven Years in Tibet* (1997), not to mention the popularity of the Teenage Mutant Ninja Turtles.[12]

Since the 1960s, coinciding with the lifting of immigration restrictions on Asians, many Americans have found in Hinduism, Buddhism, and other Asian religions a spiritual authenticity that stands in stark contrast to the materialism of the West. In this respect, they have agreed with the Hindu scholar and Indian nationalist Sarvepalli Radhakrishnan or with the Japanese Buddhist scholar D. T. Suzuki in concluding that "the West excelled materially, the East excelled spiritually."[13]

The West, in the form of the "sacred institution" of McDonald's, assured the East that its spiritual dietary requirements were met by Ray Kroc's "sacrosanct" french fry, which the anthropologist James Watson found was compatible with Asian religions, since it was "consumed with great gusto by Muslims, Jews, Christians, Buddhists, and Hindus." Unfortunately, as Hindus in America found, McDonald's fries were precooked in beef fat at processing plants before being frozen and sent to franchise restaurants. During 2001, Hindu groups, supported by vegetarian coalitions, sued McDonald's for this violation of their religious dietary requirements, but their anger was also directed at McDonald's blatant deception in representing its product as pure when it actually involved a spiritual violation.[14]

Being defrauded by McDonald's is not the only problem adherents of Asian religions have faced. In American popular culture, Asian spirituality, the lure of the mystic East, has been capitalized on, Western style, by a fraud such as Eugen Herrigel, misrepresenting the Zen master Kenzo Awa; an imposter such as Cyril Hoskin, posing as Lobsang Rampa; and an invented, fictitious Internet guru such as Sri Vendra Yallah. Understandably, with the integration of these fakes into American popular culture, Hindus and Buddhists might have become as concerned about such fraudulent celebrations of their religions as Muslims have been outraged by the denigration of their faith.

Similarly, adherents of indigenous religions, whether Native American or African, have objected to the appropriations of their traditions in American popular culture. When the Southern Baptist Convention boycotted Disney, insisting that the Walt Disney Company has become a pagan religion through such films as *Pocahontas*, Native Americans were also faced with a profound religious dilemma. Not only suffering misrepresentation, adherents of Native American religion had to contest the misappropriation of their most sacred religious traditions by

American popular culture. As many Native American religious leaders have argued, such appropriations amount to cultural genocide, the concerted destruction of indigenous ways of life.

For African adherents of indigenous religion, the global celebration of an African shaman such as Credo Mutwa, let alone the Disneyization of an African religion based on a spiritual "circle of life," did not necessarily advance their religious interests. Efforts to mix and merge various elements of indigenous African and indigenous American spirituality, whether the African shaman participated in the Native American medicine wheel or the Native American shaman brought a sacred eagle feather to Africa, primarily appealed to a globalizing American market for New Age spirituality. If these initiatives did not necessarily commit acts of cultural genocide, neither did they represent obvious expressions of indigenous religious authenticity.

RELIGIOUS WORK

Even a fake religion, as I have suggested, can do real religious work. Again, returning to the question of how religion works, we are left with tracking characteristic religious strategies of classifying persons and orienting persons in time and space.

In classifying persons, religious work entails the identification of superhuman beings, perhaps to be worshiped but definitely to be distinguished from the everyday, mundane realm of the human. As we have seen, the superhuman, even when not identified as God, can take many forms in American popular culture. Some of these forms involve strange theophanies, remarkable manifestations of God.

God, of course, has appeared on U.S. currency with the 1954 addition of the phrase "In God We Trust," but that monetary theology has been dramatically modified (for instance, by the Americans criminal gang in South Africa, who expanded the phrasing to "In God we trust, in money we believe"), so that the promise inscribed on money refers directly to its religious significance. In his reading of the "theology of the market," theologian Harvey Cox argued that money, within the capitalist economy, has acquired the basic features of divine power, knowledge, and universal presence that were previously attributed to the Supreme Being. Omnipotent, omniscient, and omnipresent—the capitalist market is just like God. Following this argument, Thomas Frank's ironic phrase for globalizing capitalism, "One Market under God," should be replaced by the formula "One Market as God."[15]

In opposition to this universalizing god of the global market, popular cultural resources have been used to identify alternative deities. Clearly, the goddess Eris of the Discordians, causing and celebrating chaos, is no help in maintaining the stability of any new world order. Most of the deities appearing in the virtual religions on the Internet, such as Ikon, Anders, Asa, Cthulu, Lord Kelvin, and Tiger Woods, perform a similar destabilizing role, even when their devotees do not address them in prayer as the "big fat zero."

By contrast, the Yoruba god, Shango, as W. E. B. Du Bois found, has performed an anchoring role, bearing a specific biography, locality, and political sovereignty. More powerful than Thor or Yahweh, this thunder god has sustained ongoing religious and cultural exchanges between Africa and Africans of the Americas.

While part of religious work entails identifying the superhuman, it also involves classifying certain entities as less than human. Animals, vegetables, and minerals might be regarded as subhuman by some, but others with an expanded scope of what counts as human might include them, for instance, a Buddhist who regards dogs, trees, and rocks as having an inherent Buddha nature. At the same time, beings who might otherwise count as human on the basis of having an opposable thumb, bipedal locomotion, and an increased frontal lobe of the brain might be classified as subhuman on the basis of religion, race, class, gender, or some other marker.

All of this is simply to say that what counts as human is not given. The human is inevitably negotiated. Popular culture is a medium of negotiation, constantly experimenting with human identity by transgressing, mixing, or scrambling conventional classifications. Attributing human qualities to animals, of course, is a common feature of popular culture. Donald, the anthropomorphic duck, is simultaneously an animal and a human, a duck with a job, house, girlfriend, and three nephews, an entity who perhaps has also acquired a kind of superhuman status in achieving Duck Consciousness. Mickey Mouse, likewise animal and human, might also have achieved superhuman status as Messiah Mickey.

In any case, this creative confusion of classifications has been variously interpreted. Following Adorno, we might see Donald Duck as an agent of the machinery of capitalist production, taking "his beating so that the viewers can get used to the same treatment." Following Benjamin, we might see Mickey Mouse as an agent of "redemption," allowing viewers to escape, if only briefly, the machinery of their ordinary world by participating in popular entertainment "full of miracles that not only surpass those of technology but make fun of them."[16] Or, if it is possible to combine these perspectives, we can recognize that popular culture enables human beings to experiment in human possibility, playing with basic classifications of the superhuman and the subhuman, the animal and the machine, but not necessarily under conditions of their own making.

Over and over again, we have seen how the human appears in American popular culture not as a stable identity but as a process of change, even as a shape-shifting, protean, or plastic process of constant transformation. Although the Human Genome Project promises the ultimate transformation, changing humans, who share their basic genetic template with apes, into deified, immortal beings through the "godlike powers" of genetic engineering, the interchange of these classifications runs throughout American popular culture.

Even a plastic person, we can assume, must have some sense of place. Generating a sense of orientation in time and space, as I have suggested, is an important aspect of religious work. The ongoing, heated controversies between biblical creationists and scientific evolutionists over the truth of human origins have deflected attention from the multiplicity of myths of origin in American popular culture. In the beginning, as these popular creation myths might be reformulated, was creation itself, the creativity of discovery and invention.

The European discovery of America, which, according to Ronald Reagan, had been hidden by God until it could be discovered by a people of a special kind, marked the origin of the world in American popular culture. In the phrase of historian Edmundo O'Gorman, this discovery should actually be regarded not as a discovery but as the "invention of America," since this myth of origin was as much a work of the creative imagination as it was of military conquest and subjugation.[17]

Inventors, as we have seen, hold a special place in American popular culture, mediating and transacting relations among the superhuman, the human, and the subhuman. In the creation myths of American popular culture, inventions stand at the origin of worlds, especially the origin of the World of Coca-Cola, McDonald-land, or Disney World. Although the Cult of the New Eve was created as a satire of the new genetic science, with its religious promise of a New Genesis, it was exactly right in identifying the American propensity for creating multiple myths of origin in popular culture.

In the analysis of American culture pioneered by W. E. B. Du Bois, a different origin is evident in conquest, colonization, and slavery. Not merely a transatlantic exchange, the middle passage of slavery was the origin of a world, a beginning with powerful mythic proportions. African American popular culture has preserved traces of that beginning, not only in the "survivals" of African religion within various musical, artistic, and performance styles, but also through cultural traditions that evoke a complex, inherently contradictory origin. Celebrated in song and legend, evoked in ritual and healing practices, High John the Conqueror, as Charles Long has recalled, was there at the beginning, coming over from Africa. "It is stated explicitly in the folklore," Long reports, "that High John came dancing over the waves from Africa, or that he was in the hold of the slave ship."[18] Obviously, those are two very different ways of crossing the seas. How could both versions be true? How could High John's origin be both slavery and freedom? A powerful myth of origin, with its specific orientation in time, however, is contained in this story that marks the beginning of America as a place of both freedom and bondage.

If America has multiple myths of origin, it also has generated different myths of destiny. The myth of manifest destiny, which drove America's territorial expansion across a continent and beyond, has been in counterpoint to other visions of the future. Throughout the twentieth century, the future was imagined as powered by better living through technology, or through electricity, or through chemicals.[19] At the same time, these imagined futures were negotiated in relation to the prevailing political reality of America. Ronald Reagan sought to redeem America, operating within the basic vocabulary of the American myth of manifest destiny, especially as it was polarized against the Soviet Union during the cold war, but the leader of an alternative religious and political movement such as Jim Jones sought redemption from America.

Visions of ultimate redemption, however, are not what they used to be in American popular culture. As America globalizes, new visions of the American future have emerged, but the plans attendant on these visions do not necessarily include America as we know it. In the aesthetics of "New Primitivism," for example, the way forward is charted along the tracks of the body, visceral and local, but is mediated by the latest developments in information technology in ways that transcend local time and space.[20] If this is an example of the posthuman, then it must appear to many Americans as alien, even though the New Primitivism resembles the appeal of the Americanization of popular culture all over the world as an embodied, localized experience of global possibility. In such transactions between the local and the global, the future is now. Along these lines, the globalization of American popular culture is generating temporal orientations throughout the world in which all of the promises of human destiny will be fulfilled in the present.

As the center of a global orientation in space, America has achieved mythic proportions. Where, we have asked, is America? As we have seen, America was the hope of redemption cherished by the American movement during the 1920s and

1930s in central and southern Africa. In the 1990s, however, America was the turf and territory of a criminal gang in the impoverished townships of the Cape Flats outside Cape Town, South Africa. In complex, multiple ways, America has also been extended through the Coca-Cola distributors, who operate in more countries than the United Nations. America has been localized in McDonald's restaurants in London and Paris, Tokyo and Delhi, Jerusalem and Riyadh, and many other locations of McDonaldland. Bearing all of the meaningful, highly charged symbolism of a global reality, America has been firmly located in the EuroDisney of Paris, the Disneyland of Tokyo, and someday soon in the Disney World planned for China. All of these commercial, cultural, and arguably religious extensions and localizations of America have reinforced America's ambiguous status as the powerful, perhaps sacred, center of spatial orientation in a globalizing world.

OUTSIDE, LOOKING IN

For better or worse, for centuries America has been invested with symbolic, even religious, meaning and significance within the human geography of the world. From a global perspective, many questions might be raised about the meaning of America, as this book's explorations of religion and American popular culture have shown. Almost anything, one might think, is possible. In analyzing the role of ideology in American history, Sacvan Bercovitch has identified "the culture's controlling metaphor—'America' as synonym for human possibility."[21] This poetics of human possibility, however, has simultaneously been the site of a politics of social conflict in which, as Giles Gunn has noted, "the term 'America' has always served the political interests of both cultural consensus and cultural dissensus."[22] In these terms, the name "America" has been mobilized as a symbol of human possibility but also as a symbol of dissent and resistance against forces that limit the realization of human possibility in the United States. Martin Luther King Jr. might have identified America as "the greatest purveyor of violence in the world," but he had a utopian dream of human realization in community that also bore the name "America."[23]

As a multivalent symbol, therefore, the significance of "America" has oscillated between fixed pattern and open promise, between limits and opportunities, between oppression and redemption. Outside the United States, people all over the world have imagined America.

The long history of the European production of images of America reveals certain characteristic strategies of symbolic representation. In the earliest "inventions" of America, dating back to the age of European explorations beginning with the "discovery" of America by Columbus in 1492, the continent and its indigenous population represented the boundary of the world. America was Europe's "other." Reports of America were used to place Europe in silhouette, to circumscribe its familiar features with images from a strange world. Travelers described America's unfamiliar topography, unknown vegetation, wild animals, savage humans, and even bizarre, semihuman monsters as if they represented the ultimate boundary of the world. Imagining America as the outer limit of possibility, as the historian Joseph Leerssen has observed, Europe was "defined in its periphery and by its margins, in its contacts with the unknown past and the alien outer world."[24] By representing America as its own boundary, therefore, Europe constituted itself as the center of the world.

In Europe as well, however, "America" could symbolize both consensus and dissent. In consensual terms, America might represent the periphery that defined Europe's central place in the world. But internal critics of European societies could also appropriate America as a symbol of alternative human possibilities. From 1500 to 1800, reports of the "New World" had a profound impact on European social thought. Their occasional descriptions of Native American societies that were in harmony with nature, without oppressive masters, exhaustive labor, private property, or greed for the accumulation of wealth, hinted at a way of life very different from the capitalist order emerging in Europe. These images of human possibility affected European notions of liberty and equality. Visions of America, such as More's "utopia," Montaigne's "noble savage," and Locke's "state of nature," were useful in gaining critical leverage on European society, providing a baseline for imagining both an original human past and a possible human future. Not merely a boundary, America could be represented as an alternative to European society.[25]

During the nineteenth century, these representations of America as both boundary and alternative proliferated in European visitors' recorded impressions of American space. Certainly, European tourists were impressed by the natural landscape. Many visitors, however, tried to represent the social landscape of America in specifically spatial terms. One of the more perceptive European visitors, the French sociologist Alexis de Tocqueville, touring the United States during the early 1830s, proposed a particular spatial representation of America by suggesting that American society was a dramatic reversal of natural order. "The Americans arrived but yesterday in the land where they live," Tocqueville reported, "and they have already turned the whole order of nature upside down to their profit."[26] By the nineteenth century, according to critics such as Tocqueville, America was not the "state of nature." American space was an inversion of nature, a mirror image of a social order regarded as natural in Europe, not merely reflecting, but actually reversing, a familiar European world.

This reversal could be celebrated or decried, sometimes simultaneously, as epiphany easily turned to irony in European representations of America. At mid-century, German novelist Ferdinand Kürnberger captured this symbolic tension between representations of America as a land of opportunity and a land of disillusionment. Kürnberger represented America as a utopian epiphany: "America! What name is as weighty as this name? Save in the sphere of imagination there is nothing loftier in the world. The individual speaks of the better self: the globe says 'America'. The word is the final chord and the great cadence in the concert of human perfections."[27] But the German novelist embedded this celebration of utopian America in a critical account of the hardships actually suffered by immigrants, underscoring the irony of his opening epiphany of America by titling his novel *Der Amerika-Müde* (Tired of America). In contrast to conventional depictions of America as a land of opportunity, some Europeans resorted to irony to represent the perceived failure of possibility in America.

More recently, Tocqueville's successor as a French intellectual tourist in America, the postmodernist critic Jean Baudrillard, pursued this use of irony by representing the entire space of America as a vast emptiness. In depicting American space, which he referred to as *l'Amerique siderale*, "astral America," Baudrillard focused on "the America of the empty, absolute freedom of the freeways." According to Baudrillard, America appeared "in the film of days and nights projected across an empty space." Most important, America revealed itself in the emptiness of its deserts. In fact, Baudrillard asserted, "America is a desert." From the outside looking in, he claimed to have penetrated the illusion of America, not by discovering the truth of the country, but by exploring the emptiness of the deserts of the American Southwest. "I know the deserts, their deserts, better than they do," Baudrillard asserted, "since they turn their backs on their own space as the Greeks turned their backs on the sea, and I got to know more about the concrete social life of America from the desert than I ever would from official and intellectual gatherings."[28]

Apparently, the American desert revealed an extermination of meaning, a void that resisted the imposition of any meaningful social, political, or moral project.

As a result, Baudrillard insisted, "Here in the most moral society there is, space is truly immoral." At the same time, however, the desert was subject to an unrestrained proliferation of meaning. Across the empty space of America, Americans were entangled in the wild dissemination of signs and images that had turned the country into a "hyperreality," a space of simulation with all the effects of the real. Because America meant nothing, it could mean anything and everything. America, the desert, was also astral America, the America of the stars.[29]

Certainly, all of these ways of imagining America—as boundary, alternative, reversal, epiphany, irony, and emptiness—have produced an "America" as an essentially mythic space. As humanistic geographer Yi-fu Tuan has argued, mythic space is not merely a realm of the imagination, a flight of fancy, because it can also produce effects by framing the everyday or "pragmatic space" in which people act and interact.[30] Mythic images of America have had practical effects. During the nineteenth century, for example, European depictions of America as a land of savagery were mythic images instrumental to governments and interest groups trying to discourage emigration. European depictions of America as a land of promise, opportunity, and equality, however, served to encourage emigration.[31] Conflicting myths of America were entangled in European social struggles, suggesting that the production of America as mythic space was integral to the production of the social and symbolic space of Europe.

Obviously, foreign perspectives on America, from the outside looking in, have not been confined to Europe. In addition to European voices, which have usually been privileged in accounts of foreign perceptions of America, many others have spoken about American space. Immigrants and refugees from Africa, Asia, South America, and elsewhere have also perceived America as a space of human possibility. Many, however, have experienced America as an empty space. To cite only one striking example: Chinese sociologist Fei Xiotong, on a tour of the United States in 1943, observed that America lacked enduring traditions that were "part of life, sacred, something to be feared and loved." As a result, in his view, American space was empty, a land without the ancestral ghosts that give meaning to the present by relating it to the past. "In a world without ghosts," Fei Xiotong remarked, "life is free and easy. American eyes can gaze straight ahead. But still I think they lack something and I do not envy their lives."[32] In these terms, American space was not full of sacred possibilities in the present because it lacked nurturing temporal connections with the past. Like Baudrillard, perhaps, Fei Xiotong found American space empty of meaning because it could mean anything. America was devoid of sacred reality precisely because everything was humanly possible.

POSSIBILITY, AUTHENTICITY

The entire field of American religion and popular culture, its machinery of production, patterns of consumption, and sacred artifacts, is poised between the extremes of possibility and authenticity. In the aftermath of September 11, the philosopher Slavoj Žižek, like Baudrillard before him, compared America to a desert, quoting *The Matrix* (1998), bidding all Americans "Welcome to the Desert of the Real." Not empty, according to Žižek, this real American desert was full of imagery, saturated with fantasy, animated by all of the images of terrorist destruction that had become commonplace in Hollywood movies, from *Escape from New York* (1981) to *Independence Day* (1996). Informed by all of these media-generated fears of terrorist devastation, Americans were still unprepared for what happened on September 11, because they harbored an even greater fear, their worst fear, according to Žižek, which resided in the lingering apprehension that behind the everyday display of their American world "the world is fake."[33]

This hard question, the question of authenticity, cannot possibly have any easy answer. It must be worked out. As I have tried to show, the authenticity of being human, in a human place, is worked out, thought out, and fought out under specific conditions of possibility.

Popular culture, as Lawrence Grossberg has proposed, enables all kinds of fake posturing, for both artists and audiences, who assume multiple, changing identities. Rather than dismissing these postures as fake, he has proposed the term *authentic inauthenticity* for their celebration of possibility. "If every identity is equally fake, a pose taken," Grossberg has argued, "then authentic inauthenticity celebrates the possibilities of poses without denying that that is all they are."[34] But American popular culture is not only about posturing and posing. It can also identify subject positions, clarifying significant locations in the broader social, political, and economic reality of America.

During the 1960s, American popular music revealed that a human being could be stuck in the snow on the East Coast, dreaming of California, or far away from a Georgia home, living in California and sitting on the dock of the San Francisco Bay. Authentically, in different ways, the Mamas and the Papas and Otis Redding confronted the American dream, entering the desert of the real, perhaps, but ending up in very different places. Whether California dreamin' or sittin' on the dock of the Bay, these musical artists worked out different subject positions in relation to America.

In the Mamas and the Papas' hit single "California Dreamin'," released in

November 1965, John Phillips, the principal writer of the song (although Denny Doherty took the lead vocal), began with the desolation of his location. He evoked winter on the East Coast of America as a dark night of the soul: the leaves were brown, the sky was gray—even when he was in motion, out walking, trying to show some sign of life, he was still enveloped by the coldness, the darkness of a winter's day. He would be safe and warm, he imagined, if he were in Los Angeles, dreaming of the "safe and sound," which Derrida has identified as recurring signs of the sacred, if not the most basic defining features of religion.[35]

In this case, the sacred, for all of its promises of safety, security, and warmth, is fixated on Los Angeles, which is the City of Angels. But it is also the City of Quartz in Mike Davis's historical account, a city of disasters, natural and social, in which catastrophic acts of God and endemic acts of political and corporate corruption have shaped a city of profound contradictions.[36]

As the holy city of desire, Los Angeles is beyond reach. The city's contradictions, however, can be enacted anywhere, even in exile on the other coast of America. This duplicity of Los Angeles, city of angels, city of demons, can be transposed anywhere. Unaware of this problem of duplicity, the writer of "California Dreamin'" duplicates it by faking religion. Longing for the Los Angeles elsewhere, Phillips describes entering a church, getting down on his knees, and pretending to pray. His pretence at praying, apparently, is not noticed by the church's priest, who simply observes that Phillips is going to remain where he is, just like the cold. Frozen in place, there he is, immobilized, dreaming of California.

We must be struck by this strange formulation: "I pretend to pray." It seems to be a conscious recognition of religious inauthenticity, an intentional admission of insincerity in faking a religious act. Although Phillips accuses himself of such religious fakery, some people have been accused by others of pretending to pray. In South Africa, for example, the first Christian missionary, George Schmidt, who began his mission in the 1730s, has long been celebrated for opening up the field of authentic religious conversion for Africans. His eighteenth-century Dutch contemporaries, however, regarded him as a fake. Specifically, they accused Schmidt of going up on top of his house, getting down on his knees, and pretending to pray.[37] As we have seen, many religious expressions in American popular culture, from New Age shamans to Walt Disney animation, have been accused of religious fakery. John Phillips, by contrast, accused himself of religious inauthenticity, admitting to his pretence and thereby, perhaps, demonstrating a greater degree of personal integrity than the original Christian missionary in South Africa. Nevertheless, as an important aspect of dreaming about California, he fakes religion.

Ultimately, in "California Dreamin'," Phillips, or at least the persona he adopts in the song, is reduced to nothing but deception. Pretending to pray to God, he avoids telling the truth to his girlfriend. "If I didn't tell her," he says, "I could leave today," reinforcing the basic undercurrent of pretence, deception, and dishonesty that defines his situation. Dreaming of being elsewhere, of being in California, and perhaps even of being in the fulfilling fantasy of the American dream, Phillips ends up stuck, in stasis, trapped by all the lies of his own making but also trapped by the lies inherent in the American dream. Freezing, frozen, and fixed in place, he remains, dreaming of California.

In Otis Redding's last record, "(Sittin' on the) Dock of the Bay," completed in 1967 three days before his tragic death in a plane crash, he begins with "Sitting in the morning sun," then traces the course of a full day, from sunrise to sunset, in which nothing happens, assuring us, "I'll be sitting till the evening comes." This particular day, like every day, is fixed. On the dock of the bay, Redding sits, motionless. He is just there. He has nowhere to go, nothing to do, nobody to be. In this song, the singer is the fixed point, not of a turning world, perhaps, but of a worldly rhythm synchronized with the sea. As the tides move in and out of the bay, he watches the ships roll in; he watches them roll away again; and he sits on the dock of the bay.

With the rhythm of every day established, Redding is just sitting on the dock, by the bay, wasting time. If time is money, and money is the god of the market, then this singer is contributing nothing to the religion of the capitalist market economy. Defying the Protestant religious ethos of work, self-discipline, and time efficiency, Redding celebrates the value, beyond all market calculations, of wasting time.

Unlike the stasis of "California Dreamin'," there is movement in Redding's song, with the tides coming in and out, the ships coming in and out, but it is not the singer's movement. Yet, we know he has moved in the past. There is a background of personal history in his song, recalling how he left his home in Georgia, heading for California, and eventually ended up in San Francisco. As a destination of desire, California in Otis Redding's case stands in stark contrast to California in John Phillips's dream about being safe and warm in sunny Los Angeles. There is nothing obviously safe and warm for Redding in sitting on the dock of the bay in San Francisco. Not a desirable destination for him, the dock of this particular bay is the end of all his desire.

Arriving at the end of the American dream, Redding sings about the reality of the ocean's tides, coming in, going out, signifying that he has nothing to live for, with nothing coming his way, because everything is finished. Nothing is going to change; everything will remain exactly the same. Refusing to conform to social expectations, let alone to do what anyone might tell him to do, Redding reaffirms his commitment, despite solitude, loneliness, to remaining exactly as he is, maintaining the same living, regular rhythm as the ocean's tides, going in and going out, while sitting on the dock of the bay.

In contrast to the persona in "California Dreamin'," who is alienated, trapped in the cold, but also trapped within the inauthenticity of his own pretence, dishonesty, and deception, stuck, dreaming of being elsewhere, the singer in "Dock of the Bay" has achieved a sublime state of stillness, doing nothing perhaps, but doing nothing extremely well. In "Dock of the Bay," Otis Redding suggested the possibility of doing absolutely nothing, soulfully, authentically.

America's "holiday from history," as Slavoj Žižek has argued, "was a fake." If this holiday from history was an illusion, a dream, what does it mean to wake up, awakening to a new, real world? In a globalizing world in which a multinational corporation such as Nike can say "Just Do It" with such powerful cultural resonance that a small religious sect in California, Heavens Gate, adopts that advertising slogan as a religious warrant for collective suicide, we might consider the possibility that doing absolutely nothing, like Otis Redding sitting on the dock of a bay, can sometimes be a good idea.

Doing nothing, of course, poses its own problems. Still, none of this is to say that American popular culture necessarily provides a program of action (or inaction) for people to follow. In all of popular culture's possibility, its authenticity, we find neither a political project for the present nor a political formula for the future. Instead, we find religion.

Religion, as both unconscious dreaming and conscious action, permeates American popular culture. In 1997 the godfather of hip-hop, Afrika Bambaataa, outlined the religious possibilities for American popular culture as it moved into the twenty-first century. He identified two kinds of religion: On the one side, there was the "go to sleep slavery type of religion," the religion of the dream. Slavery, sleep, and the American dream added up to a religion of the oppressed that sealed their oppression. On the other side, there was the religion of conscious, positive action, "like the prophets," in which "knowledge, wisdom, [and] understanding of self and others" inform a "do for self and others type of religion." Waking up from the religion of sleep, Americans might be able to participate in yet another "Great Awakening," a religious revival, in a long line of revivals, but this time they might really be awake. As the artist of "Planet Rock," Afrika Bambaataa imagined that Planet America might wake up, religiously, to the "spiritual wake up, revolutionary . . . type of religion."[38] Given his inauthentic authenticity, since he was not born in Africa, and his "Zulu Nation" was not Zulu, Afrika Bambaataa nevertheless worked out an authentic religious position in relation to the American dream.

To paraphrase Karl Marx, religion is both fake and authentic, both a dream-inducing opiate and a genuine expression of real pain and suffering at the heart of a heartless world. On Planet America, popular culture has been carrying the religious dream and bearing the religious pain through vast global exchanges, with their profound local effects, all over the world. Although conventional religious institutions remain vital, defying the predictions of their demise by prophets of modernization, religious impulses have been diffused in uncontrollable, unpredictable ways through the media of popular culture. Traces of religion, as transcendence, as the sacred, as the ultimate, can be discerned in the play of popular culture. As a result, we can conclude that popular culture is doing a kind of religious work, even if we cannot predict how that ongoing religious work of American popular culture, now diffused all over the globe, will actually work for the United States of America.

NOTES

INTRODUCTION

1. William James, *The Varieties of Religious Experience*, ed. Martin E. Marty (London: Penguin, 1982), 37–38.

2. Andrew Ross, *The Celebration Chronicles: Life, Liberty, and the Pursuit of Property Values in Disney's New Town* (New York: Ballantine Books, 1999), 296.

3. Luisah Teish, "Foreword," in Vusamazulu Credo Mutwa, *Song of the Stars: The Lore of a Zulu Shaman*, ed. Stephen Larsen (Barrytown, NY: Station Hill Openings, 1996), ix.

4. Nelson Mandela, *The Struggle Is My Life* (New York: Pathfinder Press, 1986), 72–76. See also Nelson Mandela, *In His Own Words*, ed. Kader Asmal, David Chidester, and Wilmot James (Boston: Little, Brown, 2004), 11–14.

CHAPTER 1. PLANET HOLLYWOOD

1. Michael Eric Dyson, *Reflecting Black: African American Cultural Criticism* (Minneapolis: University of Minnesota Press, 1993), 58.

2. NYCTourist.Com, "Planet Hollywood," www.nyctourist.com/topten_planet .htm (accessed April 14, 2004); Samuel Huntington, *The Clash of Civilizations and the Remaking of World Order* (New York: Simon and Schuster, 1996).

3. "Planet Hollywood Bombing," *Al-Ahram* 392 (August 27–September 2, 1998).

4. Paul Karon, "Hollywood on Alert," *Daily Variety*, August 26, 1998, www .facstaff.bucknell.edu/efaden/299/hwood_on_alert.html (accessed April 14, 2004).

5. Tarek Atia, "Bruce Willis versus Bin Laden," *Al-Ahram* 402 (November 5–11, 1998).

6. Cohn quoted in Jon Ronson, *Them: Adventures with Extremists* (London: Picador, 2001), 208. See also Neal Gabler, *An Empire of Their Own: How the Jews Invented Hollywood* (New York: Doubleday, 1989); Michael P. Rogin, *Blackface, White Noise: Jewish Immigrants in the Hollywood Melting Pot* (Berkeley: University of California Press, 1996).

7. Max Weber, *The Theory of Social and Economic Organization,* trans. A. M. Henderson and Talcott Parsons (New York: Oxford University Press, 1947), 309.

8. E. B. Tylor, *Primitive Culture,* 2 vols. (London: John Murray, 1871), 1:424; Melford Spiro, "Religion: Problems of Definition and Explanation," in Michael Banton, ed., *Anthropological Approaches to the Study of Religion* (London: Tavistock, 1966), 96.

9. Friedrich Schleiermacher, *On Religion to Its Cultured Despisers,* trans. Richard Crouter (1799; Cambridge: Cambridge University Press, 1988); Rudolf Otto, *The Idea of the Holy,* trans. John W. Harvey (1917; London: Oxford University Press, 1923); F. Max Müller, *Introduction to the Science of Religion* (London: Longmans, Green, 1873), 20; William James, *The Varieties of Religious Experience,* ed. Martin E. Marty (London: Penguin, 1982), 31–38; Paul Tillich, *The Shaking of the Foundations* (New York: Charles Scribner's Sons, 1948), 57.

10. Émile Durkheim, *The Elementary Forms of the Religious Life,* trans. Joseph Ward Swain (New York: Free Press, 1965), 62.

11. Ninian Smart, *Worldviews: Crosscultural Explorations of Human Beliefs* (New York: Charles Scribner's Sons, 1983).

12. Clifford Geertz, *The Interpretation of Cultures* (New York: Basic Books, 1973), 90.

13. Émile Benveniste, *Indo-European Language and Society,* trans. Elizabeth Palmer (London: Faber and Faber, 1973), 522.

14. David Chidester, *Salvation and Suicide: An Interpretation of Jim Jones, the Peoples Temple, and Jonestown* (Bloomington: Indiana University Press, 1988), and *Savage Systems: Colonialism and Comparative Religion in Southern Africa* (Charlottesville: University Press of Virginia, 1996).

15. David Chidester, "The Church of Baseball, the Fetish of Coca-Cola, and the Potlatch of Rock 'n' Roll: Theoretical Models for the Study of Religion in American Popular Culture," *Journal of the American Academy of Religion* 64 (1996): 743–65.

16. Richard D. Land and Frank D. York, *Send a Message to Mickey: The ABC's of Making Your Voice Heard at Disney* (Nashville, TN: Broadman and Holman, 1998).

17. Karen E. Fields, "Translator's Introduction: Religion as an Eminently Social Thing," in Émile Durkheim, *The Elementary Forms of Religious Life,* trans. Karen E. Fields (New York: Free Press, 1995), xlvi.

18. These three features of the political economy of the sacred are explained in

greater detail in David Chidester and Edward T. Linenthal, "Introduction," in Chidester and Linenthal, eds., *American Sacred Space* (Bloomington: Indiana University Press, 1995), 9–20.

19. Lawrence W. Levine, "The Folklore of Industrial Society: Popular Culture and Its Audiences," *American Historical Review* 97, 5 (1992): 1373.

20. Charles H. Long, "Popular Religion," in Mircea Eliade, ed., *The Encyclopedia of Religion* (New York: Macmillan, 1987), 11:442–52. See also Mark D. Hulsether, "Interpreting the 'Popular' in Popular Religion," *American Studies* 36, 2 (1995): 127–37.

21. Ernst Bloch, Theodor W. Adorno, and Georg Lukács, *Aesthetics and Politics,* trans. and ed. Ronald Taylor (London: NLB, 1977), 123.

22. Max Horkheimer and Theodor W. Adorno, *The Dialectic of Enlightenment,* trans. John Cumming (London: Verso, 1973), 120, 137–38.

23. Walter Benjamin, *Gesammelte Schriften,* 7 vols., ed. Rolf Tiedemann and Hermann Schweppenhäuser (Frankfurt: Suhrkamp, 1972–1989), 7:377; Miriam Hansen, "Of Mice and Ducks: Benjamin and Adorno on Disney," *South Atlantic Quarterly* 92, 1 (1993): 31.

24. Benjamin, *Gesammelte Schriften,* 2:218ff.; also quoted in Hansen, "Of Mice and Ducks," 41–42.

25. Grant McCracken, *Culture and Consumption: New Approaches to the Symbolic Character of Consumer Goods and Activities* (Bloomington: Indiana University Press, 1988), 84–88.

26. Stuart Hall, "Encoding/Decoding," in S. Hall, D. Hobson, A. Lowe, and P. Willis, eds., *Culture, Media, and Language* (London: Hutchinson, 1980), 128–38; Stuart Hall, "Notes on Deconstructing 'the Popular,'" in Raphael Samuel, ed., *People's History and Socialist Theory* (London: Routledge, 1981); John Fiske, *Power Plays, Power Works* (London: Verso, 1993).

27. Max Weber, "Politics as a Vocation," in H. H. Gerth and C. Wright Mills, ed. and trans., *From Max Weber: Essays in Sociology* (New York: Basic Books, 1958), 78.

28. Slavoj Žižek, *The Fragile Absolute: Or, Why Is the Christian Legacy Worth Fighting For?* (London: Verso, 2000), 150.

29. Ernest Renan, "What Is a Nation?" in Homi Bhabha, ed., *Nation and Narration* (London: Routledge, 1990), 8–22.

30. William R. LaFleur, "Body," in Mark C. Taylor, ed., *Critical Terms for Religious Studies* (Chicago: University of Chicago Press, 1998), 26.

31. Mark C. Taylor, *About Religion: Economies of Faith in Virtual Culture* (Chicago: University of Chicago Press, 1999), 1.

32. David Chidester, *Patterns of Transcendence: Religion, Death, and Dying,* 2nd ed. (Belmont, CA: Wadsworth Publishing Company, 2002), 122–44, 192–217.

33. See Roger Friedland, "Money, Sex, and God: The Erotic Logic of Religious Nationalism," *Sociological Theory* 20, 3 (2002): 381–425.

34. Talal Asad, *Genealogies of Religion: Discipline and Reasons of Power in Christianity and Islam* (Baltimore: Johns Hopkins University Press, 1993); Timothy Fitzgerald, *The Ideology of Religious Studies* (Oxford: Oxford University Press, 1999); Russell T. McCutcheon, *Manufacturing Religion: The Discourse of Sui Generis Religion and the Politics of Nostalgia* (New York: Oxford University Press, 1997).

35. Peter F. Beyer, *Religion and Globalization* (London: Sage, 1994); Roland Robertson, "Religion and the Global Field," *Social Compass* 41, 1 (1994): 121–35; Michael Watson and John L. Esposito, eds., *Religion and Global Order* (Cardiff: University of Wales Press, 2000).

36. Peter L. Berger, "Four Faces of Global Culture," *National Interest* 49 (Fall 1997): 23–29, and "Globalisation and Culture: Not Simply the West versus the Rest," seminar paper, Centre for Development Enterprise, 1998, www.cde.org.za/focus/global.htm (accessed September 27, 2002).

37. See Simon Coleman, *The Globalisation of Charismatic Christianity: Spreading the Gospel of Prosperity* (Cambridge: Cambridge University Press, 2000).

38. David R. Loy, "Religion of the Market," *Journal of the American Academy of Religion* 65, 2 (1997): 275–90; Harvey Cox, "The Market as God: Living in a New Dispensation," *Atlantic Monthly*, March 1999, 18–23; Thabo Mbeki, "Prologue," in Malegapuru William Makgoba, ed., *African Renaissance: The New Struggle* (Johannesburg: Mafube; Cape Town: Tafelberg, 1999), xviii; Kalman Applbaum, "Crossing Borders: Globalization as Myth and Charter in American Transnational Consumer Marketing," *American Ethnologist* 27, 2 (2000): 257–82; J. Paul Martin and Harry Winter, "Religious Proselytization: Historical and Theological Perspectives at the End of the Twentieth Century," in Abdullahi A. An-Na'im, ed., *Proselytization and Communal Self-Determination in Africa* (Maryknoll, NY: Orbis Books, 1999), 38.

39. Michael J. Perry, *The Idea of Human Rights: Four Inquiries* (New York: Oxford University Press, 1998), 11–41; Carrie Gustafson and Peter Juviler, eds., *Religion and Human Rights: Competing Claims* (Armonk, NY: M. E. Sharpe, 1999); Abdullahi A. An-Na'im, ed., *Human Rights in Crosscultural Perspective* (Philadelphia: University of Pennsylvania Press, 1993); John P. Humphrey, *Human Rights and the United Nations: A Great Adventure* (Dobbs Ferry, NY: Transnational Publishers, 1984), 67.

40. Bruce Forbes and Jeffrey Mahan, eds., *Religion and Popular Culture in America* (Berkeley: University of California Press, 2000); Eric Michael Mazur and Kate McCarthy, eds., *God in the Details: American Religion in Popular Culture* (London: Routledge, 2001).

41. Jose David Saldivar, *Border Matters: Remapping American Cultural Studies*

(Berkeley: University of California Press, 1997); Rob Kroes, *If You've Seen One, You've Seen the Mall: Europeans and American Mass Culture* (Urbana: University of Illinois Press, 1996); George McKay, ed., *Yankee Go Home (& Take Me with U): Americanization and Popular Culture* (Sheffield: Sheffield Academic Press, 1997); Reinhold Wagnleitner and Elaine Tyler May, eds., *Here, There, and Everywhere: The Foreign Politics of American Popular Culture* (Hanover, NH: University Press of New England, 2000).

CHAPTER 2. POPULAR RELIGION

1. Jeffrey K. Hadden, "The Globalization of American Televangelism," in Roland Robertson and W. K. Garrett, eds., *Religion and the Global Order* (New York: Paragon, 1991), 221–44.

2. For a useful review of literature on religion and film, see Mark D. Hulsether, "Sorting Out the Relationships among Christian Values, U.S. Popular Religion, and Hollywood Films," *Religious Studies Review* 25, 1 (1999): 3–12.

3. Colleen McDannell, *Material Christianity: Religion and Popular Culture in America* (New Haven: Yale University Press, 1995); David Morgan, *Visual Piety: A History and Theory of Popular Religious Images* (Berkeley: University of California Press, 1998); William D. Romanowski, "Evangelicals and Popular Music: The Contemporary Christian Music Industry," in Bruce Forbes and Jeffrey Mahan, eds., *Religion and Popular Culture in America* (Berkeley: University of California Press, 2000).

4. Laurence R. Moore, *Selling God: American Religion in the Marketplace of Culture* (New York: Oxford University Press, 1994); Leigh Eric Schmidt, *Consumer Rites: The Buying and Selling of American Holidays* (Princeton: Princeton University Press, 1995); Woolsey Biggart, *Charismatic Capitalism: Direct Selling Organizations in America* (Chicago: University of Chicago Press, 1989).

5. Robert H. Knight and Gary L. Bauer, *The Age of Consent: The Rise of Relativism and the Corruption of Popular Culture* (Dallas: Spence Publications, 1998); Betty Houchin Winfield and Sandra Davidson, eds., *Bleep! Censoring Rock and Rap Music* (Westport, CT: Greenwood Press, 1999); Mark Joseph, *The Rock & Roll Rebellion: Why People of Faith Abandoned Rock Music and Why They're Coming Back* (Nashville: Broadman and Holman Publishers, 1999).

6. E. B. Tylor, *Primitive Culture*, 2 vols. (London: John Murray, 1871), 1:424; Émile Durkheim, *The Elementary Forms of the Religious Life*, trans. Joseph Ward Swain (New York: Free Press, 1965), 62.

7. Geoffrey C. Ward and Ken Burns, eds., *Baseball: An Illustrated History* (New York: Alfred A. Knopf, 1994), 231; Mark Pendergrast, *For God, Country, and Coca-Cola: The Unauthorized History of the Great American Soft Drink and the Company That Makes It* (New York: Charles Scribner's Sons, 1993): 261; Fred Bronson, *The*

Billboard Book of Number One Hits (New York: Billboard Publications, 1985), 201; Dan Graham, *Rock My Religion: Writings and Projects, 1965–1990* (Boston: MIT Press, 1994).

8. Eric Benner, "Defending the 'Sport' to the Very End," *Slam: Pro Wrestling,* December 4, 1998; Bruce Lincoln, *Discourse and the Construction of Society: Comparative Studies of Myth, Ritual, and Classification* (New York: Oxford University Press, 1989), 149–59.

9. Erika Doss, *Elvis Culture: Fans, Faith, and Image* (Lawrence: University Press of Kansas, 1999); N. J. Girardot, "*Ecce* Elvis: 'Elvis Studies' as a Postmodernist Paradigm for the Academic Study of Religions," *Journal of the American Academy of Religion* 68 (2000): 603–14.

10. Michael Jindra, "Star Trek Fandom as a Religious Phenomenon," *Sociology of Religion* 55, 1 (1994): 27–51.

11. Kristin N. Weissman, *Barbie, the Icon, the Image, the Ideal: An Analytical Interpretation of the Barbie Doll in Popular Culture* (Austin: Universal Publishers, 1999); James B. Twitchell, *Adcult USA: The Triumph of Advertising in American Culture* (New York: Columbia University Press, 1995); Aaron Betsky, ed., *Icons: Magnets of Meaning* (San Francisco: Chronicle Books, 1997).

12. Dave Marsh, *Louie, Louie* (New York: Hyperion, 1993). On performance, see Catherine Bell, "Performance," in Mark C. Taylor, ed., *Critical Terms for Religious Studies* (Chicago: University of Chicago Press, 1998), 205–20.

13. Clifford Geertz, *The Interpretation of Cultures* (New York: Basic Books, 1973), 90; Pendergrast, *For God, Country, and Coca-Cola,* 400.

14. Ward and Burns, eds., *Baseball: An Illustrated History,* 231.

15. Ibid., 107–49. See also Christopher H. Evans and William R. Herzog II, eds., *The Faith of Fifty Million: Baseball, Religion, and American Culture* (Louisville, KY: Westminster John Knox Press, 2002).

16. Ward and Burns, eds., *Baseball: An Illustrated History,* xviii.

17. Thomas Boswell, "The Church of Baseball," in Ward and Burns, eds., *Baseball: An Illustrated History,* 189.

18. Ibid., 193.

19. Ibid., 189–90.

20. Ibid., 189.

21. Horace Miner, "Body Ritual among the Nacirema," *American Anthropologist* 58, 3 (1956): 503–7.

22. George Gmelch, "Baseball Magic," in James P. Spradley and David W. McCurdy, eds., *Conformity and Conflict: Readings in Cultural Anthropology* (Glenview, IL: Scott Foresman, 1978), 373–83.

23. Sigmund Freud, "Obsessive Acts and Religious Practices," in James Strachey,

ed., *The Standard Edition of the Complete Psychological Works of Sigmund Freud*, 24 vols. (London: Hogarth Press, 1953–74), 9:117–27, quotations from 117–18.

24. Émile Benveniste, *Indo-European Language and Society*, trans. Elizabeth Palmer (London: Faber and Faber, 1973), 522.

25. Thomas Hobbes, *Leviathan*, ed. Michael Oakeshot (New York: Collier Books, 1962), 69.

26. Durkheim, *Elementary Forms of the Religious Life*, 60.

27. J. Milton Yinger, *Religion, Society, and the Individual* (New York: Macmillan, 1957), 147.

28. Pendergrast, *For God, Country, and Coca-Cola*. All subsequent references to this text are cited by page number in the body of the chapter.

29. Marshall W. Fishwick, "Review: Sut Jhally, *The Codes of Advertising*," *Journal of Popular Culture* 26, 2 (1992): 155.

30. William Pietz, "The Problem of the Fetish, I," *Res: Anthropology and Aesthetics* 9 (Spring 1985): 5–17, "The Problem of the Fetish, II," *Res: Anthropology and Aesthetics* 13 (Spring 1987): 23–45, "The Problem of the Fetish, IIIa," *Res: Anthropology and Aesthetics* 16 (Autumn 1988): 105–23. See also Emily Apter and William Pietz, eds., *Fetishism as Cultural Discourse* (Ithaca: Cornell University Press, 1993).

31. Michael Taussig, "Maleficium: State Fetishism," *The Nervous System* (London: Routledge, 1992), 111–40.

32. Benedict Anderson, *Imagined Communities: Reflections on the Origin and Spread of Nationalism* (London: Verso, 1991); Eric Hobsbawm and Terrence Ranger, eds., *The Invention of Tradition* (Cambridge: Cambridge University Press, 1985); Leonard Thompson, *The Political Mythology of Apartheid* (New Haven: Yale University Press, 1985).

33. Jay R. Howard, "Contemporary Christian Music: Where Rock Meets Religion," *Journal of Popular Culture* 26, 1 (1992): 123.

34. Robert L. Gross, "Heavy Metal Music: A New Subculture in American Society," *Journal of Popular Culture* 24, 1 (1990): 119–30; Davin Seay and Mary Neely, *Stairway to Heaven: The Spiritual Roots of Rock 'n' Roll* (New York: Ballantine, 1986).

35. Bob Larson, *Rock and Roll: The Devil's Diversion* (McCook, NE: Larson, 1967); Linda Martin and Kerry Segrave, *Anti-Rock: The Opposition to Rock 'n' Roll* (Hamden, CT: Archon Books, 1988); Dan Peters, Steve Peters, and Cher Merrill, *What about Christian Rock?* (Minneapolis: Bethany, 1986).

36. David Shenk and Steve Silberman, *Skeleton Key: A Dictionary for Deadheads* (New York: Doubleday, 1994), ix; Tony Magistrale, "Wild Child: Jim Morrison's Poetic Journeys," *Journal of Popular Culture* 26, 3 (1992): 133–44; Robert Pattison, *The Triumph of Vulgarity: Rock Music in the Mirror of Romanticism* (Oxford: Oxford University Press, 1987); Lisa St. Clair Harvey, "Temporary Insanity: Fun, Games,

and Transformational Ritual in American Music Video," *Journal of Popular Culture* 24, 1 (1990): 39–64; Jon Michael Spencer, "Overview of American Popular Music in a Theological Perspective," in J. M. Spencer, ed., *Theomusicology* (Durham, NC: Duke University Press, 1994), 205.

37. Marsh, *Louie, Louie,* 74.

38. Ibid., 77.

39. Ibid., 78.

40. Ibid.

41. Ibid., 73–74; Marsh is quoting an unidentified translation of the Gospel of Thomas 70.

42. For a useful review of literature on the potlatch, see Steven Vertovec, "Potlatching and the Mythic Past: A Re-evaluation of the Traditional Northwest Coast American Indian Complex," *Religion* 13 (1983): 323–44.

43. Marsh, *Louie, Louie,* 79–80.

44. Ibid., 80.

45. Ibid.

46. Martha Bayles, *Hole in Our Soul: The Loss of Beauty and Meaning in American Popular Music* (New York: Free Press, 1994), 12.

47. Marcel Mauss, *The Gift: Forms and Functions of Exchange in Archaic Societies,* trans. Ian Cunnison (London: Cohen and West, 1969), 1.

48. Ibid., 4.

49. Victor Turner, *Dramas, Fields, and Metaphors: Symbolic Action in Human Society* (Ithaca: Cornell University Press, 1974), 262.

50. Greil Marcus, *Lipstick Traces: A Secret History of the Twentieth Century* (Cambridge, MA: Harvard University Press, 1989).

51. Georges Bataille, "The Notion of Expenditure," in *Visions of Excess: Selected Writings, 1927–1939,* ed. Allan Stoekl, trans. Allan Stoekl, Carl R. Lovitt, and Donald M. Leslie Jr. (Minneapolis: University of Minnesota Press, 1985), 118.

52. Tylor, *Primitive Culture,* 1:424.

53. *Sports Illustrated,* April 10, 1995, 92.

54. Durkheim, *Elementary Forms of the Religious Life,* 62.

55. G. Pascal Zachary, *Showstopper: The Breakneck Race to Create Windows NT and the Next Generation at Microsoft* (New York: Free Press, 1994), 281.

56. On the significance of the polythetic categories of "cluster concepts" and "fuzzy sets" for the study of religion, see Fitz John Porter Poole, "Metaphors and Maps: Towards Comparison in the Anthropology of Religion," *Journal of the American Academy of Religion* 54 (1986): 428; and Jonathan Z. Smith, *Drudgery Divine: On the Comparison of Early Christianities and the Religions of Late Antiquity* (Chicago: University of Chicago Press, 1990), 50.

57. David Chidester, *Savage Systems: Colonialism and Comparative Religion in Southern Africa* (Charlottesville: University Press of Virginia, 1996).

CHAPTER 3. PLASTIC RELIGION

1. Edward Alsworth Ross, *Social Psychology: An Outline and Sourcebook* (New York: Macmillan, 1908), 322.

2. Robert Jay Lifton, "Protean Man," *Partisan Review* 35 (1968): 13–27; and Lifton, *The Protean Self: Human Resilience in an Age of Fragmentation* (New York: Basic Books, 1993).

3. Alison J. Clarke, *Tupperware: The Promise of Plastic in 1950s America* (Washington, DC: Smithsonian Institution Press, 1999), 41.

4. Mark Pendergrast, *For God, Country, and Coca-Cola: The Unauthorized History of the World's Most Popular Soft Drink* (New York: Charles Scribner's Sons, 1993), 27.

5. Clarke, *Tupperware*, 151; Timothy B. Spears, *Hundred Years on the Road: The Traveling Salesman in American Culture* (New Haven: Yale University Press, 1995), 145.

6. Catharine Beecher and Harriet Beecher Stowe, *The American Woman's Home: Or Principles of Domestic Science* (New York: J. B. Ford and Co., 1869), 455, 459; Colleen McDannell, "Creating the Christian Home: Home Schooling in Contemporary America," in David Chidester and Edward T. Linenthal, eds., *American Sacred Space* (Bloomington: Indiana University Press, 1995), 187–88.

7. David Harrington Watt, *A Transforming Faith: Explorations of Twentieth-Century American Evangelicalism* (New Brunswick, NJ: Rutgers University Press, 1991), 84.

8. Dorothy E. Preven, "The Use of Religious Revival Techniques to Indoctrinate Personnel: The Home-Party Sales Organizations," *Sociological Quarterly* 9 (1968): 99; Clarke, *Tupperware*, 150.

9. Thomas Hine, *Populuxe* (New York: Knopf, 1986), 35; Gary Cross, *An All-Consuming Century: Why Commercialism Won in Modern America* (New York: Columbia University Press, 2000), 99.

10. Terri Lynn Main, "Of Women, Rituals, and Tupperware," *Emergence Ministries,* www.emergenceministries.org/indexframe.html (accessed April 14, 2004).

11. Régis Debray, *Transmitting Culture*, trans. Eric Rauth (New York: Columbia University Press, 2000).

12. Clarke, *Tupperware*, 3.

13. Norman Vincent Peale, ed., *Faith Made Them Champions* (Carmel, NY: Guidepost Associates, 1954).

14. David G. Bromley and Anson Shupe, "Rebottling the Elixir: The Gospel of Prosperity in America's Religioeconomic Corporations," in Thomas Robbins and

Richard Anthony, eds., *In Gods We Trust: New Patterns of Religious Pluralism in America* (New Brunswick, NJ: Transaction Publishers, 1990), 233–54.

15. Clarke, *Tupperware*, 136.

16. Alfred C. Fuller and Hartzell Spence, *A Foot in the Door: The Life Appraisal of the Original Fuller Brush Man* (New York: McGraw-Hill, 1960), 237; David G. Bromley, "Quasi-religious Corporations: A New Integration of Religion and Capitalism," in Richard H. Roberts, ed., *Religion and the Transformations of Capitalism: Comparative Approaches* (London: Routledge, 1995), 137.

17. Clarke, *Tupperware*, 137.

18. Ibid., 142.

19. Ibid., 157, 165.

20. Arjun Appadurai, *Modernity at Large: Cultural Dimensions of Globalization* (Minneapolis: University of Minnesota Press, 1996), 27–47.

21. Godin quoted in Tim Adams, "What's the Big Ideavirus?" *Observer Review* (November 26, 2000): 4.

22. Ross, *Social Psychology*, 331, 335.

23. Henri Bergson, *Laughter: An Essay on the Meaning of the Comic*, trans. Claudesley Brereton and Fred Rothwell (New York: Macmillan, 1911), 35.

24. Roland Barthes, *Mythologies* (London: Palladin, 1988), 97.

25. Ibid., 99.

26. Anthony Giddens, *The Transformation of Intimacy: Sexuality, Love, and Eroticism in Modern Societies* (London: Polity Press, 1992), 2. See also Adrian Thatcher, "Postmodernity and Chastity," in Jan Davies and Gerard Loughlin, eds., *Sex These Days: Essays on Theology, Sexuality, and Society* (London: Sheffield Academic Press, 1997), 127–30.

27. Clarke, *Tupperware*, 136.

28. Martin Regg Cohn, "Mumbai—Where's the Beef?" *Toronto Star*, November 16, 2000; Bruce Crumley and Dean Fischer, "A Mickey Mouse Operation in Paris," *Time*, September 12, 1994.

29. Michelle M. Lelwica, "Losing Their Way to Salvation: Women, Weight Loss, and the Salvation Myth of Culture Lite," in Bruce David Forbes and Jeffrey H. Mahan, eds., *Religion and Popular Culture in America* (Berkeley: University of California Press, 2000), 180–200.

30. John Perkins, "Shape Shifting," www.ethoschannel.com/personalgrowth/adventure/j-perkins/1_j-perkins.html (accessed April 14, 2004).

31. Jon Turney, *Frankenstein's Footsteps: Science, Genetics, and Popular Culture* (New Haven: Yale University Press, 1998), 147.

32. Clinton and Collins both quoted in Kevin Davies, *The Sequence: Inside the Race for the Human Genome* (London: Weidenfeld and Nicolson, 2001), 236.

33. John C. Avise, *The Genetic Gods* (Cambridge, MA: Harvard University Press, 1998).

34. Edward O. Wilson, *Biophilia* (Cambridge, MA: Harvard University Press, 1984), 14.

35. Dorothy Nelkin and M. Susan Lindee, *The DNA Mystique: The Gene as a Cultural Icon* (New York: W. H. Freeman, 1995), 41–42.

36. Lee M. Silver, *Remaking Eden: Cloning and Beyond in a Brave New World* (London: Weidenfeld and Nicolson, 1997), 235.

37. News Hour, "Multiplying Issues," transcript, January 8, 1998, www.pbs.org/newshour/bib/science/jan-jun98/cloning_1–8.html (accessed September 27, 2002).

38. John H. Campbell, "The Moral Imperative of Our Future Evolution," in Robert Wesson and Patricia A. Williams, eds., *Extended Journeys: Evolutionary Roads toward Ethical Theories and Policies* (Amsterdam: Rodopi, 1995), 79.

39. This and all the following quotations pertaining to this discussion are from the Web site Cult of the New Eve, www.critical-art.net/biotech/cone/coneWeb (accessed June 17, 2004).

40. Main, "Of Women, Rituals, and Tupperware."

41. Lois Rogers and Steve Farrar, "'Immortal' Genes Found by Science," *Times of London*, July 4, 1999, www.grg.org/rose.htm (accessed April 14, 2004).

42. Eleanor Byrne and Martin McQuillan, "Walt Disney's Ape-Man: Race, Writing, and Humanism," *New Formations* 43 (2001): 104.

43. Richard Dawkins, *The Selfish Gene* (Oxford: Oxford University Press, 1976), ix.

44. Francis Fukuyama, *Our Posthuman Future* (New York: Farrar, Straus and Giroux, 2002).

45. N. Katherine Hayles, *How We Became Posthuman: Virtual Bodies in Cybernetics, Literature, and Informatics* (Chicago: University of Chicago Press, 1999).

CHAPTER 4. EMBODIED RELIGION

1. Morton A. Heller, "Introduction," in Morton A. Heller and William Schiff, eds., *The Psychology of Touch* (Hillsdale, NJ: Lawrence Erlbaum Associates, 1991), 1.

2. Robert N. Bellah, Richard Madsen, William M. Sullivan, Ann Swidler, and Steven M. Tipton, *Habits of the Heart: Individualism and Commitment in American Life* (Berkeley: University of California Press, 1985).

3. Anthony Synnott, "Puzzling over the Senses: From Plato to Marx," in David Howes, ed., *The Varieties of Sensory Experience: A Sourcebook in the Anthropology of the Senses* (Toronto: University of Toronto Press, 1991), 63.

4. David Chidester, *Word and Light: Seeing, Hearing, and Religious Discourse* (Urbana: University of Illinois Press, 1992), 2–8.

5. Augustine, *On Free Choice of the Will*, trans. Anna S. Benjamin and L. H. Hackstaff (Indianapolis: Bobbs-Merrill, 1964), 2.14.147.

6. Emmanuel Levinas, "Language and Proximity," in *Collected Philosophical Papers*, trans. Alphonso Lingis (Dordrecht: Martinus Nijhoff, 1987), 118; Emmanuel Levinas, "Ethics as First Philosophy," in Seán Hand, ed., *The Levinas Reader* (Oxford: Oxford University Press, 1989), 79.

7. Emmanuel Levinas, "Time and the Other," in Hand, ed., *The Levinas Reader*, 51.

8. Martin Jay, "Scopic Regimes of Modernity," in Hal Foster, ed., *Vision and Visuality* (Seattle: Bay Press, 1993), 558.

9. Walter Benjamin, "The Work of Art in the Age of Mechanical Reproduction," in *Illuminations*, ed. Hannah Arendt, trans. Harry Zohn (New York: Schocken, 1968), 238.

10. Ibid., 242.

11. Ibid., 224.

12. Drawn from roots meaning either "to bind," or "to be careful," or "to re-read," the etymology of *religio* is uncertain, contested, probably undecidable, and in the end almost completely irrelevant for determining the meaning and extensions of "religion" in the modern world. In southern Africa, for example, the term *religion* did not come from any ancient Indo-European or Latin root; it came from the sea in ships, beginning in the seventeenth century, to be deployed as an instrument of denial in the European "discovery" of people with "no religion." See David Chidester, *Savage Systems: Colonialism and Comparative Religion in Southern Africa* (Charlottesville: University Press of Virginia, 1996). Although the candidacy of the root *leig* for *religion* has certainly been challenged, the mere fact that one possible etymology, *religare*, "to bind," has historically been "the subject of considerable Christian homiletic expansion" does not necessarily eliminate *binding* as a possible etymological root, or as one aspect of the etymological constellation, for the term *religion*. Jonathan Z. Smith, "Religion, Religions, Religious," in Mark C. Taylor, ed., *Critical Terms for Religious Studies* (Chicago: University of Chicago Press, 1968), 269. See also Jacques Derrida, "Faith and Knowledge," in Derrida and Gianni Vattimo, eds., *Religion* (Stanford: Stanford University Press, 1998), 33–38, 71 n. 22.

13. Edmund S. Morgan, *The Puritan Dilemma: The Story of John Winthrop* (Boston: Little, Brown, 1958), 40. See also Sacvan Bercovitch, *The Puritan Origins of the American Self* (New Haven: Yale University Press, 1975), 117–19.

14. Increase Mather, *The Times of Men* (Boston, 1675), 7.

15. Michael Wigglesworth, "God's Controversy with New-England," in Perry Miller and Thomas H. Johnson, eds., *The Puritans: A Sourcebook of their Writings*, 2 vols. (New York: Harper and Row, 1963), 2:611–16.

16. John Winthrop, "A Model of Christian Charity," in Perry Miller and Thomas

H. Johnson, eds., *The Puritans: A Sourcebook of Their Writings,* 2 vols. (New York: Harper and Row, 1963), 1:195.

17. Bill Clinton, "A Vision for America: A New Covenant," Democratic National Convention, New York City, July 16, 1992, www.ibiblio.org/pub/docs/speeches/clinton.dir/c2.txt (accessed June 20, 2004); William Clinton, "Accepting the Democratic Nomination for President," *Congressional Quarterly Weekly Report* (July 18, 1992): 21–30; Jack R. Van der Slik and Stephen J. Schwark, "Clinton and the New Covenant: Theology Shaping a New Politics or Old Politics in Religious Garb?" *Journal of Church and State* 40 (1998): 873–90.

18. Bill Clinton, "State of the Union Address, 1995," www.ibiblio.org/pub/archives/whitehouse-papers/1995/Jan/1995-01–24-president-state-of-the-union-address-as-prepared.html (accessed June 20, 2004).

19. Steven Waldman, *The Bill: Legislation Really Becomes Law in a Case Study of the National Service Bill* (New York: Viking Press, 1996), 5.

20. Clinton, "A Vision for America."

21. Émile Durkheim, *The Elementary Forms of the Religious Life,* trans. Joseph Ward Swain (New York: Free Press, 1965), 62; Rudolf Otto, *The Idea of the Holy,* trans. John W. Harvey (London: Oxford University Press, 1923), 23–24.

22. Wesley quoted in both Bernard Semmel, *The Methodist Revolution* (New York: Basic Books, 1973), 31; and W. W. Sweet, *The American Churches: An Interpretation* (New York: Abingdon-Cokesbury Press, 1945), 46–47.

23. Perry Miller, "From the Covenant to the Revival," in John M. Mulder and John F. Wilson, eds., *Religion in American History: Interpretive Essays* (Englewood Cliffs, NJ: Prentice Hall, 1978), 146.

24. Horace Bushnell, "Our Obligations to the Dead," in Conrad Cherry, ed., *God's New Israel: Religious Interpretations of American Destiny* (Englewood Cliffs, NJ: Prentice Hall, 1971), 204.

25. Fire Tribe, www.firetribe.com (accessed April 14, 2004); Wings of Fire, www.firewalking.org (accessed April 14, 2004). See also Loring M. Danforth, *Firewalking and Religious Healing: The Anastenaria of Greece and the American Firewalking Movement* (Princeton: Princeton University Press, 1989).

26. Bernard J. Leikind and William J. McCarthy, "An Investigation of Firewalking," in Kendrick Frazier, ed., *The Hundredth Monkey and Other Paradigms of the Paranormal* (Buffalo, NY: Prometheus Books, 1991).

27. Rick Gore, "Fire Walking: Embrace the Fear," NationalGeographic.Com, www.nationalgeographic.com/2000/physical/firewalk (accessed April 14, 2004).

28. Ibid.

29. Fire Tribe, www.firetribe.com.

30. Flag Burning Page, "The Flag Flames Page," www.esquilax.com/flag/

flagflames.html (accessed April 14, 2004); Jean Bethke Elshtain, "Citizenship and Armed Civic Virtue: Some Critical Questions on the Commitment to Public Life," in Charles H. Reynolds and Ralph V. Norman, eds., *Community in America: The Challenge of Habits of the Heart* (Berkeley: University of California Press, 1988), 51. See also Robert Justin Goldstein, *Saving Old Glory: The History of the American Flag Desecration Controversy* (Boulder, CO: Westview Press, 1996).

31. Peter Collier and David Horowitz, *The Fords: An American Epic* (New York: Summit Books, 1987), 52; James J. Flink, *The Automobile Age* (Cambridge, MA: MIT Press, 1988); Joseph J. Corn, *The Winged Gospel: America's Romance with Aviation, 1900–1950* (New York: Oxford University Press, 1983), 30; Douglas Curran, *In Advance of the Landing: Folk Concepts of Outer Space* (New York: Abbeville Press, 1985).

32. Philip Fisher, "Democratic Social Space: Whitman, Melville, and the Promise of American Transparency," in Philip Fisher, ed., *The New American Studies: Essays from "Representations"* (Berkeley: University of California Press, 1991), 85–86.

33. Jeff Goodell, "Lost in Space," *Rolling Stone*, April 1, 1999, 57–64, 115; Joseph Firmage, "The Word is Truth," www.firmage.org (accessed May 15, 1999).

34. Alien Abduction Experience and Research, "What Is an Alien Abduction Experience?" www.abduct.com/experien.htm (accessed April 14, 2004); C. D. B. Bryan, *Close Encounters of the Fourth Kind: A Reporter's Notebook on Alien Abduction, UFOs, and the Conference at M.I.T.* (New York: Arkana, 1996); John E. Mack, *Abduction: Human Encounters with Aliens*, rev. ed. (New York: Ballantine Books, 1995).

35. Although the Official Alien Abduction Test Site, previously at www .alien-abduction-test.com, is no longer online, screenshots of the Web site can be seen at www.west.net/~isd/screens_01.html (accessed April 14, 2004).

36. Katharina Wilson, "How My Beliefs Have Changed," *Alien Jigsaw*, www .alienjigsaw.com/yk2/beliefs.html (accessed May 15, 1999).

37. Ibid.

38. Guide to Economic Reasoning, www.apu.edu/~puerdugo.html (accessed May 15, 1999); David C. Colander, *Economics*, 3rd ed. (New York: McGraw Hill, 2000).

39. Mary Catherine Bateson and Richard Goldsby, *Thinking AIDS: The Social Response to the Biological Threat* (New York: Addison-Wesley, 1988), 30.

40. Derrida, "Faith and Knowledge," 36.

41. Marita Sturken, *Tangled Memories: The Vietnam War, the AIDS Epidemic, and the Politics of Remembering* (Berkeley: University of California Press, 1997), 247. See Steve Connor and Sharon Kingman, *The Search for the Virus: The Scientific Discovery of AIDS and the Quest for a Cure* (New York: Penguin, 1988), 2; John M. Dwyer, *The Body at War: The Miracle of the Immune System* (New York: Penguin, 1990), 39.

42. Jean Comaroff and John L. Comaroff, "Occult Economies and the Violence of Abstraction: Notes from the South African Postcolony," *American Ethnologist* 26 (1999): 279–303.

43. Zach Thomas, *Healing Touch: The Church's Forgotten Language* (Louisville, KY: Westminster/John Knox Press, 1994).

44. E. Annie Proulx, *Accordion Crimes* (London: Fourth Estate, 1996), 338.

45. David Shenk, *Data Smog: Surviving the Information Glut* (San Francisco: HarperEdge, 1997), 36.

46. Catechism of the Catholic Church, "Distraction in Prayer," www.webdesk.com/catholic/prayers/distractions.html (accessed May 15, 1999).

47. HIVpositive.com, "Non Pharmacologic Treatment of Pain in HIV: Distraction and Reframing," www.hivpositive.com/f-PainHIV/Pain/LS4.3.2.html (accessed April 14, 2004).

48. Jean Baudrillard, "Illusion of the End (or) the Strike of Events," *Canadian Journal of Political and Social Theory* 17 (1994): 191–208; and Jean Baudrillard, *Illusion of the End,* trans. Chris Turner (Oxford: Polity Press, 1994), 21–27.

49. Bruce Lincoln, "Ritual, Rebellion, Resistance: Once More the Swazi Ncwala," *Man* 22 (1987): 132–56.

50. George Lakoff and Mark Johnson, *Metaphors We Live By* (Chicago: University of Chicago Press, 1980).

51. Luce Irigaray, "This Sex Which Is Not One," in Elaine Marks and Isabelle de Courtivron, eds., *New French Feminisms* (Amherst: University of Massachusetts Press, 1980), 99–106.

52. Michel Foucault, *Discipline and Punish: The Birth of the Prison,* trans. Alan Sheridan (New York: Vintage Books, 1979); Martin Jay, "Scopic Regimes of Modernity," in Hal Foster, ed., *Vision and Visuality* (Seattle: Bay Press, 1988), 3–28.

53. Karl Marx, *The Economic and Philosophic Manuscripts of 1844,* ed. D. J. Struik (New York: International Publishers, 1972), 140–41.

54. Sigmund Freud, *Standard Edition of the Complete Psychological Works of Sigmund Freud,* trans. James Strachey, 24 vols. (London: Hogarth, 1953–74), 17:241.

55. Michel de Certeau, *The Practice of Everyday Life,* trans. Steven Rendall (Berkeley: University of California Press, 1984), 37, 88.

56. Walt Whitman, *Leaves of Grass,* ed. Malcolm Cowley (1855; New York: Penguin, 1976), 48.

CHAPTER 5. SACRIFICIAL RELIGION

1. David Chidester, *Salvation and Suicide: An Interpretation of Jim Jones, the Peoples Temple, and Jonestown* (Bloomington: Indiana University Press, 1988), 129–59.

2. See Strobe Talbott, *The Russians and Reagan* (New York: Random House, 1984), 115–16; and Ronald Reagan, *The Quest for Peace, the Cause of Freedom: Selected Speeches on the United States and the World* (Washington, DC: United States Information Agency, 1988), 55–56.

3. *San Francisco Chronicle,* November 30, 1978.

4. Robert E. Denton Jr. and Dan F. Hahn, *Presidential Communication: Description and Analysis* (New York: Praeger 1986), 68–70; Jack Beatty, "The President's Mind," *New Republic* (April 7, 1982): 12; Michael Rogin, *Ronald Reagan, the Movie, and Other Episodes in Political Demonology* (Berkeley: University of California Press, 1987), 5; Lyn Ragsdale, "Presidential Speechmaking and the Public Audience: Individual Presidents and Group Attitudes," *Journal of Politics* 49 (1987): 733. In his foundational article on civil religion, Robert Bellah noted that "sacrificial death and rebirth" was a biblical archetype that became "indelibly written into the civil religion" with the Civil War. Robert N. Bellah, "Civil Religion in America," in Russell E. Richey and Donald G. Jones, eds., *American Civil Religion* (New York: Harper and Row, 1974), 40, 31–32. With respect to Reagan, the importance of sacrificial death was ignored in the only attempt to analyze "Reagan's Civil Religion" while he was in office; see David S. Adams, "Ronald Reagan's 'Revival': Voluntarism as a Theme in Reagan's Civil Religion," *Sociological Analysis* 48 (1987): 17–29.

5. Talbott, *The Russians and Reagan*, 115–16 (emphasis added); Reagan, *The Quest for Peace*, 55–56. The emphasized passage was omitted in the latter reference, the U.S. Information Agency collection of Reagan speeches, but it reappeared in Ronald Reagan, *Speaking My Mind: Selected Speeches* (New York: Simon and Schuster, 1989), 178.

6. Reagan, *The Quest for Peace*, 41–44; see also Rogin, *Ronald Reagan, the Movie*, 15–16.

7. Reagan, *The Quest for Peace*, 217.

8. Ibid., 14–24; this quote and the previous one, 24.

9. Ibid., 38–39.

10. Ibid., 173.

11. Congressional Quarterly, *Historic Documents of 1986* (Washington, DC: Congressional Quarterly, 1987), 701–2. See also Mike Wallace, "Hijacking History: Ronald Reagan and the Statue of Liberty," *Radical History Review* 37 (1987): 119–30.

12. Reagan, *The Quest for Peace*, 228.

13. Ibid., 71.

14. Russell Watson et al., "A Tragedy in the Gulf," *Newsweek*, June 1, 1987, 16.

15. *New York Times*, November 15, 1985. See also Martin Anderson, *Revolution* (New York: Harcourt, Brace, Jovanovich, 1988), 19–21; and William A. Niskanen, *Reaganomics: An Insider's Account of the Politics and the People* (New York: Oxford University Press, 1988), 283–84.

16. For example, see Reagan's first inaugural address in Reagan, *The Quest for Peace*, 35–37.

17. David Carrasco, "The Hermeneutics of Conquest," *History of Religions* 28 (1988): 160.

18. Douglas Kellner, "Baudrillard, Semiurgy and Death," *Theory, Culture and Society* 4, 1 (1987): 126.

19. Anderson, *Revolution*, 54.

20. Jonathan Z. Smith, "The Bare Facts of Ritual," *History of Religions* 20 (1980): 124–25, and *Imagining Religion: From Babylon to Jonestown* (Chicago: University of Chicago Press, 1982), 63.

21. Rogin, *Ronald Reagan, the Movie*, 39; Ronald Reagan and Richard G. Hubler, *Where's the Rest of Me?* (New York: Hawthorn, 1965).

22. Laurence I. Barrett, *Gambling with History: Ronald Reagan in the White House* (Garden City, NY: Doubleday, 1983), 42.

23. Reagan, *The Quest for Peace*, 41.

24. Chidester, *Salvation and Suicide*, 126–27.

25. Reagan, *The Quest for Peace*, 121.

26. See Gary R. Johnson, "Kin Selection, Socialization, and Patriotism: An Integrating Theory," *Politics and the Life Sciences* 4, 2 (1986): 127–54; Gary R. Johnson, "In the Name of the Fatherland: An Analysis of Kin Term Usage in Patriotic Speech and Literature," *International Political Science Review* 8 (1987): 165–74; and G. R. Johnson, S. H. Ratwik, and T. R. Sawyer, "The Evocative Significance of Kin Terms in Patriotic Speech," in V. Reynolds, V. S. E. Falger, and I. Vine, eds., *The Sociobiology of Ethnocentrism* (London: Croom Helm, 1987), 157–74.

27. Chidester, *Salvation and Suicide*, 127–28.

28. Valerio Valeri, *Kingship and Sacrifice: Ritual and Society in Ancient Hawaii*, trans. Paula Wissing (Chicago: University of Chicago Press, 1985), 84.

29. Chidester, *Salvation and Suicide*, 109–45.

30. Edward T. Linenthal, *Symbolic Defense: The Strategic Defense Initiative in American Popular Culture* (Urbana: University of Illinois Press, 1989).

31. S. Rowland Evans and Robert Novak, *The Reagan Revolution* (New York: E. P. Dutton, 1981), 208.

32. David Chidester, "Stealing the Sacred Symbols: Biblical Interpretation in the Peoples Temple and the Unification Church," *Religion* 18 (1988): 137–62.

33. Robert G. Hamerton-Kelly, ed., *Violent Origins: Walter Burkert, René Girard, and Jonathan Z. Smith on Ritual Killing and Cultural Formation* (Stanford, CA: Stanford University Press, 1987), 188.

34. *New York Times*, November 15, 1985; Anderson, *Revolution*, 19; Niskanen, *Reaganomics*, 283.

35. Chidester, *Salvation and Suicide*, 51–57; and Chidester, "Stealing the Sacred Symbols," 146–48.

36. Reagan, *The Quest for Peace*, 57.

37. John Hall, "Collective Welfare as Resource Mobilization in Peoples Temple:

A Case Study of a Poor People's Religious Social Movement," *Sociological Analysis* 49 (1988 Supplement): 64–77.

38. Rogin, *Ronald Reagan, the Movie*, 8–9.

39. Georges Bataille, "The Notion of Expenditure," in Bataille, *Visions of Excess: Selected Writings, 1927–1939*, ed. Allan Stoekl, trans. Allan Stoekl, Carl R. Lovitt, and Donald M. Leslie Jr. (Minneapolis: University of Minnesota Press, 1985), 118.

40. Jean Bethke Elshtain, "Citizenship and Armed Civic Virtue: Some Critical Questions on the Commitment to Public Life," in Charles H. Reynolds and Ralph V. Norman, eds., *Community in America: The Challenge of Habits of the Heart* (Berkeley: University of California Press, 1988), 51.

41. Reagan, *The Quest for Peace*, 125.

42. Georges Gusdorf, *L'expérience humaine du sacrifice* (Paris: Presses Universitaires de France, 1948), 72.

43. Chidester, *Salvation and Suicide*, 127–28.

44. My distinction between "locative" and "utopian" sacrificial expenditures has been adapted from Jonathan Z. Smith, *Map Is Not Territory: Studies in the History of Religions* (Leiden: E. J. Brill, 1978), 101.

45. Reagan, *The Quest for Peace*, 41–42; Rogin, *Ronald Reagan, the Movie*, 15.

46. Norman Podhoretz, "The Future Danger," *Commentary* 71 (1981): 29, 38. See also Edward T. Linenthal, "Restoring America: Political Revivalism in the Nuclear Age," in Rowland A. Sherrill, ed., *Religion and the Life of the Nation: American Recoveries* (Urbana: University of Illinois Press, 1990), 23–45.

47. Chidester, "Stealing the Sacred Symbols," 153–55; and Chidester, "Rituals of Exclusion and the Jonestown Dead," *Journal of the American Academy of Religion* 56 (1988): 698–700.

48. C. Eric Lincoln, *Race, Religion, and the Continuing American Dilemma* (New York: Hill and Wang, 1984), 3.

49. Harold Lasswell, *World Politics and Personal Insecurity* (New York: Whittlesey House, 1935), 3–4.

CHAPTER 6. MONETARY RELIGION

1. Act Now, Inc., "Money Tracts," www.act-now-inc.com/html/money-tracts .html (accessed April 14, 2004).

2. This and the following citations of Weber come from Max Weber, "Religious Rejections of the World and Their Directions," in H. H. Gerth and C. Wright Mills, eds., *From Max Weber: Essays in Sociology* (New York: Oxford University Press, 1946), from pp. 331, 335, and 333, in order of appearance.

3. Michael Taussig, "The Genesis of Capitalism amongst a South American Peasantry: Devil's Labor and the Baptism of Money," *Comparative Studies in Society and History* 19, 2 (1977): 130–55.

4. Lisa Aldred, "'Money Is Just Spiritual Energy': Incorporating the New Age," *Journal of Popular Culture* 35, 4 (2002): 61–74.

5. Émile Durkheim, *The Elementary Forms of the Religious Life,* trans. Joseph Ward Swain (New York: Free Press, 1965), 125, 137, 188. See also Andrew Lang, *The Secret of the Totem* (London: Longmans, Green, 1905), 136–37.

6. Ken Vernon, "Soft Targets," *Sunday Times,* Johannesburg, June 20, 1999.

7. Don Pinnock, *The Brotherhoods: Street Gangs and State Control in Cape Town* (Cape Town: David Philip, 1984), and *Gangs, Rituals, and Rites of Passage* (Cape Town: African Sun Press, 1997).

8. Don Pinnock, "Rites of Passage," *Eye-Online* 19 (2000), www.cyc-net.org/cyc-online/cycol-0800-rites.html (accessed September 27, 2002); Don Pinnock, "Gangs: Fighting Fire with Fire," http://tigger.uic.edu/~huk/Gang%20History/fightingfire.html (accessed April 14, 2004).

9. David Chidester, "Mapping the Sacred in the Mother City," *Journal for the Study of Religion* 13, 1–2 (2000): 5–41.

10. Joint Committee on Printing, United States Congress, *Our Flag* (Washington, DC: U.S. Government Printing Office, 1989), 44.

11. Ibid.

12. Julia Ward Howe, "The Flag," *Atlantic Monthly,* April 1863, 443.

13. William Tyler Page, "The American's Creed," *The Book of the American's Creed* (Garden City, NY: Country Life Press, 1921); U.S. Congress, *Our Flag,* 49.

14. Thomas Paine, *Common Sense and the Rights of Man,* ed. Tony Benn (London: Phoenix Press, 2000), 27.

15. Frederick Douglass, "Reconstruction," *Atlantic Monthly,* December 1866, 761.

16. Karl Marx, "Inaugural Address to the Working Men's International Association, 28 Sept 1864," in Karl Marx and Frederick Engels, *Collected Works,* 49 vols. (London: Lawrence and Wishart, 1985), 20:13.

17. Georges Bataille, "The Notion of Expenditure," in *Visions of Excess: Selected Writings, 1927–1939,* ed. Allan Stoekl, trans. Allan Stoekl, Carl R. Lovitt, and Donald M. Leslie Jr. (Minneapolis: University of Minnesota Press, 1985), 118.

18. Henry Hyde, "Floor Statement on Referral Resolution," House of Representatives Committee on the Judiciary, September 11, 1998, www.house.gov/judiciary/091198f.htm (accessed April 14, 2004).

19. Jews for the Preservation of Firearms Ownership, "Haym Salomon: A Jew Hungry for Freedom," www.jpfo.org/jp_haym.htm (accessed April 14, 2004).

20. Paul Connerton, *How Societies Remember* (Cambridge: Cambridge University Press, 1989), 86.

21. Carolyn Marvin and David W. Ingle, "Blood Sacrifice and the Nation: Revisiting Civil Religion," *Journal of the American Academy of Religion* 64 (1996): 767,

and *Blood Sacrifice and the Nation: Totem Rituals and the American Flag* (Cambridge: Cambridge University Press, 1999).

22. Arthur Schlesinger Jr., "Back to the Womb? Isolationism's Renewed Threat," *Foreign Affairs* 74, 4 (July/August 1995): 8.

23. Paul Morris, "Judaism and Capitalism," in Richard H. Roberts, ed., *Religion and the Transformations of Capitalism: Comparative Approaches* (London: Routledge, 1995), 95.

24. Bernhard Laum, *Heiliges Geld: Eine historische Untersuchung über den Sakralen* (Tübingen: Mohr, 1924). See also William H. Desmonde, *Magic, Myth and Money: The Origin of Money in Religious Ritual* (New York: Free Press of Glencoe, 1962); and Paul Einzig, *Primitive Money in Its Ethnological, Historical, and Economic Aspects,* 2nd ed. (New York: Pergamon Press, 1966).

25. Max Horkheimer and Theodor W. Adorno, *The Dialectic of Enlightenment,* trans. John Cumming (London: Verso, 1973), 49.

26. William Pietz, "Death of the Deodand: Accursed Objects and the Money Value of Human Life," *Res: Anthropology and Aesthetics* 31 (Spring 1997): 97–108, and "The Fetish of Civilization: Sacrificial Blood and Monetary Debt," in Peter Pels and Oscar Saleminck, eds., *Colonial Subjects: Essays on the Practical History of Anthropology* (Ann Arbor: University of Michigan Press, 1999), 53–81.

27. Karl Marx, *Grundrisse,* trans. Martin Nicolaus (New York: Penguin Books, 1973), 221.

28. David Loy, "The Religion of the Market," *Journal of the American Academy of Religion* 65 (1997): 275–90; Harvey Cox, "The Market as God: Living in a New Dispensation," *Atlantic Monthly,* March 1999, 18–23.

29. Thabo Mbeki, "Prologue," in Malegapuru William Makgoba, ed., *African Renaissance: The New Struggle* (Johannesburg: Mafube; Cape Town: Tafelberg, 1999), xviii.

30. Joanna Rogers, "Notes on the Financial Statements," www.trentu.ca/trentradio/governance/_finread.txt (accessed April 14, 2004).

31. Pietz, "Fetish of Civilization," 62.

32. Luc de Heusch, *Sacrifice in Africa: A Structuralist Approach,* trans. Linda O'Brien and Alice Morton (Bloomington: Indiana University Press, 1985), 202.

33. George Santayana, *Character and Opinion in the United States* (New York: George Braziller, 1955), 97.

34. Rick Marin and T. Trent Gegax, "Conspiracy Mania Feeds Our Growing National Paranoia," *Newsweek,* December 30, 1996, 64.

35. Sarah Gertrude Millin, *Rhodes* (London: Chatto and Windus, 1933), 7.

36. Reginald B. B. Esher, *Journals and Letters of Reginald Viscount Esher,* 4 vols., ed. Maurice V. Brett (London: Nicholson and Watson, 1934–38), 4:135.

37. William F. Jasper, "Reviewing the Rhodes Legacy," *New American Magazine* 11, 4 (February 20, 1995), www.thenewamerican.com/tna/1995/vo11n004/vo11n004_rhodes.htm (accessed April 14, 2004); Dennis Laurence Cuddy, *Secret Records Revealed: The Men, the Money, and the Methods behind the New World Order* (Oklahoma City: Hearthstone Publishers, 1999).

38. Stephen Prothero, "Skulls in the Closet: What Does Membership in a Bastion of Privilege Say about George W. Bush's Character?" *Salon* (January 21, 2000), http://dir.salon.com/books/it/2000/01/21/bones/index.html (accessed April 14, 2004); Alexandra Robbins, "George W., Knight of Eulogia," *Atlantic Monthly*, May 2000, www.theatlantic.com/issues/2000/05/robbins.htm (accessed April 14, 2004).

39. David Icke, "The Reptilian Connection," www.thisistherealtruth.com/reptilianconnection.htm (accessed April 14, 2004); David Icke, *The Biggest Secret* (London: Bridge of Love Publications, 1999).

40. Gábor Klaniczay, "The Decline of Witches and the Rise of Vampires under the Eighteenth-Century Habsburg Monarchy," in Karen Margolis, ed., *The Uses of Supernatural Power: The Transformation of Popular Religion in Medieval and Early Modern Europe*, trans. Susan Singerman (Princeton: Princeton University Press, 1990), 168–88. See also Sandra Sherman, *Finance and Fictionality in the Early Eighteenth Century: Accounting for Defoe* (Cambridge: Cambridge University Press, 1996).

41. Joel Kurtzman, *The Death of Money: How the Electronic Economy Has Destabilized the World's Markets and Created Financial Chaos* (New York: Simon and Schuster, 1993).

42. David Harvey, *The Condition of Postmodernity: An Inquiry into the Origins of Cultural Change* (Oxford: Basil Blackwell, 1989), 297.

43. Jean Baudrillard, *The Transparency of Evil: Essays on Extreme Phenomena*, trans. James Benedict (London: Verso, 1993), 5.

44. Susan Strange, *Mad Money* (Manchester: Manchester University Press, 1998).

45. Benjamin J. Cohen, *The Geography of Money* (Ithaca: Cornell University Press, 1998).

46. Texe Marrs, "Old Money vs. New Money," *Power of Prophecy* (June 2000), www.texemarrs.com/072000/proin2.htm (accessed April 14, 2004).

47. Mona Eltahawy, "Egyptian Boogie Nights," *U.S. News and World Report*, December 27, 1999, 24.

48. Bill Clinton, "Speech to Parliament by President Bill Clinton of the United States of America," Cape Town, March 26, 1998, www.polity.org.za/govdocs/speeches/foreign/sp0326-98.html (accessed April 14, 2004).

49. Fidel Castro, "Speech Delivered at the South African Parliament," Cape Town, September 4, 1998, www.nnc.cubaweb.cu/discur/ingles/4sept98.htm (accessed April 14, 2004).

50. David Chidester, "'A Big Wind Blew Up during the Night': America as Sacred Space in South Africa," in Chidester and Edward T. Linenthal, eds., *American Sacred Space* (Bloomington: Indiana University Press, 1995), 262–312.

51. Zakes Mda, in "Year 2000 Supplement," *Sunday Times,* January 2, 2000.

52. Jonathan Kirshner, *Currency and Coercion: The Political Economy of International Monetary Power* (Princeton: Princeton University Press, 1995).

53. Alaina Lemon, "'Your Eyes Are Green Like Dollars': Counterfeit Cash, National Substance, and Currency Apartheid in 1990s Russia," *Cultural Anthropology* 13, 1 (1998): 34.

54. Thabo Mbeki, "Religion in Public Life: Engaging Power," Keynote Address, Multi-Event 99, Cape Town, South Africa, February 14, 1999, www.uct.ac.za/depts/ricsa/confer/me99/procs/pro_mbek.htm (accessed April 14, 2004).

55. Susan Strange, *Casino Capitalism* (Oxford: Blackwell, 1986).

56. Marc Shell, *Art and Money* (Chicago: University of Chicago Press, 1995), 80.

57. Jean Comaroff and John L. Comaroff, "Millennial Capitalism: First Thoughts on a Second Coming," *Public Culture* 12, 2 (2000): 293, 315.

58. Ontario Consultants on Religious Tolerance, "The Aftermath of the 9-11 Terrorist Attack: What You Can Do to Help," www.religioustolerance.org/reac_ter4.htm (accessed April 14, 2004).

59. Len Horowitz, "The American Red Double-cross," www.prophecyandpreparedness.com/Articles/The%20American%20Red%20Double-cross.html (accessed April 14, 2004).

60. Michael C. Ruppert, "The Bush-Cheney Drug Empire," *Nexus Magazine* 8, 2 (2001), www.nexusmagazine.com/articles/bushcheney.html (accessed April 14, 2004).

61. Reuters, "US Planes Rain Dollars, Not Bombs," *Indian Tribune,* February 15, 2002, www.tribuneindia.com/2002/20020215/world.htm (accessed September 27, 2002).

CHAPTER 7. GLOBAL RELIGION

1. Hans Koehler, preface, in Terri Morrison, Wayne A. Conaway, and George A. Borden, *Kiss, Bow, or Shake Hands: How to Do Business in Sixty Countries* (Holbrook, MA: Adams Media Corporation, 1994), viii.

2. Ibid., ix.

3. Adams Report, "Global Assignment, Americans Abroad: Doing Business in South Africa," www.globalassignment.com/10-22-99/southafrica.htm (accessed April 14, 2004).

4. Genelle G. Morain, "Kinesics and Cross-Cultural Understanding," in Louise Fiber Luce and Elise C. Smith, eds., *Toward Internationalism: Readings in Cross-*

Cultural Communication (Boston: Heinle and Heinle Publishers, 1987), 120; Morain reproduces the postures of humility from Maurice H. Krout, *Introduction to Social Psychology* (New York: Harper, 1942).

5. Edward T. Hall, *The Silent Language* (New York: Anchor Books, Doubleday, 1959), *The Hidden Dimension* (New York: Anchor Books, Doubleday, 1966), *The Dance of Life: The Other Dimension of Time* (New York: Anchor Books, Doubleday, 1983), and *Beyond Culture* (New York: Anchor Books, 1976).

6. Geert Hofstede, "The Business of International Business Is Culture," *International Business Review* 3, 1 (1994): 1–14.

7. Geert Hofstede, *Culture's Consequences: International Differences in Work-Related Values* (Beverly Hills, CA: Sage, 1980), and *Cultures and Organizations: Software of the Mind* (New York: McGraw-Hill, 1997).

8. Jeswald W. Salacuse, *Making Global Deals: Negotiating in the International Marketplace* (Boston: Houghton Mifflin, 1991), 71.

9. Arjun Appadurai, "Disjuncture and Difference in the Global Cultural Economy," *Modernity at Large: Cultural Dimensions of Globalization* (Minneapolis: University of Minnesota Press, 1996), 27–47.

10. Kalman Applbaum, "Crossing Borders: Globalization as Myth and Charter in American Transnational Consumer Marketing," *American Ethnologist* 27, 2 (2000): 257–82.

11. Thomas Frank, *One Market under God: Extreme Capitalism, Market Populism, and the End of Economic Democracy* (New York: Doubleday, 2000); Mike Davis, "The Bullshit Economy," *Village Voice Literary Supplement* (September 2000), www.villagevoice.com/vls/169/davis.shtml (accessed June 17, 2004).

12. Mark Pendergrast, *For God, Country, and Coca-Cola: The Unauthorized History of the Great American Soft Drink and the Company That Makes It* (New York: Scribner's, 1993), 261.

13. Ibid., 400.

14. Ibid., 173, 321.

15. René Girard, *Violence and the Sacred*, trans. Patrick Gregory (Baltimore: Johns Hopkins University Press, 1977).

16. Paul Landau, "Bushmen and Coca-Cola in a Cool World," *Southern African Review of Books* 36 (March/April 1995): 8–9.

17. John Tomlinson, *Cultural Imperialism* (Baltimore: Johns Hopkins University Press, 1991), 173.

18. Pendergrast, *For God, Country, and Coca-Cola*, 401.

19. Alaina Lemon, "'Your Eyes Are Green Like Dollars': Counterfeit Cash, National Substance, and Currency Apartheid in 1990s Russia," *Cultural Anthropology* 13, 1 (1998): 35.

20. Constance Classen, "Sugar Cane, Coca-Cola, and Hypermarkets: Consumption and Surrealism in the Argentine Northwest," in David Howes, ed., *Cross-Cultural Consumption: Global Markets, Local Realities* (London: Routledge, 1996), 52.

21. Ibid., 43.

22. Ibid., 39; Leonora Carrington, *The Seventh Horse, and Other Tales*, trans. Kathrine Talbot and Anthony Kerrigan (London: Virago, 1989), 182.

23. George Ritzer, *The McDonaldization of Society* (Thousand Oaks, CA: Pine Forge Press, 2000), 1.

24. Ray Kroc and Robert Anderson, *Grinding It Out: The Making of McDonald's* (New York: St. Martin's Press, 1987), 10.

25. Ritzer, *McDonaldization of Society*, 7.

26. William Severini Kowinski, *The Malling of America: An Inside Look at the Great Consumer Paradise* (New York: William Morrow, 1985), 218; see also Ira G. Zepp Jr., *The New Religious Image of Urban America: The Shopping Mall as Ceremonial Center* (Westminster, MD: Christian Classics, 1986).

27. Ritzer, *McDonaldization of Society*, 25.

28. John S. Caputo, "The Rhetoric of McDonaldization: A Social Semiotic Perspective," in Mark Alfino, John S. Caputo, and Robin Wynyard, eds., *McDonaldization Revisited: Critical Essays on Consumer Culture* (Westport, CT: Praeger, 1998), 49.

29. Ibid., 48.

30. John F. Love, *McDonald's: Behind the Arches* (New York: Bantam Books, 1986), 423.

31. Cited in James L. Watson, "Transnationalism, Localization, and Fast Foods in East Asia," in Watson, ed., *Golden Arches East: McDonald's in East Asia* (Stanford, CA: Stanford University Press, 1997), 5.

32. Ibid., 2. See also Emiko Ohnuki-Tierney, "McDonald's in Japan: Changing Manners and Etiquette," in Watson, ed., *Golden Arches East,* 161–82.

33. Watson, "Transnationalism, Localization," 24.

34. Scott Pendleton, "Giving Golden Arches Global Span," *Christian Science Monitor,* May 21, 1991, 8.

35. Alan Bryman, "The Disneyization of Society," *Sociological Review* 47 (1999): 26. See also Bryman, *Disney and His Worlds* (London: Routledge, 1995).

36. Umberto Eco, *Travels in Hyperreality*, trans. William Weaver (London: Pan, 1986), 43.

37. Stephen M. Fjellman, *Vinyl Leaves: Walt Disney World and America* (Boulder, CO: Westview, 1992), 157.

38. John van Maanen, "The Smile Factory: Work at Disneyland," in Peter J. Frost, Larry F. Moore, Meryl R. Louis, Craig C. Lundberg, and Joanne Martin, eds., *Reframing Organizational Culture* (Newbury Park, CA: Sage, 1991), 58–76.

39. Watson, "Transnationalism, Localization," 24.

40. Ariel Dorfman and Armand Mattelart, *How to Read Donald Duck: Imperialist Ideology in the Disney Comic,* trans. David Kunzle (New York: International General, 1975).

41. Eleanor Byrne and Martin McQuillan, *Deconstructing Disney* (London: Pluto Press, 1999); Michael D. Eisner, "Letter to Shareholders," December 8, 1998, www .disneyinternational.com/AnnualReport/letter03.htm (accessed April 14, 2004).

42. Richard D. Land and Frank D. York, *Send a Message to Mickey: The ABC's of Making Your Voice Heard at Disney* (Nashville, TN: Broadman and Holman, 1998).

43. Brad Prager and Michael Richardson, "A Sort of Homecoming: An Archaeology of Disneyland," in David Palumbo-Liu and Hans Ulrich Gumbrecht, eds., *Streams of Cultural Capital: Transnational Cultural Studies* (Stanford, CA: Stanford University Press, 1997), 209.

44. Michael Sorkin, "See You in Disneyland," in Sorkin, ed., *Variations on a Theme Park: The New American City and the End of Public Space* (New York: Noonday Press, 1992), 206.

45. Mary Yoko Brannen, "'Bwana Mickey': Constructing Cultural Consumption at Tokyo Disneyland," in Joseph J. Tobin, ed., *Re-made in Japan: Everyday Life and Consumer Choice in a Changing Society* (New Haven: Yale University Press, 1992), 216.

46. Ibid., 221.

47. John van Maanen, "Displacing Disney: Some Notes on the Flow of Culture," *Qualitative Sociology* 15, 1 (1992): 17.

48. Aviad E. Raz, *Riding the Black Ship: Japan and Tokyo Disneyland* (Cambridge, MA: Harvard University Press, 1999); Mitsuhiro Yoshimoto, "Images of Empire: Tokyo Disneyland and Japanese Cultural Imperialism," in Eric Smoodin, ed., *Disney Discourse: Producing the Magic Kingdom* (London: Routledge, 1994), 181–99.

49. Lamin Sanneh, *Translating the Message: The Missionary Impact on Culture* (Maryknoll, NY: Orbis Books, 1989).

CHAPTER 8. TRANSATLANTIC RELIGION

1. Melville J. Herskovits, *The Myth of the Negro Past* (New York: Harper and Brothers, 1941); E. Franklin Frazier, *The Negro Church in America* (New York: Schocken, 1963).

2. Robert Palmer, *Dancing in the Street: A Rock and Roll History* (London: BBC Books, 1996), 53.

3. W. E. B. Du Bois, *The Souls of Black Folk* (1903; New York: Vintage Books, 1990), 141.

4. Ibid., 141–42.

5. Ibid., 139.

6. W. E. B. Du Bois, *The Negro* (New York: Henry Holt, 1915), 242.

7. Ibid., 124.

8. Robert Hamill Nassau, *Fetichism in West Africa: Forty Years' Observation of Native Customs and Superstitions* (New York: Charles Scribner's Sons, 1904).

9. Du Bois, *The Negro*, 124.

10. Mary H. Kingsley, *West African Studies*, 2nd ed. (London: Macmillan, 1901), 107.

11. Nassau, *Fetichism in West Africa*, 36.

12. Du Bois, *The Negro*, 150.

13. Ibid., 188–89; Nassau, *Fetichism in West Africa*, 274. Clearly, in the passage cited from *The Negro*, Du Bois is repeating a formulation from *Souls of Black Folk*, but the problem of continuity between Africa and America will preoccupy Du Bois throughout his life.

14. W. E. B. Du Bois, *Black Folk: Then and Now* (New York: Henry Holt, 1939), 107–8.

15. Ibid., 198.

16. Du Bois, *The Negro*, 189, and *Black Folk*, 198.

17. W. E. B. Du Bois, *The World and Africa: An Inquiry into the Part Which Africa Has Played in World History* (New York: Viking Press, 1947), 79; Leo Frobenius, *Histoire de la civilization africaine*, trans. H. Back and D. Ermont (Paris: Gallimard, 1936), 79; this English translation and others of this source are by Du Bois. The 1936 edition is a translation of Frobenius, *Kulturgeschichte Afrikas: Prolegomena zu einer historischen Gestaltlehre* (Zurich: Phaidon, 1933).

18. Du Bois, *World and Africa*, 79; Frobenius, *Histoire de la civilization africaine*, 79.

19. Du Bois, *World and Africa*, 158; Frobenius, *Histoire de la civilization africaine*, 56.

20. As Robin D. G. Kelley has observed, Césaire, Senghor, and others in the Négritude movement drew inspiration from Frobenius. Kelley, "A Poetics of Anti-colonialism," *Monthly Review* 51, 6 (1999): 1–24. See also Suzanne Césaire, "Leo Frobenius and the Problem of Civilization," in Michael Richardson, ed., *Refusal of the Shadow: Surrealism and the Caribbean*, trans. Richardson and Krzysztof Fijalkowski (London: Verso, 1996), 82–87; and L. S. Senghor, "The Lessons of Leo Frobenius," in Eike Haberland, ed., *Leo Frobenius: An Anthology*, trans. Patricia Crampton (Wiesbaden: Franz Steiner, 1973), vii. If that inspiration was linked to Frobenius's critique of European inventions of the "barbarous Negro," it was also situated in the struggle to come to terms with the fetish and fetishism that provided the context for Frobenius's statement and for Du Bois's transition from rehabilitating to rejecting the fetish as the defining feature of African indigenous religion.

21. Efraim Andersson, *Messianic Popular Movements in the Lower Congo* (Uppsala: Almqvist and Wiksells, 1958), 153–54.

22. Karen E. Fields, *Revival and Rebellion in Colonial Central Africa* (Princeton: Princeton University Press, 1985).

23. George Shepperson, "Nyasaland and the Millennium," in Sylvia L. Thrupp, ed., *Millennial Dreams in Action: Essays in Comparative Study* (The Hague: Mouton, 1962), 145.

24. John Higginson, "Liberating the Captives: Independent Watchtower as an Avatar of Colonial Revolt in Southern Africa and Katanga, 1908–1941," *Journal of Social History* 26, 1 (1992): 55–80.

25. George Shepperson and Thomas Price, *Independent African: John Chilembwe and the Origins, Setting and Significance of the Nyasaland Native Rising of 1915* (Edinburgh: Edinburgh University Press, 1958).

26. Shepperson, "Nyasaland and the Millennium," 145.

27. Edwin W. Smith, *Aggrey of Africa: A Study in Black and White* (New York: Doubleday, 1929), 181.

28. Helen Bradford, *A Taste of Freedom: The ICU in Rural South Africa, 1924–1930* (Johannesburg: Ravan Press, 1987), 215. See also Kenneth King, "James E. K. Aggrey: Collaborator, Nationalist, Pan-African," *Canadian Journal of African Studies* 3, 3 (1970): 511–30.

29. Fields, *Revival and Rebellion in Colonial Central Africa*, 11.

30. Shula Marks, *Reluctant Rebellion: The 1906–8 Disturbances in Natal* (Oxford: Clarendon Press, 1970), 251.

31. Clifton C. Crais, *The Making of the Colonial Order: White Supremacy and Black Resistance in the Eastern Cape, 1770–1865* (Johannesburg: Witwatersrand University Press, 1992), 219.

32. W. D. Cingo, "Native Unrest," *Kokstad Advertiser*, September 30, 1927.

33. Bradford, *A Taste of Freedom*, 219.

34. William Beinart and Colin Bundy, *Hidden Struggles in Rural South Africa: Politics and Popular Movements in the Transkei and Eastern Cape* (Berkeley: University of California Press, 1987), 252.

35. Bradford, *A Taste of Freedom*, 217.

36. Beinart and Bundy, *Hidden Struggles in Rural South Africa*, 222–69.

37. Robert Edgar, "Garveyism in Africa: Dr. Wellington and the American Movement in the Transkei," *Ufahamu* 6, 3 (1976): 31–57.

38. Bradford, *A Taste of Freedom*, 229, 127, 218.

39. Edgar, "Garveyism in Africa," 41; Bradford, *A Taste of Freedom*, 224–28; Monica Hunter Wilson, *Reaction to Conquest*, 2nd ed. (London: Oxford University Press, 1961), 570–71.

40. Fields, *Revival and Rebellion in Colonial Central Africa,* 12.

41. Jonathan Z. Smith, *Map Is Not Territory: Studies in the History of Religions* (Leiden: E. J. Brill, 1978), 100–101, 293, 309.

42. Lamont Lindstrom, *Knowledge and Power in a South Pacific Society* (Washington, DC: Smithsonian Institution Press, 1990), 104.

43. Theodore Schwartz, *The Paliau Movement in the Admiralty Islands, 1946–1954* (New York: American Museum of Natural History, 1962), 256–57.

44. Garry Trompf, "The Cargo and the Millennium on Both Sides of the Pacific," in Trompf, ed., *Cargo Cults and Millenarian Movements: Transoceanic Comparisons of New Religious Movements* (Berlin: Mouton de Gruyter, 1990), 72.

45. *Cape Times,* February 17, 1990.

46. *International Herald Tribune,* June 30–July 1, 1990; *Daily Mail,* June 20, 1990; *New York Times,* June 17, 1990; *Vrye Weekblad,* June 29, 1990; *Time,* July 2, 1990, 12.

47. *Daily Mail,* June 20, 1990.

48. *International Herald Tribune,* July 2, 1990.

49. *New York Times,* June 24, 1990.

50. *Tennessean,* June 28, 1990.

51. *Time,* July 2, 1990, 14.

52. *Daily Mail,* June 20, 1990; *International Herald Tribune,* June 20–July 1, 1990.

53. See *Argus,* January 31, 1991, for this quote and the one in the following paragraph.

54. Victor Turner, "The Center Out There: The Pilgrim's Goal," *History of Religions* 12, 3 (1973): 191–230; Victor Turner and Edith Turner, *Image and Pilgrimage in Christian Culture* (New York: Columbia University Press, 1978), 39, 3. See also Victor Turner, "Pilgrimages as Social Processes," *Dramas, Fields, and Metaphors: Symbolic Action in Human Society* (Ithaca: Cornell University Press, 1974), 166–230.

55. Lewis V. Baldwin, *To Make the Wounded Whole: The Cultural Legacy of Martin Luther King, Jr.* (Minneapolis: Fortress Press, 1992), 203. See also George M. Houser, "Freedom's Struggle Crosses Oceans and Mountains: Martin Luther King, Jr., and the Liberation Struggles in Africa and America," in Peter J. Albert and Ronald Hoffman, eds., *We Shall Overcome: Martin Luther King, Jr., and the Black Freedom Struggle* (New York: Pantheon Books, 1990), 169–96.

56. William Minter, *King Solomon's Mines Revisited: Western Interests and the Burdened History of Southern Africa* (New York: Basic Books, 1986), 137.

57. An alternative account of how America became the "center of the world"— through African labor—was advanced by W. E. B. Du Bois: "From being a mere stopping place between Europe and Asia or a chance treasure house of gold, America became through African labor the center of the sugar empire and the cotton kingdom and an integral part of that world industry and trade which caused the Industrial Revolution and the reign of capitalism." Du Bois, *The World and Africa,* 227–28.

58. Turner and Turner, *Image and Pilgrimage in Christian Culture*, 3; *Cape Times*, January 21, 1993.

59. Achille Mbembe, "African Modes of Self-Writing," *Public Culture* 14, 2 (2002): 239.

60. Malegapuru William Makgoba, ed., *African Renaissance: The New Struggle* (Johannesburg: Mafube; Cape Town: Tafelberg, 1999).

61. TheAfrican.Com, http://theafrican.com/AboutUs.htm (accessed April 14, 2004).

62. Barbara Browning, *Infectious Rhythm: Metaphors of Contagion and the Spread of African Culture* (London: Routledge, 1998).

CHAPTER 9. SHAMANIC RELIGION

1. Dream Change Coalition, "Song of the Stars," www.dreamchange.org/programs/baba.html (accessed September 27, 2002); www.newageinfo.com/HyperNews/get/natravel/65.html (accessed April 14, 2004).

2. Eve Bruce, *Shaman M.D.: A Plastic Surgeon's Remarkable Journey into the World of Shapeshifting* (Rochester, VT: Destiny Books, 2002).

3. Plastic-Shaman-Busters.com, www.plastic-shaman-busters.com/Welcome!.htm (accessed June 25, 2004). See also Ward Churchill, "Spiritual Hucksterism: The Rise of the Plastic Medicine Men," in Churchill, *From a Native Son: Selected Essays on Indigenism, 1985–1995* (Boston: South End Press, 1996), 439–43; and Alice Kehoe, "Primal Gaia: Primitivists and Plastic Medicine Men," in James Clifton, ed., *The Invented Indian: Cultural Fictions and Government Policies* (New Brunswick, NJ: Transaction, 1990), 193–209.

4. Åke Hultkrantz, "A Definition of Shamanism," *Temenos* 9 (1973): 34.

5. Mircea Eliade, *Shamanism: Archaic Techniques of Ecstasy*, trans. Willard R. Trask (New York: Pantheon, 1964).

6. Daniel C. Noel, *The Soul of Shamanism: Western Fantasies, Imaginal Realities* (New York: Continuum, 1997).

7. Carlos Castaneda, *The Teachings of Don Juan: A Yaqui Way of Knowledge* (Berkeley: University of California Press, 1968).

8. Richard Goldstein, *Goldstein's Greatest Hits: A Book Mostly about Rock 'n' Roll* (Englewood Cliffs, NJ: Prentice-Hall, 1970), 74; see also Jerry Hopkins, *The Lizard King: The Essential Jim Morrison* (New York: Simon and Schuster, 1995).

9. Tony van Renterghem, *When Santa Was a Shaman: The Ancient Origins of Santa Claus and the Christmas Tree* (St. Paul, MN: Llewellyn Publications, 1995).

10. Bradford Keeney, ed., *Vusamazulu Credo Mutwa: Zulu High Sanusi* (Philadelphia: Ringing Rocks Press, 2001).

11. Ringing Rocks Foundation, www.ringingrocks.org/index.html (accessed April 14, 2004).

12. Healing the African Wound, www.aum.freewire.co.uk/Oneheart/SAfrica.htm (accessed September 27, 2002); *Sunday Times,* Johannesburg, November 21, 1999.

13. Rustlers, "A Tribal Gathering," www.rustlers.co.za/festivals/easter/ tipicircle2001.html (accessed September 27, 2002); *Daily Dispatch,* April 2, 2001.

14. Heart Healing Center, www.hearthealingcenter.com/earth-healers.htm (accessed September 27, 2002); *Wellness eJournal,* www.compwellness.com/ eJournal/2001/0131.htm (April 14, 2004).

15. Angela Johnson, "The Angela Johnson Interview," *Mail and Guardian,* July 18, 1997.

16. Hazel Friedman, "Of Culture and Visions," *Mail and Guardian,* March 27, 1997.

17. "Credo Mutwa, a Small Ray of Hope for Africa," www.credomutwa.co.za (accessed February 20, 2002).

18. Vusamazulu Credo Mutwa, *Song of the Stars: The Lore of a Zulu Shaman,* ed. Stephen Larsen (Barrytown, NY: Station Hill Openings, 1996), 3.

19. A. S. Brink, "Prologue," in Vusamazulu Credo Mutwa, *Indaba, My Children,* ed. A. S. Brink (Johannesburg: Blue Crane Books, 1964), xv. See also Mutwa, *Africa Is My Witness* (Johannesburg: Blue Crane Books, 1966), i.

20. Randolph Vigne, "Why It Isn't All Black and White," *Mail and Guardian,* February 9, 1999.

21. Sandra Klopper, "Mobilizing Cultural Symbols in Twentieth-Century Zululand," unpublished paper, University of Cape Town, Centre for African Studies, 1989; David Chidester, *Religions of South Africa* (London: Routledge, 1992), 204–12.

22. Friedman, "Of Culture and Visions."

23. Mutwa, *Africa Is My Witness,* 318, 319, 323.

24. Credo Mutwa, "Foreword," in Stefano Ghersi and Peter Major, *South Africa, the 51st State* (Randburg: Fastdraft, 1989), 13.

25. Mutwa, *Indaba, My Children,* 429.

26. Ibid., xiii, 455.

27. Mutwa, *Africa Is My Witness,* vii.

28. Joseph Lelyveld, *Move Your Shadow: South Africa, Black and White* (New York: Random House, 1986), 249.

29. Excite Travel, http://travel.excite.com/show/?loc = 3461 (accessed February 20, 2002).

30. Republic of Bophuthatswana, *A Nation on the March* (Melville: Hans Strydom Publishers, 1987), 19.

31. John L. Comaroff and Jean Comaroff, *Of Revelation and Revolution,* vol. 2: *The Dialectics of Modernity on a South African Frontier* (Chicago: University of Chicago Press, 1997), 1–5.

32. Ringing Rocks Foundation, "Vusamazulu Credo Mutwa," www.ringingrocks .org/html/credo_mutwa.html (accessed February 20, 2002).

33. "Audi Honours Credo Mutwa," *WildNet Africa News Archive*, August 21, 1997, http://wildnetafrica.co.za/bushcraft/dailynews/1997archive_3/archive _19970821_audi.html (accessed February 20, 2002).

34. Dolphin Society, Sixth International Whale and Dolphin Conference, Australia, 1997, http://members.austarmetro.com.au/~dolphins/icerc97.html (accessed February 20, 2002).

35. Credo Mutwa, "Keynote Address," Living Lakes Conference, U.S. Forest Service, Mono Lake Visitor's Center, Lee Vining, California, October 2, 1999, www.livinglakes.org/stlucia/credomutwa.htm (accessed April 14, 2004).

36. "Apartheid Is Dead—but 'Separatism' Is Alive and Well," http://home .intekom.com/animals/orgs/animalvoice/97aprjul/separatism.html (accessed April 14, 2004).

37. *Sunday Times*, January 2, 2000.

38. Usiko, www.cyc-net.org/cycol-0800-rites.html (accessed February 20, 2002).

39. Living Symbols of Africa, www.globaltradecentre.com/massmedia/ rerouteindex.htm (accessed April 14, 2004); TheAfrican.Com, http://theafrican .com/AboutUs.htm (accessed April 14, 2004).

40. Mutwa, *Indaba, My Children*, 559.

41. Rick Martin, "Great Zulu Shaman and Elder Credo Mutwa: A Rare, Astonishing Conversation," *Spectrum Newspaper*, October 1999, www.thespectrumnews .com/images/sb/1999/sb3-100599.gif (accessed April 14, 2004); *David Icke E Magazine* 6, www.davidicke.net/emagazine/vol6/spectmutwa.html (accessed April 14, 2004).

42. Mutwa, *Song of the Stars*, 152.

43. Ibid., 135.

44. Ibid., 142.

45. John E. Mack, *Passport to the Cosmos: Human Transformation and Alien Encounters* (New York: Three Rivers Press, 1999), 57, see also 198–218.

46. David Icke, "The Reptilian Brain," www.davidicke.com/icke/articles2/ reptbrain.html (accessed April 14, 2004).

47. David Icke, "The Reptilian Brain," www.worldwideimage.com/tragicnews/ (accessed February 20, 2002); Nicky Molloy, "David Icke's Lecture: The Biggest Secret," *Ufonet*, December 2, 1999, http://groups.yahoo.com/group/ufonet/ message/3019 (accessed April 14, 2004). See also David Icke, *The Biggest Secret* (London: Bridge of Love Publications, 1999).

48. Luisah Teish, "Foreword," in Mutwa, *Song of the Stars*, ix; Jambalaya Spirit, www.jambalayaspirit.org/ (accessed February 20, 2002).

49. Robert Mshengu Kavanagh, ed., *South African People's Plays* (London: Heinemann, 1981); S. Mngadi, "'Popular Memory' and Social Change in South African Historical Drama of the Seventies in English: The Case of Credo Mutwa's *Unosilimela,*" *Alternation* 1, 1 (1994): 37–41.

50. Teish, "Foreword," ix.

51. Diana Haecker and Nomi Baumgartyl, "Requiem for the Whales," *New World* 1 (1998), http://w3.siemens.de/newworld/PND/PNDG/PNDGA/PNDGAA/pndgaa2_e.htm (accessed February 20, 2002).

52. Mack, *Passport to the Cosmos,* 215–16.

53. Michael Taussig, "Viscerality, Faith, and Skepticism: Another Theory of Magic," in Nicholas B. Dirks, ed., *In Near Ruins: Cultural Theory at the End of the Century* (Minneapolis: University of Minnesota Press, 1998), 222.

54. Susan Stewart, *Crimes of Writing: Problems in the Containment of Representation* (New York: Oxford University Press, 1991).

55. Robin Sylvan, "Rap Music, Hip-Hop Culture, and 'The Future Religion of the World,'" in Bruce Forbes and Jeffrey Mahan, eds., *Religion and Popular Culture in America* (Berkeley: University of California Press, 2000), 281–97.

56. David Brooks, *Bobos in Paradise: The New Upper Class and How They Got There* (New York: Simon and Schuster, 2001).

57. Jim Perkinson, "The Gift/Curse of 'Second Sight': Is 'Blackness' a Shamanic Category in the Myth of America?" *History of Religions* 42, 1 (2002): 19–58.

CHAPTER 10. VIRTUAL RELIGION

1. James A. Haught, ed., *2000 Years of Disbelief: Famous People with the Courage to Doubt* (Amherst, NY: Prometheus Books, 1996), 201.

2. *Los Angeles Times,* August 8, 2001.

3. Rodney Needham, *Exemplars* (Berkeley: University of California Press, 1985), 75–116; Susan Stewart, *Crimes of Writing: Problems in the Containment of Representation* (New York: Oxford University Press, 1991), 31–65; Frank Lestringant, "Travels in Eucharistia: Formosa and Ireland from George Psalmanaazaar to Jonathan Swift," trans. Noah Guynn, *Yale French Studies* 86 (1994): 109–25.

4. On Zen master Kenzo Awa, see Eugen Herrigel, *Zen in the Art of Archery,* trans. R. F. C. Hull (London: Routledge and Kegan Paul, 1953); and Needham, *Exemplars,* 188–218. On the Yaqui shaman don Juan Matus, see Carlos Castaneda, *The Teachings of Don Juan: A Yaqui Way of Knowledge* (Berkeley: University of California Press, 1968); Richard De Mille, *Castaneda's Journey: The Power and the Allegory* (London: Abacus, 1978); and Richard De Mille, *The Don Juan Papers: Further Castaneda Controversies* (Santa Barbara, CA: Ross-Erikson, 1980). On Lobsang Rampa, see T. Lobsang Rampa, *The Third Eye* (New York: Doubleday, 1956); and

Donald S. Lopez Jr., *Prisoners of Shangri-La: Tibetan Buddhism and the West* (Chicago: University of Chicago Press, 1998), 86–113.

5. On Black Elk, see John Neihardt, *Black Elk Speaks* (Lincoln: University of Nebraska Press, 1961); and Philip P. Arnold, "Black Elk and Book Culture," *Journal of the American Academy of Religion* 67, 1 (1999): 85–111. On Ogotemmeli, see Marcel Griaule, *Conversations with Ogotemmêli: An Introduction to Dogon Religious Ideas* (London: Oxford University Press, 1975); and Walter E. A. van Beek, "Dogon Restudied: A Field Evaluation of the Work of Marcel Griaule," *Current Anthropology* 32, 2 (1991): 139–67.

6. On the category of "fakelore," see Richard M. Dorson, *Folklore and Fakelore: Essays toward a Discipline of Folk Studies* (Cambridge, MA: Harvard University Press, 1976); and Alan Dundes, *Folklore Matters* (Knoxville: University of Tennessee Press, 1989). The term *fakelore* has been applied to the invented traditions of modern nationalism in Tom Nairn, *Faces of Nationalism: Janus Revisited* (London: Verso, 1997); and to the appropriations of indigenous religion by New Age movements in Michael I. Niman, *People of the Rainbow: A Nomadic Utopia* (Knoxville: University of Tennessee Press, 1997), 131–48.

7. Émile Benveniste, *Indo-European Language and Society*, trans. Elizabeth Palmer (London: Faber and Faber, 1973), 522.

8. Charles H. Long, *Significations: Signs, Symbols, and Images in the Interpretation of Religion* (Aurora, CO: Davies Group, 1999), 3.

9. David Chidester, *Christianity: A Global History* (San Francisco: HarperSanFrancisco, 2000), 168, 172–74.

10. G. Sale, *The Koran: Commonly Called the Alkoran of Mohammed* (London: A. L. Burt, 1734), viii.

11. Leigh Eric Schmidt, *Hearing Things: Religion, Illusion, and the American Enlightenment* (Cambridge, MA: Harvard University Press, 2000).

12. Jonathan Edwards, *Religious Affections* (1746; Carlisle, PA: Banner of Truth, 1961), 17.

13. Charles. G. Finney, "Governing the Tongue," *Oberlin Evangelist* 7 (January 29, 1845), www.whatsaiththescripture.com/Voice/Oberlin_1845/OE1845 .Governing.Tongue.html (accessed December 16, 2003).

14. Michel de Certeau, *The Practice of Everyday Life*, trans. Steven Rendall (Berkeley: University of California Press, 1984), 162–64.

15. Norbert Elias, *The Civilizing Process: The History of Manners*, trans. Edmund Jephcott (Oxford: Basil Blackwell, 1978), 130, 132.

16. E. B. Tylor, *Primitive Culture*, 2 vols. (London: John Murray, 1871), 1:104.

17. Schmidt, *Hearing Things*, 51.

18. Mikhail Bakhtin, *Rabelais and His World*, trans. Hélène Iswolsky (Bloomington: Indiana University Press, 1984), 118.

19. Jonathan Swift, *A Tale of a Tub and Other Works*, ed. A. C. Guthkelch and D. Nichol Smith (1704; Oxford: Clarendon Press, 1958); this and all the following quotations from 156.

20. Phoebe Hoban, *Basquiat: A Quick Killing in Art* (New York: Penguin, 1999), 25–28.

21. Aldous Huxley, *Brave New World* (London: Chatto and Windus, 1934); Kurt Vonnegut Jr., *Cat's Cradle* (New York: Holt, Rinehart and Winston, 1963); Robert A. Heinlein, *Stranger in a Strange Land* (New York: Putnam, 1961). Although Fordianism and Bokononism might also have their adherents, the Church of All Worlds, Inc., is apparently a legally recognized pagan religion in the United States (CAWeb, www.caw.org [accessed April 14, 2004]).

22. Walter Houston Clark, *Religious Experience: Its Nature and Function in the Human Psyche* (Springfield, IL: Charles C. Thomas, 1973), 17.

23. This and all the following quotations in this discussion are from the Web site Burning Man, www.burningman.com (accessed April 14, 2004). See also Sarah M. Pike, "Desert Goddesses and Apocalyptic Art: Making Sacred Space at the Burning Man Festival," in Eric Michael Mazur and Kate McCarthy, eds., *God in the Details: American Religion in Popular Culture* (New York: Routledge, 2001), 155–76.

24. Anti-Bullshit Movement, http://home.att.net/~hugh2you/abm.html (accessed April 14, 2004).

25. Abstract Ministry, www.geocities.com/CapitolHill/9183/araman.html (accessed April 14, 2004); Andersianism, www.nada.kth.se/~asa/andersianism.html (accessed April 14, 2004); Asaism, www.users.wineasy.se/johanssons/Mikael/asaism/asaism.html (accessed February 20, 2002).

26. Margot Adler, *Drawing Down the Moon: Witches, Druids, Goddess-Worshippers, and Other Pagans in America Today*, rev. ed. (Boston: Beacon Press, 1986), 336.

27. Although Discordian sites are numerous, a good place to start for Discordian links is the self-proclaimed official site, "genuine and authorized by the House of Apostles of Eris," www.kbuxton.com/discordia/ (accessed April 14, 2004). For the first edition of their sacred text, see Malaclypse the Younger, *Principia Discordia, or, How I Found the Goddess and What I Did to Her When I Found Her: The Magnum Opiate of Malaclypse the Younger, Wherein Is Explained Absolutely Everything Worth Knowing about Absolutely Anything* (Mason, MI: Loompanics Unlimited, 1978). On the struggle between Discordians and Illuminati, see Robert Shea and Robert Anton Wilson, *Illuminatus!* 3 vols. (Leviathan, NY: Dell, 1975).

28. Church of the SubGenius, www.subgenius.com (accessed April 14, 2004); the Intergalactic House of Fruitcakes, www.tiac.net/users/ighf/index.html (accessed February 20, 2002); the Holy Church of Unified Borkism, www.borkism.com (accessed February 20, 2002); the Universal Life Church, with facility for online ordination, www.ulc.org/ulchq/index.htm (accessed April 14, 2004).

29. Jakes—Yahoo "Parody Religion" Case, www.castlechaos.com/discord/jakes/yahooparody.html (accessed April 14, 2004).

30. Agnostic Church, http://agnostic.org (accessed April 14, 2004); First Church of Rotate Your Envelope Stock, www.globe-guardian.com/dogma.htm (accessed April 14, 2004); Church of Bullshitology, www.churchofbs.org (accessed April 14, 2004).

31. Church of Nothing at All, www.geocities.com/SoHo/Square/1692/church.html (accessed April 14, 2004); Last Chance Cathedral and Discount House of _Worship, http://dragonet.com/allsaint/ (accessed April 14, 2004); Wauism www.tftb.com/deify/wauism.htm (accessed April 14, 2004).

32. Hauverism, www.geocities.com/Athens/7780/ (accessed February 20, 2002); Church of the Covert Cosmos, http://home.onestop.net/braxton/cotcc/ (accessed February 20, 2002).

33. Church of Cyberosophy, www.cyberosophy.com (accessed December 16, 2003); No Sin, http://nosin.com (accessed February 20, 2002); Church of the Covert Cosmos, http://home.onestop.net/braxton/cotcc/ (accessed February 20, 2002).

34. First Church of the Last Laugh, www.saintstupid.com (accessed April 14, 2004).

35. First Church of Cyberspace, www.godweb.org/index1.html (accessed April 14, 2004); Bastard Son of the Lord Home Page, www.bsotl.org (accessed April 14, 2004); Antichrist Bob's Family Fun Pages, http://bennyhills.fortunecity.com/fawlty/370/ (accessed April 14, 2004); Betty Bowers, America's Best Christian, www.bettybowers.com (accessed April 14, 2004).

36. True Catholic Church, www.truecatholic.org (accessed April 14, 2004); His Holiness Pope Gregory XVII, www.geocities.com/Area51/Lair/7170/ibio1.htm (accessed April 14, 2004); Landover Baptist Church, www.landoverbaptist.org (accessed April 14, 2004).

37. Jesus Seeks Loving Woman, www.datejesus.com (accessed April 14, 2004); Liberated Christians, www.libchrist.com (accessed April 14, 2004).

38. Vendraism, http://members.tripod.com/~vendra/ (accessed February 20, 2002); Alchodise, www.blackmesa.plus.com (accessed February 20, 2002); Beer Church, www.beerchurch.com (accessed April 14, 2004); Church of Our Lady of Malted Barley and Hops, www.branwen.com/01/ (accessed February 20, 2002); Blaketashi Darwish, www.blaketashi.com (accessed April 14, 2004).

39. Center for Duck Studies, www.jagaimo.com/duck/ (accessed April 14, 2004).

40. Cult Construction Set, www.fadetoblack.com/cultkit/ (accessed April 14, 2004); Diarrhetics, http://home.snafu.de/tilman/cos_fun/diarrhetics/lamp1.html (accessed April 14, 2004); Clearity is Confusion, http://home.earthlink.net/~imfalse/hcu_annex.html (accessed April 14, 2004); First Church of Appliantology,

http://home.online.no/~corneliu/extreme.html (accessed April 14, 2004); Dianetech, www.geocities.com/Athens/Oracle/5616/main.htm (accessed February 20, 2002); Apelomatics, www.apelord.com/apead.html (accessed February 20, 2002); First Electronic Church of Scamizdat, http://home.snafu.de/tilman/cos_fun/ scamchr.txt (accessed April 14, 2004).

41. Kick-Ass Post-Apocalyptic Doomsday Cult of Love, www.parody-pages .com/doomsday/ (accessed April 14, 2004).

42. Church of Elvis, www.churchofelvis.com/welcome.htm (accessed February 20, 2002); First Church of Jesus Christ, Elvis, http://jubal.westnet.com/ hyperdiscordia/ sacred_heart_elvis.html (accessed April 14, 2004); First Presleyterian Church of Elvis the Divine, www.geocities.com/presleyterian_church/ (accessed April 14, 2004); Zaragrunudgeyon, www.dial1.net/mmacrae/ (accessed April 14, 2004).

43. First Church of Shatnerology, www.shatnerology.com (accessed April 14, 2004); Second National Church of Shatnerology, www.geocities.com/Hollywood/ set/1931/shatner.html (accessed April 14, 2004); Jediism: The Jedi Religion, www.jediism.org (accessed April 14, 2004).

44. Church of Rock, www.churchofrock.com (accessed April 14, 2004); First Church of Holy Rock and Roll, http://mypeoplepc.com/members/povereem/ (accessed April 14, 2004); Church of Rock and Roll, www.churchofrockandroll .com (accessed February 20, 2002); Church of AntiChrist Superstar, www.dewn .com/mm/ (accessed February 20, 2002); Temple of the Bowie, http://ugr8.ucsd .edu/Bowie/ (accessed February 20, 2002); Partridge Family Temple, www .kapelovitz.com/pft/ (accessed April 14, 2004); Church of the Heavenly Wood, http://geocities.com/Hollywood/Boulevard/9565/ (accessed February 20, 2002); First Church of Tiger Woods, www.tigerwoodsisgod.com (accessed April 14, 2004).

45. Holy Temple of Mass Consumption, www4.ncsu.edu/~aiken/ (accessed April 14, 2004); Our Lady of Mass Consumption, http://members.aol.com/ olomc/olomc.htm (accessed April 14, 2004); Jesus Christ Superstore, www .jesuschristsuperstore.net (accessed April 14, 2004); Church of Stop Shopping, http://revbilly.com (accessed April 14, 2004); Church of Secularistic Holidayism, http://tisiphone.dhs.org/~tschap/cosh/ (accessed April 14, 2004).

46. Church of the Almighty Dollar, www.well.com/user/earl/church.html (accessed April 14, 2004); Church of the Profit$, http://home.epix.net/~jlferri/ profit.html (accessed April 14, 2004).

47. God Co., www.angelfire.com/pq/godco/ (accessed April 14, 2004); Lord Co., http://lordco.virtualave.net/index2.shtml (accessed February 20, 2002); Messiahs, Inc., www.iop.com/~thanedfane/ (accessed February 20, 2002); The Great God Contest, www.islandnet.com/~luree/contest.html (accessed April 14, 2004); Messiah

Mickey, www.iop.com/~thanedfane/ (accessed February 20, 2002); First Internet McChurch Tabernacle, www.mcchurch.com/ (accessed April 14, 2004).

48. Cthulhu, www.cthulhu.org (accessed April 14, 2004).

49. Church of the Avocado, http://members.tripod.com/~cotav/ (accessed April 14, 2004); Church of the Big Plastic Fork, http://bigplasticfork.faithweb.com (accessed February 20, 2002); Church of the Burnt Onion Ring, http://zcbor .fateback.com/ (accessed February 20, 2002); Church of the Chainsaw, http:// groups .yahoo.com/group/churchofthechainsaw/ (accessed April 14, 2004); Church of Ice Cream, www.angelfire.com/pa/FudgementDay/ (accessed April 14, 2004); Church of the Twinkie, www.geocities.com/SouthBeach/Pointe/6500/twink %5Findex.html (accessed April 14, 2004); Church of Volkswagenism, www.mvoc .com/vwism/ (accessed February 20, 2002); First United Church of the Fisher-Price Record Player, www.misty.com/people/penny/church.html (accessed April 14, 2004); Shrine of the Potato, www.dillard.com/potato.htm (accessed February 20, 2002).

50. Church of the Bunny, http://ourworld.compuserve.com/homepages/ bunnychurch/ (accessed February 20, 2002); Church of the Gerbil, www.corg.org/ main.htm (accessed April 14, 2004); Church of the Quivering Otter, http://triggur .org/coqo/ (accessed April 14, 2004); Kult of Hamstur, www.end.com/~niko/ Texts/kult.html (accessed February 20, 2002); Holy Church of Moo, http:// members.aol.com/DailyCow/indexhcom.htm (accessed February 20, 2002); Holy Turtle's Internet Cathedral, www.angelfire.com/ma2/holyturtle/ (accessed April 14, 2004); Shrine to Skippy and the Holy 'Roos, www.fi.uib.no/~alsaker/Skippy/ (accessed February 20, 2002); Temple of the Sacred Cat, www.vcnet.com/valkat/ temple.html (accessed April 14, 2004); Virtual Church of the Blind Chihuahua, www.dogchurch.org (accessed April 14, 2004).

51. First Internet Church of All, www.netzone.com/~dggannon/ficoa.html (accessed February 20, 2002); Church of Euthanasia, www.churchofeuthanasia .org (accessed April 14, 2004); Kelvin is Lord, http://zapatopi.net/lordkelvin.html (accessed April 14, 2004).

52. Church of Virus, http://virus.lucifer.com (accessed April 14, 2004); Prometheism, www.prometheism.net (accessed April 14, 2004); Techanism, http:// techanism .sourceforge.net (accessed April 14, 2004); Technosophy, www .technosophy.com (accessed April 14, 2004); Church of the Almighty Revealed in Biotechnology, www.ram.org/misc/church/church.html (accessed April 14, 2004).

53. Holy Order of the Cheeseburger, http://members.tripod.com/aslag6/ index.htm (accessed February 20, 2002).

54. Ibid.

55. Jakes—Yahoo "Parody Religion" Case.

56. Theodor W. Adorno, *The Jargon of Authenticity,* trans. Knut Tarnowski and Frederic Will (Evanston, IL: Northwestern University Press, 1973).

57. This and the following Discordian quotes in this discussion are from Jakes—Yahoo "Parody Religion" Case.

58. On the I AM movement and the Supreme Court, see David Chidester, *Patterns of Power: Religion and Politics in American Culture* (Englewood Cliffs, NJ: Prentice-Hall, 1988), 131–33.

59. Ted Kaczynski, Unabomber manifesto, http://hotwired.lycos.com/special/unabom/notes/note30.html (accessed April 14, 2004).

60. What the Heck Is It.Com, www.whattheheckisit.com/useragree.shtml (accessed February 20, 2002).

61. William James, *The Varieties of Religious Experience,* ed. Martin E. Marty (London: Penguin, 1982), 31.

62. Ibid., 37–38.

CHAPTER 11. PLANET AMERICA

1. Peter Major and Stephano Ghersi, *South Africa, the 51st State* (Randburg: Fastdraft, 1989), 239.

2. Ibid., 215, 233.

3. Ibid., 10.

4. Vicente Verdú, *El Planeta americano* (Barcelona: Editorial Anagrama, 1996), 27–28; my translation.

5. Ibid., 26.

6. Diana Eck, *A New Religious America* (San Francisco: HarperSanFrancisco, 2001).

7. Tarek Atia, "Bruce Willis versus Bin Laden," *Al-Ahram* 402 (November 5–11, 1998).

8. Jody Rosen, *White Christmas: The Story of a Song* (New York: HarperCollins, 2002), 157.

9. Will Herberg, *Protestant, Catholic, Jew: An Essay in American Religious Sociology* (Garden City, NY: Doubleday, 1955).

10. Leon T. Hadar, "What Green Peril?" *Foreign Affairs* 72, 2 (1993): 27–42, 27.

11. Leon T. Hadar, "The 'Green Peril': Creating the Islamic Fundamentalist Threat," *Cato Institute, Policy Analysis* No. 177 (August 27, 1992), www.cato.org/pubs/pas/pa-177.html (accessed June 17, 2004).

12. Jane Naomi Iwamura, "The Oriental Monk in American Popular Culture," in Bruce David Forbes and Jeffrey H. Mahan, eds., *Religion and Popular Culture in America* (Berkeley: University of California Press, 2000), 25–43.

13. Robert H. Sharf, "Experience," in Mark C. Taylor, ed., *Critical Terms for Religious Studies* (Chicago: University of Chicago Press, 1998), 103.

14. James L. Watson, "Transnationalism, Localization, and Fast Foods in East

Asia," in Watson, ed., *Golden Arches East: McDonald's in East Asia* (Stanford, CA: Stanford University Press, 1997), 24; Sam Skolnik, "Hindus, Vegetarians Sue McDonald's over Frying Process," *Seattle Post-Intelligencer,* May 2, 2001.

15. Harvey Cox, "The Market as God: Living in a New Dispensation," *Atlantic Monthly,* March 1999, 18–23; Thomas Frank, *One Market under God: Extreme Capitalism, Market Populism, and the End of Economic Democracy* (New York: Doubleday, 2000).

16. Max Horkheimer and Theodor W. Adorno, *The Dialectic of Enlightenment,* trans. John Cumming (London: Verso, 1973), 137–38; Walter Benjamin, *Gesammelte Schriften,* 7 vols., ed. Rolf Tiedemann and Hermann Schweppenhäuser (Frankfurt: Suhrkamp, 1972–1989), 7:377.

17. Edmundo O'Gorman, *The Invention of America: An Inquiry into the Historical Nature of the New World and the Meaning of Its History* (Bloomington: Indiana University Press, 1961).

18. Charles H. Long, *Significations: Signs, Symbols, and Images in the Interpretation of Religion* (Aurora, CO: Davies Group, 1999), 182.

19. Joseph J. Corn and Brian Horrigan, *Yesterday's Tomorrows: Past Visions of the American Future* (Baltimore: Johns Hopkins University Press, 1996).

20. Steve Mizrach, "'Modern Primitives': The Accelerating Collision of Past and Future in the Postmodern Era," www.fiu.edu/~mizrachs/Modern_Primitives.html (accessed April 14, 2004).

21. Sacvan Bercovitch, "The Problem of Ideology in American Literary History," *Critical Inquiry,* 12, 4 (1986): 645.

22. Giles B. Gunn, *Thinking across the American Grain: Ideology, Intellect, and the New Pragmatism* (Chicago: University of Chicago Press, 1992), 32.

23. Lewis V. Baldwin, *To Make the Wounded Whole: The Cultural Legacy of Martin Luther King, Jr.* (Minneapolis: Fortress Press, 1992), 203. See also George M. Houser, "Freedom's Struggle Crosses Oceans and Mountains: Martin Luther King, Jr., and the Liberation Struggles in Africa and America," in Peter J. Albert and Ronald Hoffman, eds., *We Shall Overcome: Martin Luther King, Jr., and the Black Freedom Struggle* (New York: Pantheon Books, 1990), 169–96.

24. Joseph T. Leerssen, "On the Edge of Europe: Ireland in Search of Oriental Roots, 1650–1850," *Comparative Criticism* 8 (1986): 109. See also Peter Mason, *Deconstructing America: Representations of the Other* (London: Routledge, 1990).

25. William Brandon, *New Worlds for Old: Reports from the New World and Their Effect on the Development of Social Thought in Europe, 1500–1800* (Athens, Ohio: Ohio University Press, 1986); Herman Lebovies, "The Uses of America in Locke's Second Treatise on Government," *Journal of the History of Ideas* 47 (1986): 567–81.

26. Tocqueville cited in Gunther Barth, *Fleeting Moments: Nature and Culture in American History* (New York: Oxford University Press, 1990), xviii.

27. Ferdinand Kürnberger, *Der Amerika-Müde: Amerikanisches Kulturbild* (Frankfurt: Meidinger, 1855), 1; cited and trans. in Hugh Ridley, *Images of Imperial Rule* (London: Croom Helm; New York: St. Martin's Press, 1983), 30.

28. Jean Baudrillard, *America*, trans. Chris Turner (London: Verso, 1989), 5, 99, 63.

29. Ibid., 9.

30. Yi-Fu Tuan, *Space and Place: The Perspective of Experience* (Minneapolis: University of Minnesota Press, 1977), 99.

31. Ray Allen Billington, *Land of Savagery, Land of Promise: The European Image of the American Frontier in the Nineteenth Century* (New York: Norton, 1981).

32. Fei Xiotong cited in R. David Arkush and Leo O. Lee, eds. and trans., *Land without Ghosts: Chinese Impressions of America from the Mid-Nineteenth Century to the Present* (Berkeley: University of California Press, 1989), 177–80.

33. Slavoj Žižek, *Welcome to the Desert of the Real! Five Essays on September 11 and Related Dates* (London: Verso, 2002), 12–13.

34. Lawrence Grossberg, *We Gotta Get Out of This Place: Popular Conservatism and Postmodern Culture* (New York: Routledge, 1992), 227.

35. Jacques Derrida, "Faith and Knowledge," in Derrida and Gianni Vattimo, eds., *Religion* (Stanford, CA: Stanford University Press, 1998), 36.

36. Mike Davis, *City of Quartz: Excavating the Future in Los Angeles* (New York: Vintage, 1992).

37. David Chidester, *Savage Systems: Colonialism and Comparative Religion in Southern Africa* (Charlottesville: University Press of Virginia, 1996), 32–34.

38. Afrika Bambaataa, "The Coming of the Next Millennium 2000: The New Age," www.geocities.com/Area51/Rampart/8569/afrika.htm (accessed April 14, 2004).

INDEX

abduction, viii, 23, 81–83, 86, 183–84
Abstract Ministry, 197–98
Acapulco, 13
Act Now, Inc., 111
Adam, 106
Adcult USA, 27, 34
Adherents.com, 1
Adorno, Theodor W.: and culture industry, 20, 220; and exchange, 118; and jargon of authenticity, 209
advertising, 27, 34, 42, 143
Aeolians, 195–96
Afghanistan, 11, 129–30
Africa: and aliens, 172, 182–84; and American movement, ix, 157–64; and Americans criminal gang, ix, 9, 113–16, 129, 215, 223; and art, 177, 185, 189; and Batokas, 132; and Christianity, 8; and Clinton, 7, 11, 170; and Coca-Cola, 42; and denial of religion, 17; and Disney, 144–45, 219; and Dogon religion, 191; and fetish, 3, 42–43, 153–57; and handshake, 132; and indigenous religion, 150–57, 177,

191; and Islam, 155; and music, 8, 150; and philosophy, 170; and pilgrimage to America, 164–70; and priest, 151; and shamanism, 9, 172–89; and spiritual tourism, 23, 173; and survivals, 150. *See also* Botswana; Cape Town; Kalahari Desert; South Africa; West Africa
Africa: An Essay toward a History of the Continent (Du Bois), 152
Africa: Its Place in Modern History (Du Bois), 152
African Americans: and Christianity, 8, 151–57, 165–66; and feminism, 185; and indigenous African religion, 151–57; and indigenous authenticity, 189; and music, 44, 188–89, 204; and Nelson Mandela, 165–66; and origin, 221–22; and slavery, 8, 150–57, 221–22
African Methodist Episcopal Church, 125–26
African National Congress, 126, 164, 166–67, 179, 186

African Renaissance, 171
Africa Square, Harlem, 169
Aggrey, James K., 158–59
Agnostic Church, 199
airplanes, 158, 161
Aladdin (1992), 144
Al-Ahram, 14
alchemy: and global economy, 125, 127–28; and plastic, 62; and Tupperware, 54–55
Alchodise, 202–3
Alien Domination Gospel Mission, 196
Alien Jigsaw (Wilson), 82
aliens: and abduction, viii, 23, 81–83, 86, 183–84; and African tradition, 172, 182–84; and David Icke, 184; as reptilians, 122–24, 184
Allah, 38, 131, 216
Amazon, 173
America: as alternative, 224; as boundary, 224; as center, 213, 260n57; as desert, 225, 227; as empty, 225–26; as human possibility, 223; as imperialism, 9; as irony, 225; as reversal, 224–25; sacrificial center of, 93–95. *See also* United States
American movement, 9, 126, 152, 157–64, 222–23
"American Red Double-cross" (Horowitz), 128
American's Creed (US Congress), 116
Americans gang, ix, 9, 113–16, 129, 215, 223
American Top 40, 14
American Youth Rising from the Waves, 97
Amerika-Müde, Der, (Kürnberger), 225
Amway, 4, 31, 58
Anaheim, 146
anarchy, 198
Anders, 198, 220
Andersianism, 198
Angeley, Ernest, 84
animals, 21

Anti-Bullshit Movement, 197
Antichrist Bob's Family Fun Pages, 202
antihuman, 82–83
apartheid: in America, 166, 169–70; and sanctions, 164, 167, 169, 213–14; in South Africa, 151, 164, 170, 176, 178–80, 182, 185–86
Apelomatics, 203
apocalypse: American, 152, 157–62; and Coca-Cola, 41; and film, 22; and Nelson Mandela, 165
Appadurai, Arjun, 60, 123, 134
Appliantology, 203
Arafat, Yasser, 167
Aramanism, 197, 210
Arbella, 97
Argentina, 8, 138
Aristotle, 72
Arlington National Cemetery, 97
Armageddon, 161
Armstrong, Neil, 214
Asa, 198, 220
Asaism, 198
Ash, Heather, 79, 88
astronauts, 97
Atia, Tarek, 14–15, 216
Atlanta, 2, 28, 34, 40, 137, 167, 175
Atlantic World, 150, 170–71
attention deficit disorder, 85
Augustine of Hippo, 73
aura, 75
Austin, 123
Australia, 113, 181
authenticity: and African religion, 3; and apartheid, 178; as aura, 75; and authentic inauthenticity, ix, 227; as control, 193–95, 209; criteria for, 209–12; cultural, 188; and fakery, 186–88; and history, 209–10; and identity, 211; and inauthentic authenticity, 231; indigenous, 9, 173, 175–79, 181–82, 185–89, 191, 219; jargon of, 209; and morphology, 210; as opacity

apocalypse, 161; and baseball, 38; and body of Christ, 87; and capitalism, 23; and cargo movements, 163; and Coca-Cola, 41; conservative, 17–18; and criteria of authenticity, 193–95; and cross, 3; and desire, 26–27; and Disney, 18; Ethiopian, 125–26, 159; evangelical, 56, 111–12, 115, 129; and fraud, 190; and gangsters, 115; and globalization, 148; Gnostic, 45, 216; and gospel of prosperity, 128; and Hollywood, 15; and home, 55–56; and interreligious polemic, 192; and Irving Berlin, 216; and McDonald's, 28, 31, 137, 142, 148, 228; and money, 111–12, 118; and orthodoxy, 192–93; and parody religion, 199, 201–2; Pauline, 87; Pentecostal, 148; and popular culture, 216; and Protestant Ethic, 28, 111–12, 229; Puritan, 75–76; and rock 'n' roll, 31–32, 43–44; and sacrifice, 24; as solid system, 52; and television evangelism, 84–85; and touch, 72–73; Zionist, 126. *See also* Baptists; Catholic Church; Christian Science; Emergence Ministries; Ethiopian movement; Gnosticism; Jesus; Methodist Church; Protestant ethic; Zionist Christian churches
Christian Science, 177, 216
Christmas, 41, 216
Churchill, Winston, 99
Church of All Worlds, 196
Church of AntiChrist Superstar, 204
Church of Bullshitology, 200
Church of Cyberosophy, 200–201
Church of Elvis, ix, 23, 192, 204
Church of Euthanasia, 207
Church of Fun, 196
Church of Holy Fucking Shit, 197
Church of Ice Cream, 207
Church of Naismith, 196
Church of Nothing at All, 200

Church of Our Lady of Malted Barley and Hops, 202
Church of Prometheus, 66
Church of Rock, 204
Church of Rock and Roll Online Chapel, 204
Church of Scientology, 203
Church of Secularistic Holidayism, 205
Church of St. John the Baptist of the Alien Artichoke, 196
Church of Stop Shopping, 205
Church of the Almighty Dollar, ix, 23, 192, 205
Church of the Almighty Revealed in Biotechnology, 208
Church of the Avocado, 207
Church of the Big Plastic Fork, 207
Church of the Bunny, 23
Church of the Burnt Onion Ring, 207
Church of the Chainsaw, 207
Church of the Covert Cosmos, ix, 192, 200–201
Church of the Heavenly Wood, 204–5
Church of the Holy Electron, 196
Church of the Profit$, 4, 112, 205–6
Church of the SubGenius, ix, 23, 192, 198
Church of the Twinkie, 3, 207
Church of Virus, 23, 66, 192, 207–8
Church of Volkswagenism, 3, 207
Civilizing Process (Elias), 194
civil religion, 6–7, 22, 96, 109–10
civil rights movement, 166–67
Clark, Walter, 196
Clarke, Alison J., 54–55, 59
Classen, Constance, 138
classification: and fake religion, 187–88; and genes, 64–66; and limits, 68; of persons, 18, 21, 219–21; and plastic, 62; and virtual religions, 207
Clearity is Confusion, 203
Cleveland, 3

Clinton, Bill: and conspiracy theorists, 7, 121; and feathers, 175; and global economy, 124–27; and Human Genome Project, 7, 53, 64–65; and impeachment, 77, 117; and inauguration, 170; and "New Covenant," 7, 76–77, 87; and South Africa, 7, 11, 170

cloning, 65, 67

Coca-Cola: and Africa, 42; and Americanization, 223; and brand-name recognition, 140; and Buddhism, 217; and capitalism, 137; and Cocacolonization, 8, 42, 135–38; and cultural imperialism, 135–38; as divine gift, 40, 54; as fetish, 32–34, 40–43, 50–51, 135; as global religion, 28; and *Gods Must Be Crazy*, 42, 136; as Holy Grail, 135; as indigenous, 138; and Islam, 216–17; and meccanization, 2–3; and museum, 34, 137, 221; as real thing, 9; as religion, viii, ix, 1, 17; and Santa Claus, 174; and translation, 135–36, 148; as transnational, 60; and Vatican, 135

cocaine, 40

Cohn, Harry, 15

cold war, 107, 109–10, 217, 222

Collins, Francis, 64–65

Colombia, 112

colonialism, 49–50, 145, 192. *See also* imperialism

Columbus, Christopher, 224

Comaroff, Jean, 84, 127–28, 180

Comaroff, John L., 84, 127–28, 180

Commission for Racial Justice of the United Church of Christ, 166

commodity: and artwork, 20; as fetish, 3, 42, 57

Common Sense (Paine), 117

communication, 8, 131–35

communism: and Coca-Cola, 137; and cold war, 217; and home, 56; and Jim Jones, 24, 110; and Moses Hess, 118;

and sacrifice, 91–92; and South Africa, 179

communitas, 47

community: and baseball, 36–37, 39; and religion, viii, 5, 2–3, 33; and Tupperware, 54–57

confession, 22, 201

Confucianism, 133

Conrad, Joseph, 110

conspiracy: and Bill Clinton, 121; of blood and money, 120–24; and George Herbert Walker Bush, 121–24; and George W. Bush, 121–23; and Hollywood, 14–15; and Jews, 14–15; as para-religion, 120

consumerism, 3, 31, 42, 57, 138, 205, 212

consumption, 20–21

Cooperstown, 2

corporations: New Age, 79; religio-economic, 31, 58; transnational, 60

covenant: and Bill Clinton, 76–77; and cargo movements, 163; and Puritans, 75–76

Cox, Harvey, 219

creationism, 221

Critical Art Ensemble, 66

Cthulu, 206, 220

Cuba, 136

cult: and anticult polemic, 203–4; and denial of religion, 17, 46; of domesticity, 55–56; and rock 'n' roll, 50; and satire, 66–67

Cult of Distraction, 196

Cult of the New Eve, 66–67, 70, 221

Cult of the Potato, 207

Cultural Imperialism (Tomlinson), 136

Currency and Coercion (Kirshner), 126

cyberspace, ix, 5, 23, 31, 192, 197–212

Cyprian, King, 178

Dada, 47, 196

dance, 174, 176

Dante, 26–27

God *(continued)*
    219, 229; and One Nation under, 215;
    and possessions, 46; selling, 31; and
    Thom McAn logo, 131; and virtual
    religions, 220. *See also* Allah; Anders;
    Asa; Cthulu; Ikon; Jupiter; Otis; Pro-
    teus; Purusha; Shango; Thor; Vishnu;
    Yahweh
God, Inc., 205
Goddess, 198–99, 209, 211, 220. *See also*
    Eris; Gaia; Kali
Godin, Seth, 60–61
Gods Must Be Crazy (1981), 42, 136
Goizueta, Roberto, 34, 41
Goldwater, Barry, 96, 99
Gore, Rick, 79
Gospel of John, 72–73
Gospel of Matthew, 206
Gospel of Thomas, 45
Graceland, 2, 33
graffiti, 189, 196
Graham, Dan, 33
Greater Ministries International, 190
Greece, ancient: goddess of, 198–99,
    209, 211, 220; myth of, 52; and theory
    of senses, 72
Gregory XVII, 202
Greys, 82, 182
Griaule, Marcel, 191
Griffith, D. W., 218
Grossberg, Lawrence, ix, 227
Guatemala, 28, 136
Gunn, Giles, 223
Guy, Sum Dum, 203
Guyana, 91

habit, 71, 75
Habits of the Heart (Bellah et al.), 86
Hadar, Leon T., 217
halal, 216
Hall, Donald, 36
Hall, Edward T., 132–33
Hall, Stuart, 21

haptics, 5, 71, 83–85
Hard Livings, 114–15
Harvard University, 183
Harvey, David, 123
Harvey, Larry, 196
Hauverism, 200
Hayles, Katherine, 70
"Heal the World" (1991), 12
Heal the World Foundation, 12
healing: faith, viii, 84; New Age, 174–
    76; and shamanism, 174–76; and
    touch, 84
hearing: ancient Greek theories of, 25–
    26; and flag burning, 80; and touch,
    72–73
heart, 78, 176
Heart Healing Center, 176
Heart of Darkness (Conrad), 110
heat, 78
Heavens Gate, 230
Hegel, G. W. F., 89
Heiliges Geld (Laum), 118
Heinlein, Robert A., 196
Herbalife, 31, 58
Herberg, Will, 216
Herrigel, Eugen, 191, 218
Hess, Moses, 118
High John the Conqueror, 222
Hinduism: and Kali, 180; and McDon-
    ald's, 141–42, 217–18; and parody
    religion, 199, 202; and spirituality,
    218; Vedic, 87; and West, 218
hip-hop, 150, 188–89, 230–31
HIV/AIDS, 83, 181
Hobbes, Thomas, 39
Hofstede, Geert, 133–34
Holley, Jim, 165
Hollywood: and Christians, 15; and Jews,
    14–15, 216; and Muslims, 14, 217; and
    sacred, 98
Holocaust, 97
Holy Church of Unified Borkism, 198
Holy Order of the Cheeseburger, 208–9

McDonald's *(continued)*
　　and arches, 3, 34; and beef-fat french
　　fry, 218; and cultural imperialism,
　　138–42; and Hinduism, 141, 217,
　　218; as indigenous, 142; and Islam,
　　141–42, 216; and Japan, 8, 140–41;
　　and Judaism, 141–42, 216; and local
　　adaptations, 141; and McDonaldiza-
　　tion, ix, 8, 138–42; and McDonald-
　　land, 221; and myth of freedom, 140;
　　as plastic, 63; and rationalization,
　　138–42, 148–49; as religion, 1, 3, 9;
　　and religious foodways, 141–42; and
　　sacrosanct french fry, 218; as transna-
　　tional, 60; and virtual religions, 206,
　　212
McPherson, James, 188
McQuillan, Martin, 69, 144
Mda, Zakes, 126
meccanization, 2–3, 13, 58–59, 70
medicine wheel, 175
Melanesia, 163–64
memes, 60, 207–8
Memorial Day, 99
memory, 36, 40
Memphis, 3
Messiah: Mickey Mouse as, 206, 220;
　　Nelson Mandela as, 165, 169
Methodist Church, 194–95
Mexico, 138
Mickey Mouse, 21, 34, 146, 206, 212, 220
Microsoft, 49
Mighty Joe Young (1998), 69
Mikhalkov, Sergei, 127
millenarian movements, 152, 157–64
Millin, Sarah, 121
missionaries: Christian, 28, 126, 137, 148,
　　154, 228; corporate, 28, 58; Muslim,
　　148, 154; and translation, 148
Mitterand, François, 98, 106
Mmkungateka, 183
money: and baptism, 112; and blood, 4–
　　5, 25, 114–15, 117–18, 122–23, 128–

30; and Christianity, 118; definition of,
112; fake, 111; and fiction, 125; geography of, 123; and God, 114, 118–19,
123, 205, 219, 229; gospel of, 85; his-
tory of, 123; and Judaism, 118; and
reality, viii; and ritual, 112; and sacred
symbols, 112–13; and sacrifice, 118–
19; as system of symbols, 4, 112; and
television evangelism, 84–85; viral,
123; and virtual religions, 205–6, 212;
and Weber, 111–12
Money Tracts, 111–12, 129
Mono Lake Visitor's Center, 181
Montaigne, Michel de, 224
More, Thomas, 224
Morrison, Jim, 6, 173–74
Moscow, 138, 143
Moses, 96
Mother Earth, 175
Mount Sinai, 73
movies. *See* film
Muhondoruka, 182
Mulan (1998), 144
Muller, F. Max, 16
mushroom, 174
music: and Africa, 8, 150; African-
　　American, 44, 188–89, 204; and
　　myth, 22; and religion, 204. *See also*
　　blues; hip-hop; jazz; rap; rhythm;
　　rock 'n' roll; theomusicology
Muslim Judicial Council, 14
Muslims: in Cape Town, 11–14, 126, 217;
　　and Coca-Cola, 137, 216–17; on film,
　　14–15, 217; and gangsters, 115; and
　　Hollywood, 14, 217; and McDonald's,
　　141–42, 216; and Thom McAn, 131;
　　and United States, 11, 14, 126, 216–17
Muslims against Global Oppression, 11,
　　14
Muslims against Illegitimate Leaders, 11
Mutende-ya-ngenge, 182
Mutwa, Credo: and aliens, 172, 182–
　　84, 187; and America, 174–77; and

apartheid, 178–79, 185–86; as author, 177–78; background, 177–78; and cultural villages, 175, 179–82; and David Icke, 124, 184–85; and environmentalism, 181; and fraud, 176, 186–88; and gangs, 115; and human sacrifice, 124; and Native American religion, 175–76; and Nelson Mandela, 9, 185–86; and New Age spirituality, 174–77; as prophet, 181; and religious work, 186–88; as shaman, ix, 5, 219; and Shango, 171; and tourism, 172–73, 177; and U.S. statehood for South Africa, 214

Mvonjina, 183

mysterium tremendum, 78

mysticism: and blood, 113; British, 203; and fire, 78; Islamic, 203; and Reagan, 95, 97; and sacrifice, 97, 111

myth: and African self-writing, 170–71; and America, 215; and American redemption, 162; and destiny, 222; and Frankenstein, 64; and genomics, 66–67; Greek, 52; and invention, 54; and music, 22; of origin, 221–22; and space, 226

Nacirema, 38

Nafu, 183

Nassau, Robert Hamill, 153–54

National Association of Evangelicals, 94–95, 106

nationalism: Christian, 24; and Hollywood, 15; and popular culture, 6–7; and sacrifice, 24–25, 117–18

National Party, 176, 178

Native Americans: and Disney, 144–45, 218–19; and indigenous authenticity, 189; and potlatch, 35–36, 45–48; and Puritans, 76; and shamanism, 175–76; and Sioux religion, 191; and tricksters, 210

nature, 210

Ndebele, 180

Needham, Rodney, 191, 210

negotiation, 19, 104–5, 134, 149, 165, 171, 220–21

Negritude, 258n20

Negro, The (Du Bois), 152–55, 157

Neihardt, John, 191

Nelkin, Dorothy, 65

Netherlands, 136

Nevada, 22

New Age: conspiracy theory, 184; and firewalking, 79; and indigenous authenticity, 219; and money, 112; and satire, 202–3; and shamanism, 9, 63, 172–77, 185, 228; spirituality, 185, 219

New Covenant for America, 7

New Hanover, 163

New Primitivism, 222

New Religious America, A (Eck), 215

new religious movements, 52

New York, 3, 165, 188

Nicholas, St., 174

Nigeria, 28

Nike, 10, 34, 230

Nixon, Richard, 123

Nonteto, 159

No Sin, 201

Not for Sale (Chidester), xi

Notre Dame, 95, 99, 109

nuclear war, 103–4

obeah, 151, 154

Official Alien Abduction Test Site, 82

O'Gorman, Edmundo, 221

Ogotemmeli, 191

O'Neil, Buck, 32, 35, 36

1 Peter, 125

1 Timothy, 112

Ontario Consultants on Religious Tolerance, 128

orientation, 18–19, 68, 221–23

Orlando, 58–59, 70, 146

rap, 31, 150

Ratcliff, 145

rationalization, ix, 138–42, 147–49; and
McDonald's, 148–49; and Tokyo Disneyland, 147

Ray, Robert B., 44–45

Reagan, Ronald: and children, 96, 101–
2; and civic ritual, 96–97; and communism, 106–7; and discovery of
America, 221; and Gipper, 93, 95, 99,
101, 109; and God, 106; and kinship
symbolism, 102; and nuclear war, 104;
as psychopomp, 98; and redemption
of America, 107–9, 222; and redemptive sacrifice, viii, 24, 92–100; sacrificial worldview of, 7, 94–100; as simulation, 6, 98–99, 107; and soul, 94–95

reciprocity: and exchange, 123; and kinship, 102–4; and revenge, 136

Red Cross, 128–29

Redding, Otis, 227, 229–30

redemption: American, 157–64; and film,
15, 21; and sacrifice, viii, 7, 23–25,
91–92

relics, 3

religio: etymology of, 75, 244n12; and
superstitio, 39, 192

religion: and awakening, 230; and belief,
198–200; and binary oppositions, 13;
and body, 25–26, 70–90; as bullshit,
208–9; as bunk, 190, 208–9; as
church, 36–40, 50–51; civil, 6–7, 22,
96, 109–10; classic definitions of, vii,
13, 15–17, 32, 39, 48–49, 211–12; and
commodification, 197; and community, 33, 54–57; and consumerism,
138; counterfeit, 193; and cross-
cultural business, 134–35; and cult,
46, 50; denial of, 50; and desire, 26–
27, 33–34; and diversity, 215–16; and
drugs, 196; as exchange, 34, 43–48,
59–61; fake, 186–88, 190–92, 197,
228; as feeling, 16; and fetish, 40–43,

50–51, 57–59; and fiction, 196; and
foodways, 141–42, 216–17; and fraud,
190–92; and globalization, 27–29;
and hip-hop, 189; and home, 55–56,
70; indigenous, 218–19; and limits,
68; and market, 4, 28, 119, 219, 229;
and Marx, 231; and money, 111; and
nature, 210; and objects, 33–34; as
oppositional term, 17–18, 39, 46, 50,
192; organized, 82; parody, 192, 199,
209; plastic, 52–70; popular definitions of, 17–19, 30, 32–33, 35–36; as
potlatch, 50–51; and pressure, 85–90;
and religious work, 15–19; and rock
'n' roll, 43–48; and sacrifice, 91; as
safe and sound, 83, 228; and satire,
195–97, 202; secular, 15, 28–29; and
senses, 70–90; as serious, 1, 211–12;
and sleep, 230; and social cohesion,
16; and stress, 86–87; as thinking, 16;
virtual, ix, 192, 196–212, 220. *See also*
classification; myth; negotiation; orientation; ritual; sacred

Remnant Church, 163

reptilians, 122–24, 174, 184

Reverend Ike, 85, 112, 206

"Reviewing the Rhodes Legacy"
(Jasper), 121

Rhema Church, 115

Rhodes, Cecil, 120–21

rhythm, 150, 171, 188–89

Riggert, Brad, 49

Ringing Rocks Foundation, 174–75

ritual: and African music, 150; and blood,
113; and Burning Man, 22; civic, 96–
97; confession, 22, 201; consumption,
21; and eating extraterrestrials, 183;
exchange, 34; expenditure, 4; and film,
98–99; firewalking, 78–80, 88–89;
and french-fry preparation, 138; and
gangsters, 115, 181; and gender, 56–
57; of gift, 34, 45–48, 59; of human
sacrifice, 124, 184; initiation, 121–22;

Schlesinger, Arthur, Jr., 118

Schmidt, George, 228

Schmidt, Leigh, 193

Science and Health (Eddy), 177

science: and god-like powers, 64–65; and virtual religions, 207–8

Scientology. *See* Church of Scientology

Scotland, 188

Seal of the United States, 116

"second coming": of Michael Jordan, 49; of Nelson Mandela, 165, 167

Second National Church of Shatnerology, 204

secularism, 15, 17, 28–29

secular religion, 15, 28–29

Seed, Richard, 65, 67

seeing: and contemplation, 74–75; and embodiment, 25–26; and flag burning, 80; and gender, 88; and modernity, 89; and strategy, 90; and touch, 72–74

Selfish Gene (Dawkins), 69

senses: and embodiment, 25–26; and media, 31; and touch, 70–90

Seven Years in Tibet (1997), 218

Sex Pistols, 47

sexuality, 27

Shaka Day, 178

Shakespeare, William, 118–19

Shaklee, 58

shaman: African, 171–89; definition of, 173; and drugs, 173–74; and ecstasy, 5–6; and firewalking, 79; New Age, 63, 228; plastic, 172–73; Reagan as, 99; and revelation of concealment, 188; and rock 'n' roll, 6, 44, 173–74; and shape-shifting, 63; Siberian, 6; and tourism, 172–73; Yaqui, 191; Zulu, ix, 9, 171–89. *See also* Morrison, Jim; Mutwa, Credo; Perkins, Jim; Santa Claus

Shamanism (Eliade), 173

Shaman M.D. (Bruce), 172

Shamwari Game Reserve, 180–81

Shango, 154–57, 171, 220

shape-shifting: and Proteus, 52; and reptilians, 122–24, 184; and shamans, 6, 172

Shekinah Tabernacle, 115

Shrine of Our Lady of Mass Consumption, 205

Siberia, 173

Siege, The (1998), 14–15, 217

Sikasa, 183

Silver, Lee, 65, 67

simulation, 98–99, 107

Singapore, 141, 216

Sioux, 191

"(Sittin' on the) Dock of the Bay" (1967), 229–30

Siva, 38

Skull and Bones Society, 7, 120–22, 124

slack, 198, 212

slavery, 3, 150–57, 221–22

Sledge, Delony, 33, 41, 135

Smith, Edwin, 159

Smith, Jonathan Z., 98–99, 105, 162–63

sneezing, 194

Soccer: Myths, Rites, and Symbols (Verdú), 214

social cohesion, 2, 16, 77

Social Psychology (Ross), 52, 61

Society of the Elect, 120–21, 124

Solomon, King, 178

Solomon Islands, 163

Sophiatown, 126

Sotho, 180

soul: and DNA, 65; and sacrifice, 94–95

Souls of Black Folk (Du Bois), 151

South Africa: and American movement, 157–62, 222–23; and apartheid, 152, 164; and Castro, 125; and Clinton, 124–26; and fetish, 153; as fifty-first state, 213–14; and gangsters, 11–12, 113–15, 215; and Islam, 11–14; and missionaries, 228; and sanctions, 167,

South Africa *(continued)*
213–14; and shamanism, 9, 172–89; and Society of the Elect, 120–21; and spiritual tourism, 172; and transition, 164–70. *See also* African National Congress; De Klerk, F. W.; Mandela, Nelson; Mutwa, Credo
South Africa: The 51st State (Major and Ghersi), 213–14
Southern Baptist Convention, 32, 144, 218
Southern Christian Leadership Conference, 166
Soviet Union, 127, 137
Soweto, 179–80
Spiro, Melford, 16
Sports Illustrated, 49
sports, 1, 22, 205. *See also* baseball; football
Springsteen, Bruce, 22
Star Trek, 2, 33, 204, 212
Star Wars, 204
state: and fetishism, 43; and power, 1; and violence, 22–23
Statue of Liberty, 97
Steel, Ronald, 140
Steevenz, Roy (Roy Little Sun), 175
Stoen, John Victor, 101
Stokes, Geoffrey, 44
Stowe, Harriet Beecher, 55
Strange, Susan, 123, 127
Stranger in a Strange Land (Heinlein), 196
Strategic Defense Initiative, 104
stress, 86–87
St. Stupid's Day, 196, 201
Sturken, Marita, 83
subhuman, viii, 18, 62, 64–65, 91–92, 187, 220–21
Sudan, 11
Sufis, 203
suicide: collective, 91, 230; revolutionary, 93, 109
Super Blue Stuff, x

superhuman, viii, 15, 16, 18, 28, 32, 49, 62, 64–66, 93, 187, 220–21
superstition, 17, 39, 55, 192
surrealism, 47–48, 138, 196
Suzuki, D. T., 218
sweat lodge, 175
Swift, Jonathan, 130, 195–96
Sylvan, Robin, 189
Syria, 197

tactility. *See* touch
Tale of a Tub (Swift), 195
Tarzan (1999), 69
Taussig, Michael, 43, 188
Taylor, Mark C., 26
Teachings of Don Juan (Castenada), 173
Techanism, 208
Technosophy, 208
Teenage Mutant Ninja Turtles, 218
Teish, Luisah, 185–86
television: evangelism, 4, 83–84, 205–6; and religion, 1, 22, 30, 204
Temple of Bowie, 204
terrorism, 100, 179
theomusicology, 44
Thomas, Apostle, 72
Thom McAn Company, 131, 216
Thompson, Charles, 116
Thor, 154, 220
Three Caballeros (1945), 143
Tiananmen Square, 144
Tibetan Book of the Dead, 27
Tillich, Paul, 16
Tocqueville, Alexis de, 225–26
Tokyo: and Disneyland, 146–47, 149; and Planet Hollywood, 13
Tomlinson, John, 136–37
Toshiharu Akiba, 146
touch: as binding, 75–77, 87–88; as burning, 77–80, 88–89; as caress, 73–74; and Christianity, 72–73; and gender, 88; as handling, 83–85, 90; and modernity, 89; as moving, 80–83,

89–90; and religion, viii, 5, 25–26, 70–90; as shock, 74–75; and tactics, 90; and Western thought, 72–73

tourism: and art, 185; and shamans, 172

transcendence, viii, 1–2, 10, 15–16, 29, 32, 49, 89

translation: and Coca-Cola, ix, 148; and missionaries, 148; and Tokyo Disneyland, 146

Treptow, Martin, 97

tricksters, 210

True Catholic Church, 202, 210

Tswana, 180

Tuan, Yi-fu, 226

Tungak movement, 163

Tupper, Earl Silas, 54–55, 57, 59–60, 68

Tupperware: and community, 54–57; as divine gift, 54; and exchange, 59–61; as fetish, 10, 57–59; and gender, 68–69; and plastic, viii

Tupperware Party: as model for global culture, 61; as ritual, 55–57

Turkey, 132

Turner, Edith, 168–70

Turner, Henry McNeal, 125

Turner, Victor, 47, 168–70

Tylor, E. B., 16, 32, 48–49, 113, 194

Tynan, Kenneth, 96

Über das Geldwessen (Hess), 118

UFOs, 82

ultimate: and "final ultimatum," 96; and human rights, 29; and religion, viii, 1, 10, 32

Umtata, 159

uncanny, 89–90

unctuousness, 121

United Church of Christ, 166

United Nations, 100, 108, 139

United States: and imperialism, 63; and Islam, 11, 14, 216–17; presidents of the, 6–7; and proposal to annex South Africa, 213–14

Universal Declaration of Human Rights (1948), 28

Universal Life Church, 199

University of the Witwatersrand, 177

Usiko, 115

U.S.S. Stark, 97

utopian: sacrifice, 109; space, 162–64

Uys, Jamie, 136

Valeri, Valerio, 103

vampires, 122–23

Van Gennep, Arnold, 120

Van Maanen, John, 147

Vatican, 135, 197

Vendramism, 192, 210

ventriloquism, 195

Verdú, Vicente, 214–15

Verwoerd, H. F., 178

Vietnam, 143–44

Vigne, Randolph, 178

virtual religions: as antibelief systems, 199–200; as anticult systems, 203–4; and authenticity, 208–12; as belief systems, 197–99; as Christianesque systems, 201–2; as entertainment systems, 204–5; as market systems, 205–6; as New Age systems, 202–3; as object and animal systems, 207; as practical systems, 200–201; as scientistic systems, 207–8

Vishnu, 38

vodou, 150–51, 154

Vonnegut, Kurt, 196

Vulgar Boatmen, 45

Walesa, Lech, 95

Watch Tower Bible and Tract Society, 158

Watkinson, A. S., 177

Watson, James, 218

Watt, David, 56

Wauism, ix, 192, 200

Wavy Gravy, 196

Compositor:	BookMatters, Berkeley
Text:	Fournier
Display:	Fournier

CPSIA information can be obtained
at www.ICGtesting.com
Printed in the USA
LVHW03s2142260618
582000LV00004B/5/P